The Senator Next Door

The Senator Next Door

A Memoir from the Heartland

Amy Klobuchar

University of Minnesota Press
Minneapolis
London

First published in 2015 by Henry Holt and Company

First University of Minnesota Press edition, 2016

Published by the University of Minnesota Press
111 Third Avenue South, Suite 290
Minneapolis, MN 55401-2520
http://www.upress.umn.edu

ISBN: 978-1-5179-0227-8

A Cataloging-in-Publication record for this book is available from the Library of Congress.

Designed by Kelly S. Too

Printed in the United States of America on acid-free paper

The University of Minnesota is an equal-opportunity educator and employer.

22 21 20 19 18 17 16   10 9 8 7 6 5 4 3 2 1

To John (the best husband in America)
and
Abigail (I wrote this for you)

CONTENTS

The Senator Next Door

Prologue

In my early campaigns people would sometimes come up to me at a grocery store or at a shopping mall and say, "I know you from somewhere." They would look at me intently and ask, "Is it the PTA? Do you live in my neighborhood?"

Always trying to be respectful, I would say things like, "I don't think so, but maybe you saw me on TV. I'm your county attorney." Or, "Actually, I'm running for the United States Senate."

"No," they'd respond, "that's not it. Are you sure you don't live down the street?"

As the years went on I figured out it was much easier if I just answered, "I don't *exactly* live on your block, but you can always think of me as the senator next door."

I got the idea for the title of this book from my husband, who has heard me talk to many constituents over the years and shares my view that politics is at its best when you listen and learn from the people you represent. To me a public servant should have both the grounding and the compassion to carry the common sense and good will of his or her neighbors into the political arena. And when in that arena, whether it be a city hall or the U.S. Senate, that public servant should be expected to work honestly and collaboratively with others who were presumably elected to do the same thing.

I know this description of American government might seem better suited to a high school textbook than a contemporary political memoir. And I am well aware that our polarized politics—egged on by supersized outside spending by interest groups on the left and the right—has taken us further and further away from the ideal of value-based and, for that matter, neighbor-based governing. But that is the very reason I wrote this book. At a time when our politics has become increasingly pungent, and politicians are more often lampooned as cartoon caricatures than portrayed as public servants, it is worth remembering why we have this representative democracy in the first place. As elected officials, we were sent to the halls of government by our neighbors to do their work—and much work needs to be done. Remembering our shared experiences with the people we represent makes us better and more accountable civil servants.

So this is my story about how I went from leading my suburban high school's prom fundraiser, a Lifesaver lollipop drive, to winning a seat in the United States Senate. It's about tackling all the obstacles I encountered along the way—my parents' divorce, my father's alcoholism and recovery, tough decisions as a prosecutor, my political campaigns, and Washington's gridlock—with good intentions and, whenever I could, some good humor.

It's about my immigrant grandparents who settled in Milwaukee, and my Slovenian-American grandpa who spent his life working fifteen hundred feet underground in the mines in Ely, Minnesota. He never graduated from high school, but he saved money in a coffee can so he could send my dad to college. Both my mom's and my dad's parents devoted their lives to making sure their children had a better future. My mom and dad carried on from there, both serving the public—she as a teacher, he as a newspaperman. They taught me not only to approach my work with a public purpose, but also to set expectations high for myself, my family, and for everyone I work with.

When our daughter, Abigail, was four years old, she had a neighbor girl over and they were playing with dolls. The other girl was a little older than Abigail and as I walked by my daughter's room, I heard the older girl say to her: "One day soon I'm going to have a baby, just like this doll."

I stopped in my tracks, stacked towels in hand, and thought, this is it, this is the moment . . . maybe not "the" moment, given that she was only four, but certainly "a" moment. What is she going to say?

Brushing her doll's hair with much calm, my daughter looked up at that girl with a sweet little smile and said: "Well, I'm going to have a baby, too, but not for a long, long time. Because you can't have a baby until you run for office and win an election."

Okay, that was a minor mom victory. Standing outside my daughter's bedroom door that day, I knew we'd set expectations high enough in our household.

And I knew something else. "You can't have a baby until you run for office and win an election" was not the answer I would have given growing up in Plymouth, Minnesota, in the 1960s and '70s. Back when I was in fourth grade I was actually kicked out of my cherished suburban public school—Beacon Heights Elementary—for having the audacity to be the first girl to wear pants. This was—mind you—in Minnesota, where I walked to school up the Bezenars' hill and through the woods, rain or shine, 10 below or worse.

That bold pants-wearing move landed me in the principal's office, where I was called in for my bell-bottomed reckoning by Mrs. Quady, our beehived principal. Peering down above her cat-eyed black glasses, in what to me at that moment looked larger than a beehive (picture a wig the size of a construction cone), she called me out with so much scorn that I could feel it bouncing off my mod, multicolored flowered pants: "Amy Klobuchar, you can wear your culottes and your knickers and your trousers at home, but at Beacon Heights School you wear dresses."

I wish I could say that I talked back or started a girls-can-wear-pants petition drive, or even more dramatically, a lawsuit. But since I was the good girl who had never been called into the principal's office before, who didn't really know how to take on the likes of Mrs. Quady and talk back, I simply cried. I got a permission slip, walked home, put on a skirt, and returned to school.

Now, all these years later, I get to tell my story of how I learned to talk back, stand my ground, and start that petition drive. It's a story about beating the expectations of our culture and our times, trying my best to stay grounded in the values I learned growing up, and actually getting some things done along the way.

The hardest chapters to write were the two about my time in the U.S. Senate, partly because there's so much to tell, partly because it's an unfinished chapter of my life, and mainly because I have a lot of mixed emotions about what's happening in American politics right now. As a U.S. Senator, I've tried my best to practice politics the way I think it's supposed to be practiced—always looking for common ground, and truly enjoying the people I meet along the way. I believe in my heart that courage in our nation's capital is not about standing by yourself giving a speech to an empty chamber. Courage is about whether or not you're willing to stand next to someone you don't always agree with for the betterment of this country.

That's why the first thing you see when you visit my office in the Senate is a smiling photograph of former Minnesota Senator and Vice President Hubert Humphrey in front of his campaign plane emblazoned with his famous nickname, "The Happy Warrior." I hung it there for a reason. I am convinced that now, more than ever, our nation needs a good dose of the courage and optimism and moral purpose that defined Hubert Humphrey's life.

Humphrey's own words are etched on his grave in Minneapolis: "I have enjoyed my life, its disappointments outweighed by its pleasures. I have loved my country in a way that some people consider sentimental and out of style. I still do. And I remain an optimist with joy, without apology, about this country and about the American experiment in democracy."

When you read my story I have one hope: that you will come away from it with some of that Humphrey joy and, despite our turbulent times, a renewed respect and love for our great "American experiment in democracy." And then, if I was really convincing, I hope that you will find some way, somehow, to be a part of it. For those who are already a part of it, my wish is that you will care for it just a little bit more.

Beginnings

When Everything Was New

My parents wallpapered the last room in their house on 1315 Oakview Lane in 1960 when everything was new. The house was new, Oakview Lane was new, and even the frontier-town-turned-Minneapolis-suburb of Plymouth, Minnesota, was looking new. Barns and silos were giving way to tracts of attached-garage houses, and what were once cow paths had become streets with names like Kirkwood and Evergreen and Jonquil. With its exposed wood ceiling, my parents' three-bedroom, one-bathroom house was so 1960s modern that one visitor—my grandma—would always ask my dad, "Jim, when are you going to finish that ceiling?" Every single appliance in the house—from the butter yellow–colored oven to the aqua countertop stove to the side-by-side washer and dryer—was new, fully paid for by my dad's GI loan.

And yes, I was new, having come into the world on May 25, 1960. That last room they wallpapered? It was for me.

The scrapbook my mom religiously kept for years features all kinds of data about my early months. The birth certificate from suburban Methodist Hospital is pinned down securely with pink paper picture corners. (Thanks, Mom! I'll never have to contest that in an election!) The Western Union telegram of congratulations from my grandparents in Milwaukee is preserved, envelope and all. I smiled at three and a half weeks, blew bubbles at thirteen weeks, and didn't walk until I was fourteen months old (my mom always told the neighbors that crawling for a long time made a child a better reader). All polio and smallpox vaccines are recorded by month; of key interest, I ate an egg yolk when I was four months old.

As idyllic as that all sounds, in truth I cried a lot, and for months I hardly ever slept. My mom would look longingly across the street to Dan and Ila Ronning's perfectly kept home, where their infant son Bryan's shades would go down like clockwork every afternoon at 2:00 p.m. That wasn't happening at 1315 Oakview Lane. I slept so little as a baby that one hot summer Saturday afternoon, when our neighbor Mr. O'Fallon started mowing his lawn just after my mom had finally managed to get me down for a nap, my dad ran outside to rebuke him for the noise.

"Who mows their lawn on Saturday afternoon?" my dad yelled over the roar of the mower.

Mr. O'Fallon responded with the obvious answer: "Everyone, Jim, everyone."

My parents, Rose Heuberger and Jim Klobuchar, had met through friends in the Minneapolis Hiking Club. She was a kindergarten teacher from Wisconsin who had moved to Minnesota to teach at an elementary school in Minneapolis. He was a newspaperman with the Associated Press who had gotten his start at the *Bismarck Daily Tribune* in North Dakota and served in Germany during the Korean War.

On my parents' first date, they went to a minor-league Minneapolis Millers baseball game. After that blind date, they courted for a while until my dad spontaneously proposed one rainy night after yet another sporting event—this time, an NFL exhibition game at Parade Stadium in Minneapolis. Both in their late twenties, they got married in 1954—the year that Elvis Presley recorded his first songs, CBS News broadcaster Edward R. Murrow took on Joe McCarthy, and Willie Mays made his famous over-the-shoulder catch in the first game of the World Series.

For the six years before I was born, my dad established himself with the AP and my mom cooked and cleaned and taught school. My mother was a great teacher, and the only reason she stopped teaching in early 1960 was that in those days the Minneapolis school district, like practically every district in the country, had a rule that you could only teach until you were five months pregnant. Of course the teachers who got pregnant back then—according to my mom's longtime friend and fellow teacher Gwen Mosberg—would always stretch the alleged due date so school officials would allow them to work weeks, sometimes months, past the five-month limit.

For the next fifteen years, my mom stayed home. My sister Beth was born in 1963. She was a spunky, cherub-cheeked baby with curly, dark hair. For the most part my mom was happy raising her two girls and hanging out with the neighbors. But sometimes it got frustrating, especially since we only had one car and my dad was gone a lot. My mom didn't really push the car issue, though, because she didn't like to drive anyway and was never very good at it. She depended on her husband and her neighbors and her friends for transport.

Since there was no bus service on our dirt road, my mom walked everywhere. The nearest grocery and hardware store was a mile away, and when we couldn't get a ride, we would walk or take a cab. I was the only kid in my suburban elementary school, in fact, who went to piano lessons in a cab. On Sundays, my mom, my sister, and I would also take a taxi to go to church.

"It's cheaper than buying another car," my mom would tell people, rarely mentioning that she didn't have a driver's license.

My job on those trips was to make sure the cabdriver always got a tip by saying, "Add fifty cents, please." My mom had always told me to say that, and to this day I associate going to church and piano lessons with those words and the dread that I would miss the moment and forget to add the tip, thus depriving the driver of his well-earned money. Only years later did I learn that my mother actually prepaid for the rides, including the gratuity. She wanted to be sure I never forgot the importance to workers of adding a tip.

Although they didn't have two cars, my parents got plenty of use out of the one they had. And just as America was ready to take on the world, so were Jim and Rose Klobuchar. President Eisenhower was about to pave the country from east to west with the interstate highway system, but my parents still found a way to drive their brand-new Plymouth west for their honeymoon to the Black Hills of South Dakota and Wyoming's Teton National Park. Their car also made it possible for them to build their house in the suburbs as part of the massive wave of suburban 1950s and '60s migration that followed Eisenhower's highways.

Both my mom and dad came from families that struggled during the Depression. My mom's immigrant parents converted recycled pie syrup into homemade jelly and sold the jars of jelly to help feed the family. My dad's dad worked day after day fifteen hundred feet underground in the iron ore mines in northeastern Minnesota. That's why, for my parents, the memories of difficult times were never far behind. From the Depression and World War II to the Korean War and the Cold War, the economic and security fears still haunted them. The possibility of another Depression and the ever-present fear of a run on the banks? More than enough reason for my dad to stash a wad of cash in the woodpile in the garage well into the next century. And his mom and dad? They kept a good part of their life savings in coffee cans in their basement in Ely, Minnesota.

For my parents' generation, another disaster was always looming right around the corner: the banks could fail; an atomic bomb could land in St. Paul; and the hazards from the past were as close to my mom and dad's present as the cars stretching behind them in the glistening rearview mirror of my dad's beige four-door. But the sheer joy of even having that rearview mirror—of being able to afford that car—was reason enough to leave the past behind. In a country filled with the exuberance of a new decade and the promise of upward paths for all, my parents counted their blessings.

Breaking News

Nothing embodied that youthful exuberance in the year I was born more than the man who would win the election for president, John F. Kennedy. Early on, this wasn't a great Minnesota story: Senator Kennedy outran and outmaneuvered our own beloved Senator Hubert Humphrey, culminating in a humiliating defeat in the 1960 West Virginia primary. Humphrey once lamented during the course of the primaries that with Kennedy's well-organized team and the entire Kennedy family canvassing the country, the election made him feel like "an independent merchant running against a chain store."

But once the primaries were over, it was Kennedy vs. Nixon. And for my mom, who'd moved to Minnesota from Wisconsin because of the stronger teachers' union and better pay, and for my dad, who'd been raised

Catholic in an iron ore mining town, the 1960 election was truly about the future—their future.

When America woke up and went to vote on November 8, 1960, no one knew what the outcome would be—this wasn't the age of instant data crunching or computer election modeling and exit polling. As Election Day turned into election night, and November 8th became November 9th, it became clear that this would be the closest presidential election since 1916. The country held its breath. Results came in slowly. And somehow, in that year when everything and anything was possible, it all ended up on my dad's desk, in the hands of young Jimmy Klobuchar, graduate of Ely Junior College and the University of Minnesota journalism school.

On Election Day morning my dad had gone climbing with a friend on the rocks above the St. Croix River, the scenic waterway dividing Minnesota from Wisconsin. When he showed up at work later that day, his assignment was not the typical sports, crime, or public interest story he normally covered. Instead, his task was to work with his boss and bureau chief, George Moses, along with Adolph Johnson, the AP's state capitol reporter and resident expert on Minnesota politics, to write stories on the election returns for Minnesota and North and South Dakota.

By the morning after the election, Kennedy was still five electoral votes shy of victory, and three states—Minnesota, Illinois, and California—were too close to call. The three sleep-deprived Minneapolis reporters confronted this reality: Nixon and Kennedy were running dead even in the state, but tens of thousands of votes were still unreported in Duluth and on northern Minnesota's Mesabi Iron Range, my dad's home turf.

My dad told George Moses that he had little doubt the region would go for Kennedy. "If you grew up on Minnesota's Iron Range in the middle of the twentieth century," he later said, you knew, first, that the area had "as many bars as churches," and second, that "Dick Nixon's prospects in northeastern Minnesota in 1960 were as bright as the temperance movement's chances in West Duluth." Both he and Adolph Johnson emphatically told Moses that in northeastern Minnesota, a working-class Catholic stronghold, Kennedy would most likely pick up more than two-thirds of the vote and thus win the state. And if Kennedy won Minnesota's eleven electoral votes, that would put him over the top.

After hearing his two reporters out, Moses placed a call to the AP's general desk chief in New York, Sam Blackman.

"We're going to elect Kennedy," he told Blackman.

Silence followed. "I've got two words for you guys in Minneapolis," Blackman finally said, pausing before adding with great emphasis: "*Be right.*"

So it was that my dad, the go-to wordsmith of the hour, then in his early thirties, got the chance to write the national story that declared John F. Kennedy the victor in Minnesota, and thus the next president. His sweaty fingers flew across his old Underwood typewriter, hammering the keys furiously with no time to follow the usual protocol of three carbon copies underneath. To beat the AP's chief competitor, United Press International, to the punch, my dad would hand a page to Moses containing only a single paragraph at a time. Moses would check the copy for typos and then run it over to the teletype operator paragraph by paragraph.

Without a carbon to review, and with each page including only a small piece of the story, my dad kept yelling to Bob Mexner, the teletype operator, "Bob, how did that last paragraph end?"

Through dazed eyes after a night of little sleep, Bob would yell back, "With a period, Jim, with a period."

My dad's story calling the election for Kennedy—sent out across the wires at 12:33 p.m., Eastern time—appeared in newspapers across the country. As James Reston of the *New York Times* explained the next day, the calling of the race in Minnesota was monumental. "At 12:33 o'clock," Reston wrote, "Senator Kennedy clinched Minnesota and the election. Thirteen minutes later, Mr. Nixon made his formal concession."

After Nixon conceded, my dad celebrated his groundbreaking story with Moses and Johnson. "Nice work doing the story," Moses told him. "I almost died twice and barely missed a hernia."

But the party was brief. My dad went to lunch at a nearby Swedish cafe and then returned to the office. There he was given his next assignment: three pigs were stuck in a mud pit near Faribault, Minnesota. He dug in and wrote his story.

So that was the year I was born—a year of endless possibilities. A year of new houses and new cars and new refrigerators. A year when a kid from the Iron Range of Minnesota could write a story calling the presidential election. A year when the country took a risk and elected a youthful and vigorous leader—and a Catholic at that. It was a good year to be born in.

My Mom

My earliest memory in life is of my mom the day President Kennedy was killed. People a little older than me remember seeing the coverage of the assassination and the funeral procession on TV—the horse-drawn caisson with the casket, little John-John's salute, the black veil—but I don't recall any of that. I only remember my mother on the floor of our basement laundry room, crying over her pile of *Life* magazines, clutching a cover showing Jackie Kennedy in a nice suit and pearls with the president in the background. I was three years old, and I remember it because I was upstairs calling for my mom and she didn't answer (a rarity). So I climbed down the stairs to the basement by myself (also a rarity) and found her in the laundry room. Crumpled on the cement floor, sobbing between her magazines and her laundry, my mom couldn't have been further removed from the glamorous lifestyle of the Kennedys. But this was *her* president.

Whenever I think of that day, I recall an old story that Eleanor Roosevelt used to tell about President Roosevelt's funeral in 1945, when a man fell to the ground in grief as the funeral procession proceeded down Constitution Avenue. The stranger standing next to the man asked him simply, "Did you know the President?"

"No," the grieving man answered, "I didn't know the President, but he knew me. He knew me."

My mom, a teacher and a union member and the daughter of immigrant parents, was a loyal Roosevelt and Kennedy Democrat. And even though she had never met these presidents, she knew that they were looking out for her. My mom also saw the Kennedys—with their youth and excitement and love of music and art—as icons, as extraordinary, as uniquely American. Perhaps Mrs. Kennedy summed it up best for my mom immediately after the president's death. "There'll be great Presidents again," she told journalist Theodore White, "but there'll never be another Camelot."

That quote appeared in the December 6, 1963, issue of *Life* magazine. Almost fifty years later, while we were cleaning out my mother's house after she died, my husband and I found a copy of that issue on a shelf in my mom's basement laundry room. The only other magazine she had saved was the August 13, 1973, edition of *TIME*. Its cover story featured Minnesota's beaming Governor Wendell Anderson holding up a northern pike with the bold title "The Good Life in Minnesota."

My mother was born in Milwaukee on St. Patrick's Day, 1926, the daughter of Margaret and Martin Heuberger, both Swiss immigrants. My mom's parents had met in Monroe, Wisconsin—"the Swiss Cheese Capital of the U.S."—and were married in Milwaukee less than five weeks before my mom was born. (I figured this out in 1992 while sitting in the pew of the church at my grandmother's funeral. Thanks for the heads-up, Mom!)

Three years after my grandparents were married, the stock market crashed and the country fell into the Depression. My mom and her younger brother, Dick, grew up in hard times. The family moved from one rented place to another, but through it all my grandpa kept his job at Milwaukee's Porth Pie Company. At some point, he convinced his boss to let him take home the syrup left over from the pie production. It was that syrup that my grandpa and grandma, frugal Swiss that they were, would convert into jelly. They'd sell the jars out of a little wagon they pulled up and down the street.

Despite their limited means, the Heuberger family made the best of their circumstances. Always a spirited girl, my mom sang and played the cello. As her high school yearbook entry noted, "Say it with music—and Rosie will!" She was third in the National Honor Society at Milwaukee's West Division High School. According to my uncle, this ranking bothered her greatly. She always believed the choirmaster had marked her down a few points and thus denied her the honor of being class valedictorian.

My mom's streak of naughtiness and her competitive feelings toward her younger brother were legendary. One day during the Depression her brother and my grandpa decided to teach her a lesson by playing a trick on her. Using a needle, they inserted citric acid my grandpa had brought home from the pie company into one of the chocolates nestled in a box in the basement. Chocolates were a special treat in their home, and this box had been hidden away for a future party. The prank was risky, because if Rose took the wrong chocolate, they'd be out a precious candy. How did they know which one she would steal? That was easy: they picked the biggest chocolate. In no time at all she was wailing from the bowels of the basement.

Teacher of the Year

After high school my mom attended the Milwaukee State Teachers College. Her class included seventy-six kindergarten and primary school teachers, all women. She did well in school, and she found a teaching position soon after she graduated in 1947.

Her first permanent job was at the Custerdale schools in Manitowoc, Wisconsin. The classrooms were built for a new forty-one-acre federal housing project constructed during World War II to house the families of the submarine builders at the Manitowoc Shipbuilding Company. (The workers were hired to build twenty-eight submarines, and streets in the new development were named after the subs.) As a sign of how much teachers were respected back then, the local "Kindergarten Mother's Club" held an afternoon tea for the new teachers at the beginning of the school year, complete with a brass sextet. One hundred mothers showed up to meet my mom and the other kindergarten teachers to discuss the coming school year.

Two years later, at age twenty-three, my mom got a job in Minneapolis at the 18th Street School, later known as Tuttle Elementary School. It was a public school, and because of its location in the southeastern part of the city, she taught the children of many University of Minnesota professors and several Minneapolis Symphony Orchestra members. As a talented cello player and member of the Cecelian Singers, she loved having those orchestra kids in her classroom.

In January 1951 my mom participated in a Minneapolis teachers' strike. A newspaper photo from that time shows her and other teachers walking the picket line, followed by grim-looking kids in plaid jackets carrying signs that read WE WANT SCHOOL. (To me, the students look like they would rather have been sledding, but their parents sent them out with the signs.) The day after the photo appeared in the newspaper, and twenty-two days after the teachers walked out of their classrooms, then Minnesota Governor Luther Youngdahl settled the strike for a $100 annual salary increase for each teacher, along with a promise to try to get more state aid for schools.

My mom was proud of her union membership, which she held until she retired. She would often recall going to union rallies and hearing

Hubert Humphrey speak. She and her friends would stand on folding chairs just to get a glimpse of the great man.

But what my mother loved most was teaching, being *in* the classroom. People often talk about how women in the 1940s and 1950s really only had three major career choices: nurse, secretary, or teacher. I always believed my mom would have chosen to be a teacher anyway because she loved it so much.

She taught school until I was born and then went back to teaching around the time my parents were getting divorced. For the last twenty years of her career she taught kindergarten and then second grade in the suburban Wayzata schools, the district that included Plymouth, my hometown. In 1993 she was named the Wayzata School District's "Elementary School Teacher of the Year." When she retired at age seventy, she was still teaching thirty second graders.

To this day I still meet people who remember my mom as their favorite teacher. She would always find the best in each student. She spent time with her kids' parents and loved including parent volunteers in the classroom. She made learning memorable and fun, welcoming every single animal her kids wanted to bring to class—from bunnies to snakes to a live penguin.

The scrapbooks of each class tell it all. Wrote second grader Bryce: "Today a squirrel visited our class. It was cool. Mrs. Klobuchar made us wash our hands when he left." Or eight-year-old Boris Kessler: "Mrs. Klobuchar, I'm happy to be in your room. You've taught me a lot. You're the best teacher I ever knew." "One more thing," he added, "I know how you like monarch butterflies so if you ever go to Cub Foods there might be some monarch cakes for $3.00."

The monarch butterfly unit was my mom's favorite. Every year she gathered milkweed for the fuzzy caterpillars that would eventually spin their chrysalises until one day a butterfly would burst out in all its orange and black glory. My favorite photograph is the one of my mom surrounded by second graders all looking up at the blue sky as she releases a new monarch after weeks of patient waiting. "Fly, monarch, fly," my mom would say to her wide-eyed students.

The highlight of the butterfly unit was the day my mom dressed as a monarch in an orange and black outfit with antennas on her head and a sign saying To Mexico Or Bust. After school on those days she would always visit the Cub Foods store in her monarch outfit and stroll the aisles with her sign. It was only after she died that I found out why she went to that particular store.

At my mom's visitation, the mother of a grown man with disabilities came over to me in tears, her family at her side. She told me that after graduating from high school her son got a job bagging groceries at the store near the school. He loved my mom's class in second grade and he particularly loved the monarch butterfly unit. Long after having him in class, my mother would go to the store every year and stand in his line with her groceries, all decked out in her monarch costume. When she saw him, she would always give him a big hug.

That's why she went to the grocery store. That was my mom.

The Swiss

After teaching and her family and her house, the other thing that mattered most to my mom was her Swiss heritage. She loved to hike, and during every trip to Minneapolis's Theodore Wirth Park, she'd wear her alpine hiking hat with a Swiss flag pin.

She also loved cheese. She would host annual craft parties and serve fondue or raclette, a Swiss dish featuring melted cheese on boiled potatoes. Every August 1st we would be the only family on Oakview Lane to dutifully celebrate Swiss Independence Day. Every Christmas she made stollen, a German bread laced with candied fruit, and exchanged it for Norwegian and Swedish treats from her neighbors. My grandpa constructed beautiful miniature Swiss chalets out of tiny pieces of wood, and during the winter my mom would take his handicrafts and make an elaborate Swiss village, complete with lights and snow made out of sheets of cotton.

She got all of this, of course, from my grandma and grandpa in Milwaukee. My mom's parents were blessed by that immigrant exuberance—they were what people now call "immigrant strivers," having come to our country with an unfailing belief that even without a high school education they could make it in America. They were certain that the country would give their children a better shot at a future, something they passed on to my mom and to me.

Both my mom's parents came to America from the German-speaking part of Switzerland. My grandma Margaret was brought over as a baby by her parents, Bertha and John Wuthrich. John was an accordion player who had learned to make cheese in his hometown in Switzerland. Once in America, he and his wife settled in Illinois and later Wisconsin, where John worked as a farmer and a cheese maker. But life was hard. According to a local newspaper, they reportedly "lived at several cheese factories about the city." John Wuthrich often got drunk, and his marriage to my great-grandma Bertha ended in divorce. That didn't seem to dampen my grandma's spirit, though. With her letter writing and piano playing and all-around zest for life, she was always a lot of fun.

The story of my Swiss grandpa, Martin Heuberger, was different than my grandma Margaret's. He, too, was a Swiss immigrant but he wasn't brought over as a child to our country. Instead, he made the choice to leave Switzerland at the age of twenty-two after serving in Switzerland's Red Cross. In October 1923 he set sail out of Cherbourg, France, traveling with a friend. Martin arrived at Ellis Island in New York with $70 in his pocket, a stated destination of Toronto, Canada, and a reported occupation as a chef's assistant.

With U.S. quotas for Swiss immigrants already filled for the month, Martin and his friend were both detained in New York. The only way the two of them would be allowed to leave Ellis Island was if they agreed, with the blessing of Canadian immigration officials, to continue on to their listed destination. The next day, the two young men traveled by train from New York to Toronto. They clearly had no intention of staying in Canada—just a week later, they boarded a train to Detroit, again applying for admission to the United States. This time Martin was admitted as a resident "alien" but not as a U.S. citizen. He made his way to Monroe, Wisconsin, where he would find a job and meet my grandma. Later, they would move to Milwaukee, get married, and have my mom and her brother.

It now seems fairly obvious that my grandpa went through Canada merely to get into our country. That wasn't unusual in those days. According to Canadian immigration sources, during the 1920s Canada was used as a "back door" for entry to America when Congress cut back on the quota of European immigrants to be allowed into the United States.

Perhaps because he was anxious about the circumstances surrounding his arrival, my grandfather lived in this country as an "alien" for almost twenty years and didn't apply to be a U.S. citizen despite marrying my grandma, who was an American citizen. Even then, he didn't attempt to change his alien status until he had to.

Everything changed with a letter in the mail. In 1940, as World War II was raging in Europe, my grandpa received a letter that, according to my uncle Dick, caused a great deal of consternation in the family. The letter said that my grandpa was required to officially register as an alien. (Earlier that year, Congress had passed the Alien Registration Act, which made it illegal for anyone in the United States to advocate overthrowing the government and gave the government the power to track those who were not U.S. citizens.)

My grandpa wanted nothing to do with overthrowing the government. He was happy just to work at the pie company and raise his kids. But the letter created a lot of angst. The family feared that my grandpa, a Swiss-German and non–U.S. citizen with issues related to his entry into the United States, would somehow be deported during World War II.

Luckily, my grandpa was able to register as an alien without a problem. On the part of the form that was meant to weed out Communists—where they asked the applicant to "list memberships or activities in clubs, organizations, or societies"—my grandpa listed only one: he was a member of a "Swiss male choir."

The next year, my grandpa applied for citizenship. After clearing up a number of issues related to the circumstances of his entry into the country, he got his naturalization papers on November 18, 1941. The photograph taken for his official naturalization certificate shows a handsome, clean-shaven man wearing a suit and tie. Less than three weeks later, the Japanese bombed Pearl Harbor and our country declared war against Germany, Japan, and Italy.

As the debate over immigration has raged on in Congress, I have often thought about my grandpa Martin and all of my immigrant relatives. In 2007 Ted Kennedy asked me to join the bipartisan group working on a bill that would at last provide meaningful immigration reform. Despite Senator Kennedy's and then President Bush's valiant efforts, the bill never passed the Senate. In 2013, as a member of the

Judiciary Committee, I was also part of the effort in the Senate to successfully pass a comprehensive, bipartisan bill, one that included a path to citizenship. Unfortunately, that bill never made it through the House, which in 2014 led to President Obama's later-contested executive action granting temporary work permits and deferring deportation for approximately five million people. During my floor speeches advocating for the Senate bill in 2013, I often made the case for immigration reform by talking about my ancestors. But back then, I did not understand or actually know about my grandpa's decades-long "alien" status.

My grandpa, a Swiss immigrant and pie maker and later the father of two, clearly stretched the rules when he entered our country. I know now that he wasn't completely honest on his immigration forms about how he came into the United States, initially neglecting to mention how he first entered our country. If my grandpa had come in under these terms today— an alien, entering the country twice to beat the quotas, at one point filling out a form without giving all of the correct details on his place of entry—I often wonder what would have happened to him. Would he have eventually become a citizen, as he did in 1941? Probably not. Would he have been deported after living in the country for eighteen years? Maybe. Would he have been affected by the anti-immigrant sentiment so commonplace now? Absolutely. What would he have thought about people calling him a "drain on the economy" and a "border-jumping criminal," as they do on my Facebook page whenever I post anything on immigration reform?

Just like so many immigrants who have come to this land, my grandpa simply wanted a better life. He paid his taxes, provided for his wife and children, and worked hard to the end.

This country was built by immigrants and the sons and daughters of immigrants. We all stand on their shoulders.

The Slovenians

The immigrant experience was central to my dad's life, too. His grandparents on both sides came to this country from Slovenia—a small country surrounded by Austria, Italy, Croatia, and Hungary—around the turn of the last century. Like so many others from that part of the world, they made their way to Minnesota to work in the underground mines.

Klobuchar means "hatmaker" in Slovene, indicating that at some point in the centuries past, my ancestors were in the haberdashery business, a risky trade back then since they called the "mad hatter" mad for a reason. Until the process was banned in the first half of the twentieth century, the mercury used to manufacture felt hats would often lead to insanity.

Back in the old country, Slovenians worked as miners and farmers and woodworkers. But for my ancestors, America brought the promise not only of steady work but of better lives for their children. In America, the Austrians (who, for centuries, ruled Slovenia as part of the Habsburg Dynasty) would no longer be able to tell them which of their kids could go to school. In America, they would be paying taxes to *their* country, not to foreign monarchs, and every child would get a good education.

On northern Minnesota's Iron Range—a vast landscape of forest and lakes, rich in iron ore and ethnic culture—my great-grandparents found not just fellow Slovenians and Serbs and Croatians, but also Finns, Swedes, Norwegians, Poles, and Bulgarians. They had all traveled thousands of miles in hopes of finding a job, and they'd heard that northeastern Minnesota "looked just like home." That was something of an exaggeration, since in its early years, the Range was mostly a collection of frontier shantytowns, complete with brothels and illegal stills. Life was hard and keeping warm was a major struggle. Yet my great-grandparents never really complained about their lot. As my dad once said: "If the New World was not deliverance to them, then it would be for their children. They would study in American schools, understand this country and not only work for it but make it work." In time, unions would battle management, wages would go up, mines would open and close. Life was never easy, but over the years it slowly got better.

Of all my relatives on the Range, my grandpa Mike best embodied the miner's hard life: the red rock, the work boots, the lunch bucket with the meat pasties, the freezing walks home, the drinking binges on Saturday night followed by mass on Sunday morning. His face was strong and chiseled like a miner's version of one of the presidents on Mount Rushmore. His hands were enormous and stiff and the nerves of his left thumb had been permanently damaged in a mining accident. On the Range many likened him to Spencer Tracy, especially when he wore a hat. Into her eighties, my grandma Mary would always tell me, "Your grandpa was a handsome man, Amy, he was a handsome man."

My grandpa grew up in Ely, Minnesota, a small town on the Range not far from the Canadian border. In the eighth grade, he got As in math, and my guess is that in another time and place he would have been destined for college. He dreamed of a life at sea and wanted a career in the Navy. But at age fifteen he had to drop out of school to help support the family, first as a teamster driving a delivery wagon, and later with a job in the mines.

And the family—there were ten children—needed a lot of extra help. Mike's mother died of cancer when he was nineteen and his father died of a heart attack less than two years later. Mike, the oldest son, was barely in his twenties when he became responsible for taking care of himself and all nine of his siblings. Life was so hard that the family decided to send the youngest child—ten-year-old Hannah—to an orphanage in Duluth for a brief time. But less than two years later, just as he'd promised, my grandpa borrowed a car, drove to Duluth, and brought Hannah back home.

To provide for their siblings, my grandpa and his brother John worked in the Zenith Mine. The mines in those days were extraordinarily dangerous. Every time a siren would go off the whole town would come running to see who had been injured, who had been killed. Miners would die in cave-ins and dynamite blasts. My dad still remembers seeing the coffins of victims at St. Anthony's Catholic Church.

Mike Klobuchar was a hard worker. He did well in the mine and was soon made a shift foreman. Somewhere along the way, he met my grandma, Mary Pucel, oldest child of the eight Pucel children, graduate of Ely Memorial High School, and bookkeeper at Grahek's Grocery and Meat Market. They married in October 1927, only two years after my grandpa lost his father. Not only did my grandma walk into a situation where she was expected to help care for my grandpa's siblings, but at the time of her marriage she was already pregnant with my dad, who was born on April 9, 1928. (Nothing like doing a little research only to find out that not one but *both* of your parents were conceived before marriage!)

Mike and Mary had a second son, Dick, four years after my father was born. One day when the kids were young, my grandpa drove to the closed-down Babbitt mine to buy a boarded-up house for the family. He bought it for $100, loaded it up on the back of a flatbed truck, and drove it to Ely. To give you an idea of the neighborhood they lived in, when a man across the alley decided he wanted a basement for his new house, he got his hands on some dynamite and blew a big hole in the ground. But he used too much, and decades later my uncle Dick—who witnessed the explosion—still vividly remembers how flying rocks knocked his mother Mary's wash off her clothesline, prompting the man to apologize to Mary and offer to buy her new sheets. That's the thing about Iron Rangers—they never forget.

My grandpa Mike loved being outdoors. He liked to fish, and he enjoyed hunting deer and partridge. He loved walking in the forest and gathering blueberries. He spent most of his life in the underground mines (followed by stints in logging and lumber after the mine closed), but he would always cherish those times outdoors, including the once-a-year weekend trips when the family would borrow Uncle Joe's blue Chevy and drive to Lake Superior to hike at Gooseberry Falls.

My grandpa also liked to drink. Drinking was part of life on the Range. He drank beers and brandies with the other miners at Garni's Bar. Sometimes he drank way too much and came home in a rage, yelling at my grandma about all kinds of grievances. As the years went on, his drinking became a little more moderate, but it was still a major part of my dad's childhood. My dad remembers the shouting and the carrying on, he remembers trying to break up the arguments, and he remembers my grandpa's regret and remorse.

But in the end I always think of my grandpa in those underground red rock caverns, producing the iron ore that made the cars and won the wars. I think of him supporting his orphaned sisters and brothers, supporting his family. He would go to work every day with his black lunch pail and descend fifteen hundred feet down the mineshaft in a cage in the darkness. As the cage went down the shaft, how often did he think of that life he wanted at sea, of that career in the Navy? How often did he think of a path in the woods, of the sun coming through the trees?

In 2006, when I returned to Ely to campaign for the U.S. Senate, I was eating lunch at Vertin's Cafe and happened to meet a man whose father had worked with my grandfather. He remembered how his dad would always tell him that my grandpa was a strong and kind boss. But he especially remembered my grandpa's courage. Looking directly at me, his eyes filling with tears, the man said, "Whenever it was time to explore a new part of the mine, all the miners knew it would be dangerous. That's why most of the mine foremen would stand at the top of the mine and radio down to the miners below, telling them where to go. Not Mike Klobuchar. He would always go with the miners. He would always go with his guys. And he would always go first."

My Dad

While my grandpa would go to work every day, lunch pail in hand, it was my grandma Mary who would make that lunch, run the house, and raise her boys with a vast reserve of energy all tucked inside her five-foot, hundred-pound frame. If my grandpa Mike was a rough-hewn Spencer Tracy, my grandma Mary was a tiger mom before anyone had heard of tiger moms.

My grandma's guiding principle in life was her stubborn insistence that her two sons—Jim and Dick—could make it in America. They would do their homework, do their chores, and practice their piano. If they did those three things every day—and went to church every Sunday and confession when necessary—they would succeed.

Her first plan for helping her older son move up in life involved the piano. After my grandpa bought a piano for $15 from another miner's family, my grandma dreamed that my dad—her young Jimmy—would someday become a concert pianist. My dad loved music, but after he'd played and practiced for a few years my grandmother realized that Juilliard wasn't in her son's future.

Then she noticed his interest in the *Duluth Herald*. At age twelve he started reading the newspaper every day after it arrived at the front door. He was insatiably curious and also a very good storyteller.

"Son," she said to him one day, "you know what I'd like? I'd like to see you writing in the newspapers and magazines like a very famous man who grew up here in Ely. His name is Simon Bourgin."

At the time Simon Bourgin was reporting for the military in Europe for *Stars and Stripes*. Later he became a special correspondent covering central and eastern Europe for *TIME* and *Life* magazines, but from my grandma's perspective, what mattered most was that he had grown up in Ely and gone on to make something of himself. Simon's family also lived in the Slovenian part of town—they had come from Russia, and they were one of only six Jewish families in Ely. The way my grandma saw it, if Simon could do it, Jimmy could, too. Journalism, she decided, was a career worth pursuing. It would satisfy her son's desire to see the world and also bring in a salary. Maybe she would even see the Klobuchar name in print someday.

My dad got his start in the newspaper business delivering *Grit*, a weekly paper targeted at small-town subscribers. He watched George Sanders in Alfred Hitchcock's *Foreign Correspondent* and imagined himself an intrepid reporter exposing Nazi spies in England, just like Sanders's character. In high school he wrote stories for the *Ely Hi-Lites* and was enthralled with his Finnish tenth-grade literature teacher, Tyne Souja. He remembers the passion she brought to reading the words of the great poets: Keats, Shelley, and Wordsworth. As Miss Souja would read the poem Wordsworth wrote from a London bridge, it was as if central London was just outside the window of her Ely classroom:

Never did sun more beautifully steep
In his first splendour, valley, rock, or hill;
Ne'er saw I, never felt, a calm so deep!
The river glideth at his own sweet will;
Dear God! the very houses seem asleep;
And all that mighty heart is lying still.

My dad wanted to write like that. And my grandma wanted him to write like that—or at least like Mrs. Bourgin's son.

After graduating from high school in the mid-1940s, my dad enrolled in Ely Junior College, just as Simon Bourgin and so many other Iron Range kids had done. Hardly anyone considered Ely Junior College a training ground for poets or foreign correspondents, but two very important people in the world were true believers: the mothers of Simon Bourgin and Jimmy Klobuchar.

It was while attending Ely Junior College that my dad first crossed paths with the famous conservationist Sigurd Olson, then the college's dean. Olson, who had worked as a canoe guide and outfitter in Ely, would later spearhead efforts to preserve Minnesota's forests and parks. In the 1950s he wrote a book of essays called *The Singing Wilderness*; in 1963 he became the president of The Wilderness Society. In 1977, in the midst of bare-knuckled political battles between environmentalists and many locals and lodge owners, Olson was hanged in effigy in his hometown. But one year later President Jimmy Carter signed into law Hubert Humphrey's bill to create the Boundary Waters Canoe Area Wilderness. In the years leading up to the bill's passage, my dad wrote over a dozen columns about the issue. He and Olson remained friends for life.

After Ely Junior College, my dad attended the University of Minnesota journalism school. My dad's first job in his new trade was at the *Bismarck Daily Tribune*. His starting salary was forty dollars a week. The paper was the oldest in North Dakota and even had a Pulitzer in its past (for dust bowl reporting in 1938). He was the wire editor, putting headlines on scores of stories each day and editing them down to size.

My dad loved the work, but the Korean War put his career on hold. About six months after he got to Bismarck, he was drafted into the Army and sent to Fort Riley, Kansas, for training. Afterward he was assigned to a new psychological warfare unit in Stuttgart, Germany, that wrote anti-Communist material in an effort to influence the hearts and minds of citizens of Soviet-bloc countries. To this day he feels guilty that he served in Germany when so many of the other young men he trained with were sent to Korea.

After eighteen months in Germany, where he fell in love with mountain climbing, he returned to North Dakota for another short stint at the Bismarck paper. Soon he was recruited by George Moses, the Associated Press bureau chief in Minneapolis, and he went on to happily work for the AP for eight years. Then, in 1961, he joined the *Minneapolis Tribune* as a sports reporter, beginning his decades-long coverage of professional sports. His main beat was the Minnesota Vikings, which had just become a National Football League franchise.

My dad had great fun writing about the Vikings' early days. He had a wild relationship with the Vikings' first head coach, Norm Van Brocklin. The two of them once got into such an intense argument in a hotel lobby that Van Brocklin summoned my dad to his hotel room to settle the fight man-to-man. (In the end, the only thing that got broken after the punches were thrown was the hotel TV.) My dad also wrote about the Vikings' raucous training camps in Bemidji and Mankato; Jim Marshall's infamous 1964 fumble recovery (after picking up the ball, Marshall ran 66 yards into the end zone, but he ran *the wrong way* and scored a safety for the San Francisco 49ers); the scrambling quarterback Fran Tarkenton; the irascible Joe Kapp; the stoic, beloved coach Bud Grant; the glory days of the Vikings' great defensive line, nicknamed the Purple People Eaters; and all four of the Vikings' Super Bowl losses. In 1977 my dad wrote a book called *Will the Vikings Ever Win the Super Bowl?*—sadly for Vikings fans the world over, his question is still relevant well into this century.

In June 1965 my dad left the *Tribune* and moved to the competing paper, the *St. Paul Pioneer Press.* A few months later John Cowles, the publisher of both the *Minneapolis Tribune* and the *Minneapolis Star,* enticed him back across the river, this time with an offer to write a regular column on anything he wanted for the *Star,* the afternoon paper. My dad would join Barbara Flanagan, a local society reporter, in a rotating column. The paper promoted them as "the twin columnists for the Twin Cities," and they were once described in a local magazine as the "Fred and Ginger of daily newspaper columnists." The two of them had fun with that for years.

Later my dad was off on his own, writing five or six days a week. This was print journalism's heyday, when local newspapers could afford to send reporters—and in particular popular columnists—all over the world. During the height of the Cold War, my dad spent a week reporting from Moscow, with a Soviet Intourist guide assigned to him at all times. He covered the murder and funeral of Aldo Moro, a prominent politician in Italy. He reported from Venice and Scandinavia. He climbed mountains across the world, from the Himalayas to the Andes, and returned home to write about it.

He loved to do crazy things and write about his experiences. A sharpshooter once shot a piece of chalk from between his pursed lips. He paraglided before it was safe, flew airplanes and a hot air balloon, and took on Rudolf Wanderone—better known as "Minnesota Fats"—in a pool game. He covered a nudist colony and an air service with topless flight attendants. He appeared as a reporter in the movie *The Wrestler* with Ed Asner.

Occasionally he got into hot water with his bosses. He was twice suspended from the newspaper: once for a week because he'd crossed the line and gotten involved in politics by writing an inaugural speech for his fellow Iron Ranger, Governor Rudy Perpich; and once for ten days because he made up quotes and attributed them to a Vikings official just before the team's last game in Bloomington at their longtime home field, Metropolitan Stadium. Before the game, the Vikings expressed concern that the fans would tear up the stadium to take home mementos. In response, my dad wrote a humorous column in which he claimed the Vikings' ticket manager, Harry Randolph, had said: "If they are going to carry off their seats, we prefer handsaws to the standard Black & Decker ripsaws in the commercials." Although he apologized later, it was clear that my dad saw the column as a bit of mirthful satire.

My dad also drank too much. His columns contained scattered references to bars and beer—a Munich hofbrauhaus and Mousey's Bar on 12th and Hennepin, to name but two. He was colorful and irrepressible, and for a long time his drinking was a big part of his public persona. But it was also a sign of trouble ahead.

In the mid-1970s my dad was charged with a couple of alcohol-related driving offenses. He tried to stop drinking several times after that, but in 1993 he got a DWI. By then society's attitude toward drunk drivers had changed. This time he lost his license for a while. And this time it was possible he would actually go to jail, so it was essential that he get treatment and remain sober.

The newspaper's management didn't seem particularly upset by my dad's first offenses, but their response to the 1993 arrest was different. Right after my dad was charged, the paper's editor, Tim McGuire, published my dad's apology to his readers on the front page. McGuire also wrote a note to the paper's readers saying my dad's drinking and driving had "endangered lives" and that his decision to seek treatment was one the paper agreed with and would "insist upon."

That's when my dad finally got sober. He tossed out all the booze in his house, went to inpatient treatment and AA, and started going to church again. His renewed faith in God was a major part of why he stayed sober.

It also helped that his readers forgave him. In fact, it was his very flaws that made my dad so appealing to them. His rough-and-tumble life growing up and his personal struggles had a huge influence on his writing.

That's why he was at his best when he wrote about what he called the "heroes among us"—ordinary people doing extraordinary things.

One of my favorite columns of his appeared in 1967. Later published in his first book, *The Zest (and Best) of Jim Klobuchar*, it was about a five-year-old girl who had a brain tumor. She loved trains, and during what would be one of the last weeks of her life, her mom took her on a train ride from Minneapolis to St. Paul. The twenty-six-year-old mother's love for her daughter and her brave attempts to comfort her child by keeping a smile on her face throughout the ride is heartbreaking. The description of the little girl draws you in from the beginning:

> Her fingernails were gaily polished red, her checked dress freshly pressed. In her hair was the blue clasp she wore to birthday parties.
>
> She was cradled in her mother's lap on the observation car of the Milwaukee Road's Hiawatha, a tidy young lady.
>
> A dying little girl, taking her last train ride.

I'm sure my dad's readers were as touched as I was by that column, and I bet many of them saved it and tacked it up on their refrigerators. So many people kept his stories. I still get yellowed newspaper clippings from people with Post-it notes attached: "Your dad helped my aunt get her job back." "Your dad wrote about my teacher." "This column is about me when I got married." "This story meant a lot to my grandpa before he died."

In 1995, after forty-three years in journalism, including thirty years as a columnist, my dad retired. When word of his decision got around, a *StarTribune* reporter named Chuck Haga wrote that many in the newsroom had doubted he would ever retire and instead predicted that he would be "writing his last column a week or two after his death, filing from Heaven or Hell, drawing comparisons with Hibbing" (the town on Minnesota's Iron Range where Bob Dylan grew up). But retire my dad did, though he never stopped writing. During the next twenty-plus years he wrote for the *Christian Science Monitor* and for *MinnPost*, an online publication. He covered the Salt Lake City Olympics and climbed more mountains. By the time he retired he had written fourteen books; at last count, the total was up to twenty-three.

When my dad left the paper, he wrote a number of questions for himself about his career. The first one was, "Was it worth it?"

Was his job worth, as he put it, the "dead-of-night plane flights, writing against the clock, absorbing the jocks' screaming curses in the losers' dressing room, keeling over from the cops' tear gas in Miami outside the Republican convention, trying to keep the mother of a dead marine on the phone although she was crying and alone in the house while I struggled with my revulsion for doing this."

Was it worth it?

His answer: "God, yes."

When his career as a journalist finally came to an end, my dad had written eighty-four hundred columns and about twelve million words. He'd been a finalist for NASA's program to send a journalist into space before it was canceled after the *Challenger* disaster. He was voted the nation's "outstanding columnist" in 1984 by the National Society of Newspaper Columnists. And then there was the note that William F. Buckley wrote after my dad featured him in a column. In the note, Buckley effectively told my dad he was the only person as witty as Buckley himself.

The defining characteristic of my dad's work was described best by Dave Nimmer, the *StarTribune*'s former managing editor, who said my dad was "a champion of those on the outside." The influence of his Slovenian ancestors ran deep. My dad took on the causes of those he grew up with, continuing the struggle of his immigrant grandparents and their sons and daughters. Whatever the topic of a column or an article, his work so often reflected the bedrock belief that if you worked hard and tried your best, you would get ahead in America.

On the day my dad retired from the Minneapolis *StarTribune*, he packed his box with his belongings, turned off the light in his small office, and closed the door. He had refused the offers for an office party and said he just wanted to leave quietly. But as he was walking out, his box clutched in his hands, Steve Ronald, the paper's deputy managing editor, got on the newsroom's PA system and announced, "This is Jim Klobuchar's last day. That is forty-three years of journalism going out the door." Every reporter in the room spontaneously stood up and clapped. And my dad? He paused and smiled and waved, and then he just walked out the door.

That's a nice way to say good-bye.

Growing Up

Beacon Heights Elementary

The walk across Oakview Lane, through the Bezenars' yard and up the hill to Beacon Heights Elementary School, was really just a stroll through the woods. But for a young kid walking that path alone, it was one big hill in one dark forest. The school got its name, after all, because it was located right near the high-elevation beacon light that used to guide airplanes to the nearby Minneapolis airport before the days of radar.

But long before the hilltop was named Beacon Heights, it already had a school—a one-room log schoolhouse built in 1858, the same year that Minnesota was admitted to the Union. Plymouth was a pioneer town back then, and students would walk to the school from as far away as three miles. The schoolhouse, with enough benches for twenty-six students in grades 1–8, was replaced by a new wood-frame building in 1872, a structure that stood until 1940, when it was replaced by a two-room brick school. By the 1960s the school had expanded twice, adding eleven classrooms, a gymnasium, a kitchen, and a new wing with a library. At every step of the way the Plymouth community would herald the new additions and modernization of the school.

So as I made my daily trek on the leaf-covered path through the woods (and in the winter, hopscotched the path's gigantic boot prints left by the older kids), I was walking the path of history, one that pioneer kids had walked over a century before. But no matter how many wild animals those pioneer kids encountered, they never had to deal with the Bezenars' scary black lab, Y'all. No matter what time of day I passed, Y'all would emerge from her doghouse in the Bezenars' backyard and then bark and growl as I ran by on the path. It didn't matter if I tiptoed or took the biggest possible steps, she would always know it was me and chase me as far as possible. After my parents' attempt to get Agnes and Bill Bezenar to chain up the dog failed, my mom told me that when the dog barked I should just yell back, "Hi, Y'all!" and then run as fast as I could.

Over the years a host of hazards awaited me when I actually got to the schoolyard at the top of the hill: a boy named Jeff taking my purple Vikings cap and throwing it up in a tree (he wanted to prove to the other kids that the "Amy + Jeff" they had stomped in the snow couldn't have been more wrong); the President's Physical Fitness Test and accompanying 600-yard dash (you could actually see my heart pounding through my t-shirt); the softball throw (in fourth grade I was second to the worst, beating out only Gretchen Johnson); and the scariest of all, the track-and-field hurdles.

But nothing was as challenging as trying to meet the high expectations of my first teacher, Miss Alexander. For a brand-new kindergarten teacher, she was pretty intense. When I couldn't tell her the year of my birth, she was not pleased. I still remember walking along the path to school the next day and repeatedly chanting the numbers "1-9-6-0" so I could rectify the situation.

I had a host of problems that first year. I couldn't sing on key. I had a lisp. I wasn't very good at printing my first name—the *Y* was always way too big. Miss Alexander actually noted that on my kindergarten report card.

But my worst crime was that I had no artistic ability. I vividly remember the moment when Miss Alexander assigned the task of coloring a page of grapes with a purple crayon. Trying to impress her with my ability to complete the assignment quickly and efficiently, I decided to color all the grapes in one big collective mass instead of individually. I was the first one finished, and I'll never forget how stunned I was when Miss Alexander clearly disapproved of what I'd done.

It didn't help that I was small and shy and younger than a lot of the other kids in my class. But Miss Alexander *was* direct and to the point.

After the infamous grape-coloring episode, she told my mom that I'd never be more than an average student. Fortunately, my mother wasn't having any of it. Years later she told me that Miss Alexander was wrong to extrapolate that verdict from a bunch of grapes. But in one sense Miss Alexander was good for me. She made me understand that you have to rise to challenges, and for that I will be forever grateful.

All was salvaged by my first-grade teacher—the stern but kind Mrs. Mooney, a wonderful teacher who had the whitest of hair, as only a Mrs. Mooney would have. Thanks to her, I came to love reading. I still remember the first real book I read, *Little House in the Big Woods*. I read the whole book in one sitting and got a headache. Laura Ingalls Wilder's *Little House* books enthralled me because they were based in Minnesota, Wisconsin, Iowa, and the Dakotas and I felt surrounded by history. I was so taken with reading that I soon decided to be a librarian when I grew up. In an old tin recipe holder of my mom's, I started my own card catalog of the books I'd read.

Mrs. Mooney was also intent on helping me to pronounce words that ended in "ing" (I was saying "kin" instead of "king"). She even sent me for a while to a speech therapist who visited the school once a week. Over time, she solved the "ing" problem and as an added bonus stopped me from making my "th's" sound like "s's." She did it firmly but with much white-haired kindness.

It was also gentle Mrs. Mooney who one day rescued me from the heavy front doors to Beacon Heights School. It was a below-zero day in January, and my mittens—wet from the snow I may or may not have eaten on the way up the hill—had somehow frozen to the school doors' steel handles. The mittens had been knitted by my great-grandma, and she fastened them together with a long string of yarn that ran under my coat and along each arm so I wouldn't lose them. But this made the mittens very difficult to get off, and now I was attached to the school like a little first-grader magnet. When Mrs. Mooney looked out the window and saw me stuck to the doors, she came outside and extricated me by unzipping my jacket so I could get my hands free of the frozen-on mittens.

All my teachers at Beacon Heights Elementary School were strict, but they were also conscientious and enthusiastic. I loved school, and I was especially challenged by my fourth-grade teacher, the red-haired Miss

Kalionen, who was a cross between a Catholic school nun and the similarly red-haired and then-popular comedienne Carol Burnett. Ruling her classroom in a manner that would never be accepted today, Miss Kalionen tested us with math problems I wouldn't see again until eighth grade. And it was Miss Kalionen who taught me how to speak in public. She would stand at the back of the class and yell, "Speak louder! I can't hear you!" Whether it was a presentation on the history of dairy farms in Minnesota or my show-and-tell story about our summer vacation to the Black Hills, she would stand there and yell, "Speak louder! I can't hear you!"

Miss Kalionen put a premium on achievement and doing your best, and she didn't seem to care how many little egos she bruised along the way. She made us give flutophone concerts that were like an early 1970s version of *Survivor*: we would all start out playing together, and then song by song one student after another would have to drop off until the best student would be left standing for a solo at the end. For a while she actually had our desks arranged in the order of our math scores. And once, after one boy had really acted out, she dramatically upended his desk in the middle of class. His desk was chock-full of stuff and everything came flying out, including all his Hot Wheels. After a fleet of the miniature cars spilled out and rolled down the rows of desks to the front of the room, she looked at him and said, "Charlie, all that's between those ears is cold mashed potatoes and gravy."

I never forgot Miss Kalionen and we stayed in touch over the years. During my first U.S. Senate campaign, she would send me notes of encouragement. She still had that same spidery handwriting I'd seen on every quarterly fourth-grade report card, and although her later comments about my performance in campaign debates were generous, her notes on my fourth-grade report cards weren't nearly so nice. After the first quarter she wrote, "Speak up and out! L-O-U-D-E-R." After the second quarter she wrote, "Same prayer. Amen." And, bringing back memories of Miss Alexander from kindergarten, she added, "Pursuits in art leave something to be desired."

But she also added some praise: "A well-turned phrase is a thrill not too often enjoyed at this level." And: "The comprehension of the printed word is thrilling to Miss Prim" (by that she meant herself).

Miss Kalionen and the other Beacon Heights teachers gave me the gifts of discipline, order, and respect. They made me want to do my best, and if I didn't, they were more than ready to give me a not-so-gentle reminder that I could do better. There was no "you are great no matter what you do" mantra at Beacon Heights School. It was more like "every so often, you are pretty good, but most of the time, you need to work on it."

Bluebirds and "Flying Up"

If Miss Kalionen and our teachers taught us to learn, behave, and excel, Camp Fire Girls taught us to serve others and have a little fun while doing it. My mom, along with her friend Mary Beaudin, put together our nine-girl Bluebird group in 1967. The group included my best friend, Amy Scherber, and Mrs. Beaudin's two girls. My sister, Beth, also attended the meetings, and, with a few other girls joining us as time went on, my mom kept the group together through junior high. (By that time, of course, we were no longer Bluebirds but full-fledged Camp Fire Girls.)

We played games and made holiday crafts and decorations; learned how to make candy, applesauce, pumpkin bread, and cranberry relish; made yarn dolls and bird feeders; and went on hikes, picnics, and winter cookouts. One of the girls in our group recorded the following in our Bluebird scrapbook:

> At our 2nd meeting we sang the blue bird wish song. Then we started our nature hunt. Then we ate our treats. We went back to Amy Klobuchar's house and we drank termite tonic. Yum! Yum!

"Termite tonic" was my mom's nickname for her red Halloween punch.

Each summer we would spend a week at Camp Tanadoona on the shores of Lake Minnewashta, where we would learn how to use a saw, build a campfire, hunt for fossils, horseback ride, and swim on our backs. Every night we sang around the open fire. My favorite round from that time was

> *Make new friends*
> *but keep the old;*
> *one is silver and the other gold.*

As the years went on the girls in our group learned square dancing, performed German folk dances, and tried out pow-wow steps in keeping with the Camp Fire respect for the Native American culture. (Having already taken several years of ballet and tap at Marilyn Thomson's neighborhood dance studio, I especially liked the dancing.) We held father/daughter dinners, and my dad would always come. And we went on many field trips. One that stands out was a Children's Theatre Company production of *Little Women* that was dedicated to the memory of the late singer Janis Joplin.

We took on a lot of service projects, and I kept careful track of everything I did in a logbook, because each completed project added another bead to my Camp Fire vest. We made Mother's Day cards for the Ambassador Nursing Home residents. We made crayon holders for the children's ward of the county hospital. We would visit kids with disabilities, plant tulips at the school, sing Christmas carols for seniors, and collect toys for orphans in Thailand. Every year at Halloween we would all trick-or-treat for UNICEF with little orange boxes. In 1967 our combined efforts brought in the whopping sum of $22.87.

But above all, we followed "The Law of the Camp Fire Girls" (and pledged to continue doing so after we "flew up" from Bluebirds):

WORSHIP GOD

SEEK BEAUTY

GIVE SERVICE

PURSUE KNOWLEDGE

BE TRUSTWORTHY

HOLD ON TO HEALTH

GLORIFY WORK

BE HAPPY

When I look back now at my experiences as a Bluebird, I'm struck by how simple life seemed. The rules were so straightforward, and they were just like the ones I learned from Mrs. Mooney and Miss Kalionen in Beacon Heights School. Always do your work as best you can. Get your work done but favor quality over speed. Speak up but respect others. Give service and you will be rewarded (maybe with some beads for your vest). Be trustworthy, pursue knowledge, and "glorify" your work.

All these years later, I often find myself thinking about those old Camp Fire and Beacon Heights School rules. They don't just belong at summer camp and in the classroom. We need to tack them up in the Senate cloakroom!

Glorify Work

Since the Law of the Camp Fire Girls required that I glorify work, I was determined to rise to the challenge. It began with babysitting, and I took an early interest in the trade by watching my little sister, an adorable and impish baby and toddler. By the tender age of six, I knew the difference between the right way and the wrong way to change a diaper, as evidenced by this "secret" note I left for my mom at the bottom of the stairs on one of those rare occasions when my dad had been left alone to watch my sister and me:

Dear Mom
When dad put the dipper on Beth I think he put it on tight or something because Beth acted a little funny. I could see where it would hurt.
    Dad dos'it know about this note or how he put on her dipper. I din't want to hurt his feels by telling him that he put the dipper on wrong. I wrote this secrtly. Please cheak Beth before you go to bed.

                                               Love, Amy

Sure enough, when my mom went up to "cheak" Beth, she discovered that my dad had put the plastic pants on the inside and the diaper on the outside.

By the age of twelve, I had taken a preteen course in babysitting offered by the Camp Fire Girls. I was very proud of the certificate I was given upon completing the course. In our neighborhood, the going rate for a babysitter at the time was 75 cents an hour. I started working for the Tiedts across the street, with easy access to my mom in case something went wrong. I was pretty good at taking care of the kids, but after they went to bed I never missed an opportunity to raid the refrigerator.

One time I made myself a huge bologna sandwich and brought it down to the Tiedts' basement family room so I could watch TV. A few minutes later, I heard the telltale sign of the garage door opening. The Tiedts had come home an hour early! Believing this half-eaten sandwich could seriously hurt my chances of getting future work as a babysitter, I hid the sandwich, plate and all, on the shag carpet under the couch. A week later I returned to the Tiedts' for another Wednesday night job and was relieved to learn that my income stream was safe. The seven-day-old sandwich was still wedged underneath the couch, exactly where I had left it.

At the Wagensteens', Amy Scherber and I would raid the ashtrays and collect used cigarette butts and later take them out to the woods for a pathetic try at smoking. At the Salmelas', the highly organized Mrs. Salmela would yell up the stairs as she left for the evening, "It would be great if you could do a load of dishes." This request always provoked paralyzing fear. What Mrs. Salmela didn't know was that I had no idea how to operate a dishwasher. We didn't have one at home and I was petrified that I would use too much soap and the suds would come pouring out of the machine like in an *I Love Lucy* episode. Finally I turned to one of my wards—Mrs. Salmela's six-year-old son—for a dishwasher tutorial.

But nothing compared to babysitting for Mr. and Mrs. Rogers, the parents of six children, four boys and two baby girls. It's not at all clear why six children would be left in the hands of such a young sitter, but it was the 1970s and the Rogers did. Or at least they did until the "Kevin Rogers ran away down Murder Hill naked while the babysitter was there" incident. That was when they starting hiring two girls at once.

Naturally the story about four-year-old Kevin Rogers running away naked became the talk of the neighborhood. And although it's true that this notorious incident occurred on my watch, it really was explainable. At the time I was engrossed in a valiant effort to extricate the entire family's toothbrushes from the toilet, shortly after Kevin had attempted to flush them down, creating a major clog. I had four Stouffer's chicken pot pies in the oven, mashed bananas on the kitchen counter, a baby in the crook of my left arm, and all the older kids watching as I tried to unclog the toilet.

"Mom and Dad are going to be really mad at you when they try to brush their teeth!"

"How will you ever clean them off now?"

"What will we use to brush our teeth tonight? A hairbrush?"

Meanwhile, Kevin, knowing he was going to be in big trouble, took off without a stitch of clothing on and headed down Murder Hill, the nickname given by the neighborhood kids to the very steep hill on which the Rogers family lived. Luckily, before I even knew Kevin was missing, one of the neighbors found him two blocks away and brought him back.

From then on Amy Scherber and I handled the babysitting duties at the Rogers' house together. By then, the two of us had already established ourselves as not only a good team but true babysitting entrepreneurs. With our Camp Fire babysitter certificates and our well-established neighborhood connections, we got more jobs than we could handle. The summer we were twelve, we joined forces with our friend Laura Norris and started a babysitting service. We would go from house to house collecting neighborhood kids, instructing them to hold on to a long rope, and then bring them to Laura's backyard, where we would organize games and activities.

Every entrepreneurial venture needs a goal, and we had one. We wanted to use our babysitting earnings to visit Laura's grandparents in Kansas City—and we wanted to go there alone. But first we needed to convince our three moms that this visit would be a really good idea. What better way to persuade them than by presenting our plan while serving up a special mom/daughter lunch? Using a recipe we'd seen in a magazine—chicken salad served up in halved, carved-out pineapples—we won them over. A month later, the three of us—all twelve-year-olds—traveled alone on a Jefferson Lines bus to Kansas City, where we were greeted warmly by the Norris relatives.

In seventh grade I had a new goal: after months of saving my babysitting wages in a shoe box, I used the money to pay for my spot on the class trip to Washington, D.C., the only time I would visit the East Coast until I applied to college. I wish I could say that Mr. Hoffman and Mr. Danielson's seventh-grade trip to Washington was instrumental in my decision to run for the Senate more than thirty years later. But all I remember now are the junior high boys, the Virginia battlefields, and posing for a Polaroid picture in a life-size astronaut cutout at the Air and Space Museum.

Finally at age fifteen I got my first real job. The summer after ninth grade I was a root-beer-mug washer and carhop at the Wayzata A&W. I would ride my bike five miles to that job and five miles back. My job for A&W involved cleaning the mugs by plunging them into a series of vats of hot water with varying concentrations of soap. Then I would put them in a freezer and, voilà, they were frosty, just as advertised. The only problem was that we hardly ever changed the water and it didn't even stay hot for very long (two dubious practices that have long since been changed).

In addition to washing an endless number of mugs, I would occasionally get to carhop. The shirts of our required uniform were tight and to the point. On our chests were emblazoned the words "A&W Root Beer. Take home a jug of fun." I have met many a woman my age who remembers wearing these shirts—and many a man who remembers seeing them. And as with the dishwashing techniques, it's good to know that these shirts have been replaced by new and improved models.

From A&W I advanced to waitressing and pie cutting at Poppin' Fresh Pies. I worked there through high school, as did Amy Scherber, our friend Heidi Bergsagel, and the third Amy in our circle, Amy Schatzke. Heidi kept winning "waitress of the month" awards (along with homecoming princess), and the three Amys kept getting in varying degrees of trouble.

Amy Schatzke once spilled hot coffee on her leg and had to go to the emergency room. Amy Scherber kept having to fend off boys who would show up at the restaurant. They played games with the ketchup bottles, put salt in the sugar holders, and wouldn't leave the booths. But I set the all-time record: I once spilled four ice teas on *one* customer. The people I'd been serving left a penny tip and I was demoted to pie cutter.

Being a pie cutter at the restaurant wasn't really that bad. For one thing, you were very popular. Every time you damaged a pie, an employee got to take it home. Mysteriously, the desserts that seemed to get damaged more than any other were the ever-popular Chocolate French Silk pies. Being a pie cutter also gave you constant access to the freezer, where the frozen menu items such as Strawberry Supreme pie and Sour Cream Raisin pie were kept. Also stored there was the gigantic bowl of whipped cream, and nothing was better than standing in that freezer with the dishwasher boys, dipping spoons in the whipped cream bowl between pie cuttings.

My earnings from Poppin' Fresh Pies financed the most memorable girl trip of my life. Amy, Amy, Heidi, and I spent our entire senior year of high school saving and planning for a spring break trip and at last we met our goal. We had enough tip and wage money for four Greyhound bus tickets to Florida. Our destination? The Days Inn in Fort Lauderdale.

When we arrived, the three-story hotel and its pool were teeming with boys and beer can pyramids. Earlier we had decided to pretend we were in college, hoping that would improve our chances of meeting older boys. That worked fine until we met our match—four boys from Janesville, Wisconsin, all with mustaches and all claiming to be in college. After an evening out, the truth was discovered—they, too, were high school students, and their mustaches were fake. In fact, they were stick-ons, though I won't describe which one of us figured that out and how.

The mid-1970s was clearly a more trusting time—what mother today would allow her high school daughter to travel with three of her friends by Greyhound bus to Fort Lauderdale for spring break? Somehow, though, we all survived. Maybe our parents gave us enough independence that we had no choice but to learn how to make our own good judgments. Maybe we were stronger and more mature because we had each other. All I know is that despite the stolen cigarette butts and the keg parties, despite the bus trip to Florida and the encounters with the fake-mustached boys, in the end all four of us followed our dreams and came out fine—just as our parents always believed we would.

Amy Schatzke—the best dancer in our high school chorus line, which won the state championship our senior year—became a national champion ballroom dancer and the co-owner of a successful local dance studio along with her dance partner–husband, Scott Anderson. Heidi Bergsagel, who was always everyone's trusted confidante and best friend, became a career counselor and associate dean at an arts college and is still everyone's trusted confidante and best friend. Amy Scherber, after getting her start on the front lines at Poppin' Fresh Pies, trained as a baker in New York and Paris and then started up her own bakery. Amy's Bread has now been in operation for more than twenty years, and it's one of the most successful and beloved bakeries in New York City.

So maybe our parents got it just right!

1315 Oakview Lane

As I was growing up and making my way through the hallways of my middle school (Ridgemount Junior High) and my big public high school (Wayzata High School)—not to mention the freezer at Poppin' Fresh Pies—life at 1315 Oakview Lane remained pretty much the same, with a few notable updates. A color TV replaced the black-and-white one, and I still remember the first movie I ever watched in color: *The Wizard of Oz*, featuring Minnesota-born Judy Garland. My sister and I would watch after-school reruns of shows like *Petticoat Junction* and *The Beverly Hillbillies*, and we waited all week for the super cool ABC Friday night lineup: *The Brady Bunch*, *The Partridge Family*, and *Love, American Style*. (To this day I remember David Cassidy's birthday from the Partridge Family album: April 12.) If we were really lucky, my dad would make his Friday night fried flour tacos with crumbled hamburger meat, and we would start the lineup with our TV trays in front of us, tacos in hand.

My parents also bought a piano and for ten years I took lessons. Despite my inability to play music by ear, I was good at memorizing and playing classical pieces with flair. I earned some awards in state contests, but there's no question that my piano career peaked at age sixteen in an onstage performance at the University of Minnesota's Northrop Auditorium, when I was one of twenty intermediate students who played Poulenc's *L'embarquement pour Cythère* simultaneously—on twenty dueling grand pianos—under the direction of the famous Minnesota conductor Philip Brunelle. My mom and my grandma from Ely beamed.

Our house in Plymouth changed with the times. The closely cut gray carpet that had been installed in the late 1950s was replaced by stylish burnt-orange shag. My parents built an addition on the back that included a modern dining room, family room, and deck. We finally got air-conditioning, which led to years of mother/daughter fights over the nighttime temperature. We also got a dog, a soft-coated wheaten terrier that became a favorite of my sister. Molly had boundless energy and a tendency to bark at the least provocation. She would become the subject of several of my dad's columns in the 1970s.

Every summer we would take a family vacation. We'd drive to northern Minnesota or the Black Hills or the Grand Tetons and Yellowstone. All these trips featured long, arduous hikes, ranger talks, and fishing. We'd pack a tent and sleeping bags and strike out on three- to four-day backpack trips through the Grand Tetons' canyons, aptly named Cascade and Paintbrush and—my personal favorite because it sounded so hard—Death. We'd take in scenes of wildflowers, glacier lakes, and an occasional moose. "I am exhausted," my mom confessed in a postcard to her parents, written from Red Lodge, Montana, on the way home from one trip out west.

On all our trips, my dad always insisted we get up early, no matter how late we'd been up the night before. In another postcard to my grandparents, my mom wrote:

> Left at 6AM! Got up at 5 after going to bed at 1:30. Jim is stewing in the car cause the girls just had to have some breakfast. They had instant B at 5:30 and that seems ages ago to them.

My dad would often write columns about our family trips, and his high-profile job with the newspaper brought some notoriety to our family. This was good and bad. The good part was that whenever my dad had two extra tickets to a Vikings game, I got to bring along a boy from school. The bad part was that he would sometimes mention me in one of his columns, which wasn't always easy for a teenager. Once, after watching a Monday Night NFL game on television with me, he wrote a column featuring a debate we'd had about a player who'd suffered a serious injury during the game. I insisted that it was a groin injury, he was certain that it wasn't, and the question wasn't settled until later in the game when the announcers confirmed that it was, in fact, a serious groin injury. Two days later, as I walked into the junior high cafeteria, I encountered a group of boys laughing uproariously at my dad's latest column: he'd outted me as the one who'd spotted the groin injury on the field.

Talk about living in the public eye.

Over time, my dad became a local celebrity. He had one of the first talk radio shows in the Twin Cities and one of the first local TV talk shows, *Jim Klobuchar's Merry-Go-Round*. The show competed against *The Honeymooners*, *Bewitched*, and *Wild Kingdom*. Among the show's best-known episodes was the one when nationally known wrestler Verne Gagne put my father into a sleeper hold on live TV.

Booze

But my dad's high-flying job and exhilarating fame had some serious drawbacks. He was gone a lot. He missed family gatherings. Even on evenings when he was in town, my mom often had to call him and ask when he was coming home.

But the biggest problem was that he started to drink more and more.

A lot of journalists drank to excess in those days, especially sports-writers. Alcohol was part of the reporter's culture—you drank with your buddies, with politicians, with cops, with coaches and players. My dad had seen a lot of drinking at home when he was growing up, and he always enjoyed his wine and a few cocktails. And for much of my parents' twenty-two-year marriage, his drinking wasn't an issue at all.

In the early 1970s that began to change. I remember one of my birth-day parties when he came home two hours late. We blew out the candles and ate the cake without him. I remember several Christmas Eves when he didn't seem right, and one Christmas morning when we waited for him to come home so we could open our presents. As my sister and I hung over the back of the living room couch and looked out the picture window facing the driveway, my mom said over and over again, "Who works on Christmas morning?"

For years I was too young to understand what was happening, but by my early teenage years it became clear to me that his drinking had gotten out of control. The first memorable incident occurred when I was in junior high. My dad and I went to a Vikings game in Bloomington at the old Met Stadium. On the way home from the game, we stopped at the Monte Carlo bar in Minneapolis so he could visit his friend and the bar's owner, Steve Critelli. While my dad and his buddy Steve had drinks upstairs, I sat at the bar on my own, a twelve-year-old sipping a 7UP. On the drive home, my dad was weaving all over Highway 55 and he ended up putting his car in a ditch right near our house. When the police came, they let him go home and that was the end of it. But I was scared. He told me he was sorry and that he would never do it again. I remember he cried.

Then came the drinking-related driving offenses in the 1970s. He didn't go to jail or even lose his license, but the charges were mentioned in the paper and got some attention. (After the first one, a classmate carved the words "drunk" on the front of my junior high locker. The boy allegedly had a crush on me and must have imagined that this would demonstrate his undying affection. A janitor sanded off the graffiti two days later.) After the second one my dad pledged to join AA. He told everyone he wasn't drinking anymore, but in fact he'd stay sober for a while only to fall off the wagon. Holidays or major events were especially hard. He would sometimes go a year or more without drinking and then go back to it. He did most of his drinking in secret. My mom found liquor bottles hidden in the laundry room. For almost two decades, my father kept his drinking problem out of the public eye, but he was unquestionably an alcoholic.

On more than one occasion we had an argument about it on the way up to Ely to visit my grandma. Twice after I got my driver's license I caught him taking a drink out of a bottle stashed in the trunk of his car. When I confronted him, he would say that it was mouthwash. I would call him out on his lie. I would take the keys from him and drive, and we wouldn't speak for hundreds of miles.

My dad would always say that his drinking never affected his writing or his work. For the most part that was true, and in fact his career and his fame kept getting bigger. But it did affect things. It hurt his marriage. It made it really hard growing up, especially for my sister Beth. It nearly ruined both my high school and college graduations. It was really sad for my mom.

Twenty years after my dad's first encounters with the law, he was, as he put it, "pursued by grace." Thanks to the stricter laws in place by the 1990s, and also due to good substance abuse treatment, his faith, his friends and family, and AA, he finally quit drinking once and for all.

I grew up seeing my dad climb the highest of peaks and then, because of his drinking, fall into the lowest of valleys. Like many alcoholics' kids, the experience has given me a low tolerance for lying and a deep-seated desire to try to fix every problem that comes across my path, even when it isn't possible.

A Marriage Ends

I was sitting in the living room on the couch doing my homework when I heard my dad ask my mom for a divorce. I was fifteen and in tenth grade, focused on school, my friends, and boys (and not necessarily in that order).

It was Thanksgiving weekend. My mom and dad and my grandma Margaret were sitting at the dining room table drinking coffee. My mom had just done the dishes. Leftover pumpkin pie sat on the table, and paper mache turkeys hung from the ceiling. In the background, a football game played on TV.

I don't know why my dad picked Thanksgiving weekend to ask my mom for a divorce. I also don't know why my grandma from Milwaukee (my mom's mother) was sitting at the table with the two of them. But the biggest mystery was why my dad didn't look around the corner into the living room to see if my sister and I were within earshot. After all, it was a holiday weekend and it was snowing. We didn't have a lot of places to go.

When I look back at that moment now, I am convinced that my grandma Margaret was there for a reason, that my dad had persuaded her to join the conversation so it would be easier for my mom to handle. Fair or not, his marriage to my mom had come to an end, and I suspect he wanted her mother to be there to comfort her after he delivered the news.

Later my dad would write that although he initiated the divorce, "[t]here was no provocation for it," describing himself as "another middle-aged man with wanderlust." Less than a year later, the day the divorce was finalized, he would explain the decision to end his twenty-two-year marriage in a column called "Four Days Short of an Anniversary." "There are times when lives must take another direction," he wrote, "when the mind's resistance to this change yields to an intuitive force that sometimes governs the person in ways he does not totally understand but has come to accept." Not surprisingly, my mom wasn't a big fan of that column, but he wrote it with much pain and with much affection for her.

I remember the night my dad asked for a divorce with perfect clarity. My mom's immediate response was to ask, "Why are you doing this at Thanksgiving?" and then she burst into tears. Her next words were not full of rage or betrayal. She simply said, "How can I afford this? How can I stay in the house? How can I pay for a car?"

"I will take care of you," my father answered. "I will take care of Amy and Beth. You can do this. You like teaching. You can learn to drive."

My mom responded to this earthquake in her life with no anger about the past, no resentment about affairs or drinking. It just was. I remember my grandma trying to convince my mom that this was going to be okay and saying something about some savings. To that my mom replied that she had just cashed out all of her Minneapolis teachers' pension money to build the deck and the addition on the back of the house.

That was when I got up from the living room couch really, really quietly, went down the stairs, grabbed my winter ski jacket with all the Afton Alps ski tags on it, and ran into the night. I particularly remember that for the first and only time in her life, Molly the dog did not bark.

A light snow was falling. It was beautiful, brand-new Thanksgiving snow. No one was out. I ran through the snow and down Oakview Lane and past the houses of all the people I babysat for—the Tiedts, the Salmelas, the Rogers. I ran around the pond and up the big hill toward the new development, Ravenwood, where all the houses had two-car garages and where my best friend Amy Scherber lived on Windemere Curve.

I had never run away before, not even close.

Everything was rushing through my head. First, there was the scourge of divorce itself. Divorce may have been sweeping the country at the time, but it hadn't quite made it to Plymouth, Minnesota. None of my friends' parents were divorced and my closest encounter with divorce at Wayzata High School was going to a keg party thrown by a guy whose parents were divorced. On an ominous note, we were all told at the time that the reason he could have the keg party was because his "parents were divorced and no one was home."

Divorce meant trouble. Divorce meant unsupervised keg parties. But divorce also meant no family vacations. And especially because my dad was gone a lot, our family vacations were really important. We *always* took a summer vacation. I planned all the dried food for the backpack trips and what we would eat each day for breakfast, lunch, and dinner. I made charts.

After a while I stopped running and just walked through the snowy darkness. Finally I reached the Scherbers' house and rang the doorbell. I hadn't called ahead and they had no idea I was coming. Then, just as Amy's dad answered the door, a car pulled up in the driveway. It was my dad. I ducked into the house and ran by Mr. Scherber and yelled back, "I don't want to talk to him. My parents are getting a divorce."

Tony Scherber, trim Pillsbury executive and cross-country skier that he was, was no match for my stocky dad as he came barreling through the door. But somehow Mr. Scherber's calm business manner slowed my dad's forward momentum. Mr. Scherber left my dad in the front hall and then came and found me in Amy's room. After talking with me for a while, he went back to my dad and explained that I didn't want to see him that night but that I would talk to him the next day.

I guess everyone decided that since I had run away for the first and last time in my life, at least I should be allowed to sleep over.

Amy's mom, Pat, got out the sleeping bag, and I slept on the floor in Amy's room surrounded by her mod yellow- and orange-circled wallpaper with the inlaid foil. We really didn't talk that much. We just went to sleep.

When I woke up the next morning Mrs. Scherber made pancakes. She also served me powdered milk, something they'd always had from back when they didn't have any money. They'd all gotten used to it, but I never did.

I remember staring into that glass of powdered milk knowing I was going to have to go home.

After breakfast, Amy and her dad drove me back to the house.

When we got to 1315 Oakview Lane, there was my mom, outside shoveling snow in the driveway by herself, just as she did most times when it snowed.

The driveway needed to be cleared, but I'm sure it was also my mom's way of saying that life would go on.

And it did.

Jaunts with Jim

After my parents got divorced, there were really only two choices for dad/daughter outings. One was the awkward once-a-month divorced dad dinners—"your mom says you really like your English teacher"—at Latuff's Pizzeria in the strip mall a mile from our house.

The other was long-distance bike rides. After a while we dropped the pizza dinners and just did the bike rides.

These outings typically involved much more than just a couple of loops around nearby Medicine Lake. In fact, the template for our many adventures together was our first long-distance bike ride, which we took before the divorce. This was a marathon trek from Plymouth to Ely to visit my grandparents. Total distance? 255 miles. Days traveled? Two.

Before that day I had never ridden a bicycle more than twenty-five miles. Clad in strawberry-patterned pink shorts, wearing no helmet, and riding my ten-speed orange American Arrow bike—which my dad had purchased that spring at a "fire sale" at the Jewish Community Center where he played racquetball—I left the house at 6:00 a.m. and began following my dad down the road. Early on, I realized that only the top five of the bike's ten gears worked, but that was okay because the terrain was relatively flat and the wind was at our backs. By midday, riding like crazy, we made it to Hinckley, the site of a historic firestorm that killed more than four hundred area residents in 1894.

Hinckley was supposed to be our overnight stop, but at some point my dad decided that we could actually complete the trip to Ely in two days instead of three and surprise my grandparents. But that would require reaching Cloquet by nightfall, and getting to Cloquet—the home of a major paper mill, not to mention the world's only gas station designed by Frank Lloyd Wright—would mean that on that first day we would have to bike a total of 145 miles.

For the last twenty miles I was really dragging. At one point I actually got off my bike, laid it on the highway shoulder, and pretended that I'd fallen.

"Come on, get back on the bike!" my dad yelled back at me. "We have to get there by dark!"

I got my second wind.

As darkness fell, we pitched our tent near the historic gas station. Soon we were eating Cheez Whiz and salami on Ritz crackers.

The next day, undeterred by a thunderstorm and repeated flashes of lightning, we covered another 110 miles. Toward the end, we had to climb a lot of hills, and as my own little show of rebellion, I walked most of them. Arriving in Ely in late afternoon, we were welcomed by my grandpa's big open arms and my grandma's famous Slovenian sour meat and homemade noodle soup.

My dad loved taking long, challenging bike trips. He once bicycled around Lake Superior in only seven days, pedaling the entire time with a large pack on his back. In later years he and I bicycled in Slovenia and Russia; rode eleven hundred miles in ten days from Minneapolis to Jackson Hole, Wyoming; and, after my freshman year in college, cycled from New Haven en route to Minneapolis, although our trip ended prematurely near Flint, Michigan, when my dad fell and broke his cheekbone. In the mid-1970s, he started up an annual "Jaunt with Jim" bike trip and pro- moted it using his newspaper column. As many as two hundred people would join him, and the annual trek would continue for thirty-nine years.

For three years in a row during high school, Amy Scherber and I joined the trip. We loaded all our gear on the backs of our bikes and covered an average of eighty to ninety miles a day. About twenty-five kids our age would come on the trip; on the first day, that number would be divided almost evenly between girls and boys. By the end of the next day, several girls would drop out. By the end of the third day, Amy and I would pretty much have fifteen high school boys to ourselves.

The days were long and the weather was often scorching. Highway shoulders were not exactly bicycle friendly back then. There were a lot of bicycle-on-bicycle crashes and plenty of tire blowouts. As the leader of the "Jaunts with Jim," my dad was always a strong and omnipresent bike war- rior. Sometimes I would ride side-by-side with him down the highway, but for the most part he left Amy and me alone.

The "Jaunt with Jim" bike trips with my dad gave me a lifelong love of the far reaches of our state. On one trip we bicycled along Lake Superi- or—a lovely route I would put up against an ocean-side trail any day—all the way up to the Canadian border. We bicycled from the Twin Cities to the headwaters of the Mississippi at Lake Itasca, the place where you can actually walk across the Mississippi River. We took river rides in the shad- ows of pine trees and spruces, traveled the farmlands of southern Min- nesota (narrowly missing many a barking farm dog), and rode the rolling hills and bluffs in southeastern Minnesota and Wisconsin.

My dad's sincere efforts to make peace with me after the divorce, and in so many ways with my mom, were good ones. They were the right way to reach out to a miffed teenager. He shared not just his time but his love for the woods and our beautiful state. It was a gift.

Stairway to Heaven

Wayzata High School in the 1970s was not exactly a hotbed of political activism. Watergate and Nixon's resignation were behind us. The Vietnam War had ended. Minnesota Senator Eugene McCarthy, an eloquent opponent of the war and once one of the most prominent Democrats in the country, was no longer a force to be reckoned with. And Hubert Humphrey, our "Happy Warrior," was laid to rest in 1978.

With the exception of Humphrey's death and the 1976 election of Walter Mondale to the vice presidency, the truth was that, for my friends and me, national politics was little more than a blip in the top-of-the-hour news break during Casey Kasem's *American Top 40*, a show that played nearly nonstop on our transistor radios.

For the most part our high school political debates were confined to meandering discussions in Mr. Lewis's social studies class, once-a-year visits from our local Republican legislator, and late-night ruminations on the meaning of the lyrics to "Stairway to Heaven." No matter how many times we listened to that eight-minute Led Zeppelin track, it never got much clearer. As the song repeatedly intones, *"Ooh, it makes me wonder."* And wonder we did.

Even the feminist movement, then in full swing elsewhere in the country, received little attention during my high school years. Wayzata had begun to offer more girls' sports, but a good part of the student body cared mainly about boys' football, basketball, and hockey. Girls engaged in highly competitive tryouts for the girls-only cheerleading squad and chorus line. (Amy and Amy were sure bets for the chorus line. I tried out but didn't make it because I couldn't do the splits.)

The one area where equality reigned was academic achievement. Of the top ten honors students in our graduating class of 522, six of us were girls. But no matter how many "way to go" signs we got from our teachers or how many smiley faces appeared on our papers, they carried little weight compared to the premium placed on good looks, invitations to class dances, and getting a red carnation delivered to you in the middle of class during Heart Week, a five-day tribute to Valentine's Day.

Thankfully, much has changed since I attended high school in suburban Minnesota, but in the mid-1970s many girls had three short-term goals:

1. Wear your hair long and straight (I passed) or, if it suited you, sport a Dorothy Hamill haircut (see 1976 Olympics, figure skating).
2. Develop a dark, *even* summer tan, best achieved by spending hours on

    your roof covered in baby oil and lying prone in a cardboard box lined
    with tin foil. (I achieved this goal, too, and I only had to make one visit
    to the doctor for severe burns. My husband still does not believe I did
    this. I did. And yes, I now know it is bad for you.)

3. If you really hit the jackpot, marry your senior prom date (several of
   my friends succeeded in pulling that one off).

In the end, as I'll explain shortly, I failed to meet only goal number three: I never married my high school prom date.

My association with the senior prom actually began in my junior year, when I was elected secretary-treasurer of our junior class. It was our class's job to raise the money for the seniors' prom, and we soon came up with the brilliant idea of launching a Lifesaver lollipop drive. After learning that we could purchase the lollipops in bulk at a very reduced rate from the local dime store, we organized students to sell them for months during lunch outside the cafeteria at triple the cost to us. I had organized trips and babysitting joint ventures in the past, but the Lifesaver lollipop drive was my first major political field operation. The cash poured in, and by the spring we'd raised enough money to give the seniors a fancy prom at the Leamington Hotel in downtown Minneapolis.

But as is often the case with the administration that follows a highly successful one, the next class of juniors faltered badly. They raised so little money that our senior prom had to be held in the common area of the Ridgedale Mall, where we were expected to dance around the mall's center fountain, surrounded by the romantic after-hours lighting of Woolworth's, Hallmark, and the Orange Julius store.

My prom date was my friend Steve Bergman. He and I double-dated with our friends Heidi Bergsagel and Steve Dick. In keeping with the times, Heidi and Steve went on to wed. They are still happily married and very good friends of mine to this day. I've always admired how they embraced their last name. For years their doormat in Plymouth read "Welcome, the Dicks."

For our senior prom Heidi and I dressed in matching pink dresses. Steve and Steve wore maroon tuxes and pink carnations. We took pictures in the backyard and went out to dinner. Afterward we went to the mall, and by the time we got to the dancing part of the prom, my date,

Steve, was very focused on one thing. He wanted me to dance with him in the mall fountain.

"No," I said, "I absolutely will not do that."

Why would I ever want to ruin my pink polyester dress and matching shoes and shawl by dancing in the mall fountain? After all, I was certain that one day I would wear them again in all their glory. But Steve was on a mission. He was furious that the juniors had screwed up our prom and that we had to hold it in the Ridgedale Mall, and he was going to make them remember it forever. He soon found a willing accomplice in Sally Lundin, who was wearing a much prettier dress than mine. (Like I actually remember. Okay, I do remember—it was a gorgeous silky satin pastel green dress. There was no shawl.)

Steve and Sally whooped it up in the fountain and got sopping wet. The entire senior class gathered around and cheered them on.

In what was surely one of the lowest moments of my high school career, if not my life to date, the assistant principal and head chaperone, Dr. Sommers, walked over and asked me if I needed a ride home from one of the parent chaperones.

"No, Dr. Sommers," I said, "I can take care of myself. I can get a ride home from Heidi."

As my daughter would say years later when I told her the story to cheer her up after some equally mortifying school experience, "Awkward, Mom, awkward."

Looking back at those years, I'm amazed that more didn't go wrong. The wrong party or the wrong boy or the wrong turn in the wrong car with the wrong driver could set you back for life. The sexual revolution had finally reached the Twin Cities suburbs, resulting in memorable truth-or-dare games in the basement of the kid whose family ran the trailer court. Hickeys were seen as an early teen status symbol. (I have a very strong recollection of one of my friends telling her mother that the mark on her neck was from the suction of a vacuum cleaner nozzle when it whipped out of her hand while she was babysitting.) Couples were making out in the hallways of the high school.

Drive-ins were really hot. Until my senior year I was allowed to borrow my mom's red Comet, and I especially liked to take friends with me to see movies at the local drive-in. But my privileges came to an abrupt end after

I borrowed the car for a double date with my friend Amy Scherber and two boys named Mike. Somehow during the course of this Amy/Mike, Amy/Mike escapade, the driver's-side heating vent got kicked in, and for the rest of the car's life only the passenger-side vent worked. Every winter my mom would drive to work wearing a hat and mittens inside the freezing red Comet with the busted heating vent, vociferously complaining about the day she loaned me the car for the drive-in. She never let it go.

And then there were the pranks. The night before our last day of classes at Wayzata High, seven of us had an ingenious if ill-advised idea for a senior prank. We commandeered an elephant kiddie ride outside the local Kmart, loaded it onto the back of a pickup truck, and brought it into our school for our classmates to ride.

We intended to return the machine the next afternoon—we really did. But just before the end of our final day of school, the Plymouth police showed up and loaded us into a couple of police cars. As it happened, the entire school witnessed this humiliation, because someone had just celebrated the last day of class by lighting a smoke bomb, setting off the fire alarms and sending everyone outside.

We were taken to the Plymouth Police Department and questioned about—you guessed it—the theft of an elephant. The police actually impounded the elephant ride as evidence. They used a stolen car sheet for record-keeping purposes, and on the line that said "COLOR" they filled in "GRAY." On the line that said "MAKE AND BODY DESCRIPTION" they wrote "FAT."

Fortunately cooler heads prevailed, and upon learning of the nature of the prank the managers of the local Kmart decided not to pursue the matter. We forked over the money to get the elephant out of the impound lot and returned it to Kmart. The store even made a nice little profit. While the kiddie ride was at the high school, a great number of Wayzata students had paid a dime to ride the elephant.

Lessons Learned

Looking back on my years at Wayzata High, I think three things got me through. First, although in those days our school was neither racially nor religiously diverse (I actually remember meeting my first Jewish friend,

Michael Siskin), it was demographically diverse. That evened the playing field and caused the school to be accepting of all kinds of kids, including me. Every day felt like an Election Day voting line. Everyone was mushed together—at your locker, at your bus stop, in your typing class. That's how you met the kids who became your friends.

And I did have lots of true and trusted friends, both girls and boys. My friends' dads worked in hardware stores, sold Kraft Foods, worked as firemen, and ran companies. Some came from wealthy families, some grew up in low-income families, and a number lived on farms or at least in the rural part of the district. Most of us were somewhere in the middle. We lived in modest suburban homes with one- or two-car garages. We got spider bikes in junior high and ten-speeds in high school. We never had a lot, but we always had enough.

Second, the teachers at Wayzata—just like those at Beacon Heights—truly cared about us. They were demanding, but they also went out of their way to bolster our confidence. I will never forget walking into my advanced chemistry class the first day. Only a few girls had signed up for the course, and the room was filled with boys ready to realize their teenage dreams by setting off an explosive chemical reaction or, at the very least, a stink bomb. But my teacher, Mr. Hembre, was used to that and took it all in stride. He was generous and attentive, and he went out of his way to make sure I liked the class.

In his V-neck sweater and relaxed Scandinavian way, Jim Hembre taught me that I could "lean in" and do better than those boisterous guys, long before anyone knew what "leaning in" was all about. Mr. Hembre was the best. Knowing that a teacher cared about a girl doing well in advanced chemistry was all I needed to succeed. And it didn't end there. Years later, my former high school chemistry teacher regularly showed up at precinct caucuses and fundraisers and rallies—and he always sported my campaign bumper sticker on his pickup truck.

The last reason I survived high school was that my parents had taught me the importance of striving to do my best. Like my teachers, they instilled in me a "you can always do better" drive that kept me going. I would study for a test even if no one else did. I would do my utmost to write a really good paper. I would bicycle every day to my job. Just like my mom, I would aim high, and in the end I achieved the goal that had just barely eluded her—I became the valedictorian of my class and gave the graduation speech.

Instead of cutting out wedding pictures for my bedroom wall—I once slept over at a girl's house whose room was inexplicably plastered with photos of Tricia Nixon in her wedding gown, Tricia Nixon with her wedding cake, and Tricia Nixon on the White House lawn with her parents and new husband—my mom was pinning my report cards on the kitchen bulletin board. She never talked about weddings or Prince Charmings or asked me if I was going to a dance. She was much more focused on my piano recitals, my science projects, and my history reports.

And my dad? He was hugely proud of my grades at Wayzata High and always urged me on to greater things. One day after school I was riding down the elevator at my dad's office when one of his coworkers casually asked me where I was going (meaning at that very moment). Without missing a beat, my dad answered, "She's going to college."

Between my friends, my teachers, and my parents, I somehow managed to buck the norms of the 1970s. I decided not to adopt the permanent tan. I gave up on the seven-bananas, seven-eggs, and seven-wieners three-day rotating diet. I even gave up on going to The Who concert in Johnny Royer's van (although the time we went to Aerosmith . . . well, that was really fun).

I learned a sense of balance in high school that has served me well throughout my life. I learned the value of trusted friends, and I learned that mixing it up with people who are very different from me makes the world a far more interesting place. Most important, I learned the lyrics to "Stairway to Heaven."

From New Haven
to Hyde Park

College

During high school I rarely thought about college. I worked hard and both my teachers and my parents seemed to believe that college was in my future. I assumed I'd go, but no one gave me any specific advice, and right through the end of my junior year my parents and I never discussed where I should apply.

In the fall of my senior year I borrowed a copy of *Guide to Colleges* from the guidance counselor's office. That's the first time it occurred to me that maybe I should at least think about applying to colleges beyond Minnesota and Wisconsin. As I paged through the book, I had no idea which college was in which state, which one was urban or rural, which one was big or small. I certainly didn't know their faculty/student ratio; I didn't even know what that was.

By this point I knew that my parents, proud graduates of Midwestern public colleges, hoped I would stay in Minnesota, mainly because they wanted me to be close to home. But they also wanted me to take advantage of the $500 in-state local teachers' scholarship they knew I'd get because my mom was a teacher and I had good grades. Given today's tuition costs, that may not seem like a lot of money, but my parents' divorce had made our financial situation shaky, so every dollar counted.

By mid-fall I decided to take the tests that were required for the fancy

Ivy League schools. At the time nearly all Minnesota kids took the ACT, but since the East Coast schools mostly required the SAT, my prom date Steve and I had to drive to a neighboring school district to take the test. Not familiar with the nearby suburb, we got lost on the way and arrived too late, leaving very few options for future testing dates. Somehow we managed to take the test later that fall, and we both did well.

Armed with some good scores, good grades, and recommendations from Mrs. Johnson, my piano teacher, and Mr. Hembre, my chemistry teacher, I somewhat randomly selected eight schools and applied to them. As I remember it, I was more focused on not racking up more than eight application fees than on which college might be right for me. I never visited any of the schools I applied to, so my most vivid memory of this period was typing the applications and the accompanying essays in our basement while I ate orange popsicles.

A few months later, I got some exciting news. Among other places, I got into Yale, Dartmouth, and Brown. Neither of my parents wanted me to go to an Ivy League school; my dad thought the $7,500 annual fee for tuition and room and board was way too steep, and he and my mom actively worked with Wayzata's guidance counselor in an effort to steer me elsewhere. But by then I was determined to attend a school far from home. Having a dad who was always in the news wasn't easy, and I really wanted to go someplace where nobody would know my name.

Then good fortune intervened in the form of my dad's new boss. One day in the spring of my senior year I was visiting my dad at work when we happened to encounter the brand-new editor of the newspaper, the intimidating Steve Isaacs. When Mr. Isaacs asked me where I was going to college, I said I didn't know. When he asked me where I got in and I told him, he seemed shocked. He immediately said, "Well then, you're going to Yale." My dad shook his head and said, "No, it's really too expensive." Mr. Isaacs, who was always quite blunt, told my father he was out of his mind.

Finally my dad agreed to allow me to see one college out east—it was up to me to pick the one we'd visit. I chose Yale, and when the two of us arrived in New Haven, Connecticut, our first stop was the university's financial aid office. As my dad stood in his brown polyester pants playing with the coins in his pocket, the financial aid officer looked up from his desk and stared him down. "I am sympathetic about your divorce and all, sir, but you are simply caught in the middle-class crunch. You don't qualify."

We then had a brief meeting with David Papke, an American studies professor. Soon after I'd received my acceptance letter, he had written me a kind note saying that he liked my application essay. But I could tell my dad was still riled up about our encounter at the financial aid office, so I found it hard to concentrate on our conversation with Professor Papke.

Ready for a break, we checked into the local Holiday Inn, where my dad promptly got in a huge fight with a clerk at the front desk when the man innocently asked him for a credit card. With his Depression-era upbringing and libertarian streak, my dad strongly believed that if an American citizen had cash or a personal check and a driver's license, he should not have to pay a monthly fee to a credit card company to prove his creditworthiness. While arguing that he ought to be able to pay for our room with a check, my dad blew a gasket as only an Iron Ranger could do, and finally the rather timid desk clerk slunk away to the manager's office. My dad was delighted when the clerk returned and said he could indeed pay by check.

A week later I accepted Yale's offer. After days of discussion and a great deal of grumbling, my dad had finally agreed to put up the money as long as I agreed to take out student loans and keep any extraneous expenses to a minimum. In the end, my dad was always a strong supporter of my education, and for years he proudly wore the Yale Bulldog tie I gave him for his birthday.

Two Suitcases and a Trunk

I flew to New Haven the following August. Alone, I loaded my trunk and two suitcases into an airport van. For some reason the van dropped me by the train station, a mile from campus. Problem: how to get to my actual destination? Picking up both suitcases, I walked a block down what was then a rather run-down Chapel Street and left the suitcases near the next corner. Then I went back for the trunk. I repeated this routine block after block after block. Two suitcases, then the trunk. Two suitcases, then the trunk. In keeping with my dad's demand for frugality, the idea of taking a cab didn't even occur to me.

It was an unorthodox way to enter Yale's campus, with all of its gargoyles and Gothic architecture. Continuing my two-suitcases-and-a-trunk forced march, I made it to the Old Campus—a large public square surrounded by dorms—and walked to the bronze statue of American Revolutionary War hero Nathan Hale. Looking down at the base of the statue of Hale, a young schoolteacher and Yale alum, I read the words he is said to have uttered before being executed by the British in 1776 for being an American spy: "I only regret that I have but one life to lose for my country."

The statue reminded me that I had come all this way for a reason: I wanted to make something of myself. But at that particular moment I wasn't inclined to spend a lot of energy on lofty thoughts. Instead, I was just very focused on the two heavy suitcases, the trunk, my sore shoulders, and whether I could even make it to my assigned room.

I finally found Farnam Hall tucked in the corner of the Old Campus square by Battell Chapel. I took the suitcases and the trunk up several flights of stairs to my assigned dorm room—Farnam Hall, A entryway, third floor, room FA32.

My four freshmen roommates were all from the East Coast. One had attended Andover and another had graduated from Miss Porter's School for Girls. As I walked into the dorm room I realized that these four girls were not merely the only people I knew at Yale, but the only people I knew on the entire East Coast. I was the Iron Ranger's daughter from Minnesota, the girl who had never met a kid from a private school and had no idea that squash was a sport as well as a vegetable. And at the bottom of my trunk was the fanciest piece of clothing I owned: thinking I might need it, I'd actually packed that pink polyester high school prom dress.

I never did wear the dress again, but the major adjustment ahead of me could be summed up in one exchange that occurred only a few weeks after I got to Yale. Late one afternoon I came upon one of my freshmen neighbors as she was trying on her designer debutante dress. She was very upset: the New York ball was approaching and she was convinced that her dress was a failure because she wasn't flat enough on top. I tried to reassure her that the dress looked great.

"How would you know, Amy," she said through the tears, "you've never been to a debutante ball."

"That's true," I said, "but that's because they don't have them in Minnesota."

"Yes, they do," she sobbed. "You just weren't invited."

Years later, I checked with a number of Minnesota's old-money families—the Pillsburys, the Cowles, the Wintons. Yes, years ago they may have had some debutante balls in Minnesota, although they were mostly well before my time. But on one count the girl was right: if there had been one in 1978, I'd never have been invited.

We were an eclectic mix in room FA32. One of my roommates was a classic preppy, one was a crew jock, one a Russian Studies major, and one a chemistry whiz. And me? I was the girl the freshman counselor called when someone was needed to make peace because the other four weren't getting along. In the end, it all worked out fine. Yale's residential college system—the school divides the thirteen hundred incoming freshmen into twelve different colleges—made it easier for someone like me to meet people and make new friends. Assigned to Jonathan Edwards College, I had a place to eat and a place to call home.

I went to Yale knowing I would have to work really hard. From the start, I loved my classes and my professors. In the first year I took everything from international relations to French to calculus. I spent many long days and nights studying in Yale's majestic Sterling Memorial Library, taking copious notes on yellow legal pads under the chandeliers and high-arched ceilings of the library's cavernous Reading Room.

Determined that no one in my family would come to regret my decision to go to an Ivy League school, and driven by a conviction that I had a lot of catching up to do after high school, I treated every assignment as an opportunity to learn and excel. I went on to take statistics, economics, international law, and several political science and writing classes. I read late into the night, methodically typing up my class notes, and preparing for tests by filling out lined index cards in small all-caps print.

Unlike some of my fellow students, I didn't arrive at Yale academically "burnt out." Instead, I had spent a good chunk of the previous three years hanging out with my friends after school, waitressing, and going to rock concerts (whether in vans or otherwise). I was just incredibly happy to be there.

Life Outside the Library

I had never considered myself or my family lacking in resources, but compared to some of my classmates, I was. Having gone to a public high school with kids from all sorts of backgrounds, I knew this new world of privilege and secret societies was a kind of parallel universe. But that never really bothered me. Besides, being of modest means gave me more opportunities to meet people in college, since for me there was no winter break ski trip to Aspen, no warm-weather vacation in March, and no family summer house.

To save money, I spent several of my Thanksgiving and spring breaks at Yale. Since there was no dining hall service, I would eat at Claire's Corner Copia or Yorktown Pizza or just buy Ritz crackers and cheese. I also recall a couple of great Thanksgiving dinners in New York. One time my friend Joel Paul, a Haitian immigrant who had even less money than I did, took me to his secret society and we made dinner in the kitchen for ourselves. At Christmas, I would sometimes take the Greyhound bus back to Minnesota, a time-consuming but effective cost-saving measure.

Twice a month, my parents would send me a $25 allowance, so every other Friday I would stand in line at a New Haven bank to take out the money. And all through college, I found innovative ways to make extra money. I signed up to be the paid subject in science experiments, which often brought in as much as $25 a pop, and even more for the one where I breathed in cotton dust. I typed senior essays for a dollar a page, which was easy except when they were in German and had lots of umlauts. I was such a fast typist that I joined a temp service in Minnesota and got hired to work as a temporary secretary over Christmas breaks.

Summer jobs also provided critical income. I spent one summer working construction with the Minnesota Highway Department. No sign-holding for me—I pounded surveying stakes into the ground with an eight-pound maul. And just to be sure I wouldn't fall behind my classmates, some of whom spent their summers studying in London or Paris, I would pull out *30 Days to a More Powerful Vocabulary* at lunchtime and regale my fellow construction crewmembers with the new words I'd learned in the book.

All my summer jobs paid a wage, but they maxed out at about $5.00 an hour. I worked at the Hennepin County Public Defender's Office answering phones and filing papers. I worked at the Minnesota Attorney General's Office as a clerk, but my bosses there actually allowed me to do some undercover investigator work. Several times I visited stores and checked the prices of appliances; my best case involved a fraudulent dog scam where people were duped into buying dogs and breeding them after being told they were purebreds. Every household I called in my search for evidence featured dozens of dogs barking in the background and really angry dog owners.

I was so busy with my classwork and my moneymaking ventures that I had very little spare time. I did take on a couple of extracurricular activities, but not nearly as many as kids do today. I was part of College Democrats and in 1980 canvassed for the Carter/Mondale campaign. I also joined the Yale bike team for a brief time. But on the day our coaches planned to teach us how to fall off our bicycles, my friend Maggie Jackson and I decided we had better things to do with our time.

Somehow I always made time for friendship, and at Yale I was lucky to have a lot of very good friends. Alex (the Miss Porter's School girl) and I went on to room together for three years. I met a lot of interesting people through Alex, including Jón Tómasson, the dashing son of an Icelandic diplomat. Jón and I have remained friends for decades, and back in college he introduced me to a bunch of suave European types, including a group of his friends who started up "The Deposed Monarch League." This club was founded somewhat in jest, of course, but not entirely!

Alex and I had a memorable roommate during our sophomore year: Becca Lish, daughter of former *Esquire* fiction editor Gordon Lish. Becca was a brilliant student with a flair for the dramatic. While neither of them remembers this thirty-five years later, I distinctly recall one major Alex/Becca argument that culminated in Becca throwing a number of Alex's shoes out the window and into the courtyard. This penchant for the theatrical was undoubtedly one reason Becca was a superb actress, and during the spring of that year she was cast in a play called *Getting Out* with one of Yale's most famous students at the time, Jodie Foster. Just as the play was set to open, the news broke that John Hinckley Jr.—a stalker—had shot President Ronald Reagan and that Hinckley had done so in part because of his obsessive infatuation with Jodie Foster. Everyone on campus was shocked, but in the best tradition of show business, Becca and her acting partner made sure the play would go on.

My roommate senior year was my forever friend Meg McFarland, who later became Meg Symington after marrying her senior-year boyfriend, John Symington, the grandson of Stuart Symington, the well-respected former senator from Missouri. Meg went on to get her PhD in biology at Princeton and to study monkeys in Peru; she now heads up the World Wildlife Fund's Amazon program and regularly leads trips there to fight rain forest deforestation.

John, meanwhile, became a doctor specializing in infectious diseases, but my fondest memory of him dates to our days together at Yale. John was a member of the Whiffenpoofs, Yale's best-known a cappella singing group, and in 1981 *Saturday Night Live* invited the Whiffenpoofs to appear on a holiday show and sing a boisterous round of Christmas carols. Unbeknownst to them, the show superimposed fictional phrases under their faces as they sang. Under the face of a particularly dapper young man ran the words "Dates Kennedys you never even heard of," and as my friend John sang his heart out, up popped a set of invented SAT scores, "390 Verbal; 418 Math," and the words "Dad made a few calls."

During my four years in New Haven, I made friends I would see for the rest of my life. But I never thought of college as a place to make connections; instead, I looked at it as an opportunity to learn. To me, Yale was an eye-opening and often mind-boggling experience, a place to study and think and debate. And it sure was a long way from the senior prom at the Ridgedale Mall.

A Political Education, Part I

I grew up learning about politics from my dad. One summer we took a family vacation to Wyoming, and we listened to the Senate Watergate hearings on the radio all the way there and back. As my sister and I squabbled over who got what space in the backseat, my dad would ask us to be quiet while he did his best to follow the proceedings. He would get especially furious when, somewhere in the middle of South Dakota, the reception would go bad. And it would always happen at the juiciest part: just as one of the president's men was testifying about taped conversations in Nixon's White House, the static would take over. Dad would turn the radio dial incessantly and punch every button he could find, including the heat controls, until we got the coverage back.

My dad covered politics for many years, and as a child I grew accustomed to answering the phone and taking messages from political leaders when they would call my dad back in the evening or on the weekend.

"Klobuchar residence, Amy speaking," I would say.

My mom saved one message I took when I was eight years old. A month before the momentous 1968 Humphrey vs. Nixon presidential election, I had taken down the particulars in my slanted, second-grade handwriting:

Call callect, Jhon Heritage with the Vice Prestint. All they wanted to know was if he'd be with VP in Detrit.

Translation: My dad was supposed to call John with the vice president's office if he planned to join them in Detroit.

That same fall, I remember that at recess some kids would chant "Nixon, Nixon, he's our man, Humphrey belongs in the garbage can." Later, of course, Humphrey went on to win Minnesota and lose the national election to Nixon. But in Minnesota we always subscribed to the theory that the election was so close that if Californians who voted for Black Panther Eldridge Cleaver had voted for Humphrey, Humphrey would have taken California, won the election, and been our president. (Alas, that was no more than a pleasing fiction: the record shows that even then Humphrey would have lost California.) More plausibly, if Eugene McCarthy— the former presidential candidate from Minnesota who served with Humphrey in the Senate—had chosen to endorse him before October 29, 1968, just a week before the election, Humphrey might have actually won.

As a junior high and high school student, I worked on several state legislative races. In 1974 I knocked on doors for Emily Anne Staples, a Democratic state house candidate who had once been a Republican. Her slogan: "Put It Together with Staples." Two years later, she won and became the first Democratic woman to serve in the state senate. I also marched in parades and carried the banner for former Kennedy agriculture secretary Orville Freeman's son Mike, who ran for Congress in 1978 and lost. Years later, Mike would become my predecessor—and my successor—as Hennepin County Attorney, my first job as an elected official.

My interest in politics and policy really blossomed in college. I was particularly inspired by Yale political science professor Robert Dahl, author of the 1961 book *Who Governs?*, a study of politics and power in New Haven that I read for his class. Professor Dahl was sometimes described as the dean of American political scientists, and his theories about how American politics worked opened a whole new world of ideas for me. He believed that government decisions were not driven by the actions of a power elite (a view held by academic C. Wright Mills) but instead were the result of power struggles among various political groups, a theory also known as pluralism.

In Professor Dahl's class I was entranced by the idea that despite the increasingly negative feelings about interest groups, democracy could succeed as long as everyone participated and representatives were held accountable for their actions at the ballot box. Dahl would also write about the methods by which people and interest groups influence decision-makers. He rated the methods on a sliding scale that went from good to bad and then from really bad to felonies. At the top of the scale was rational persuasion (a method used all too rarely in politics!); on the bottom was physical force (last employed in the U.S. Senate in 1856 when Representative Preston Brooks of South Carolina, in a dispute over slavery, beat Massachusetts Republican Senator Charles Sumner with a cane).

Another favorite college class was one about the U.S. Congress, which was taught by Steve Rosenstone, who went on to become the chancellor of the Minnesota State College and University System. I saved the notes from that class, and one day a few years ago I showed them to Dick Durbin, the Democratic whip, so I could point out all the amusing things I had written about his job. In my idyllic academic world, the whip could do everything, including "ensure party discipline," "guarantee attendance," "count votes," and "persuade wavering members to support a certain position."

In my junior year, I took a seminar from my future Senate colleague

Joe Lieberman. At the time he was in between political jobs; in the 1970s he had served as Connecticut's Senate majority leader, and the previous year he had run for Congress but lost, a victim of the 1980 Reagan landslide. His Yale class was called "The Democratic Party in the United States," and at the end our major project was to write a strategy paper for a presidential candidate. I picked Walter Mondale.

The last Yale professor who played a major role in my life was Ted Marmor. I took Ted's class, "The Politics of Medicare," as a junior. We spent a great deal of time discussing Ted's superb book, *The Politics of Medicare*, which explained how a major piece of legislation that had initially been so controversial ultimately received the bipartisan support of sixty-eight senators when it passed in 1965. (Fifty years later, Medicare continues to be extremely popular.) We also tried to better understand how those involved in politics make compromises. I was fascinated to learn about how the American Medical Association eventually came to support Medicare, despite their vehement early opposition to the program. And finally, of particular interest to me, we talked a lot about how Medicare was actually implemented after the bill passed.

The following year Ted took my friend Matt Hamel (later a fellow student at the University of Chicago Law School) and me under his wing. On Sunday evenings, Ted conducted weekly tutorial sessions with just the two of us: sitting in wingback chairs set around the fireplace in his campus home, we discussed the senior essays Matt and I were writing. Both of us felt a deep sense of purpose about our essays and never missed a session, especially since Professor Marmor's advice would always be accompanied by a glass of red wine.

Our subjects were not exactly a matched pair. Matt's thesis was about the Swedish health care system; mine was about the politics behind the building of the Hubert H. Humphrey Metrodome, the professional sports stadium in Minneapolis. But for both of us, the essays were life changing. During our senior year, Ted recommended Matt for a Fulbright Scholarship to study the health system in Uppsala, Sweden. Matt won the scholarship and spent a year in Sweden, and though in the end he didn't enter the health care field—he became a fine and accomplished lawyer instead—he did take enough time away from his foreign studies to meet his Swedish wife, Lena.

For me the senior essay was life changing in a different way. It brought together so many things in my life: my deep interest in the academic disciplines I had studied at Yale, my love of my home state and its politics, and my fascination with professional sports, which my dad had passed on to me. Maybe that's why my vision of the essay grew more ambitious by the day. Originally I thought I would write a paper of about thirty pages, but in the end it topped 200 pages, 215 to be exact.

The essay and later book—called *Uncovering the Dome*—told the story of the decade-long political struggle behind Minnesota's effort to build a new sports stadium. I wrote the essay based on academic and newspaper research, and I tape-recorded interviews with many Minnesota political and business leaders during my summer and winter breaks. For every interview, I would wear the used gray business suit I had purchased from a secondhand clothing store in New Haven. After sitting down with each interviewee, I would pull out a long list of handwritten questions (much to his or her chagrin, I'm sure). After an interview I would transcribe every word on the electric typewriter I had set up on a card table in my bedroom. I would then cut up the transcribed interviews, paste them on recipe cards, and code them by color for each chapter.

I interviewed everyone from Minnesota state legislators to Harvey Mackay, the stadium booster and entrepreneur who would later become famous for writing business advice books, including *Swim with the Sharks Without Being Eaten Alive*. I interviewed the team owners, the union presidents, John Cowles Jr. (the publisher of the Minneapolis paper, who had fought hard for the project), and many other decision-makers. All my interviews were aimed at understanding the macro story (the state government's view of the project and the economics of professional sports), the political story (the battle among various interest groups at the legislature), and the micro story (the motivations and views of those serving on the commission who decided where the stadium would be built and how it would look).

In the end the book was a lot of fun to write, mainly because I became so caught up in the effort to understand how the ambitious public project had come to be. It wasn't easy and there were a lot of bumps along the way, but ultimately the construction of the Metrodome was an unqualified success: it was built on time and under budget. The total cost of the project was around $70 million. In today's dollars, that amount would probably not be enough to pay for a new stadium's upper-deck bleacher seats!

My own project suffered a few bumps of its own. While I was working on the essay during my senior year, the stadium's inflated roof collapsed due to excess snow, though it was later fixed without too much difficulty. When my book came out, stadium vendors tried selling it next to the purple inflatable swords for a while, but that wasn't really its target market. For years it's been used at several colleges, including at Brown University where it has been one of the assigned texts in the big American government class. The professors told me that they loved discussing the book in part because they would say to their students, "She wrote this when she was just a year older than you are." Even now, after the recent demolition of the Metrodome and the construction of Target Field, the Twins' beautiful new baseball ballpark, as well as the Vikings' under-construction football stadium, the book lives on—albeit mostly in the basements of former students who post used copies for sale on Amazon.

A Political Education, Part II

My work on the essay and the book, along with my studies at Yale, gave me a solid understanding of how things could and should work in politics. But my best political experience during college—by far—was working as an intern for Vice President Mondale in 1980, the summer before my junior year and the last year of the Carter-Mondale administration. That job paved the way for my friendship with Fritz Mondale, who became an incredibly important mentor. It also allowed me to get to know his staff, inspired me to think about a future in politics, and encouraged me to believe that someday I could actually run for office.

My political career didn't exactly get off to a glamorous start. I rented a room that summer in the George Washington University Phi Delta Phi fraternity, which at the time was populated by swimmers, crew jocks, and only four other girls. It cost me $100 a month to live at 2020 G Street, and every day I walked the four blocks to my job at the Old Executive Office Building. There I shared adjoining offices with three other interns: Pat O'Connor, the son of former Democratic Party treasurer Patrick

O'Connor; Steve Befera, a soon-to-be University of Miami law student who had grown up in Minnesota; and Tom Nides, a student at the University of Minnesota.

Tom and I would become friends for life, and he would go on to be House Speaker Tom Foley's chief of staff, U.S. Trade Representative Mickey Kantor's chief of staff, and the number two in the State Department under Hillary Clinton, with a lot of business experience in between. But back then he was just a gritty, aggressive kid from Duluth. When I walked into the office for my first day as a brand-new intern he sat sprawled in his chair, his feet up on the desk, his vice presidential pin on his lapel. I watched him answer the phone and say "Tom Nides with the vice president" in a tone that would convince anyone that he was no twenty-year-old intern. No, he was already the chief of staff.

Tom had gotten off to a fast start, and he was already handling actual casework back in our home state—weighty matters like working with pizza tycoon Jeno Paulucci on the preservation of a foghorn in Duluth. My first assignment was a little less glamorous. I was told to conduct an inventory of every piece of furniture residing in the offices of every staff member who worked for the vice president. This task required that I crawl under hundreds of desks and chairs—and look under multiple lamp stands and sofas—and dutifully check off each item on a list of serial numbers.

The project took weeks, and when it ended I learned two important lessons: (1) true to his reputation, Vice President Mondale is a very honest man, and not a single piece of government-issue furniture was missing; and (2) it pays to take your first job very seriously, because you never know where it will lead. That internship was my first government job in Washington. My seat in the U.S. Senate was my second.

In addition to meeting some great new friends who would help me throughout my life, I also got to experience my first political convention—the 1980 Democratic Convention in New York City. Mrs. Mondale had an intern named Marianne Herrmann. By August, she and I had become fast friends. Marianne and I traveled to New York, rented a somewhat seedy room at a hotel near the official convention hotel, and spent our days sitting side by side at a table on the vice president's hotel floor. Our job was to open the packages sent to the VP from well-wishers.

At the time we believed that we were the first line of security. After all, we did actually open the packages, and even in pre-anthrax days that seemed a little scary. In retrospect, my guess is that the packages were in fact screened and X-rayed, but I still don't know that for sure. All I know is that our work made Marianne and me feel very important—and very glad when we finished each day.

Fortunately our bravery was rewarded with visits to the convention itself. I vividly remember the excitement of entering Madison Square Garden, floor pass strung around my neck. Squished between delegates carrying Carter/Mondale signs, I watched with pride as Vice President Mondale, his wife Joan, and their children, Eleanor, Teddy, and William, took to the stage. I cringed when President Carter mistakenly referred to Hubert Humphrey as "Hubert Horatio Hornblower," and cheered Ted Kennedy's rousing speech from the podium (never imagining that one day my desk in the Senate would be just three rows away from his).

I came away from that convention and that summer feeling enormous admiration for Vice President Mondale: I looked up to him then, and I've looked up to him ever since. He had a dignity about the way he practiced politics. He treated everyone with respect, including the interns. He did things for the right reasons, whether by intervening as a young state attorney general and arguing for the right to counsel in the landmark *Gideon v. Wainwright* case, or, as a senator, fighting for fair housing and investigating CIA abuses.

That summer in Washington wasn't easy for him. He knew Carter's campaign for reelection was not going well. Four years later, it wasn't easy for him to run against Ronald Reagan, knowing that Reagan would probably win. And in 2002, after the tragic death of Minnesota Senator Paul Wellstone just eleven days before an election he was expected to win, it wasn't easy for Mondale when he chose to come out of political retirement and run for Wellstone's seat for the sake of his party and his country. But Walter Mondale did all that. He did it with grace and good purpose—and he always did it for the right reasons and in the right way.

To this day I still listen to the advice of Walter Mondale. And I will always believe that whether my job was taking inventory of the furniture or opening packages, working in his office was a great way to get my start in politics.

Law School

At age seventeen I titled my college application essay "A Different Look at the Law." Striking what I must have believed was an appropriately sober note, I began my essay as follows: "For the past three years, I've been interested in law as a career." (Age fourteen seems a bit young to be plotting a legal career, but then again, I always was a planner.) I also mentioned watching *Perry Mason* reruns, my attraction to the legal profession as portrayed on TV, and my fascination with how, at the end of the courtroom shows, "goodness always prevailed."

The heart of my essay was about a visit I paid to the courtroom of Hennepin County Judge Neil Riley after my junior year in high school. As I wrote in my essay, the visit "destroyed my preconceived ideas about the drama and excitement of the courtroom since these were real people, not actors." Sounding a touch let down, I noted that "the defendants weren't smartly dressed and the prosecutors weren't smug."

My time in Judge Riley's courtroom forced me to confront the realities of the criminal justice system. I saw people with little hope and even less money, and their problems seemed intractable. I saw people who had stolen things and forged checks and who had been in and out of jail. They had few opportunities, and bad choices had only compounded their problems. At the end of the essay I wrote about how the visit made me realize that the legal system was flawed and that judges try their best, but no single decision will fix the lives of the people before them. I then asked whether I actually still wanted to become a lawyer. My answer: "to be part of an imperfect system, to have a chance to better that system," was a career worth pursuing. "The courtroom may not always have been exciting," I wrote, "but I think the law itself became even more exciting to me."

What I realized as a young kid visiting a courtroom—and later when I worked with the Hennepin County Public Defender's Office and the Minnesota Attorney General's Office—is that the answers in criminal cases, as with legal problems in general, are not always easy or clear-cut. The truth is hard to find. It was the same thing I had learned when watching my dad struggle with his alcoholism or my mom grapple with her divorce.

What I had also learned by that time was that standing up for your principles really matters. I had seen my dad stand up for people when he wrote about their lives in his columns. I had seen my mom stand up for kids in her class. I had seen my grandparents, who had so little, stand up to everything the world threw at them. I had seen inspirational public figures like Hubert Humphrey and Walter Mondale stand up for the people of our state and our country. I believed that becoming a lawyer would help me to do the same thing.

And so it was that four years later, my undergraduate days nearly behind me, I applied to law school. But this time I knew that my dad—recently remarried to Lois, a widow whose husband had been killed in a car accident—couldn't possibly afford to pay for three more years of my schooling, in large part because he was now helping to raise three more kids. So when I was asked by the various law schools what factors would help me to choose their school over others, I gave only one answer: financial aid and scholarships.

Financial aid was a major reason I ended up attending the University of Chicago Law School, which offered me both an attractive aid package and student loans. For my first two years, with my dad's help, I rented an apartment in a brownstone in Hyde Park—the neighborhood on the city's south side that is the University of Chicago's home—from my Yale professor and senior essay adviser Ted Marmor. (He used to teach at the University of Chicago, and he'd kept his place there.) Then, during my last year of law school, I landed the Illinois Women's Bar Association scholarship, which was awarded each year to aspiring lawyers in the state's law schools. Without the financial aid, the scholarships, and the student loans—not to mention the great room rate from my Yale mentor—I never would be where I am today, and for that I am eternally grateful.

But financial assistance wasn't the only reason I ended up going to the University of Chicago. First, it is a really good law school. Second, it was in the Midwest—I knew I wanted to go back to Minnesota eventually, and Chicago was halfway there. Finally, it was very different from Yale politically, and I thought that was a good thing. While Yale is known for its liberal bent, the University of Chicago Law School was and is known for being a pretty conservative place. I liked the idea of going to a school where I would be exposed to different ideas and different people. I wanted to be somewhere that would take me out of my comfort zone.

The University of Chicago has long been known for its study of "Law and Economics," a legal framework that applies economic theory to the study of laws. The basic idea is to assess laws by performing a cost-benefit analysis. The field was founded by the university, and the law school offered seminars on economic theory as early as the 1930s. One of its most famous adherents is Judge Richard Posner, who started teaching at the University of Chicago Law School in 1969. By the time I arrived in 1982, Posner had just been appointed to the 7th Circuit U.S. Court of Appeals by Ronald Reagan, but he was still teaching part-time at the law school.

I studied law at Chicago in part because I wanted to be exposed to the ideas of professors like Posner and Frank Easterbrook, another scholar, and later federal appellate judge, who embraced the concept of "Law and Economics." I was excited to be part of discussions that didn't feel like another meeting of the Yale College Democrats. Sitting in Easterbrook's class, or listening to my classmates' debates, or even going to the Friday night "wine mess" and seeing my classmate Nelson Lund (who never seemed to wear a pair of jeans without his NRA belt buckle and who later went on to clerk for Justice Sandra Day O'Connor), allowed me to expand my world beyond a single set of ideas.

The University of Chicago Law School wasn't a place for students who wanted a low-pressure academic experience. The law professors all used the Socratic method: they asked students formidable questions and expected answers on the spot. Many of our first-year classes included the entire class of 185 "1L" students, so there was nowhere to hide and reputations were made within days. Some of the students were "gunners"—they constantly raised their hands—but the rest of us were just trying to survive one class at a time.

Professor Richard Helmholz, our first-year property professor, was the scariest. Although I later came to understand that he was actually a pretty nice guy, we all called him "The Hammer." He terrorized students with his sharp responses when they gave the wrong answer, or, worse, when they gave no answer at all. When he called on someone who hadn't read the assigned case, he would stare straight at the student, purse his lips, and allow an excruciatingly long moment to tick by. Then he would slowly move his head to the other side of the room and say, "Can you answer that question for us, Ms. Brett?"

My last name is hard to pronounce, and with a paucity of Slovenian scholars teaching at the law school, I didn't get called on as much as some of the other students. But woe to "Mr. Johnson" or "Miss Kraus" or any of the other students with easy-to-pronounce names who would sit near me when we were placed in alphabetical order.

Not every professor avoided calling on people with difficult last names. Professor Richard Epstein, my often provocative first-year torts professor, was more than willing to call on anyone and everyone, regardless of whether he got their name right or wrong. Early in our first year, Professor Epstein described a hypothetical set of facts and asked which legal theory applied. Having done all the reading and highlighted what seemed like every sentence of the assigned cases, I pounced. When he saw my raised hand, Professor Epstein called on me immediately.

"Foreseeability," I gulped. "That is the theory that should apply in this case."

From my reading, I knew that foreseeability involves holding people responsible for damages based on whether they could have foreseen that their actions could have caused those damages. But what I did not know as my hand shot up in class that day was that Professor Epstein was not a fan of this particular legal concept. (In fact, he would later publish an article called "Beyond Foreseeability," which criticized its use in contract cases.) What happened next became class lore. In fact, to this day I have yet to attend a law school class reunion where someone did not bring up "the time when Klobuchar gave the 'foreseeability' answer in Epstein's torts class."

Seconds after I uttered the word "foreseeability," Professor Epstein went wild. In front of the entire ninety-student class he started shrieking the word "foreseeability," alternating between a high-pitched scream and a cow-like bellow. Prancing around the room, swinging his head, he spoke the word over and over again. At some point he started addressing me in a feigned French accent.

"Miss Klo-BOOSH-er, Miss Klo-BOOSH-er, do you really think the answer is FORESEEABILITY?" he yelled as he launched into a diatribe about why the theory should not be applied to his hypothetical. Then, in a move that shocked even the most jaded Professor Epstein observers, he lay down on his back on the long table that stood in the front of the classroom, tilted his head, put his fingers in his mouth, and pretended to gag himself, all the time calling out "FORESEEABILITY. FORESEE-ABILITY."

No one ever volunteered the word in class again.

Despite that "tort room" trauma, I learned a lot from Professor Epstein, just as I did from all of my University of Chicago law professors. I took civil procedure from the late David Currie, a man known for his encyclopedic knowledge of America's founding era. I learned about criminal law—and the Fourth Amendment protection against "unreasonable searches and seizures"—from professors Franklin Zimring and Geoffrey Stone. I had only two women law professors, but I liked them both: Mary Becker, who taught contracts, and Mary Ann Glendon, who taught a class on family law.

But the professor I got to know best was my law review comment adviser, Cass Sunstein. I took four classes from Cass: constitutional law, constitutional interpretation, administrative law, and welfare law. I still remember paying a visit to his office to ask him to be my adviser on my law review comment. His office was located on one of the school's upper floors, tucked away behind racks of bookshelves. That was fitting because that's how I found Professor Sunstein, buried behind a stack of books on his desk. When I asked him whether he'd serve as my adviser, he graciously said yes. Years later, I was delighted to return the favor when Cass asked two of my colleagues and me to help move his nomination through the Senate confirmation maze after President Obama nominated him to be in charge of the Office of Information and Regulatory Affairs. One of the most prolific and cited legal scholars in the country, Cass was perfect for the job. He got confirmed on a 57–40 vote despite some resistance from the NRA after it was discovered he'd once coauthored a book on whether animals had rights. That experience taught him something I, too, learned the hard way: Washington is a tough place. But the University of Chicago Law School helped prepare me—and him—for the challenges ahead.

Fun in Hyde Park

Despite the law school's well-earned reputation for intensity and high academic standards, my classmates and I still managed to have some fun. We knew from the outset that the University of Chicago was not exactly known as a party school. Before our time, in fact, the school lounge's chairs and couches were arranged so they faced back-to-back, a not-so-subtle message that students should be studying rather than socializing. We set out to change that reputation by planning multiple social events, including, thanks to our classmates Linda Benfield, Jeff Pecore, and Josh Hornick, reinvigorating the Law School Musical. We were so successful in bringing some life to the place that some of our professors started calling us "the happy class." At the time we thought the nickname was intended as a compliment, but we later learned it was actually code for the unstated but shared belief among some of our professors that our class wasn't likely to produce many Supreme Court clerks.

This was the 1980s, and Blondie, Madonna, and Cyndi Lauper were hot. My friend Kate Herrmann and I would host dance parties, and my classmate Mark Sexton and I could dance for hours. We always celebrated Halloween and one time I took first place in a costume party when I dressed as "Purple Rain" (thank you, Prince) and won a dance with the runner-up—a guy dressed as "the bathroom wall."

One unsanctioned university-wide Hyde Park party was particularly memorable. The University of Chicago was then famous for its Lascivious Costume Ball, an annual event that featured costumes that left little, if anything, to the imagination. In fact, for those who decided to go that route, clothes were optional. (No, that was not me.) One year the winning entry was a guy wearing a bagel.

Our friend Karen Cornelius had a car, so whenever we had some free time, we would explore Chicago's neighborhoods, shop downtown, or go to Cubs or White Sox games. My dad conducted a weekly "football clinic for women," and once every fall he would load two hundred of his adult female students on buses and bring them from Minnesota to the Vikings/Bears game at Soldier Field. He would save two extra tickets for me, and I would always bring a guy from law school to the game. My disbelieving law school guests could never quite get over it when my dad showed up with two hundred women.

Our University of Chicago class was full of amazingly talented people. There was Bill Fisher, a witty guy from New Jersey who is now a judge in Minnesota; Leslie Shad, later the general counsel of the nonprofit humanitarian aid group CARE; Tim O'Malley, who went on to head up Minnesota's Bureau of Criminal Apprehension; and Richard Hertling, who worked as chief counsel for my future colleague Senator Arlen Specter. Another classmate, Adam Emmerich, would go on to be so helpful during my Senate campaign that a reporter once asked me how I had raised such a large sum of money from his New York law firm, Wachtell Lipton. It's nothing nefarious, I told him, I just know a great guy from law school who has done really well at that firm.

And finally there was my classmate and *Law Review* colleague, Jim Comey, now the head of the Federal Bureau of Investigation. Jim served as Attorney General John Ashcroft's deputy in the Bush administration, and during Ashcroft's hospitalization in 2004, Jim resisted enormous pressure and refused to "certify" portions of the National Security Agency's domestic wiretapping program. Later, after President Obama nominated him to be the FBI director, I got a chance to talk about Jim's character at the Senate Judiciary Committee hearing. As I said that day, I hoped that our law professors, who didn't always hold out much hope for "the happy class," were watching us at the hearing at the Capitol: Jim as the nominee for the director of the FBI and me as a U.S. senator.

While the friends and the classes and the characters are what I remember best from the University of Chicago Law School, my time there also provided me with an invaluable education. Law school taught me not only the importance of lawyerly skills but also how to anticipate arguments and understand both sides of a case. I learned how to put myself in someone else's shoes and in their political mind-set, or at least on their side of a lawsuit. When I graduated in 1985, with my mom and dad both there with me in Chicago to celebrate, I felt a little like my parents did back in the 1950s: I was ready to take on the world.

4

The Real World

The Firm

I spent almost fourteen years working in the private sector. And, to paraphrase my Senate colleague Al Franken when he talks about his forty-years-and-counting marriage to his wife, Franni, "many of them were happy."

Actually, I wouldn't take back any of those fourteen years in private practice. They showed me how commerce and the business world work. I learned a lot about management and accountability. I represented and came to know a number of Fortune 500 companies, many of them based in Minnesota—from General Mills to SuperValu, from First Bank (now U.S. Bank) to Northwest Airlines (now Delta Airlines). I also got the opportunity to work with my law firm's nonprofit clients, including such Minnesota treasures as the Mayo Clinic and the University of Minnesota.

I entered the private sector when I started working at Dorsey & Whitney four months after graduating from law school. Formed more than a century ago, Dorsey—as the firm's lawyers call it—is one of Minnesota's best-known law firms. Back when I started there, it was also the largest, with around 250 lawyers. Several judges had gotten their start at the firm, including U.S. Supreme Court Justice Harry Blackmun.

Dorsey has long been a top-notch, full-service law firm. Headquartered in Minneapolis, today the firm has offices in more than ten U.S. cities and in Canada, Europe, and Asia. But when I started my legal career, the firm was smaller and less international. I had been recruited through the firm's summer associate program, which—in the 1980s, with the economy booming—involved wine-and-cheese receptions, a boat outing on Lake Minnetonka, Minnesota Twins games, and a trip to Mayslack's Polka Lounge. But once I accepted the job, some of that fun was over. I was paid to work—and work I did.

As a new associate, I got my start in litigation, working with a number of high-powered litigators such as Tom Tinkham and John Levine. I wrote research memos, drafted pleadings and motions, and handled pretrial depositions, taking sworn testimony from witnesses. Like lawyers at most big firms, the Dorsey litigators kept time sheets that accounted for all their billable hours in fifteen-minute increments, which in the beginning took some getting used to.

Mostly I did a lot of legal research, and in those days some was by computer and some by book. I will never forget the day former Dorsey partner Jack Mason (who went on to become a federal magistrate and died way too young) asked me to research an obscure legal point. Jack was known as a funny and pretty intense guy. He also had a bit of a temper. So I was more than a little anxious when he called me into his office not long after I became an associate and said firmly: "I know there is a case out there that says such-and-such [referring to an obscure legal point], and I need it for a brief I am filing tomorrow. Your job is to find it and to find it soon."

The legal point Jack mentioned was so obscure that there was no obvious way to research it. I stayed up all night and looked back through a century of Minnesota law. And somehow, some way, I found a Minnesota case from decades ago that mentioned the exact point Jack wanted to make in his brief. While it wasn't the strongest precedent, I was sure it was the case Jack had in mind.

Walking into Jack's large office the next morning—with no sleep—I proudly handed him a photocopy of the case.

He shook his head and laughed. "I cannot even believe this case exists," he said. "I was pretty much making it up. I never thought you'd find anything."

Welcome to the world of a big-time law firm.

Dorsey had its share of major litigation cases, and the firm's partners needed a lot of young associates to staff them. I once spent weeks on a case up near the Canadian border in Warroad—Minnesota's own "Hockey-town, U.S.A." The case involved a big-dollar dispute over window sealant between Warroad-based Marvin Windows and Norton, a large out-of-town company that was Dorsey's client. The lawsuit, like so many complex cases, would go on for years. I plowed through what seemed like truckloads of papers, staying at the Marvin family–owned Patch Hotel and eating in the Marvin family–owned Patch Restaurant, which once a week featured a lunchtime special of chipped buffalo on croissant. Even though Marvin was suing our client, the company still treated us nicely.

Most of the litigation work at Dorsey was rigorous and intellectually challenging. But ultimately I decided that the process-oriented world of big-case civil litigation was not for me. In a bit of law firm rebellion—which isn't easy to get away with if you're a young associate who wants to keep her job—I gradually stopped working on the big cases and instead built my own practice based mainly on the regulatory work I was doing in the fast-growing and specialized area of telecommunications law. Most of that work involved complicated telecom cases before the Minnesota Public Utilities Commission.

Within four years I transferred out of the trial department, rejecting the litigators' advice that the move wouldn't be the best thing for my career. Before long, I carved out a nice niche for myself doing regulatory hearings and administrative law work. In that role I worked extensively with the beloved Warren Spannaus, a former taxi driver who went to the University of Minnesota Law School and later became a three-term Minnesota attorney general.

Warren was a unique figure at a buttoned-up law firm. He would always sit back in his chair and put his feet up on his desk, and the soles of his shoes would inevitably have holes in them. He kept a tin of shoe polish and an old cloth in his desk drawer, and he would often shine his shoes while we talked about work or, more often, politics. For years he and his pal Judge Gerald Heaney—a northern Minnesota political powerhouse and a federal appellate judge—would regularly talk on the phone at great length, Warren from the law firm, Judge Heaney from his chambers in Duluth. The topic was always the latest political battle.

The two old friends would end every conversation by simply hanging up the phone, often before the other person had finished talking. Saying good-bye, or even politely winding down their discussion, was not worth their time or part of their shared culture. To this day, my friend Colleen Short (one of Judge Heaney's former clerks) and I pay tribute to Warren and the judge by ending our conversations in the same manner. We don't say good-bye; we just hang up.

Like Judge Heaney, Warren never forgot where he came from. At least once a month a man with disabilities who Warren had helped back when he was attorney general would stop by. Warren would always give him a little cash for lunch. Later, when Warren's friend (and my former boss) Walter Mondale came to the firm in 1989, the two old friends were inseparable. It is a lasting testament to their friendship that when Vice President Mondale learned that the University of Minnesota Law School wanted to name its new building after him, he insisted that the student lounge in the building be named after a true friend of the man on the street, Warren Spannaus.

With Warren's help and support, I built up a healthy regulatory practice at Dorsey. I represented a number of telecommunications companies, and my main client was MCI, an aggressive, innovative long-distance telephone company that was determined to disrupt the telecom industry by competing with the local monopoly carriers. In 1989 I became the chief Dorsey lawyer for the company, and in that role I worked closely with MCI's director of regulatory affairs, Bill Levis.

It was an exciting time to be representing a hungry young company. MCI's scrappy lawyers viewed themselves as cowboys of sorts, fighting for consumers and lower prices and taking on local telephone monopolies around the country. Back then, Bill Levis was based in Denver and later Chicago, and he and I became good friends as we fought the company's battles together. Appearing regularly before the Public Utilities Commission on MCI's behalf, we were often on the same side as the consumer representatives and agencies. Bill played an instrumental role in my success at Dorsey, going out of his way to tell the firm's partners that I was doing a good job with MCI's legal work.

While building my law practice, I also kept up my work in politics. Walter Mondale's arrival at the firm was a great thing for me, and a couple years after he came to Dorsey I got the chance of a lifetime—and one that would later shape my political future. The former vice president had become so busy at the firm that he needed an associate to work with him on business development, speeches, and other civic activities. He chose me for the job, and during 1989 and 1990 I divided my time between Vice President Mondale's work and my regulatory cases. With Walter Mondale and his next-door officemate and buddy, former Attorney General Spannaus, I had found a political oasis in the corporate hallways of the big law firm.

Another opportunity at Dorsey also made a major difference in my career. The firm wanted its young associates to get trial experience, and the Minneapolis City Attorney's Office, which was chronically over-stretched, needed prosecutors to handle misdemeanor and gross misdemeanor cases. This led to a good, commonsense public-private partnership, and when the opportunity to serve as a prosecutor came along, I jumped at it. Among other things, the work for the city gave me the chance to handle six criminal jury trials.

It was a thrilling, humbling experience to argue—and present evidence—before twelve people sitting in a jury box. The trials included domestic assault, drunk driving, and theft charges, and I got convictions in all of them. Not every Dorsey lawyer liked the messiness of the city attorney's program. In fact, some of them couldn't wait for it to end so they could get back to the more complex civil work. But I loved being a prosecutor, and I wanted more. Years later, that four-month stint in the City Attorney's Office was helpful to me in understanding the inner workings of the courthouse when I ran for Hennepin County Attorney.

Dorsey also gave me the chance to work with some great mentors. In addition to Vice President Mondale and Warren Spannaus, I worked closely with Becky Comstock and Mark Rotenberg, two of the firm's many talented lawyers. With Mark's help, I developed my expertise in telecommunications law, and with the help of Becky, Mark, and many others, I learned the art of business development, what lawyers at big firms call "rainmaking." Sadly, one of my most important mentors at Dorsey—a lawyer by the name of Jan Sanderson—died suddenly of a brain aneurysm less than three weeks after giving birth to her son. Her death, which occurred five years after I got to the firm, was a real blow to all of us, but it was especially hard for the firm's women lawyers. There weren't many of us to begin with, and when Jan died we lost a true friend and confidante.

Back when I first started at Dorsey, all the women at the firm wore suits with skirts. As was then customary, we also wore bow ties, but they were really hard to tie and looked pretty silly. I was so bad at tying mine that they ended up looking truly comical—not to mention floppy. Luckily for me, given that no one really wants to hire a floppy-looking lawyer, those bow ties went out of style just a few years later.

Workplace attire was a minor issue compared to the host of challenges faced by working women. It was a new era, and in the 1980s the few Twin Cities women lawyers with kids were constantly struggling with brand-new "work/family balance" issues. While the men would be commended or at least admired for going home once in a while to, as they put it, "babysit" for their own children, the women were viewed very differently. For female attorneys in those early years, the daily departure for pickup at day care was often seen as a limitation. There was a lot of angst—as of course there still is—for moms who were trying to "do it all."

My favorite work/family balance story from that era was about the time my friend Allison Humphrey—the only other female associate in the corporate/regulatory department on the nineteenth floor—went to pick up her three-year-old daughter, Claire, at day care. The assignment for the day was for the toddlers to tell the teacher what their mom did for a living. The teacher had pinned Claire's drawing up in the classroom and written Claire's description of her mom's job on the picture: "My mom is special. She waits for foxes." It included a drawing of her mom with foxes.

The teacher told Allison she couldn't figure out what Claire meant, but she was clearly very proud of her mom's animal-related job. It took a few minutes, but Allison finally figured out what her daughter meant. Every time she brought Claire to the Dorsey office she told her they were almost ready to go home, but they had to "wait for a fax." Her daughter had envisioned not a fax but a pack of foxes in the neighboring conference room, hungry and waiting for Allison's attention.

We all tried our best to balance.

My time at Dorsey taught me many things, but perhaps the most valuable lesson was that relationships matter. They *really* matter. To be effective, lawyers must maintain good relationships with their clients, their colleagues, and, yes, even with opposing counsel. In the telecommunications industry (as in many other industries), you would find yourself opposing a government agency or a competing business on one day, and then fighting side by side with that agency or business the next day. If you burned bridges, you would soon be left standing alone on the wrong side of the river.

Sadly, I've found that in Washington, D.C., people all too often neglect the relationships that are most needed to make our country work effectively. They choose to burn the bridges. People are friends and then they aren't. People destroy years of a friendship for one appearance on TV, and then they don't just disagree with their colleagues, they attack them personally and impugn their integrity. People forget that you can disagree without being disagreeable.

Another crucial lesson I learned in my fourteen years in the private sector is that successful entrepreneurs work incredibly hard to build their companies. We live in a global economy, and commerce often moves at lightning speed. The pace of the business world is frenetic. At Dorsey, the lawyers were expected to keep up with the swiftly moving current. A client would ask a question and expect a prompt, well-informed answer. And if a client was working on getting a deal done, it was the lawyer's job to facilitate, not impede, the transaction. Sometimes I wish more elected officials—and people in government generally—had an appreciation for the fast pace of the commercial world, the need to be agile and move quickly, and especially the benefit of being consistent so that our U.S. businesses can plan and compete in the global marketplace.

While I was at Dorsey, some associates got hooked on the adrenaline rush of litigation and last-minute deals. Others found a quieter practice somewhere in the firm, and still others worked until they paid off their student loans and then decided to go to a company as an in-house lawyer or to leave the law altogether. As for me, I stuck around longer than a number of my classmates. I worked hard to become a partner, striving to achieve the goal that I'd set for myself. I drafted business development plans; I managed cases, arbitrations, and litigation matters; and I supervised the work of others at the firm. Because of the niche I had carved out for myself, I brought in significant billings and major clients, at the time something of an unusual accomplishment for a woman.

I came up for partner in 1992. There were no guarantees: with each performance review, every associate was reminded "that admission to the partnership is at the sole discretion of the partnership" and that we, as associates, had "no right, contractual or otherwise," to join it.

I had worked hard and done well, and in the winter of 1992 the management committee asked me to join the firm as a partner. I accepted. By then, my relatively care-free summer associate days—promoted in the firm's 1984 recruiting brochure with promises of "dinner parties, lunches, visits to Garrison Keillor's *A Prairie Home Companion*, late-night swims, and many TGIF sessions"—were far behind me. After seven long years I had made partner and I was proud of that. But even then, I knew I had a few other things I wanted to do with my life.

Meeting John

Nineteen ninety-two was a pretty good year. Not only did I make partner at the firm, but I was a Mondale Fellow at the University of Minnesota's Humphrey Institute, giving me the chance to meet all kinds of national political types. I was also a first-time delegate to the Democratic National Convention in New York City and a surrogate speaker for the Clinton campaign in Minnesota. And it was a big thrill when Bill Clinton was elected president. But if Clinton's victory was by some measures the year's most significant event, for me it was meeting my husband, John, over beers at the Coyote Cafe in Minneapolis.

John grew up in Mankato, Minnesota—a college town about one and a half hours south of the Twin Cities—in a family of six boys. His dad, Bill Bessler, was a biology professor at Mankato State (now known as Minnesota State) who presided over the family's dinners with the same loud booming voice he would use to teach his freshman Bio 100 course. Even when teaching classes with as many as three hundred students, Professor Bessler never used a microphone.

John's mom, Marilyn, came from a family farm outside of tiny Gaston, Indiana. While attending Ball State Teachers College in Muncie, Marilyn met Bill in a social dance class. They had little to their name, but they got married in their senior year and moved to a mobile home court in Mankato when Bill landed a teaching job at the college.

Marilyn and Bill had four boys over six years, with John arriving as boy number three. After the fourth boy Marilyn really wanted a girl and got pregnant again. The result? Identical twin boys. In typical Bessler fashion, Marilyn and Bill solved the problem of how to house the twins in their crowded single-wide trailer by setting up bunk beds and personally building an "addition" onto the mobile home. As John's brothers would note years later, who builds an addition onto a mobile home? The Besslers, of course.

All six boys attended Catholic schools. John, who liked playing baseball and basketball but who was a bit of a bookworm compared to his brothers, was always on the lookout for a quiet place to read and write on the family's Smith-Corona electric typewriter. He wanted some privacy from the household chaos, his five brothers, their friends, and the Boy Scout troop all six boys joined and their dad led. (Five of the six boys would go on to become Eagle Scouts, but I never say which one didn't make it because I don't want to embarrass my husband.)

When the family moved to a small house on Mulberry Street, John begged his mom to let him sleep in a crawl space wedged under the eaves in the attic between the wall and the sloped roof. When his mom vetoed the idea, explaining that not only would it be too small but also potentially suffocating because of the extreme heat and lack of ventilation, he cried.

What John really wanted was to see the world. And while there wasn't any money to do that, at least he could run as far as his legs would take him. John was a natural athlete and good at almost every sport. He had a particular talent for running, and as he trained for cross-country and track and field, he would run up and down Good Counsel Hill, dodging the retired nuns of the School Sisters of Notre Dame as they tended their gardens.

During his high school runs, John would often see the state-supported "career trailer" outside the school. One day he stopped in and saw the brochure on the University of Minnesota's early admissions program. He immediately hatched a plan to enroll in college a year early so he could at last get a room of his own.

Once in college, John worked his way through the University of Minnesota in only three years, taking extra classes every semester, studying by day and staffing the Walter Library front desk by night. Eager to see the world, he applied for and was accepted to a one-semester-long Minnesota Studies in International Development program in Kingston, Jamaica. Unfortunately that adventure came to an abrupt end when he came down with mono after making out with a girl from Florida in Jamaica's Blue Mountains.

Even in college, John was a thinker and a dreamer. He also collected many friends along the way. Most of all, he was a nice guy with an incredible work ethic. Everything he did, he did on his own. Everywhere he got, he got there on his own. The proof was right there in our checkbook: even into my forties, we were still paying back his $60,000 student loan debt.

Having graduated a year early from high school and a year early from college, John arrived at Indiana University's law school in Bloomington at the age of twenty, still under the drinking age. At IU he was named senior managing editor of the *Indiana Law Journal*, and after graduation he went on to join the prestigious Minneapolis law firm of Faegre & Benson, starting there as one of the youngest lawyers ever. His interest in the law was matched by an interest in politics—even in high school, many of his friends thought he would one day run for office. During college, he interned for both a Republican state legislator from Mankato and former U.S. Congressman Don Fraser, then the mayor of Minneapolis.

In some ways politics brought the two of us together. The night I met John, I had just attended an all-day Mondale Fellow session at the Humphrey Institute that featured, among others, the famous *New York Times* national political correspondent R. W. Apple Jr., National Public Radio host Linda Wertheimer, and *Meet the Press* moderator Tim Russert. Afterward, some friends and I went to the Coyote Cafe and John happened to be there, too. We had a great talk. I was excited about the conference, and John seemed genuinely interested. At some point that evening I learned that John was a second-year associate at Faegre, but what I didn't realize until much later was that John was actually seven and a half years younger than I was. And by the time I put that together, it was too late to worry about it.

John and I met again a few weeks later through another group of mutual friends—John and Kathleen Sheehy and John Sheehy's brother

Jim—at a pool hall called City Billiards. Not long after that, we went on our first date. It was a double date, or maybe I should call it a one and a half date. A friend of mine at Faegre, Kristin Karls, was supposed to invite John for me. It was my job to invite another guy for Kristin, but when that didn't work out (too late, I discovered that the guy she wanted me to invite for her already had a girlfriend), the three of us went out on "our" first date together.

For our Friday night out, John, Kristin, and I went to see the movie *Wayne's World*. After that we went to dinner at an Italian restaurant, but halfway through I decided that John wasn't really interested in me. Thinking "why bother?" I went into the restroom, took out my contact lenses, and replaced them with my glasses.

Either I was wrong or John really liked the glasses. He called me the next day and we've been together ever since.

Soon after my dad met John, he said, "This guy is a really good guy." That was not only dad code for liking John, it was also a needling commentary about the endless array of actors, fellow lawyers, and the occasional ne'er-do-well that I'd dated for the past decade. The guy I had dated the longest before John—still a friend—had broken up with me on Halloween. Just before a party, he told me he wanted to get married and that unfortunately he considered me—with my alcoholic dad, my divorced parents, and my keen interest in politics—a high risk for a future divorce. He delivered this news while I stood there in my Halloween costume. I'd just gotten ready, and I was dressed as a Christmas tree, decked out in a green turtleneck, green tights, brown shoes, and brown socks. I was covered in ornaments, and I had a star attached to a ruler on top of my head. I'd topped everything off with a blinking string of lights that I'd plugged into the wall with two extension cords for maximum mobility. But who remembers? Looking back, I do acknowledge that it may have been my outfit that actually scared him off.

The dating scene was so challenging that at one point my friends Susan Segal (now happily married and the Minneapolis city attorney) and Kathryn Quaintance (ditto on the marriage and now a state court judge) and I started the "5'4" Brunette's Club," a tongue-in-cheek group formed to compete with Minnesota's many tall, blond Scandinavian women who seemed to win the hearts of all the best guys. I also got occasional help from a friend at a competing law firm who, for the sole purpose of identifying potential suitors, would surreptitiously send me résumés of the men her law firm was recruiting. She especially enjoyed sending me the ones that included LSAT scores, circling the scores in red ink with somewhat sarcastic comments about the potential a particular applicant would bring to a marriage.

But very quickly I knew that John was in fact the guy—and I never did find out what his LSAT score was. I loved how nice and generous he was to everyone he met and knew—his brothers, the neighbors, the grocery store checkout guys, the sometimes zany people in politics. If someone who was a bit odd started an endless conversation with us at a political event, John would always bring out the best in the person and half an hour later I would be the one dragging him away.

John was really patient. A few months after meeting him I called one day and told him, "The Russians are coming." By that I meant that we would soon be getting a visit from a small but hearty band of Russians who had hosted my dad and me when we had traveled to Russia a year earlier for a bike trek along the Volga River to Moscow. Somehow John— who had not participated in our bike trip—was assigned to ferry the Russians around the Twin Cities for a week. He ended up nursing the guys' hangovers after they consumed every bottle of vodka they had brought for gifts; consoling my mom over the phone in the middle of the night when two of the guests she had graciously agreed to host accidentally walked into her bedroom and scared her to death by sitting on her bed; and talking down the manager of a restaurant after one of the Russians unwittingly made off with two pieces of banana cream pie from a revolving refrigerated display case.

John was also levelheaded and practical. One day soon after we started dating, we discovered that his brand-new Toyota Corolla was missing. He had parked it right outside my house, and the only clue to the car's whereabouts was a small pile of shattered glass and taillight shards on the street. When we arrived at the Minneapolis impound lot we were told that his car was in Lot 10C. As we wandered from Lots 1A to 2B, the cars got progressively more beat up. When we finally arrived at Lot 10C we learned the truth: his new car had been totaled by a twelve-seat van, hit so hard that parts were everywhere and there was little to salvage. Even the motor was dislodged.

But John? As he went through the car's wrecked interior for his personal effects, he was as calm as could be.

At one point I stared at him in utter disbelief. He was picking up coins off the floorboards. "You just lost your whole car," I said, "and you're looking for pennies?"

"No," he replied, "I'm only taking the quarters. They are really useful for the meters."

Most of all I loved John's curiosity about the world around him. He was interested in even the most esoteric political questions and captivated by the enthusiasm he saw in the characters that gravitated to politics. He loved our country and its history, which is why it made perfect sense that he proposed to me at a bookstore in St. Paul on February 12, 1993. Forget Valentine's Day, even though it was only two days later. John, a big fan of Abraham Lincoln, wanted to ask me to marry him on his favorite president's birthday.

He also liked the name of the bookstore—The Hungry Mind—and took care to propose in the store's nonfiction aisle. When you start a marriage, he told me, you want to be realistic. The nonfiction aisle was a good place to start.

Mylo, Omer, and Dan

As John and I started our lives together, we spent a great deal of time with his family, and I really enjoyed getting to know the Bessler clan. We also saw a lot of my parents. One of the blessings in my life has been the fact that my parents reconciled after their divorce and then remained friends for the rest of my mom's life. Through two subsequent marriages, my dad never missed a Christmas Eve at my mom's house with my sister and me. He rarely missed a Thanksgiving. He even came by for a few Easters. We always had two parents, and it made such a difference that they were able to maintain a strong bond with each other.

Part of it was their shared interests—in the outdoors, in politics, in sports, and in their kids. They didn't do things together anymore, but there was always something to talk about, something they genuinely wanted to

tell each other. It probably helped that both my parents went their separate ways and made new lives for themselves, and there never seemed to
be any bitterness or jealousy. Beyond that, they both believed that you treat
someone you shared a life with—in their case, twenty-two years and two
children—with dignity and devotion. It seemed to me it was almost a
religious tenet—they may not have stayed married as they promised God,
but they were going to do their best to live out those vows in spirit. They
would be honest and respectful toward each other, and although the marriage had ended, the promise to take care of the other person "until death
do us part" had not.

My sister Beth (who later changed her name to Meagan) went through
a difficult time during this period, which was hard on both my parents,
especially my mom. My sister left home a lot and ultimately dropped
out of high school. She worked a series of different jobs. For years she
struggled with drinking and other challenges. Finally she ended up in
Iowa, where with her GED she enrolled in her thirties at a local community college. That changed her life. Like my dad, she first got her two-
year degree and then completed a four-year degree. After graduating, she
took the Iowa state accounting exam and got an award, receiving the
highest score in the state that year. She got a good job as an auditor, which
she still has today. Our whole family was proud of all she accomplished.

Postdivorce, my mom was very happy to be teaching again. She was
well respected at school and frequently mentored the younger teachers.
Her red Comet—and later her blue Honda Civic—gave her a freedom
she'd never had before. Driving a car opened the door to new adventures,
including the first time she took the Comet out for a spin and a car wash.
She was so nervous that she drove through—and completely shattered—
the car wash's gigantic plate-glass window at the local Amoco station.

She became very active in our church choir, practicing every Wednesday and rarely missing a Sunday. She also went to plays and concerts
with her friends and took cross-country vacations with her best friend,
Mary Beaudin. One time Mary and my mom rented an RV and went
to California's Baja Peninsula for the sole purpose of getting the best
vantage point to watch a total eclipse. Another time I saved frequent
flyer miles for a year and then took my mom to Switzerland to visit her
relatives.

My mom never showed any interest in remarrying. She never even talked about wanting to go on dates. By age fifty she had come to be extremely utilitarian about what she needed from the men in her life. And to be honest, it was mostly about home maintenance.

There were three Mr. Fix-its on Oakview Lane to whom my mom turned in time of need. There was Omer Oestreich, husband of Hilma, a plumber who oversaw all projects related to sprinklers, the water heater, and leaky faucets—really anything related to pipes. There was Dan Ronning, husband of Ila, who lent his expertise in a number of areas that required a lot of patient tinkering: snowblower maintenance, grounded sockets, and mailbox repair, to name a few. But it was Mylo Hoisve, husband of Marilyn, who provided the most crucial help. Mylo, a telephone company engineer who owned the tallest extension ladder on Oakview Lane, took charge of all operations involving hard-to-reach places, that is, anything related to our house's redwood exterior, roof, or chimney.

It was Mylo whom my mom turned to for help during what she called the "siege of the woodpecker." I first heard about the problem when my mom called me one day and announced: "A female downy woodpecker is demolishing our house. She has drilled five holes under the kitchen window, all more than two inches deep."

For weeks she had tried different defensive approaches culled from the pages of home repair columns. She had leaned out the kitchen window and hammered mousetraps with suet to the side of the house. She had tacked up mobiles of can lids under the window. Nothing worked, so now it was time to call in her most reliable fix-it man.

She assigned Mylo to take his ladder, climb up to the second floor, and hammer large pieces of tin over the holes. According to my mom, the woodpecker sat perched in a nearby birch tree, chirping with glee throughout the entire operation. Right after Mylo left, the bird began drilling new holes into the house that were three inches to the right of the tin barricades.

Refusing to encase the entire house in tin, my mom knew what had to be done. For a woman who staged a yearly classroom "adios party" for butterflies flying south and caught basement-bound chipmunks in "Have-a-Heart" traps, the idea of gunning down a woodpecker was deeply unsettling. But she was a single mom protecting her home, and she felt she had run out of options. She first called the Minnesota Department of Natural Resources and sorted out the necessary legalities. Then she headed down to the garage and found the old BB gun. She had always threatened to use the gun against invading animals, and this time she was going to do it.

In the garage, she loaded the gun with BBs. Then, in a shock to herself, the neighbors across the street, and every mouse residing in our attached basement, she accidentally set the gun off right in the middle of the garage. The BB that blasted out of the gun's barrel pierced the family globe.

My mom had literally blown up the world.

She was so shaken by the incident that after spending an hour regrouping and plucking pieces of various oceans out of the family badminton net, she decided against using the BB gun.

Instead, she found an old rainbow-colored wind sock on the garage shelf and hung it from the kitchen window. As if to say "give peace a chance," the bird retreated within a week.

That's how my mom got by for decades—a little ingenuity, a lot of independence, some great friends, and a few good men (as in Mylo, Dan, and Omer).

Pursued by Grace

My dad, on the other hand, was off to the dating races. He ended up marrying Lois, a registered nurse, while I was in college, and for many years he helped raise her kids in Chaska, Minnesota. They enjoyed travel and home life, but from time to time they separated, in large part due to my dad's alcoholism. Their marriage lasted twelve years. When it ended, he moved back to a bachelor condo he owned in the neighboring suburb of Minnetonka. Unlike his divorce from my mom, this one had little effect on me—except when he stopped by my apartment one day to retrieve the condo's original microwave and vacuum cleaner, both of which he'd loaned to me during his second marriage.

"Really, Dad?" I said.

"You were just borrowing them," he said.

In December 1992 my dad had quadruple bypass surgery, and that's when his midlife romantic chaos all came to a head. John and I were together by then, and on the morning of the surgery we went to the hospital and visited with my dad just before they wheeled him away for what would be a six-hour operation.

I held his hand tightly and said, "Is there anything I can do for you?"

With the sedative already taking effect, he looked at me through drowsy eyes. "Have you been out in the waiting room?" he asked.

"No," I replied.

"It's a little messy out there. Could you mediate things?"

That was the last thing he said before he went into his open-heart surgery.

Out in the Abbott Northwestern Hospital waiting room I found: 1) my mom; 2) Lois, from whom my dad was getting a divorce; and 3) the current girlfriend. The three of them were perfectly cordial to each other, but I sensed trouble ahead—and I had to make good on my dad's pre-op wishes.

I walked up to the nurse at the front desk and asked about the rules regarding who could visit a patient immediately after heart surgery.

"Only immediate family," she said.

I drew close to her desk. "We have kind of a situation here," I said, motioning to the three women. "Could you please be lenient in how you interpret 'immediate family'? My dad has a number of different women here who he wants counted as family."

I then explained each relationship. After hearing me out, the nurse nodded and said, "Of course."

That afternoon, we got the good news that the surgery had been successful. My mom and John and I visited my dad. He was hooked up to several machines and still oblivious to his surroundings and all the women-in-waiting. After a while we left and went down to the cafeteria.

We returned an hour later. Both Lois and the girlfriend were gone. Presumably they had already stopped in to see him. But as my mom and I returned to his hospital room, we were surprised to find another woman at his bedside. She looked familiar but I couldn't quite place her.

"I'm Sally Furness and I live down in Albert Lea," she said. "My husband and I go on your dad's bike trips. We're here at the hospital because our daughter just had a baby, and when we heard your dad was having surgery, we stopped by the waiting room and asked the nurse for an update."

According to Sally, the nurse looked down at her notes, glared at Sally's husband, and said, "You stay in the waiting room."

Before she could even make a request, Sally was ushered into my dad's room for a visit.

The nurse had truly taken my words to heart. She was allowing every woman who stopped by the waiting room to enter into my dad's room, even those who hadn't asked.

Nine years later, I found the perfect opportunity to tell that tale—I featured it in my toast at the brunch before my dad's third wedding. His bride, Susan Wilkes, didn't know him at the time of his heart surgery, and fortunately she's got a good sense of humor, so the story worked. Happily, so did my dad's third marriage. He and Susan have now been together for thirteen years.

But the open-heart surgery was not the end of my dad's troubles during that time. The following year—five months after the open-heart surgery and still in the midst of his divorce from Lois—he was diagnosed with prostate cancer. A week before that scheduled surgery, he got arrested for a DWI in Maple Plain, Minnesota. When he got to the station, he called my mom. She drove to the Maple Plain police station in the middle of the night, picked him up, and brought him home. And to our enormous relief, that arrest and all of its consequences marked the turning point in his long battle with alcohol.

He later wrote about the day he went to court for his 1993 DWI. Accompanied by his minister and me, he met with the chemical dependency court evaluator before the hearing, where he dubbed me "the prosecutor." He described the encounter with me this way:

> She told of the times when as a child she'd seen me tight at home. She told of the damage my divorce had inflicted on her, her sister, and her mother. She told of the lies she'd heard from me when she brought up the subject of drinking. She told of seeing me lift the trunk door of the car, pretending to examine something in the car, and taking a drink during the charade. She spoke with fury and sorrow and in tears. I was stunned by her arraignment . . . by the litany of my deceptions. When

she finished, she . . . took my hand, and said, "I love you. You can save yourself."

With great pride, I watched my dad go to treatment, join AA, and start a new life. In his own words, which he captured in the title of a book he wrote about his alcoholism and renewed faith, he was "pursued by grace." In 2001, my dad married Susan, an adviser to nonprofits on philanthropic giving, a cofounder of Up with People, and a reformed alcoholic herself. He stayed pals with both of his ex-wives and made amends with most of the people in his life. He joined a Bible study group and, through his church, led many faith trips. Through his adventure club, he led treks all over the world, including one to Nepal at age eighty-six.

So when people ask me why I do a lot of legislative work on drug courts, treatment, and drunk and distracted driving, the answer comes pretty easily. When they ask me why I go to the Senate prayer group, that answer comes easily, too.

It took a while, but late in life my dad taught me that no matter how many times you mess up, you can still get things right. He taught me that faith in God and redemption are real. And he taught me that standing up for someone means something—even when it is for your own dad.

My dad taught me how to do that. He taught me to want to do that.

Just Married

John and I got married on July 10, 1993. We held the wedding at my dad's church, University Lutheran Church of Hope, even though John is Catholic, I was baptized Catholic, and I was raised and confirmed in a Congregational church. The only problem? Right across the street from the Lutheran church is a Catholic one. When our guests arrived, a few of John's Indiana relatives initially went to the Catholic church, thinking the wedding was there. But everyone was in their seats by 5:00 p.m. when the service started.

John and I had met with my dad's pastor, Mark Hanson, several times before the wedding, and I made only two requests: no lawyer jokes and no politician jokes. A lot of our lawyer friends would be there, and I also knew that Walter and Joan Mondale—as well as quite a few elected officials whom I had met on campaigns and in my political work—would be in the pews.

Naturally, the minister began his remarks at the service by making a lawyer joke, one of those about how many lawyers does it take to do something or other. And then, to my eternal mortification, with Walter Mondale seated in one of the front pews, the good pastor offered: "Who knows where this couple might end up? Summit Avenue [the street in St. Paul where Minnesota's governor lives]? Pennsylvania Avenue?"

Then, as I stood at the altar, with a face as bright pink as the brides-maid dresses I had personally picked out at Talbots, he made note of my request that he not make such jokes. "Amy has a way of wanting to be in charge of things," he said.

Lesson learned the hard way: it's never a good idea to try to dictate what a pastor can say in his own church!

The Reverend Mark Hanson went on to become the presiding bishop of the Evangelical Lutheran Church of America, so I guess he knew what he was doing. After all, everyone laughed at the lawyer joke. Of course they did: who doesn't love a good lawyer joke?

True to form, I had done my best to plan every moment of the ceremony and the reception, right down to the boundaries of my mother-in-law's videotaping and the pace of my walk down the aisle. We were, in fact, trying to stage a relatively large wedding on a limited budget. I was bound and determined to pay for the whole affair—dress, invitations, wedding rings, decorations, cake, food for 250 guests, drinks, gifts, and dance band—on a $10,000 budget, and I did it. There was certainly no room in the budget for a wedding planner, so I took on all details myself.

John and I personally folded hundreds of invitations and attached the gold sticker seals. The dress was a "sample" from Dayton's department store, purchased at a steep discount since it was last year's model gown and had been tried on by hundreds of hopeful brides. Our rings cost less than $2,000, and I am still proud of my little brown diamond from Australia and the tiny white diamond that serves as a symbol of our engagement (and thus allowed us to forgo the expense of a second ring). The band was affordable, the caterer was a deli in the western suburbs that my mom liked, and I found the cake at a Korean bakery next to the St. Paul bus depot. The beer and wine came from a liquor wholesaler who sampled each glass of wine with John and me at ten in the morning, and let's just say we weren't his first appointment.

We held the reception in the atrium of the Humphrey School of Public Affairs, with multicolored balloon decorations courtesy of the family-owned Tuthill's Balloon Emporium. The atrium had never been used for a wedding reception before, but John went to the University of Minnesota, both of us had always admired Hubert Humphrey, and the U of M's Humphrey School was just a short drive away from the church. Besides, we got a good deal, and they even opened up the Humphrey exhibit space during the reception. Our friends took some great pictures in front of the '68 protest displays.

But creativity? That was free.

The rehearsal dinner—dubbed the "Unrehearsed Dinner"—was a brats and beer event in Minneapolis's Theodore Wirth Park pavilion. My mom made gift bags for all of our out-of-town friends. For those who brought their kids, she included copies of a children's book called *The Pigs' Wedding*, featuring the nuptials of Porker and Curlytail.

For the morning of the wedding we planned a series of activities (called "Wanderings in the Wilderness" on the wedding invite) for the out-of-town guests. My mom and John's dad, Bill, then the biology chair at Mankato State, led a nature hike at the Minnesota Landscape Arboretum. John's mom and my dad led a canoeing adventure on the Minneapolis lakes, with my dad decked out in a commodore's uniform—gold sash, Royal Navy hat, and all.

The wedding program featured the "best men" and the "better women" with tongue-in-cheek descriptions of the bridesmaids (my grade school friend Amy Scherber, college roommate Meg Symington, and law school buddy Kate Stacy) and groomsmen (John's friends Bruce Beddow and Rob Hendrickson, and his brother Greg). The wedding colors were red and purple, which I knew would cheer up the reception's institutional setting.

Paying meticulous attention to every detail did have a downside, of course. Among other things, it meant that I had to personally manage every problem that arose. One of the trickiest involved the lodging for all of our out-of-town guests. After we set the wedding date and reserved the church, we learned that the Lions Club International was hosting its worldwide annual convention in the Twin Cities on the same weekend. Tens of thousands of Lions Club members would descend on Minneapolis/St. Paul, and I soon discovered that nearly every hotel in the area was booked for that weekend. But after a lot of frantic calling around, we finally found enough rooms, including at one hotel that the Lions Club chose not to book because it was under the management of a Chapter 11 bankruptcy trustee.

Our no-frills option was the Gopher Campus Motor Lodge, where we reserved rooms at the bargain rate of $35 per night for one to four guests. Near the University of Minnesota campus, the concrete-block lodge overlooked the 35W Interstate and featured a large smiling Gopher statue. As we would later learn, the hotel was also the site of more than a few crime scenes over the years. We intended the rooms for John's friends who were looking for deals, but of course it was my grandma from Ely—and her eighty-plus-year-old sisters—who promptly booked the Gopher rooms and refused to move.

I dodged another glitch only three hours before the wedding. Just at the moment when I was putting on my wedding gown, the phone rang. It was the Korean bakery. In broken English the baker kept asking me if I had changed my mind and wanted the "plastic swans."

"No swans," I said. "Please, no swans. No plastic swans."

Then came a series of unfortunate events: First my dad began walking too fast as he accompanied me down the aisle. "This isn't a two-minute drill," I said, kicking him gently in the shin. "Slow down, I don't do this every day." Then came the minister's lawyer joke, followed by the reception where my mom's friend Gwen unintentionally threw uncooked rice in my dinner, almost chipping one of my teeth. Then I realized that I'd forgotten to pick a "first song" for our first dance. Then my grandma and her sisters were spotted walking through the party carrying pieces of sheet cake they had cut for themselves long before we'd even taken our first bite of our own wedding cake. (Hey, they eat early in Ely.) Then my dad threw down the microphone after he finished his toast, breaking it, so Vice President Mondale couldn't use it when he gave his. (A true pro, the VP just yelled his toast, but not before making a Watergate-related joke that engulfed the room in laughter. "Is Donald Segretti in the audience?" he quipped.)

My dad left the reception before the dad/daughter dance. My high school prom date Steve gathered the hundreds of red and purple centerpiece balloons and prepared to release them for good luck, causing my mom to break down in tears because it would be bad for the environment. And finally, my college roommate Meg, who'd had her third child only three weeks before, went into an understandable panic because her breast pump was missing from the refrigerator along with the milk she'd stored. It turned out that the Korean bakery had packed it up along with the cake stand and plastic pillars.

I kept my cool throughout. I talked Steve into not releasing the balloons, calmed my mom down, and located the baker and the breast pump bound for St. Paul. I never did find my dad or a new microphone.

As for John? Blissfully unaware of all these little disasters, he was standing by the keg drinking beer with his college buddies.

When it came time to leave the reception, I carried my shoes as we headed to our Saturn, which John's brothers had adorned with an enormous tissue wedding bell and white crepe paper streamers. Almost as soon as we got in the car, the skies opened up. It was not a light rain, not even a heavy rain—it was as if buckets of waters were being poured from the sky.

Just at this moment John turned to me and sighed happily. "Wasn't it a great wedding?"

That was it. Just as the skies had brought down the waters from above, so came the tears. For twelve hours straight, I had been the perfect wedding planner and the perfect bride. But now I had had it.

"Great?" I said. "*Great?*"

Through sobs over sobs, I described each of the calamities—the forgotten first song, the broken microphone for Mondale, the grandmas eating the cake too early, the fiasco with the balloons, and, of course, the missing breast pump. John looked for a Kleenex in the car but couldn't find one. In an act of great wedding-night chivalry, he stepped outside into the pouring rain, grabbed the soggy wedding bell from the front windshield, and gave it to me to use as a gigantic tissue.

For better or for worse, for richer or for poorer, 'til death do us part, our married life had begun.

A Big Decision

John and I went to Europe for our honeymoon. I was thirty-three years old and my husband, at age twenty-five, still qualified for a youth Eurail pass. We hiked in the Alps near Kandersteg, Switzerland. We visited my Swiss grandpa Martin's nephew Toni Heuberger and his wife, Gracious, staying with them in their centuries-old farmhouse in northern Italy. From there John and I traveled by train to Germany and by boat along the Rhine River, marveling at the luminous Marc Chagall choir windows at St. Stephen's Church in Mainz. We also rode the rails to Vienna and Prague, eating a lot of sausage, noodles, and Wiener schnitzel along the way.

Refreshed from our trip, we returned to our lives at the Dorsey and Faegre law firms, only to face one of those out-of-your-control, life-changing decisions that so often come at the most unexpected times—like the day after you get back from your honeymoon. In my case, on that day, I was called into the office of Dorsey's managing partner Tom Moe. At a firm with over 260 lawyers, this was not an everyday occurrence, so I immediately suspected that something important was up.

Tom Moe is a big guy—a smart, no-nonsense type who worked his way to the top of the firm after a highly successful sports career, first by lettering at Edina High School in three sports and then as a football and baseball star at the University of Minnesota. After congratulating me on my wedding, Tom Moe told me that the firm truly appreciated the practice I had built up by representing MCI and the other competitive local exchange companies. But then he informed me that an exciting new business opportunity had arisen out of the firm's Denver office, a new office set up to accommodate the firm's most important client, First Bank (now U.S. Bank). The potential business involved representing what at the time was MCI's archenemy—the dominant regional local telephone company U.S. West (formerly Northwestern Bell). He told me that Dorsey's top management had decided that U.S. West would be a better fit for its expansion into the western states than MCI, and that therefore the firm was terminating the future legal work of MCI and all of my other telecom clients that had cases against U.S. West.

I knew this decision was the result of a conflict with a new partner in the firm's Denver office who, earlier in the year, had wanted to bring in a relatively minor case for U.S. West involving phone service to a small transportation company. Understandably, MCI objected to Dorsey's representation of U.S. West on a telecommunications matter but said it would be fine for the firm to handle any non-telecom legal work for U.S. West. But the new partner was well connected in Denver and he wanted his way.

I tried valiantly to make the case that it would be a mistake to end Dorsey's relationship with MCI and the other companies. The firm's work for these clients had resulted in hundreds of thousands of dollars in steady billings every year; they were also loyal clients who always paid their bills. Besides, FCC and court rulings and state and federal legislation were constantly changing the competitive landscape, and that meant future work for years to come.

Tom Moe was firm. The decision had been made.

I went home and called Bill Levis, then director of public policy for MCI's western division, and read off the words I had written down during my meeting with Tom Moe: the firm would no longer take any new work for MCI. The firm was obligated to finish the twenty-some cases that were ongoing, of course, but any future relationship was being severed, and it would therefore be best if MCI sought new counsel for its work in Minnesota.

Bill Levis was livid. "They're firing us?" he fumed. "They're *firing* us? Usually clients fire law firms, law firms don't fire clients. And we have always paid our bills." Then, without a moment's hesitation, he added, "If you want to leave we will go with you wherever you want to go."

The telecommunications work was about half my practice, but, unlike some of my other work, it was *my* practice. Still, Tom Moe and the Dorsey partners had followed up the news about their decision to terminate MCI by making me a very nice offer. I would remain a full-time partner but, by way of acknowledging that they had eliminated half my practice, for the next three years I would be expected to bill only half my hours and use the rest of the time to build up a new practice. They pledged to help me make this transition and I believed they would do it.

It was purely a business decision. There were moments when I wanted to yell down the hushed hallways, "You are destroying a practice I've been building for years," but I never did. I was working at a business, Dorsey had made a decision that was strictly about business, and now I would have to make a business decision of my own.

I had strong support at the firm, and a lot of lawyers voiced opposition to the decision, both behind closed doors and to me in writing. Many believed it would have been financially smarter for Dorsey to keep MCI. One of my favorite e-mails was from Ken Cutler, then a fellow partner but now the firm's managing partner, who wrote that he was "amazed and appalled" about what had happened, telling me he felt the firm had made the wrong decision.

Giving up a partnership at the biggest law firm in the Twin Cities only a year after earning it? That wasn't easy to do. But in the end, despite the real and generous offer to rebuild my practice and the fact that I liked so many people at Dorsey, I decided I needed to go my own way. No matter how much money I could make, I didn't want to walk the firm's hallways clientless and the object of pity and charity.

I promised myself I would keep up my friendships with my pals at Dorsey, tell the story of why I resigned truthfully, and never bad-mouth a stellar law firm that had been so good to me for so many years. They returned the favor—I kept in close touch with all my friends there, and to this day the people who have contributed the most to my political races are those who work at Dorsey & Whitney.

Gray, Plant, Mooty, Mooty & Bennett

Within a month I had several offers for partnerships at major law firms. In most cases, it's not ethical to search for a legal job and show your client billings, but when clients are in the midst of being terminated, the rules are quite different. In the end I chose Gray, Plant, Mooty, Mooty & Bennett, the firm I had clerked with after my first year in law school. Gray Plant had long been known as one of the Republican firms in town. John Mooty, one of the kindest men I've ever known, had been the chair of the Minnesota Republican Party when political beliefs were, well, a little more moderate. He was a smart businessman, too. In 1970, he led a group of investors who paid $5 million for Dairy Queen, which later became one of the firm's biggest clients. In 1997 he and his investors sold the business to Warren Buffett for $585 million while keeping the legal business with Gray Plant.

MCI liked Gray Plant and agreed to follow me there. It was fun to show up for my first day of work at the new firm with MCI, several smaller telecom companies, and other clients in hand—as well as a brand-new Coach briefcase that Dorsey had given me as a going-away present.

When I started at Gray Plant, the firm had a reputation—as it still does today—for being a nice place to work. Though it now has sleek modern offices in Minneapolis's IDS Center, back then the firm had three floors in the International Multifoods Tower, with dimly lit hallways, dark wood paneling, and lots of lake- and animal-themed art. When I would bring my mom to visit, she would always remark loudly that they "need to turn up the lights" and that I should "get one of those miner's headlamps to see down the hall." She would also note that the conference rooms (labeled A, B, C, and D) located on each of our three office floors (32, 33, and 34) were actually incognito bra sizes.

"You don't think it's strange to meet one client on 32B and the other on 34D?" she asked with great amusement. Years later the firm renamed the rooms after their law firm partners.

I made a bit of a splash in my first weeks at the firm. Gray Plant was pretty traditional in those days, and when I looked at the letterhead and spotted my name all the way at the bottom of a long list of dozens of partners—including some well-loved but deceased ones—I thought the letterhead would make it difficult for me to establish my credibility when trying to bring in new business. I decided to format my own letterhead, one that simply listed the firm's five named partners at the top and left out all the other names, including my own. I'd used similar letterhead at Dorsey.

After someone mentioned this breach of protocol to the Gray Plant office manager, she was very unhappy. She immediately paid me a visit, telling me sternly that altering the letterhead simply wasn't allowed at the firm. Within an hour this now weighty matter caught the attention of Gray Plant's managing partner—the jolly and straight-as-an-arrow Mike Cunningham. Mike soon appeared in my doorway.

"You do whatever you need to do to bring in business," he said.

The next day Mike Cunningham sent out a firm-wide memo inform-ing all the lawyers that from that day forward it would be acceptable to use the optional letterhead.

Then there was the e-mail system. This was the early 1990s, and big law firms were only just starting to use e-mail. Dorsey was already well along in the transition from fax to e-mail, but at Gray Plant e-mail was something of a novelty, used mostly as an interoffice version of the want ads, with staff selling everything from used mattresses to high chairs.

Most lawyers didn't use e-mail at all, but for me it wasn't a choice. My client MCI was a telecommunications company, and the company—with all respect to Al Gore—had actually hired the guy who was consid-ered by many to have been one of the inventors of the Internet: Vinton Cerf. While at MCI, he also developed the first commercial e-mail system (MCI Mail), so MCI was all-in on e-mail, sending me dozens of messages a day regarding legal inquiries and case documents. When an e-mail arrived a "ping" would go off and I would immediately check the computer in case it was a new message from someone at MCI. The problem for me was that at Gray Plant half the pings were for "everyone" e-mails, containing such all-important requests as "Does anyone have directions to the air-port?"

One day I finally fired off my own e-mail to my sparring partner, the office manager, asking her to look into an "everyone" e-mail that asked all employees of the firm to search for a single spoon that had been taken from one of our conference rooms. Noting that the firm's cutlery appeared to be quite inexpensive, I suggested that it was time to do a cost-benefit analysis measuring "the benefit of finding one spoon against the cost of the lost productivity" of all lawyers and staff at the firm reading the e-mail. Knowing that my words might truly send her into a bureaucratic orbit, I ended by suggesting that we needed a better way to triage personal and for-sale all-firm e-mails. Until that happened, I asked that she take me out of the "everyone" e-mail group.

Within a day, Mike Cunningham and the office manager paid me another visit. They informed me that some would take umbrage to my unorthodox request, and that although it was technically possible to remove me from the "everyone" e-mail group, taking that step would present a problem.

"Why?" I asked.

"Well, because if we removed you from the group, it would no longer be everyone."

"I don't want to be 'everyone,'" I said. "I don't want to buy a mattress or look for a spoon. I just want some peace so I can do my work."

The next day the "everyone but Amy" e-mail group was quietly launched. That was fun while it lasted, but a few weeks later Mike Cunningham sent out an e-mail announcing the creation of an all-firm electronic bulletin board. He also declared that it was no longer permissible to send "everyone" e-mails to inform people about personal sales or to make minor requests. Those types of missives would be relegated to the bulletin board.

Gray Plant joined the modern e-mail age and I rejoined "everyone."

As I adjusted to the firm, my business boomed. Three years after I got to Gray Plant, Congress passed the Telecommunications Act of 1996—a law that sought to open up telecommunications markets and pave the way for companies like MCI to compete more effectively. After that, my telecom billings, already strong, grew larger. MCI became the third-biggest client at the hundred-lawyer law firm, and I soon had one junior partner and a number of junior associates and legal assistants working with me to manage my clients' business.

Just as I did at Dorsey, I worked with some wonderful lawyers at Gray Plant. In addition to Mike Cunningham and the whole Mooty clan, I was fortunate to collaborate with a lot of terrific colleagues. At Gray Plant, I made friends for life, built a business, and started a family. I also gained another opportunity to mix it up with people who held varying political views. Perhaps best of all, the Mooty family's history with the Republican Party meant that Gray Plant's managing partners believed that politics and service were compatible with the firm's mission. I had found a firm that considered running for office and being involved in public service to be a good thing, for both the firm and the broader community it served.

A Mom and a Candidate

A Political Education, Part III

While my early political education involved studying textbooks, interning in government offices, writing my senior-thesis-turned-book, and working one-on-one with Vice President Mondale at Dorsey & Whitney, the next decade ushered in some real-world political campaigns and, ultimately, my own run for office.

One of my first political jobs was working as a volunteer on a 1987 city council race for a guy named Bruce Bataglia in St. Louis Park, Minnesota, a suburb west of the Twin Cities about halfway between Minneapolis and my hometown of Plymouth. My work consisted mainly of calling ward and precinct captains and making sure they turned out Bruce's supporters. Bataglia won the race but later moved to Florida before his term ended. Nevertheless, I got some valuable experience, learning that every call makes a difference and that grassroots politics works best when you have a lot of people on the team.

From there, I launched myself into the big time, or so it seemed to me then. In 1988, while still a law firm associate, I volunteered to manage the reelection campaign of State Representative Gloria Segal, mother of my Gray Plant law firm friend Susan. Elected to the Minnesota House of Representatives in 1982, Gloria would routinely win in a landslide. When I took up the reins of her campaign, she was running for her fourth term.

The district was predominantly Democratic and the epicenter of Minnesota's Jewish community. During her years in the legislature Gloria took on several key issues, including the provision of mental health services, pay equity, and funding for girls' sports. She was also known for her big heart and the personal attention she paid to her constituents whenever they were in need.

That personal attention extended to her political opponents, and though she was expected to win big, neither of us planned to slouch through the election. Nearly every morning between 6:00 a.m. and 7:00 a.m. the phone would ring in my apartment. It was always Gloria. Maybe she was checking up on me—at the time I was still single, and Gloria was not beneath meddling in everyone's romantic affairs—but it was jarring to wake up to her phone call each day. She would never offer a greeting and always began the same way: "Amy, I think it's time we knock my opponent's street again." She loved to torment her opponents by door-knocking all their neighbors, and, even better, getting a bunch of her lawn signs put up in the yards on the blocks leading up to their homes.

That campaign provided me with my first real opportunity to "rally the troops." At Gloria's annual corn feed, with nearly one hundred campaign volunteers dutifully gathered in Milt and Rosalie Goldstein's living room on a hot September afternoon, my job as campaign manager was to give them an update on the race and marching orders for the fall. In my brand-new red suit and white silk blouse, buttoned to the top despite the sweltering temperature, I stood at the front of the room and told Gloria's supporters how important it was for them to sign up for phone calling, lawn signs, and door-knocking.

After I finished, I asked if there were any questions. A hand shot up from the back. It was Sophie, Gloria's eighty-six-year-old mother. I called on her and she came to the front of the room and stood next to me. I had no idea what she wanted to say; maybe, I thought, she wants to organize an event at her senior housing complex at Menorah Plaza.

"Amy is a very smart girl," Sophie began.

"Amy is also a very nice girl," she added.

A long pause, and then finally the punch line: "Does anyone have a boy for her?"

There I stood, decked out in my new suit, clipboard in hand, and looking out at a living room filled with the St. Louis Park Democratic power structure—it still goes down as one of my most embarrassing moments in politics. Nothing but an awkward silence followed Sophie's plea until I filled it by asking the bemused crowd if there were any other questions. Hearing none, I signed up a ton of people for lawn signs.

Soon I added Gloria's victory to my clipboard, and before long the size of my political territory expanded once again. In 1990, I managed a county commissioner race in a district that covered the southern part of Minneapolis and St. Louis Park. My candidate, Mark Andrew, was a popular, high-energy, and environmentally focused Hennepin County commissioner seeking reelection, and my job was to make sure we raised money, got his literature out, and spelled his name right in the ads in the local newspapers.

Mark had a lot of enthusiasm for his work and he taught me one memorable lesson: if you have an opponent no one knows, never spend your time talking about him. And, if you can avoid it, never even use his name. Mark gave me very specific instructions. Whenever anyone asked me about his opponent, I was to say: "Oh, do you mean 'the kid'? He's so new to politics that everyone just calls him 'the kid'!"

To this day I don't remember the guy's name.

Wellstone, Clinton, and a Party on the Move

By the early 1990s my political work broadened beyond local campaigns. It was an exciting time to be involved in politics—Bill Clinton's campaign for president was under way, and across the country Democrats were resurgent. After years of Reagan and Bush and two Republican senators representing Minnesota, everyone was talking about a new Democratic Party with new ideas.

In 1990 we showed the country the power of Minnesota populism in Paul Wellstone's come-from-behind victory led by campaign operatives John Blackshaw and Pat Forciea, with Paul's signature green bus and his amazing passion and energy. That populist spirit was reflected in Wellstone's terrific ads, the brainchild of Minnesota adman Bill Hillsman. There was "Fast Paced Paul," with the make-you-smile theme that Paul had to talk twice as fast as anyone else because he had so little money and so few ads to buy. Then there was "Looking for Rudy," an ad in which they filmed Paul trying and failing to find his opponent—Republican Senator Rudy Boschwitz—all across Minnesota. ("They say he's in the Cities," a smiling Wellstone said, speaking to the camera. "I don't know where he is. He's not in Minneapolis. They say he's campaigning. Then I go to St. Paul, they say he's in Milwaukee.") But the most memorable ad for me was one showing little kids sitting in chairs trying to write checks with colored markers to demonstrate how children and regular people need someone in Washington to represent them.

The enthusiasm in Minnesota Democratic politics didn't end with Paul's election. Around that time I took over as president of the Minnesota DFL Education Foundation, a think tank that ran independent of our Minnesota Democratic-Farmer-Labor Party. Through the foundation work I got to know Dave Lillehaug (now a Minnesota Supreme Court Justice), who would go on to become a friend and longtime political strategist and adviser. Walter Mondale was the honorary chair of the board and Minneapolis Mayor Don Fraser and his wife Arvonne were the heart and soul of the group. In an interview I gave about the foundation in 1991, I explained that the foundation's mission was to promote more citizen involvement in politics. "In this era of sound bites and quick fixes to problems," I said, "people are yearning for something more substantial in the way they talk about issues."

We sponsored issue forums and put out a quarterly newsletter called the *Idea News*, landing an interview with Paul Wellstone right after he got elected. By publishing question-and-answer sessions with many of the state's leading Democrats, our newsletter spanned the ideological spectrum within our party, from southern Minnesota's fiscally conservative Democratic congressman Tim Penny to the liberal representative Marty Sabo in Minneapolis. Producing the *Idea News* also brought me into what was then considered the cutting-edge world of computer layouts and direct mail. St. Paul volunteer activist Jules Goldstein would lay out our newsletter on his computer at home, and then Mondale aide and my future press secretary Ross Corson and I would spend an entire day in my living room on our hands and knees stacking our three thousand newsletters by zip code and binding them together with the twine required by U.S. Postal Service protocols. Especially since we were a nonprofit, we saved money however we could, and years later it gave me a great story to tell campaign volunteers, reminding them that the bulk mailings were even harder in the "good old days."

My early political work was far from glamorous, but people began to take notice and I was given more and more responsibility on campaigns. I put together young professional events for the Clinton/Gore team in Minnesota and was elected chair of the suburban senate district that included Gloria Segal's turf. My extensive work for the Clinton campaign led to my election as a delegate to the 1992 Democratic National Convention in New York, where I roomed with State Senator Ann Rest. To save money she brought her own cereal, and every morning we would eat it dry because we didn't have any milk.

The 1992 Clinton/Gore campaign, which inspired so many people to believe our country could move forward again, had a major impact on my decision to stay involved in politics and step up to the next level. The campaign handled economic issues especially well, and it also had an innovative nationwide grassroots "rapid response team" to counter false attacks. I memorized the Clinton economic plan so I could talk about it on the road. I liked Bill Clinton's emphasis on jobs and fiscal responsibility, and I liked Hillary Clinton's strength and her hands-on approach to policy.

I still remember when Walter Mondale introduced me to President Clinton right after he was first elected. Referring to our work together at the law firm, the former vice president said with much pride, "Amy is my partner," using a term that was coming into vogue at the time as a way to describe people who were dating but not married.

Bill Clinton looked at me and smiled.

"He means at our law firm," I said.

My First Run for County Attorney

My first run for public office didn't turn out exactly the way I'd planned. I didn't lose, and I didn't win, but in the long run it was all worth it.

By 1994 I had turned down offers to run for the state legislature. I had also decided not to wait for what would eventually be an open seat for Minnesota Secretary of State. I was told these jobs would be good "stepping-stones" for other offices, but I knew I didn't want to run for a job just because it would be a good stepping-stone. I wanted to run for an office where I thought I could make a difference. I wanted a job that I actually wanted. Otherwise, why do it?

One job seemed particularly appealing. Serving as the chief prosecutor for Hennepin County, which encompassed Minneapolis and its forty-four surrounding suburbs, was the equivalent of a DA's office in another city, but even better. The Office of the County Attorney not only handled about five thousand adult felony prosecutions and twelve thousand juvenile cases a year, it also had civil jurisdiction. Of the four hundred employees in the office, about half were assigned to criminal work. The other half made up the civil division, which represented the county board, handled all child protection and child support matters, and litigated all civil cases for a county of over one million people, including those involving the state's largest public hospital, Hennepin County Medical Center. In past decades, Hennepin County residents had elected lawyers to the job from both political parties. They had come to the position from outside the office, and over the years county voters had accepted the idea that this worked out pretty well.

I had the civil legal management background and at least some criminal prosecution experience from within the courthouse. I had chaired or served on several nonprofit boards, including the one for my neighborhood, and I had a lot of ideas about how to make the County Attorney's Office more accountable to the people it served. It helped that I had lived in both the suburban and urban parts of the county. And even though a woman had never come close to being elected to this major office, I had watched Paul Wellstone win his election on a shoestring and then been hugely inspired by Bill Clinton's victory. Anything and everything seemed possible.

I decided to run for county attorney in the fall of 1993. Thanks to my work with nonprofit groups and my experience in both business and politics, I quickly lined up lots of support. Eventually I received the endorsement of the Minneapolis Police Federation, several labor groups, and a lot of elected officials, particularly in the suburban communities. Many of the lawyers in my Republican-leaning law firm also supported me.

The theme of my campaign was "turning ideas into action," and I outlined a number of new initiatives. Crime was becoming a major issue in the county. I promised that I would go after violent offenders and set up a community prosecution program similar to the community policing program that Bill Clinton had proposed and later put in place on the federal level. I ran on a law-and-order platform; the job was essentially about crime fighting, and we had some major crime issues.

But no matter how good my platform, I would never become county attorney if I couldn't get on the ballot that November. And that was contingent on a factor over which I had no control: the Democratic endorsement for a candidate for governor.

Politics is complicated—that was as true then as it is now. In 1993, Hennepin County Attorney Mike Freeman was one of several Democratic candidates who had decided to take on Minnesota's incumbent governor, moderate Republican Arne Carlson. Freeman was seeking the support of our DFL Party, a crucial endorsement that would be determined at our state party's convention. He was the odds-on favorite, so if he got the endorsement, the Hennepin County Attorney's seat would be open.

Here was the catch: Freeman had made clear that if he did not get the DFL's endorsement for governor, he planned to run again for Hennepin County Attorney. So if for some reason he was unsuccessful in getting the endorsement, I would have nothing to run for, since the DFL's Hennepin County convention was scheduled to take place after the DFL's state convention in June. But having decided that Freeman had a good chance of winning the endorsement, I took the risk and ran.

I announced my bid for Hennepin County Attorney on a Saturday morning in January at the Matthews Recreation Center, an inner-city neighborhood community center just six blocks from where John and I lived on Milwaukee Avenue. Of course John and I had mailed out invitations to the event well in advance. But when the day for my announcement arrived, it was very cold. No, not very cold—bitterly cold. The average temperature that day in Minneapolis was 17 degrees below zero.

Don Fraser, then the former mayor of Minneapolis, introduced me, and standing next to us were key supporters: Tom Johnson, the former Hennepin County Attorney; Matthew Little, the former head of the Minneapolis NAACP; and Ember Reichgott Junge, a state senator who represented the northern suburbs and who served with Don as my campaign cochair. "I used to work for the city of Minneapolis," Don said, drawing a laugh. Then he talked a bit about my recent political work, emphasizing my credentials and telling the audience about how I'd worked closely with him on the DFL Education Foundation and neighborhood issues.

In my speech I welcomed everyone to the Matthews Center—everyone, that is, who managed to get their cars started. Standing in front of professionally printed blue signs that read "Amy Klobuchar for Hennepin County Attorney," and standing behind my six-year-old neighbor Sarah Brown, who was holding up a handmade sign, I quipped that this might be "one of the first announcements in history where the candidate came with jumper cables."

"This place and the public park which surrounds it," I said, "are the heart of our neighborhood, the Seward neighborhood of Minneapolis. Kids get together here and play softball and basketball in the summer; they skate and take art classes in the winter. Adults use the center for neighborhood meetings and community education courses. My six-year-old neighbor Sarah Brown goes to school next door at Seward Montessori and comes over here every afternoon for Latch Key."

Then I got to the heart of my message. "I am running for county attorney," I said, "because I believe that Sarah Brown and her friends should have the right to walk the six blocks between their house and this center without fear. They should have the right to keep their windows open on a hot summer night. They should have the right to be kids."

"As county attorney," I continued, "I pledge to you that I will work to give them what is their right: I want to put the dangerous criminals far away from these streets and this center. I want to create a spirit of responsibility in every neighborhood in this county so that both kids and adults know that if they do something bad, there will be consequences."

For the die-hard Minnesotans who managed to make it that day, the atmosphere—at least once inside the Matthews Center—was upbeat. I joked that my dad, who had made it from the western suburbs, one day hoped to be known everywhere as "the father of Amy." The rest of my family, as well as many of my longtime friends, were wonderfully supportive as well.

That morning, my new in-laws, Bill and Marilyn, had driven all the way from Mankato to the Twin Cities to be there. That meant a lot to me, but my favorite part was the crowd of kids carrying the handmade "Pre-schoolers for Klobuchar" signs. Running for office is a major undertaking, and my friends had gone out of their way to make sure that my campaign got off to a good (if really cold) start.

Not an End, but a Beginning

We had no paid staffers on my first campaign for county attorney. With lots of help from family, friends, and a boatload of volunteers, John and I did pretty much everything. We typed up handouts and distributed them ourselves. Attorney John Eisberg agreed to serve as the campaign's treasurer (after, more notably, serving as Bill Clinton's finance chair for Minnesota). We also put together a nearly twenty-person campaign steering committee that was especially helpful with advice and fundraising.

In that election year of 1994, Minnesota's precinct caucuses took place on March 1st. Caucuses are a Minnesota tradition, and both the DFL and the Republican Party have them. They get people out to meet their neighbors, and the caucuses then elect delegates to send off to nominating conventions, including the Hennepin County convention. Since they take place all over the state, we did our best to line up supporters to go to the caucuses, doing everything from setting up phone banks to sending out letters to likely caucus attendees. We had a small budget, but enough money to produce a professional-looking, two-color brochure.

The caucuses went well, and lots of my supporters were elected as delegates and alternates to the Hennepin County convention. But I took nothing for granted: my worthy opponent for the endorsement was Bill Richardson, an experienced prosecutor in the Hennepin County Attorney's Office who had worked on a lot of Minneapolis-based campaigns. So while still working full-time at Gray Plant, I conducted a series of community meetings throughout the county. I also spent several months of my evenings and weekends calling the thousand-plus delegates and alternates, reaching nearly all of them personally. I kept track of my numbers on a spreadsheet (listing how many definitely supported me, how many were likely to support me, how many were neutral, etc.), and in the end I knew I had the numbers to prevail at the convention.

But then fate intervened in the form of a state senator named John

Marty. At the state gubernatorial endorsing convention in early June, the grassroots candidate Marty upset the more rank-and-file candidate Mike Freeman, the man I wanted to replace as county attorney. John Marty— a good government and reform-oriented state senator—would go on to lose to Arne Carlson, the Republican governor.

When I announced my campaign on that bitterly cold day in January, I had pledged not to challenge Mike Freeman in the event that he reentered the county attorney's race. I'd been a volunteer for Mike's congressional race when I was in high school and one of the cochairs of his 1990 Hennepin County Attorney campaign. I had always intended to keep my word, and that is what I did. On June 8, 1994, our campaign— just ten days out from the county convention—sent out a final press release in which I noted that "while it is disappointing to close down the campaign at this stage, I view this not as an end, but as a beginning." And in my closing letter to friends and supporters, I thanked everyone and told them I had no regrets about the past five months of hard work.

The following November Mike Freeman was reelected as county attorney. I actively campaigned for him, and in 1998 Mike would return the favor by strongly supporting my next run for county attorney. Years later, he also backed my candidacy for the U.S. Senate. And another Freeman—Mike's son Matt—would be the field director in my U.S. Senate reelection bid in 2012.

Patience and picking my moments have served me well in politics. Back in 1994, I was resolved to try for the job again, but I had four years to wait. Besides, I had my law firm practice, my friends, my husband, and plans to have a baby. What they say about politics is true: it's all about timing.

Abigail

In the fall of 1994, nearly five months after my campaign for county attorney had ended, I found out I was pregnant. In the months leading up to our daughter's birth, we were your typical excited parents preparing for the big event. We went to the birthing classes at Abbott Northwestern Hospital. I practiced my breathing exercises, and John rehearsed his coaching skills. We took an infant care class, and I even dragged

John along to a three-hour breast-feeding class, arguing that he would be one of the "cool" dads who dared to accompany his pregnant wife to the class. He came all right, but the cool part was questionable.

I borrowed maternity clothes, bought a few loosely fitting work suits, and purchased the latest edition of *What to Expect When You're Expecting*, reading it cover to cover. Thanks to our family and friends and some generous baby showers, we were equipped with all the latest gear, including a safe crib and a diaper disposal contraption. Everything was set to go: we even put a fresh coat of yellow paint on the walls of the baby's bedroom. I didn't want to know if the baby was a girl or a boy, and I spent hours listening to other people guess. By the end, I was sure it was a girl, and I was right.

When John and I got to the hospital in the middle of the night on June 19, 1995, he was so excited he ran through the hallway and got way ahead of me. "What are you doing?" I yelled down the empty hallway, waddling far behind him and already in labor. "Nothing will happen unless I am there."

"There are papers to sign," he yelled back, only then realizing that perhaps it would be a little strange for him to arrive at the maternity ward a full ten minutes before me.

The pregnancy had been uneventful, but in the final few months the doctors realized I had a fairly rare condition called polyhydramnios, which involves an excessive accumulation of amniotic fluid and can signify a swallowing problem for babies. At the time my doctor was not really worried about it, so my only problem was that I was carrying so much water weight up front that a lot of people asked if I would be having twins. For the most part, though, everything seemed fine, and I kept working at Gray Plant right up to the end.

I went into labor two weeks early. The labor lasted more than fifteen hours and although all moms will know what I mean when I say that it was really hard, let me put it this way for everyone else: I had once spent ten days riding my bicycle eleven hundred miles from Minneapolis to Jackson Hole, carrying twenty pounds of gear on my bike and much of the time pedaling against the wind and uphill—and those ten days were nothing compared to those fifteen plus hours.

Abigail was finally born at 6:00 p.m. She was a beautiful little girl who had all her fingers and toes. Initially she seemed quite healthy except for some phlegm in her throat.

We called our parents, and then convinced my grandma Mary in Ely that it was okay to name our daughter Abigail—she had never heard of a baby being given that name. We filled out seemingly endless hospital forms. We had a late snack, but I was really tired and could barely walk. We finally got a little sleep around midnight.

About three hours later, we were awakened by the pediatrician on call. "All the liquid we put in her mouth goes out her nose," he said. "We think she needs emergency surgery because her esophagus may not be hooked up to her stomach." The nurses—who had seen just about everything—confessed to John that they'd never come across anything like this before.

We hurried to the nursery, and we were up the rest of the night as the doctors and nurses conducted tests and took numerous X-rays—hardly the ideal way to welcome a new baby into the world. It was finally decided that Abigail didn't need emergency surgery, but the doctors still couldn't figure out what the problem was. They thought it might be a small tumor or a muscular condition or a genetic problem—in truth, they had no idea.

The next day was a blur of pain, fear, and more tests. A tube was inserted in Abigail's nose, bandaged to her cheek, and snaked down to her stomach so she could be fed the breast milk I was told to pump out every few hours. We spent almost no time in our hospital room and instead careened from doctor to doctor and procedure to procedure. I never slept.

As the day went on, I remembered that despite the emergency nature of the situation, insurance company rules still required that I be sent home within twenty-four hours. Back in the mid-nineties, as a cost-saving, profit-boosting measure, insurance companies across the country had instituted twenty-four-hour hospital stay policies for both new mothers and their babies. "Drive-by births," as they were known at the time, worked all right for some parents. But especially for first-time moms, it was hardly realistic to expect that an exhausted mother could learn all she needed to know to take care of a brand-new baby and also recover enough to go home and begin caring for her baby within twenty-four hours of birth. The rule was particularly problematic when the baby was ill.

Friends and relatives, many of them unfamiliar with the twenty-four-hour policy and thus unaware that we were leaving that day, kept calling to see if they could stop by. "We're out of here in a few hours," I'd say.

By the end of the afternoon it was clear that Abigail, still plugged into a battery of machines, would be staying the night. In fact, she ended up being transferred to the infant specialized care unit in Abbott Northwestern Hospital and later the adjoining Minneapolis Children's Hospital. She remained there for a week, and over the next year she spent many other weeks there, too.

At 11:00 p.m. that night, the hospital kicked us out. We kissed little Abigail good-bye, loaded our duffel bag and the two plants I'd received just hours before onto a cart, and headed out through a long tunnel to a non-hospital room in a different building. Among other issues, we were told that it was very important for our sick baby to get my breast milk, yet the room—which we were paying for—had no refrigerator in which to store the milk. Early the next day and every day for a week we returned to the hospital, hanging on to the doctors' and nurses' every word of advice.

When the week was done, they sent Abigail home with her nose tube and a nighttime heart monitor. Later we moved to an oxygen-level finger alert, a device to measure her oxygen saturation and pulse. She would return to the hospital within weeks. Six months with a nose tube was followed by a year with a surgically inserted stomach tube, which made things much easier because we no longer had to feed her a couple ounces of milk multiple times during the day and night. The scary part was when the doctor told us that it took kids an average of three days to learn to swallow for every day they had a stomach tube.

We carted Abigail from doctor to doctor, swallowing expert to swallowing expert. All we knew for sure was that until she learned to eat—which didn't happen until she was about a year old—everything she would try to swallow would come out her nose. She was so small, she didn't have the strength to crawl until her first birthday, and for nearly two years she was in the bottom one percent for weight. Our main goal was to make sure she got the nutrition she needed so that her condition didn't affect her development.

What was the problem? No one really knew. The doctors told us they thought it was a muscular weakness, although one expert—who ended up being wrong—was sure it was cerebral palsy. In the end they concluded that Abigail probably developed the condition in the womb—explaining my polyhydramnios—but some thought it was possibly caused by a never-established neck injury at birth.

One specialist recommended surgery, claiming her soft palate was hanging loose like "a hunk of bacon." The doctors at Minneapolis Children's Hospital—ENT experts Sidman and Brown, stomach doctor Ferenci, and our extraordinary pediatricians Inman, McLeod, and Moore—counseled the opposite. They believed in caution and patience. I consulted a number of experts across the country and they all agreed: it would be best simply to wait and take our daughter in to see swallowing therapist Susan Fields every other week. For someone who really isn't very patient (that would be me), waiting was the hardest part of all.

The Gifts

We were blessed with many gifts during those years. The first and most obvious one was our little daughter. Through the nose tubes and the stomach tubes and the ear tubes and the barium swallows and the surgeries, she never gave up. Even though she didn't really swallow for six months and then could hardly do it right for another year, she kept her spirits up. When she would pull out that nose tube in anger—which only caused the visiting home care nurse to reinsert it and cause yet more pain—she kept testing the limits. They tried making her wear mittens so she would stop pulling at the tubes, but she would just pull off the mittens.

After the tears, she would smile and laugh and jump up and down and move around in her play Exersaucer on wheels. She'd learn words, babble away, and refuse to let the tubes and the bandages and the occasional stares from strangers get her down. The doctors would always express surprise at how alert and bright she seemed, and I would always feign disbelief and say, "Why are you so surprised?"

The second gift was the incredible generosity of our family and friends, as well as the extraordinary care provided by the doctors and nurses who helped us. When you have a baby with a serious illness, the concept that "it takes a village" to raise a child applies in a very special way. Our parents and in-laws were always there, with Bill and Marilyn Bessler staying at our house for weeks to help with the on-the-hour nose tube feedings. Abigail's godmother, Kathleen Sheehy, would often stop by, as did so many other friends. Eventually, when I finally went back to work, Andrea Murrill—who loved and hugged Abigail no matter how sick she was— would watch her during the day. She was followed a year and a half later by Jayme Kellington, who would keep such careful track of Abigail's feedings and progress that I came to believe that Jayme literally willed Abigail to swallow.

And then there was John. Having a sick child can take a toll on a marriage, but John never wavered. I returned to Gray Plant after a leave that lasted much longer than I had expected, but John actually left his job at his law firm and then did contract work for another firm and clerked for a federal magistrate so he had more normal hours. He was there for our daughter every step of the way. In Hebrew the name Abigail—as our Jewish friends later told us—means "my father's joy." Even though we didn't know that when we named her, we couldn't have picked a better name.

The third gift from Abigail's illness was the most intangible—the gift of faith and understanding. Being confronted with an illness that no one can diagnose, much less cure, makes you question all your knowledge and beliefs. Every time we tried to be "normal" parents, something would go horribly wrong. We would go to a park and she would pull out the nose tube. We would take her to the zoo and she would throw up because of too much milk in the tube. We would take her to the mall and forget the syringe. But we took solace in the one thing we knew for certain: every milestone—from Abigail's baptism to her first Christmas to her first birthday—was a gift from God.

We'd always wanted to take Abigail on a driving trip out west for our first family vacation, and after a year of being essentially homebound, we decided to take the plunge. Abigail was doing better and we took off on the trip in such high spirits that it didn't occur to us that gas stations and small grocery stores in South Dakota and Wyoming might not sell the special frozen pureed baby food we'd finally gotten her to eat. But one thing they did sell was pudding. I have many fond memories of that trip: in my mind's eye, Abigail, always a bit hungry, is sitting perched in a restaurant high chair in a Billings, Montana, diner or a Rapid City, South Dakota, Perkins and yelling *"Pudding!"* at the top of her lungs. Pudding— in all flavors—seemed to be the only thing she would eat on that adventure, and she somehow managed to survive on it for an entire week.

In the end, after two years of struggle, Abigail got better. Despite all the early problems, her disability didn't became permanent. In fact, no one who meets her today—she's now a healthy, happy, successful college student—would ever guess that her first two harrowing years even happened.

But what a gift those years were. They gave me such respect for everyone who cares for children with disabilities—whether they are parents, teachers, or health care workers. The experience also gave me enormous empathy for those who have lost children. Having sat for hours in those children's hospital waiting rooms, having spent time in neonatal infant care units, having known the feeling of waiting for the doctor to tell you something was mortally wrong, I often think of the unspeakable tragedies experienced by parents whose children don't recover.

When you spend a lot of time with those who care for very sick children, you see up close the depth of their faith and their belief in spiritual healing. It runs so deep that all the tests and studies and credentials fade into the background. I remember the exact moment this happened to me. Abigail was about a year and a half old, and during the annual Christmas Eve morning "muffins and grog" party we hold at our house for our neighbors and friends, a neighborhood girl came downstairs to tell me that Abigail's stomach tube had accidentally fallen out. I remember running up the stairs to where the children were playing. I remember exactly where they were sitting and what they were wearing.

I knew that if the tube wasn't reinserted within three or four hours the incision would close up. I immediately called the home number for Dr. Jim Moore, who specialized in the treatment of kids with disabilities. He was fully up to speed on Abigail's condition and knew that after eighteen months of nose and stomach tube feedings, we had gotten to the point where we only used the stomach tube for one supplemental bottle a night. Otherwise, she was drinking the rest of her milk like any other child.

After listening to my panicky account of what had happened, Dr. Moore said, "It's Christmas Eve. Let's chalk it up to a miracle and leave the tube out."

Knowing that this wonderful doctor's faith in little miracles was backed by an equal grounding in scientific facts, I didn't hesitate to question his reasoning.

Even when we found out that Abigail got chicken pox from another child at our party, and even when that case of chicken pox landed her in the hospital for another week because she was still so frail, I remained certain that Dr. Moore had made the right decision. Sure enough, it was the last lengthy hospitalization she would ever have.

It was Christmas Eve. It was a miracle.

A Mom in Tennis Shoes

One of my favorite political stories is about Patty Murray, now the senior U.S. senator from Washington State. Before she held elective office, Patty advocated for environmental and educational issues in her home state. One day, when she went to the state capitol to advocate for a local preschool program, a Washington State lawmaker told her that she "couldn't make a difference" because she was just another "mom in tennis shoes." She later turned that label to her advantage, first winning a seat on the school board, then joining the state legislature, and finally taking those tennis shoes all the way to the U.S. Senate. "A mom in tennis shoes" has been the symbol throughout her campaigns.

Abigail's "drive-by birth," where I was forced by insurance rules to leave the hospital after twenty-four hours with no sleep and a sick baby in intensive care, became my own "mom in tennis shoes" moment. As John wheeled me out the hospital door that night—dizzy, scared, exhausted, and still in pain—I asked him whether he thought this would be happening to the wife of an insurance company executive under these same circumstances. Answering my own question, I told him I didn't think so.

Once Abigail's health began slowly improving, I spent a lot of time thinking about what had happened and decided that I didn't want any other mom to go through what I had experienced. Even though I wasn't an elected official and had never even testified at the state capitol before, I became determined to change the policy. I went to the state legislature and worked with two great Minnesotans—State Representative Joe Opatz, whose wife had had a similar experience, and State Senator Don Betzold— to pass one of the first laws in the country guaranteeing new moms and their babies a minimum forty-eight-hour hospital stay. I testified in support of the bill before both houses of the legislature, summoning the courage to talk about episiotomies and breast pumping in front of TV cameras. And I quickly realized that my testimony had the advantage of being so embarrassing to a still male-dominated legislature that it was nearly impossible to *not* pass the legislation.

Noting the support for the bill by pediatricians and ob-gyns alike, I concluded my testimony before one Senate committee by appealing for bipartisan support and pointing out that New Jersey's Republican governor Christine Todd Whitman had made such a bill one of the centerpieces of her legislative agenda. "Certainly the women and babies of Minnesota," I said, "should be protected as much as the women and babies of New Jersey."

After a bill with slight variations passed both houses, only one obstacle remained: the conference committee where the House and Senate legislative conferees would work out the differences. Although no one wanted to oppose the legislation publicly, I knew that the insurance companies wanted to delay it for a year. I showed up at the meeting of the conference committee with six visibly pregnant friends so they would outnumber the insurance lobbyists two to one. When the legislators asked when the bill should take effect—in Minnesota bills normally go into effect on August 1st—the pregnant moms all raised their hands and said, "*Now.*"

And that is what happened. The forty-eight-hour maternity hospital stay rule became law the day after Governor Arne Carlson signed the bill on March 20, 1996.

To this day Minnesota moms still thank me for that law, which was later adopted on a national level under President Clinton's leadership. In the end Abigail wasn't the only one born on June 19, 1995. That day also brought the world a new mom and a person who became firmly committed to the simple idea that change can happen. And I was determined to make sure that politics—at least my politics—would be about getting things done for people.

On the Ballot

By the fall of 1997, Abigail, now a little more than two years old, had turned the corner. She was growing and happy and our trips to the hospital had nearly come to an end. "What better way to celebrate our life returning to normal," I joked with John, "than running another campaign?"

That's exactly what we did. On November 15, 1997, I announced my candidacy for Hennepin County Attorney for the second time, once again choosing the Matthews Center for my campaign kickoff. It snowed that day, but it was quite a bit warmer—at least by Minnesota standards—than it was when I announced my candidacy in 1994. This time it was a balmy 22 degrees. And this time there was a new addition to our announcement team: Abigail. We even had a t-shirt made for her. It said, "Vote for my Mommy."

By the time I announced that day, I had already done all the groundwork and knew I would face no opposition on the Democratic side. The seat was open and my party wanted a strong candidate. People knew after the endorsement battle in 1994 that I could deliver the delegates and had the gumption to win. Before announcing, I had lined up a broad base of supporters within and outside the party structure, including elected officials, former prosecutors, and community leaders. I had also already secured the endorsement of the Minneapolis Police Federation and the AFL-CIO.

One of the ads that captured the breadth of my support during that 1998 campaign was a full-page newspaper spread. The ad's background listed one thousand lawyers' names, including that of John Mooty, my law firm partner and former State Republican Party chair. The names had been painstakingly gathered and double-checked by my husband, and we had signed statements of support from every lawyer in the ad. In bold type in the middle of the page the copy read: "More than 1,000 lawyers, a dozen former bar association presidents, nine present and former chief prosecutors, and one former Vice President agree . . . Amy Klobuchar has the experience, judgment, and integrity to be a great Hennepin County Attorney."

And then in even bigger type: "Who says lawyers don't agree on anything?"

I had the operations and logistics down from the last campaign. We had our colors (blue—as in police blue—and white, with a touch of fluorescent green). Our parade sticker design was oval, more or less out of necessity so my long last name would fit. And this time John's younger brother Andrew, a graphic artist, designed a website, which seemed like a big deal at the time. John even convinced me to do a little Web advertising on news sites. We were told by the *StarTribune*, the Minneapolis paper, that we were the first campaign to do that in the state.

My themes and ideas had evolved and expanded since the last campaign. Two years before, an article in the *New York Times* referred to Minneapolis as "Murderapolis," calling it a "nice city" with a "nasty distinction" after the city recorded ninety-seven homicides in 1995, meaning that the city's per capita murder rate was almost 70 percent higher than New York City's. It was hard for Minneapolis to live that article down, and even though the murder rate had declined a bit since 1995, it was still a major concern for city and county residents in 1998. That's why in this campaign, just like in the last one, my plan for the County Attorney's Office continued to focus on violent offenders, convicted felons who illegally possessed guns, and the need to reform the juvenile justice system. But this time I would go with a tougher slogan. Instead of "Turning Ideas into Action," we used "Safe Streets, Real Consequences."

Since my previous campaign for county attorney, I had spent quite a bit of time working on a leadership plan for the office. I had developed a lot of new ideas gleaned from dozens of meetings with law enforcement officials, school leaders, and prosecutors across the state and around the country. Among other things, I wanted to establish a community prosecutor program for property crimes, integrate police and prosecutor computer systems, place a bigger emphasis on school truancy, better connect the domestic violence prosecutions with child protection cases, do more police training, and make changes to our drug court. In early October, a month before the election, I released a forty-eight-page leadership plan, a comprehensive package of crime-fighting and civil reform proposals that would make the County Attorney's Office more accountable to the community.

I knew from the start that this campaign would be different from the last one in one crucial respect: this time I would get the chance to actually face the voters. When Mike Freeman announced his candidacy for governor in February 1998, he simultaneously announced that he wouldn't be seeking reelection as county attorney. In June he would be endorsed by the DFL state convention, but three months later he would come in second in the DFL primary to then Minnesota Attorney General Skip Humphrey. Skip, the son of Minnesota icon Hubert Humphrey, would go into the November general election as the favorite, facing Republican nominee and then Mayor of St. Paul Norm Coleman, as well as Reform Party nominee and former Brooklyn Park Mayor Jesse "The Body" Ventura.

One of the more memorable parts of that year was witnessing Jesse Ventura's completely unexpected rise to power. Given that the two of us had much less money and staff than our well-financed opponents, we would often find ourselves together in parades and at festivals, usually at the end of the line or at least at the end of the program. His election theme was "Retaliate in '98," and I happened to be speaking to Minnesota's Reform Party convention the weekend he was endorsed. I saw his campaign evolve from a few volunteers carrying signs to long lines of adoring fans at the Minnesota State Fair to a grassroots victory at the ballot box. For me, it was an important lesson in how quickly things change in politics. In less than a year, Jesse Ventura went from the back of the line in the Minneapolis St. Patrick's Day parade to the front of the national news coverage, inauguration feather boa and all.

There were no feather boas in the 1998 Hennepin County Attorney's race, but it did get a lot more attention than it had in the past. Although the Office of the County Attorney is nonpartisan on the ballot, both political parties had traditionally endorsed candidates. And though no woman had ever campaigned to become the chief prosecutor of Minnesota's biggest county, that year featured not one but two women on the ballot. The Republicans chose a formidable candidate: Sheryl Ramstad Hvass, a former prosecutor and former judge who'd headed up the state bar association. She was also the sister of Jim Ramstad, the very popular Republican suburban congressman.

The Democrats chose me.

Race to the Finish

It was a novel campaign: for the first time, two women were running for one of the most important jobs in the state. From the beginning, I knew it would be a tough race. Jim Ramstad, the sitting U.S. congressman, not only already represented more than half of Hennepin County voters, he was also on the ballot at the same time as his sister. His advertising that year, which included crime-themed ads, would help Sheryl. And Jim, I knew, was not only a talented fundraiser but a nice guy who would be eager to support his sister and allow her to tap into his Rolodex.

So Sheryl had her experience, her brother, and access to funds. My advantages? I had a lot of ideas for reforming the criminal justice system, a great law firm that supported me, a lot of friends, recently retired parents who were eager to volunteer, and a husband with five brothers (who were a big help hammering in lawn signs). I also had a head start on Sheryl: I had already run for the office once and I was very familiar with the issues.

But money was clearly going to be a problem. The race would be expensive, and the measly $30,000 I had raised in my last campaign wasn't exactly going to scare Sheryl off. My family didn't have anything like a fundraising Rolodex. It was an advantage that my dad's name was well known from his columns, but outside of an event at his house that raised about $10,000, I was basically on my own when it came to bringing in the cash to pay for the campaign.

Up to that point, with strict election year limits of $500 per donor, around $200,000 was the most anyone had ever raised for a Hennepin County Attorney's campaign. I knew Sheryl would raise much more than that, so in April 1998, I asked her to agree to a three-part proposal: (1) limit campaign spending by each candidate to $321,000, the base spending limit set by state law for the Minnesota Attorney General's race; (2) restrict "soft money" contributions; and (3) limit out-of-state contributions to 20 percent of all campaign funds.

When Sheryl promptly rejected this proposal, I knew I would be badly outspent over the course of the race. I would have to be nimble, bring in lots of small contributions, and use my money carefully. One of my first dilemmas involved TV advertising, which could quickly get very expensive. With an ad budget of less than $50,000, we decided to do something that was fairly innovative, which was to run some ads on cable TV channels. At the time cable ads were really cheap. Advertising on cable allowed us to target our advertising to areas within the county, whereas ads on network TV went to half the state and were much more costly. True, fewer people saw our ads, but those who did see them saw them over and over again. Or, more accurately, they saw the *same ad* over and over again.

Not only did we broadcast only one ad, we produced it on a shoestring budget. We had no money for a crew so we shot no video. Instead we used black-and-white still photos, including one of me with police, one with my family, and one with me sitting in front of a lot of law books. The ad also featured a male narrator whose voice was so melodramatic that he sounded like the prize announcer on the game show *The Price Is Right*. The sole special effect involved the word "WON," which was printed in bright red and whooshed onto the screen at the end of a sentence such as, *"She took on a big telephone monopoly and WON"* or *"She prosecuted criminals before juries and WON."*

And that was our multimedia campaign. Years later, when I first ran for the United States Senate, I sent that ad to Mandy Grunwald, the widely respected political consultant and media adviser. She called shortly after getting the VCR tape in the mail. "Instead of the mock-up version of one ad," she implored, "will you send me the actual ads so I can see all of them?" I replied: "There was only one ad, and that is not a mock-up. That *is* the ad."

With Sheryl running glossy network commercials, I knew that we would lose the ad war; the only way we could win was on the ground. In Wellstonian fashion we poured our time and limited budget into lawn signs, parades, billboards, bus signs, and human visibility. My dad and I personally door-knocked the homes where the backyards bordered on major highways.

"You have a really nice garden back there," I would say. "Do you mind if we put up one of our signs in the very back overlooking the highway? It won't get in the way at all, and I'll make sure our volunteers don't walk through the flowers."

At one point we had miles of large four-by-eight-foot lawn signs on Highway 169—a major thoroughfare that runs north to south through the county.

Among other lessons, the campaign taught me that parents of candidates are obsessed with lawn signs. My mom and dad would become very unhappy if Sheryl out-signed us—even in the most Republican of areas—and they would personally go to neighborhoods in search of sign locations. They would target the houses that displayed no signs for any candidate and plead with them to take mine. Their passion for signage was indulged by the cool and collected Jeff Blodgett—who ran Paul Wellstone's campaigns and helped me through 1998 and many other election years to come—but he would always note, "Remember, Amy, lawn signs don't vote."

Billboard placement was also an issue. Through her brother, Sheryl had an in with the billboard company, so we didn't get the best locations. One night from midnight until four in the morning, John and I personally drove around the county and scouted out locations while Abigail slept in her car seat. My sweet-tempered husband later blew a gasket when one of the locations we requested was changed to another that was completely covered by a tree. You literally couldn't see it unless you parked the car by the highway and got out and looked behind the tree.

Most important, though, I went everyplace that would have me, including a dunking booth at New Hope's "Duk Duk Daze" festival. I held meetings with prospective voters and shook hands at street corners, grocery store entrances, and bus stops. Thanks to Paul Wellstone, I learned how to campaign on city buses. What a joy it was to get on a bus with him, shake everyone's hands, and then get off a few blocks later, only to get on a bus going the opposite way. That was how we did it—up and down Minneapolis's Nicollet Mall. And we paid every time!

I also went places that weren't necessarily eager to have me. If festivals or fairs wouldn't allow signs, I would simply walk through the crowd accompanied by big guys with t-shirts emblazoned with my name. My favorite companion for these events was Dominick Bouza, son of former Minneapolis police chief and once gubernatorial candidate Tony Bouza.

Dominick was so big and so tall that he was a walking billboard—everyone would see his "Amy Klobuchar for Hennepin County Attorney" t-shirt.

My favorite event was the Minneapolis Aquatennial. Officials wouldn't let political candidates into the parade, so I just walked along the crowded barricaded route right before the parade began. Next to me walked two guys with signs, and we all acted like we were actually in the parade. Just in case I was kicked out, I made sure to walk close to one side of the route. That took some moxie but it gave us great visibility.

That was just one of many parades I attended. Hennepin County, an area of 611 square miles, has lots of annual parades. Of course there are dozens of Fourth of July parades, but there are also the parades that celebrate the Robbinsdale Whiz Bang Days and the Hopkins Raspberry Festival—not to mention the Long Lake Corn Dog Days, the Brooklyn Park Tater Daze Festival, and the Crystal Frolics.

In our news updates to volunteers, put out by our loyal campaign manager Laura Sether and workers Theresa Sheehy and Sarah Rathke (who originally got involved in my campaigns when her dad sentenced her to help after she'd been truant from high school), we encouraged our friends and supporters to march with us. Once, when we had two parades at the same time, my friend and law firm colleague Sarah Duniway, who looked a bit like me, went to the parade I couldn't attend and walked down the middle of the street pushing her baby in a carriage. She never said she was me, but a lot of people thought she was.

Eventually, as the race heated up, Sheryl and I squared off in a series of debates. To say the debates were "lively" would be something of an understatement—"combative" would be a more accurate description. We would argue about endorsements—we had both been endorsed by the Minneapolis Police Federation, but she also had endorsements from the airport police and the park police. Sheryl would stress her experience as a prosecutor and a judge and I would stress my experience in the private sector and my work in the neighborhoods. She would brush off my claims of experience by saying things like, "I was trying cases when you were still in diapers." I would emphasize my ideas and my detailed leadership plan.

Two other points of contention emerged toward the end of the campaign that ultimately proved helpful to me. The first involved a dispute over changing the law so that prosecutors would get the last word in closing arguments in jury trials. At the time, Minnesota was the only state in the country that gave criminal defense lawyers the final word in jury trials—prosecutors did not have the right to rebuttal.

Prosecutors across the state had long been unhappy about what they saw as an unfair procedural disadvantage created by this rule. Given their grave responsibility to prove a defendant guilty beyond a reasonable doubt, prosecutors felt they should have the opportunity to rebut a defense attorney's closing argument. The rule made it possible for defense lawyers to take potshots at a prosecutor's case, or at the victim of a crime, or at the testifying police officer, and criminal defense lawyers were well aware of this advantage. As one out-of-state attorney who'd defended a 1960s homicide case in Minnesota once said to his fellow lawyers: "If any of you get hasty with a girlfriend and knock her off one night, get the body up to Minnesota, because that is the place to go on trial; there the defendant gets the last word."

Nearly every recent candidate for county attorney in the state had argued for changing the rule. That made perfect sense to me, and I made changing the rule one of my campaign platforms. I was lobbied by criminal defense lawyers to oppose the change, but I figured I wasn't running to be a criminal defense lawyer. In fact, I went so far as to pledge not to accept any campaign contributions from criminal defense lawyers.

Sheryl, on the other hand, did accept money from a number of prominent criminal defense lawyers. Then, in a surprising move late in the campaign, she declared that the law didn't need to be changed. I raised the issue in several debates and argued that she was out of step with other prosecutors. I also made the point that she had accepted money from criminal defense lawyers and was now embracing a position that was clearly theirs.

The second issue that emerged was more bizarre. In late October I received the endorsement of the Minneapolis *StarTribune*. Shortly thereafter Sheryl and I participated in a debate on a popular show on WCCO radio, and at one point she claimed I had gotten the endorsement of the paper because my dad and "my brother" worked there. I began my response by explaining that my dad had retired and had nothing to do with the endorsements. As for her mention of "my brother," I was stumped.

I waited twenty seconds before responding: "I don't have a brother, so that's interesting."

She responded that in fact I did have a brother—"a stepbrother"—who worked at the paper. Claiming she had done the research, Sheryl would not back down and actually repeated the claim the next day during a Minnesota Public Radio debate.

The minute I got in the car after the debate, I discovered that I had already received a message from Cheryl Johnson, better known as "C.J.," the *StarTribune*'s gossip columnist. In her message, C.J. said she was calling from the cubicle of a young sports department intern named Tim Klobuchar. Suddenly swept into the vortex of a tumultuous campaign, the poor guy had already received numerous calls.

"He says he's distantly related," C.J. said in her message, "but he is not your brother. Do you have a comment?"

In the car with me was Tim O'Malley, a friend from our time together at the University of Chicago Law School and then a law enforcement officer. Tim had volunteered to drive around with me that day, and after I relayed the message to him he took a long, thoughtful pause. "Am I thinking what you're thinking?" he asked.

"Yes," I said. "I need to call my dad before I call the gossip columnist."

Soon I had my dad on the phone, and in an awkward but memorable conversation I asked him if he was in fact this young man's father. I wasted no time on niceties—I needed an answer and I needed it quick.

"No, of course I am not his father," he said. "I know his parents." Then he explained some distant second-cousin relationship to our family involving a lot of Mikes and Marys and Johns.

I called C.J. back and told her that although I had always wanted a brother, it simply wasn't in the cards. Tim Klobuchar was not my brother.

Campaign research can be hard. And in the heat of a campaign sometimes things get said before all the facts are checked.

Election Day

Even on Election Day I never stopped. I campaigned on the skyways and in the food courts of downtown Minneapolis. I shook every hand within reach, determined to sprint hard to the finish line.

Grandma and Grandpa Heuberger with my mom and her younger brother Dick in Milwaukee in the early 1930s.

My grandpa Mike Klobuchar. By age twenty, he was already working in the iron ore mine to support his nine orphaned brothers and sisters.

ELY-WINTON HISTORICAL SOCIETY

Grandpa Mike and his fellow miners in 1936 at the Zenith Mine in Ely, Minnesota.

My mom in class, 1946. She's the teacher to the right of the elephant!

Here she is fishing up north.

My mom loved teaching.

My dad served in the Army during the Korean War. He was stationed in Germany.

With his trusty typewriter he covered everything from pro football to presidential politics, becoming a daily columnist for *The Minneapolis Star,* later the *StarTribune.*

Here's my dad with Hubert Humphrey in 1970 on St. Patrick's Day.

My dad has climbed mountains all over the world. This photo was taken on the summit of the Matterhorn.

My mom and dad on
their wedding day in
Milwaukee, 1954.

1315 Oakview Lane in Plymouth,
Minnesota. This is the house
I grew up in, complete with
car and camper.

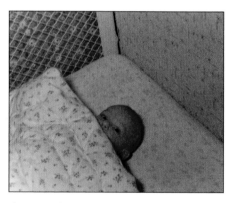

I've never been a good sleeper!

In my grandparents' garden
in Ely, Minnesota.

With my grandparents, Mike and Mary Klobuchar, on their front steps. When my dad was young, my grandpa drove to a nearby town where an iron ore mine had closed down, bought this house for $100, and moved it to Ely.

With my best friend, Amy Scherber.

I earned a lot of beads as a Camp Fire Girl.

My sister Beth and me. In fourth grade I was sent home for wearing these bell bottom pants to school.

Always a diligent student.

My babysitting partners and I getting off the bus in Kansas City at age twelve. We made the trip with no parental supervision.

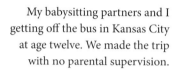

HEIDI BERGSAGEL

Amy Schatzke, Amy Scherber, and I tap danced our way through "Once in Love with Amy" at the high school talent show.

In 1977, as juniors in high school, we held a Lifesaver lollipop drive to raise money for the senior prom.

As a student at Yale.

My college roommate Meg and I with her future husband, John (on far right), and our friend Matt.

As an intern for Vice President Mondale in 1980.

With my friend Kate at our graduation from the University of Chicago Law School in 1985.

In the early 1990s I headed up Minnesota's DFL Education Foundation and edited its newsletter.

While working as a lawyer at the Dorsey & Whitney law firm I worked closely with Walter Mondale.

My dad and I took many long-distance bike trips together.

John and I on our wedding day, July 10th, 1993.

When our daughter, Abigail, was born she couldn't swallow. She spent her first week in the neonatal intensive care unit.

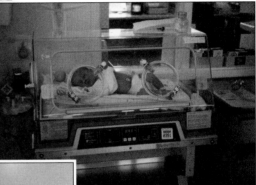

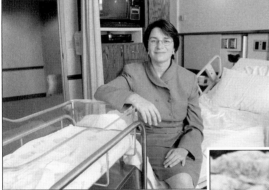

I was the lead advocate for a law guaranteeing new moms and their babies a forty-eight-hour hospital stay.

By the time Abigail was two, her health had finally improved. We celebrated by taking a family hiking trip to the Black Hills of South Dakota.

At my announcement for
Hennepin County Attorney.

Marching in a
parade in the
summer of 1998.

Abigail on the
campaign trail.

Election Night, 1998.
We didn't find out
that I'd won until the
next day.

Abigail was very proud of her
Bible-holding duties on
the day I was sworn in as
Hennepin County Attorney.

Hennepin County has more than thirty police
departments. Here I am with the Minneapolis police.

One of the issues I focused on as County Attorney was fighting truancy.

At my annual corn roast with
U.S. Senator Paul Wellstone.

Campaigning in 2004 in St. Paul for John Kerry.

Ice fishing with Cass County
Attorney Earl Maus and his
wife, Jean, on the day I decided
to run for the U.S. Senate.

I announced my campaign for the Senate in 2005.

At the Minnesota State Fair with Abigail.

In the fall of 2006 I debated my opponent on NBC's *Meet the Press*.

After my election, Senator Barbara Mikulski invited me to join the women of the Senate in her office. Barbara is on my right, and my Republican mentor, Senator Olympia Snowe, is on my left. Then Senator Hillary Clinton, sitting to Senator Lisa Murkowski's right, was there to greet me as well.

Speaking out for ethics reform right after I got to Washington.

In April 2009, John McCain, Lindsey Graham, and I traveled to Vietnam. We visited the prison in which McCain was held as a prisoner of war for more than five years.

Abbey Taylor, the Minnesota girl who died after being injured in a pool. She inspired me to work on a pool safety bill that was signed into law in 2007.

The nine brothers and sisters from the Philippines adopted by Tim and Renee Merkouris. I got the law changed so the family could stay together.

On August 1st, 2007, the I-35W Mississippi River Bridge collapsed during rush hour, killing thirteen people and injuring more than a hundred others. Minnesota's citizens and first responders rushed to the scene to aid the survivors, and I fought to secure funding to replace the bridge, which was rebuilt just over a year later.

At Justice Sonia Sotomayor's confirmation hearing in July 2009.

Arriving in Minnesota on Air Force One with the President, Senator Al Franken, and Congresswoman Betty McCollum.

Celebrating Abigail's high school graduation, 2013.

That night we had a party at our neighborhood deli, Kramarczuk's, a popular Ukrainian restaurant and a Minneapolis landmark since the 1940s. Best known for its Eastern European smoked sausages and its sauerkraut and stewed cabbage, Kramarczuk's serves really good homemade food. It was a great place to be on election night. The Kramarczuks' Ukrainian immigrant experience was inspiring to me, and the stories of their journey to America were very similar to those of my own immigrant relatives.

Beyond its food, Kramarczuk's is famous for an amazing mural. The Kramarczuks are so proud of their adopted country that a huge image of the Statue of Liberty covers an entire wall of their restaurant. I'd always loved the mural, and if the Kramarczuks were proud of their adopted country, that night I was equally proud to be running for office in such a country.

We saw a lot of Lady Liberty that night. The outcome of my race remained in limbo for a long time: 10:00 p.m. turned into 11:00 p.m., which turned into midnight, and then one and two in the morning. Sometime during the evening, as people at my party gathered around the not-so-big TV screen, Jesse Ventura was declared the victor and our next governor. He had pulled off a major upset and beaten both Norm Coleman and Skip Humphrey.

In my race, I was pulling more votes than expected in the suburbs and in some Republican areas. The night went on, but still the race was too close to call. Right before I planned to give one of my "it's just too early to know if we have won but things are really looking good" speeches to rev up the crowd, a bit of a disaster occurred. Standing in the back room of Kramarczuk's, only feet from where they were busy making their famous sausage, I was looking over my notes and holding Abigail, now three, in my arms. She had eaten a lot of chocolate "victory" cake, and just before I was due to address the crowd she threw up all over my red suit.

John ran back to our house to get me a blue pantsuit. My second speech of the night was delayed while I stood in the bathroom and waited for the new clothes. When John came back, I changed into the pantsuit and gave my pep talk to all of my campaign supporters. Then I headed straight to the bar thinking, well, I tried my best. I really wasn't sure if I was going to win the race, but I decided that no matter what happened, it would be okay.

Eventually, with the outcome still unclear, we went home and went to bed. In the morning, a reporter from a local radio station called our campaign headquarters. The staff had been up all night waiting for the results, and they, too, had finally called it quits and gone home. So when the call came the only one there was my mom, who had dropped by and found the door unlocked and the place empty. Taking it upon herself to answer the phone, she fielded the call from the reporter, who was broadcasting live. He asked my mom if I had won.

"Well," she said, "I have no idea. Do you know?"

Sometime in the middle of the day they finally called the race. I had won—by less than one percent of the vote. I had won, but by an average of fewer than nine votes per precinct.

I learned so much from that campaign, but two lessons stand out. The first is to respect your opponent. Though the race was strongly contested and often heated, it was never sleazy. Sheryl's staff was polite to our staff. Sheryl was a worthy opponent, and in time she would use her skills in other ways when Governor Pawlenty appointed her first as the Commissioner of Corrections and later a state tax court judge. And at age sixty-three, she would get her master's of nursing degree from the University of Minnesota and go on to a second career as a nurse.

I never burned bridges with the Ramstads, and over the years I worked with Sheryl's brother Jim on a number of occasions, both when he was in Congress and after, as Jim continued to lead the fight for drug court funding. It's a useful reminder that there's more to life than politics. Human relationships—and the betterment of society—are more important than any heat-of-the-moment squabbles between political rivals.

The second lesson I learned from that campaign was never to give up and to go with your strengths.

In the end, my opponent raised nearly $700,000 and outspent me by a ratio of two to one. Most people—including many of my supporters—didn't think I had much of a chance of beating Sheryl because of my fundraising disadvantage. But I proved them wrong, and after winning the race by such a slim margin, I felt certain that every sign, every parade, and every pancake breakfast counted. When the campaign ended I drew up a tally: twenty-nine parades, three thousand lawn signs, and eighty-five pancake breakfasts, lutefisk dinners, and fall festival picnics. And one—and only one—dunking booth.

To this day I am convinced that if I had attended five fewer parades, or hammered in three hundred fewer signs, or skipped that dunking booth, I wouldn't have won. When you win by fewer than nine votes per precinct, every vote really does count.

I also knew that without a devoted staff, an army of determined volunteers, and the hard work I had put into understanding the issues and coming up with new ideas, I wouldn't have had a chance.

But I got my chance. And I will forever be grateful to the people of Hennepin County for giving it to me.

Certified election results in hand, I was ready to get to work. I had enjoyed the campaign, but now came the best part. It was time to put my ideas into action.

The Chief Prosecutor

Swearing-In Day

What I most remember about my county attorney swearing-in ceremony was Abigail holding the Bible. When we got to the courthouse, she wouldn't put it down and she wouldn't let it go. At age three she was taking her job very seriously and she was going to do it without any help from anyone.

It was my dad's Bible and it was big. It was so big that when it came time for her Bible-holding debut, my daughter could hardly hold it straight, much less high enough. I had to lean way down so my left hand could actually touch the top of it while U.S. District Judge Ann Montgomery administered the oath.

The other thing I remember is having Vice President Mondale there. It meant a lot to have him speak at the ceremony and stand at my side for my first day in public service. "In my years in government," he recalled, "I've noticed that with lawyers and politicians, they either grow or they swell."

I remember holding my breath and hoping against hope that I didn't look like I was "swelling." Mondale finished off the thought with this: "Amy is someone who grows and keeps growing."

That was nice, though it took a few years for me to fully appreciate what he meant about people "swelling" in public life. My friend, former North Carolina Senator Kay Hagan, once summed it up in a very amusing way.

"In Washington," she said, "there are two kinds of senators. There are those that spend all this time getting their hair and make-up done before they go on TV—and then there are the women senators."

Okay, that was a good joke, but Mondale's warning about knowing the difference between growing and swelling was not a joke. It was something important to think about at the beginning of a life in public service: politics is about doing things for people, not about doing things for your own political pride or personal aggrandizement.

Walter Mondale also taught me another lesson that I did my best to follow while serving in the County Attorney's Office. Political leadership isn't all about giving soaring speeches and punchy sound bites. Although speeches are the lifeblood of the profession since they allow an elected official to communicate a message, you actually learn a lot more from listening than you do from talking.

The only way you can fix problems for the people you represent is by understanding them to begin with. How could we work with police on a new way to reduce auto thefts if we didn't know what kind of criminals were stealing the cars and where they were doing it and if the court would accept evidence from "bait cars" (a newfangled approach that allowed us to catch thieves in decoy cars)? How could we work to improve truancy rates if we didn't understand what the schools did when kids were not showing up for class? How could we reduce lawsuits against the county if we didn't listen to the county department heads about how we could prevent the problems that led to the lawsuits in the first place?

Over the eight years I served as county attorney, I learned that the value of public service is not found in grandiose rhetoric or the big headline. Sometimes you do your best work when you simply help people by righting a wrong or giving them the courage and the wherewithal to move on with their lives. We did a lot of that in the County Attorney's Office. Whether it was giving a rape victim strength by making clear that she had single-handedly put a sex offender behind bars so he couldn't hurt anyone else, telling a kid that the community truly cared if he went to school, helping a family pay the rent by making sure the child support check came in, or retrieving an elderly couple's money from a fraudster who had ripped them off, our job was to do justice for the people we served.

But before I could get to any of that, I needed some basic tools. First,

I needed an actual office. My predecessor Mike Freeman had been in the job for two terms. He had done good work, hired some great people, and accumulated a lot of stuff. He was actually in his office packing his boxes into the wee hours of the night before my swearing-in. John and I had visited him once that afternoon and left a few of my boxes on the floor, but that night we really needed to hang some things on the wall so the office wouldn't look empty the next morning when my friends and family would be stopping in to say hello after the ceremony.

After finding Mike still packing up his things, I called my mentor Secretary of State Joan Growe from a phone booth on the ground floor of the courthouse to inquire about the protocol. Did she think it was okay to go back after dinner and hang a few pictures and documents even if Mike was still there?

"Of course it is," she said. "It's just hard for him to say good-bye, and that's why he's still there."

"I don't think so," I said. "I think it's because he's got the NFL playoff games on while he's packing. The Green Bay Packers wild card game is close and I think it's distracting."

"You need to look in charge starting tomorrow," Joan said. "Go hang up your stuff—at least get your diplomas on the wall."

Mike was more than gracious when John and I stopped by at about nine that night with a few pictures, the diplomas, and a hammer and nails. Mike just kept packing, and we kept hammering.

They vacuumed the office early the next morning and I moved in two hours later, throwing out the decades-old drink umbrellas I found in the back of one of the desk drawers.

Management

After an office, the next thing I needed was a management team. I had thought long and hard about managers, and I knew that to hit the ground running I needed a mix of managers from inside and outside the office. Mike had been in office for eight years, and his predecessor, my friend and neighbor Tom Johnson, had served a total of twelve years before that. I knew that making changes would not be easy.

But I wanted to try some new things, and I knew I couldn't do it alone.

To make the changes I believed were necessary, not only would I have to appoint some great managers, I would also have to get the buy-in of the dedicated 160 attorneys and 240 staff members of the Hennepin County Attorney's Office. Because we represented the county with the largest and most diverse population in Minnesota—serving nearly a quarter of the state's more than five million residents—the workload of the office was, and is, enormous. Fortunately, the office was staffed with a steady group of workers and there wasn't a lot of turnover. In fact, the entire office was made up of civil service employees, and many of the employees, including nearly all of the attorneys, were part of the American Federation of State, County and Municipal Employees, commonly known as AFSCME, the nation's largest public service employees' union.

With two sets of rules—civil service and union—any changes I wanted to make had to be made within the context of those rules. And as I knew from working in the private sector, getting a large group of lawyers to move in the same direction can be . . . well, let's just say, not so easy. As Pete Cahill—my longtime deputy and later chief judge of Hennepin County District Court—used to say about managing lawyers, they can be "fearless in the face of supervision."

I got all kinds of advice. When I first arrived, one of our civil lawyers, Marty Munic, kept telling me that I should watch reruns of a British comedy show called *Yes Minister*. One of the show's signature bits is that every time the minister leaves his office to visit an employee or one of his managers, an assistant puts out an alert telling employees that the minister is on "walkabout," so they should all look like they are incredibly busy. Another lawyer reminded me that most of the staff would inevitably outlast me. He called them the "We Bes," meaning "We be here before you came, and we be there after you leave." And then there was the counsel provided by my neighbor and former Hennepin County Attorney Tom Johnson. Tom had left the office years before I arrived, but many of the people he hired were still there. Whenever I would visit Tom to get his advice on how to manage a particularly difficult employee, I nearly always got the same response.

"Oh," he would say, "sorry, he was that way the day I hired him. But let me tell you what he's good at."

Tom's point was well taken: so many of our employees were amazing and good at a lot of things. But if I wanted to make changes, I needed to set them in motion fairly quickly, not six months after I got there.

Picking my two top deputies would be critical. To manage the civil side of the office, I hired Cindy Jesson (now the state commissioner of Human Services). To manage the criminal side, I chose Kathryn Quaintance (now a district court judge). Both had public and private sector experience, which was really important to me.

Cindy was coming from outside the office, which I also liked. She had been a partner at the Twin Cities firm of Oppenheimer Wolff & Donnelly but also a Minnesota deputy attorney general. We didn't know each other, but we immediately clicked when I interviewed her for the job. Among other things, she told me she had four sons. I figured anyone who could balance raising four boys and a law firm partnership could probably manage the county's legal work. Kathryn, on the other hand, was a longtime friend who had spent a number of years at Robins, Kaplan, Miller & Ciresi before moving to the County Attorney's Office in 1990. She became a respected violent crime prosecutor, managed a trial team, and prosecuted scores of murder and sex-crimes cases. Also, she knew all of the personalities in the office.

I still remember bringing my two deputies together for the first time. I set up a lunch for the three of us at the Nicollet Island Inn shortly before my swearing-in. They had never met, but I was hopeful they would make a good team. I was so proud. Here I was, the first woman Hennepin County Attorney, having an inaugural lunch with my two women deputies. I hadn't set out to hire two women, but as it turned out, they were simply the best people for the job.

The waiter came over to the table. "How are you three little gals doing?" he asked. "Are you taking a break from work?"

Maybe this job wasn't going to be as easy as I thought.

Undaunted, the three of us soon went to work. We assembled a great management team, putting a well-respected lawyer from within the office in charge of each division. We "flattened" the management structure and put more people on the front lines, allowing us to increase the number of criminal trials while slightly reducing the number of employees over the long term. We greatly decreased the amount of county funds spent on outside counsel for civil lawsuits; by the end of my eight years as county attorney, each attorney's caseload had gone up, and our out-side counsel costs had gone down markedly, resulting in a savings of over $5 million to county taxpayers.

Pretty good for "three little gals."

By the Numbers

I came into the office with a forty-eight-page leadership plan and I was very serious about getting it done—so serious that it took some in the courthouse by surprise. I think they thought the plan was just a grab bag of campaign promises. But I had spent years putting it together, with help from people inside and outside the office, and I was determined to make good on my promises.

A few weeks after I started we put out hundred-day and year-end goals, and I said we would follow these with twice-a-year public reports of results. That's exactly what we did every year, and at some point people started to believe that I was serious about keeping my promises.

In that first plan our goals included "Aggressively enforce the new law imposing five-year minimum sentences for felons in possession of a gun." By the time we were a hundred days in, we'd already made significant progress, and throughout my two terms we continued to show a high rate of mandated sentences for gun crimes. Seven years in we were at a 75 percent rate for mandated gun crime sentences vs. 63 percent for the state as a whole.

One of my 1999 hundred-day goals was to go to the legislature and change the law so that Minnesota joined the rest of the country in allow-ing prosecutors to have the last word in final arguments before juries. It had been a high-profile issue in my campaign. And everyone remembered the quote from famed criminal defense lawyer F. Lee Bailey when he appeared on *The Tonight Show* with Johnny Carson and was asked by Carson what he would do if he had committed murder. Echoing what other criminal defense lawyers had said, Bailey replied, "I'd drag the body into Minnesota." With State Senator Randy Kelly and House Majority Leader (and later Governor) Tim Pawlenty as the lead bill sponsors, in one hundred days we changed Minnesota's 124-year-old rule and Gover-nor Ventura signed the bill into law.

I also set out to improve coordination with the police departments. We assigned the responsibility for police training to full-time prosecutor and former sheriff's deputy Fred Karasov. It was Fred's job to help resolve some of the tensions that existed at the time between our office and law enforcement. After gathering complaints from all the police departments in the county, he brought our prosecutors into a special meeting and used an overhead projector to put up every single complaint on a screen. People listened. Over time, relations between the County Attorney's Office and the police improved.

At the end of each year we spelled out twenty new goals for the following year. We would increase the number of trials; we would create a property crime team; we would accelerate child support and protection cases. And I would always put my signature at the end of the report as a way of sending an unmistakable message that we would let the public know what we had planned to do, what we had accomplished, and what we still needed to work on.

I had a plan. I had well-meaning and skilled employees and a professional courthouse. I had the managers. But to truly steer the big ship that was the Hennepin County courthouse, I needed real numbers.

Coming from the private sector, I had learned that numbers matter. Back then, numbers were annual billings and time sheets and law firm goals. In the prosecutor's office they were even more important: they could literally mean the difference between life and death. They mattered for public safety, and they mattered for getting grants to support the work of the office. How could we change our practices if we didn't know whether they were effective? How could we measure progress in a bureaucracy without numbers? How could we go to the Justice Department or a foundation and ask for financial support for the office without benchmark data?

During my first year in office, I got a call from a reporter who had heard about the increasing number of murder cases going to trial. The reporter asked how many murder convictions we'd gotten since the beginning of my term. That was a reasonable question, because we had made prosecuting murder cases—some of which had been in the office for a long time—a major priority. I was proud of the work our prosecutors had done, and I knew they had won a lot of cases. I asked our press person,

Ross Corson, to check in with the Violent Crimes Division and ask them how many murder convictions they'd gotten.

Ross came back an hour later. Dismayed, he simply said, "They don't know."

"What do you mean they don't know?" I said. "A murder conviction is a big deal."

"Well," he said, "historically they don't keep track except by a Robinson Crusoe–type series of hash tallies on a piece of paper. They aren't caught up and there's a lot of confusion."

By the end of the day, we had the data. Our incredibly skilled prosecutors got sixty-nine murder convictions in 1999, some of which involved crimes that had been committed years earlier. Our attorneys deserved to be recognized for their work, and from that day forward we began recording the relevant statistics. And not just for murder convictions—we gathered and then published data related to every function of the office, from the dispositions of property crimes to the time it took to complete the adoption of a foster child.

Recording statistics allowed us to keep another promise. When I published my first set of goals, I said that accountability would be a core value of the County Attorney's Office. Now we had the benchmarks and the numbers to measure our results.

Marathons and Sprints

These changes led to better results, but they also led to another roadblock, one that I had long anticipated: institutional resistance. Every change we made was noted not just by our office but by the entire courthouse, affectionately known to many as "Hennepin High."

The Hennepin County courthouse, designed in the shape of the letter *H* in honor of the county's name, looks more like a giant toaster than the eighth letter of the alphabet. Two parallel towers rise up twenty-four floors, and in between the towers is a glass-walled atrium stretching all the way to the top. One tower is called the "courts tower" and the other the "administration tower." On some of the floors, crosswalks—bridges of sorts—stretch between the court and administration towers.

It was generally understood that if someone working in our offices on the twentieth floor of the courts tower made a managerial change or issued a new policy, the news would travel over to the administration tower within two minutes. In another five minutes it would shoot down the elevators and arrive three floors below. Within ten minutes it would leak back over the bridge to the lower floors of the courts tower.

Faster than a hamster racing through a gigantic Habitrail, the gossip would pass from employee to employee, crisscrossing multiple floors, sky bridges, elevator banks, and offices. Of course, within three hours the news would be totally mischaracterized, with the truth butchered somewhere between the seventeenth-floor skywalk and the fourth-floor elevator bank. You could never trace how it happened.

About two months after I started, I received my own version of a Hennepin High hazing when I decided to rearrange the furniture in the County Attorney Office's main reception area. This was where our customers visited—police, other prosecutors, social workers, criminal defense lawyers, and, yes, sometimes criminal defendants themselves. You never knew who was going to be sitting in the lobby.

Back then, many people were still using landlines, and the phones were awkwardly placed at some distance from the chairs. One weekend Cindy Jesson and I decided to move the furniture around a bit. When we came in the next day, it had all been moved back. I asked the woman at the front desk how this could be when no janitorial staff had been on duty. She laughed and told me that in fact some of the staff members had done it.

"They like how it was before and not how you changed it. They said it's always been that way."

Without missing a beat, I moved the furniture back. Within an hour, someone had returned a chair to its original position. I moved it again. Two hours later the receptionist came into my office with a tally sheet of comments. I hadn't asked her to compile this, but she'd found the whole episode quite amusing. Sparing her fellow employees, she hadn't used names. She divided the comments into categories. In a two-hour period, she reported that two employees said they liked the new furniture arrangement, fifteen said they didn't, and eight said it was "dangerous." They said people would trip and fall.

I was immovable. The furniture would stay where it was. And for the record, I note that during my eight years as county attorney, no one tripped and no one fell due to the new furniture arrangement. Everyone got used to it.

My goal-oriented approach was well received by the local neighborhood groups and other law enforcement offices. The elected county commissioners—three were Republican, three Democratic, and one an Independent—were big allies. The county's sheriff, a Republican named Pat McGowan who'd supported my opponent in the county attorney's race, was a solid partner from the moment I arrived. From the outset, the sheriff and I agreed that we would keep all of our policy disagreements (and there weren't many) between us and never criticize each other publicly. That proved to be a great way to work together, and over time he would help me to implement many of the reforms. After four years we were both running for office again. We actually rode in parades together—except when he was on his horse.

The thirty-plus police chiefs of Hennepin County were also a really good group. I started going to the chiefs' meetings from day one, and we met for lunch every month. The first time I went to lunch with the chiefs, I arranged to meet the University of Minnesota police chief (and later Minnetonka police chief) Joy Rikala at the beginning of the lunch.

"How will I know who you are?" I asked.

"It won't be hard," she said.

She was right. Joy was the only woman chief at the lunch that day. The good news is that the number of women chiefs has greatly increased since then.

Compared to the reception from law enforcement, the initial response from the county's judges to my plans for change was a little less enthusiastic. Most of our discussions about court reform were constructive, but after I issued our first hundred-day results report, Chief Judge Kevin Burke, who had made some great reforms of his own, sent me a letter. He was nothing if not to the point. "You need to start viewing your time as County Attorney as more of a marathon than a sprint," he warned.

"It's a sprint, too," I replied.

I didn't mean to be disrespectful, and in fact I agreed with his point about the job being a marathon. Reform requires persistence and patience. It can take a long time to make changes in government, and experienced leaders like Judge Burke are crucial partners in the effort to make change a reality. But I also believed that if you didn't set your expectations high from the get-go, bureaucratic stagnation would quickly set in. So I would start every year with a hundred-day sprint because that was the only way to win the marathon.

Doing Justice

Accountability to the public depended on the numbers, but behind every number was a victim of crime. How we treated those victims—regardless of whether we won or lost their cases—is what mattered the most.

By the end of my eight years in office we would record nearly four hundred homicide convictions. Behind every conviction was a heartbreaking story, such as the case involving the convenience store clerk who was shot seven times because he dared to tell a gangster to stop making fun of a mentally disabled man. And then there were the three children whose father stabbed their mother to death right in front of them. In one act of rage they lost both their parents—their mom to murder, their dad to prison. A few months after the murder, two of the kids came to visit me in the office. They were really good kids and their guardian told me proudly that they were still getting As in school. They'd suffered an unimaginable loss, but there we were, talking about grades and teachers and sports.

Some cases were incredibly gruesome. A sixth-grade Hmong girl named Pa Nhia Lor from St. Paul was raped, choked, and stabbed in a park, and then taken to a garage and suffocated with garbage bags. Five teenagers then concealed her naked body by covering it with sticks. After the young girl's body was found, the Hmong community was understandably outraged. Karel Moersfelder of our office handled the case well and got convictions against all of the defendants, with the ringleader, Michael Medin, pleading guilty to first-degree murder.

As the case moved forward, I met with members of the Hmong community and told them that this girl's murder was being handled by one of our best prosecutors and that we would put the murderers in jail. Minnesota is a state of refugees. We have the second-largest Hmong population in the country and the largest Somali population. As county attorney, my job was to assure these new citizens that they could trust the system. We would respond to crimes against their people in the same way we would respond to white victims. Over a decade later, both ethnic groups are still a major part of our community, with Hmong and Somali elected officials now serving in state and local offices.

Some of the most horrible crimes were completely random, like the murder spree perpetrated by Jonathan Carpenter, who was high on meth, and Christopher Earl. Carpenter committed his first two homicides in our county, slitting the throats of an eighty-eight-year-old man and his adult daughter. Later the men drove to rural Todd County, where Carpenter—accompanied by Earl—murdered Holly Chromey and her two teenage children by tying them up, beating them with a hammer, and cutting their throats. Before killing the eighteen-year-old girl, Carpenter raped her. Our prosecutor, Judith Hawley, assisted Todd County by jointly trying the case with the Minnesota Attorney General's Office. Jonathan Carpenter ended up killing himself in prison after pleading guilty, and Christopher Earl received three consecutive life sentences for aiding and abetting the murders.

For one of the initial hearings, Judith and I took a trip out to Todd County. After driving through a thunderstorm, we forgot to turn the car's lights off. The Todd County sheriff had to give us a jump, and I remember watching the Todd County deputies trying to disguise their amusement at the sight of big-city prosecutors coming out to help the country lawyers and needing a jump start. But Todd County Attorney Gaylord Saetre was grateful for the help, and of course he always remembered the car story.

So many of the crimes took place in low-income neighborhoods. One of the first major cases we handled when I got to the office involved the murder of eleven-year-old Byron Phillips, a young boy with a sweet smile who was killed on his friend's front porch in a gang-related drive-by shooting. The murder had taken place in 1996, three years before I became county attorney, and the residents of north Minneapolis—many of them African American—were very upset that the County Attorney's Office and the police had not moved forward with the case. I remember one of the community members saying to me at a crime meeting, "If Byron Phillips was from Edina"—a predominately white suburb—"this case would have been prosecuted years ago."

Committed to seeing justice done, the community put up billboards with Byron's face on them and the words "You know who killed me.

Why won't you help?" to remind everyone—including neighborhood residents—that the killer had not yet been brought to justice. The citizens refused to let the gangs rule their neighborhood.

The billboards had proved helpful. A year after Byron was killed, they generated a new witness who had heard several gang members talking about the murder. But the case was hardly open-and-shut, and we knew that we were taking a risk when we decided to go to trial against Kawaskii Blanche and his fellow Bogus Boyz gang member. Thanks to the excellent work of prosecutors Al Harris and Carrie Lennon, the jury convicted Blanche of first-degree murder, and he received a life sentence. The other gang member was also found guilty of conspiracy to commit murder.

So many of the crimes were senseless and completely unexpected. Grieving family members would have to come to terms with the fact that they had lost their loved one simply because he or she was in the wrong place at the wrong time with the wrong person. Melissa Schmidt, a young and earnest police officer, was gunned down by a sixty-year-old woman in a public housing project when Officer Schmidt kindly agreed to escort the woman to the bathroom. A young woman named Pamela Ragland died when a twenty-one-year-old man—a man engaged in a dispute with her boyfriend over specialty SUV tire rims—shot at her and her boyfriend multiple times. The boyfriend survived; she did not. Conservator Shelley Joseph-Kordell, the daughter of former U.S. ambassador to the Netherlands Jeri Joseph, was shot and killed by her mentally ill cousin. In fact, she was murdered in our courthouse, just three floors below my office.

Crimes like these always made me step back and think about how quickly things can go wrong. And when they go wrong, the victims and their families must feel confident that the legal system will do everything in its power to deliver justice.

A Cold Case

Sometimes, though, the wheels of justice move very slowly. A number of cases on our docket had been dormant for years because there simply wasn't enough evidence to go forward. Unexpected DNA "hits" would solve some of these cold cases long after the fact, but others were solved by an investigator or prosecutor who just wouldn't give up. Sometimes a new prosecutor or police officer would hear about the case and decide to dig into the file for the first time in years.

When important new evidence came to light, I would ask that a cold case be reopened. That's what happened with an unforgettable twenty-four-year-old arson case. In 1977 two Minneapolis firefighters—Captain Jack Crothers and firefighter Grant Benson—were killed in a raging blaze at Vic's Auto Shop in south Minneapolis. Police and prosecutors had always suspected that the owner of the shop, Victor Cossette, had hired someone to set the fire to collect insurance money. Three years after the two firefighters died, Robert Eisenbise, a petty criminal known to have associated with Cossette, told the FBI that he had set the fire. But the case fell apart the next day when Eisenbise was found dead with his car running in his garage. At the time, his death was ruled an accident.

Minneapolis firefighters had long wanted justice in the Cossette case, as had arson investigators and the victims' families. Glen Miller, an arson investigator in our office, had been haunted by the deaths of the two firefighters for years, and after assembling the critical evidence, he brought the case to my attention. I authorized a reopening of the case which was expertly handled by a pair of prosecutors in our office, Pete Connors and Andy LeFevour.

One of the more interesting new witnesses in the case was a former arsonist whom Cossette had originally approached to torch his business. The guy had turned down the work all those years ago, but because of his other criminal activity he had never come forward. But now, with the statute of limitations having run out on his own unrelated crimes, he was willing to talk. He and his associates weren't the most cheerful of potential witnesses, though—they were so crabby, in fact, that we called them the "grumpy old men."

In the end, thanks to the tenacious work of Glen Miller and our prosecutors, we charged the case. Because of the thorough investigation and the reams of new evidence it produced, Cossette pleaded guilty to two counts of third-degree murder in connection with the arson. He was sentenced to six years in prison, which was the guideline sentence for such a crime back when it was committed.

The day he was sentenced, Cossette spoke about his crime with much remorse. I sat with the families of the two firefighters in the courtroom. They had waited a long time for this moment.

"I don't know how to feel," James Benson, Grant Benson's father, said to the Minneapolis *StarTribune*. "After all this time, there was some closure; now there's some resurrection, too."

Ann Crothers, the widow of Captain Crothers, was similarly thoughtful: "The day is finally here. . . . I'm nervous. I always thought that I didn't need to know every little detail—but I was wrong, I do. Maybe it was always something I needed to know but had just stuffed in the back of my mind to get on with life."

Victim Advocates

Helping people get on with their lives was part of our job, and one of the groups I was most proud of as county attorney was our victim-witness team. It was their responsibility to work with families like the Crothers and the Bensons, and they went to extraordinary lengths to provide sympathetic assistance to victims and keep them informed of our efforts to bring perpetrators to justice. Those who served on this team were the heart of our office.

A few years into my tenure, I put Lolita Ulloa, a lawyer who'd been running our domestic abuse service center, in charge of the victim-witness group. She followed in the footsteps of Micky Cook, another passionate victim advocate. Lolita did a great job, and over time she and I came to understand that in many cases faith in the system is not based solely on whether a prosecutor succeeds in bringing a charge and getting a conviction. Also important is whether victims of crime trust that there's a caring, competent person on their side. At times I personally met with victims and their families to explain why we couldn't bring a particular case to trial or why we were going to have to plead it out to lesser charges.

All of our victims' surveys showed that while charges and convictions were the gold standard and of course the best outcome with regard to public safety, trust in our office was still an important intangible quality that determined how victims felt about "the system." That was a lesson I shared with the White House and our military leaders during the recent debate about sexual assault in the military. I told them that bringing cases whenever possible is key, but that carefully reviewing all of the evidence and explaining your reasoning to the victim is critical for building trust, even if a case can't be brought.

We would always explain to victims that even when the County Attorney's Office didn't have enough evidence to bring charges, the decision to come forward and provide assistance still mattered and made a difference. Their evidence would be kept on file, and it might prove to be a deciding factor in a future case. Years later, that's why I fought hard to add provisions to federal law to preserve records of sexual assaults in the military.

Under Lolita's leadership in the County Attorney's Office, we also built on the successes of our award-winning domestic abuse service center by partnering with the Hennepin County Medical Center to train employees to spot victims of domestic abuse. We also cross-trained police on child protection issues so that those cases would be pursued in conjunction with domestic violence prosecutions. In addition, we expanded our work with immigrant victims.

Our victim advocates often got close to the families of crime victims, especially in cases involving longer trials. Sometimes, right after the crime occurred, they accompanied a family to the victim's funeral. Occasionally I would go with them.

I particularly remember visiting with the family of Svetlana Pedash, wife of Pyotr Shmelev, before Svetlana's funeral. An engineer, Shmelev stabbed and killed his wife in their apartment in Eden Prairie while their four-year-old daughter slept in her bedroom. He then placed his wife's body in the bathtub, drove to Home Depot, bought a saw, and came back and cut his wife's body into pieces. He put the body parts in a trash bag and drove to Missouri, where he dumped the bag in a reservoir. In an act of complete depravity, he kept his wife's head in the trunk of his car. Weeks later, with the head still in his trunk in a bowling ball bag, he confessed to the police.

On the day of the funeral, very few people paid their respects to the family at the Russian Orthodox church. Svetlana, an immigrant from Russia, had not made many friends. But Svetlana's parents and her identical twin sister had come all the way from Russia, and just before the service began, I met with the family and our victim advocate, Jeanne Werenicz.

That day I heard the poignant story of when the four-year-old daughter met her Russian relatives earlier in the week. When the little girl saw her mother's identical twin sister, she ran to her and hugged her tight and said, "Mommy, Mommy, Mommy."

These stories would make anyone cry. But for years I never cried. I never cried at the victims' funerals and I never cried at press conferences. I never cried in front of the families. I trained myself not to cry, no matter how many people were crying around me. One time I literally bit my tongue so I wouldn't cry in front of a family. Being strong was a big part of my job.

A Visit to the White House

Beyond the personal challenges that came with the county attorney's job, there were also the professional challenges of partnering with other law enforcement offices, from the local police departments to my fellow county prosecutors. I especially enjoyed working with the U.S. attorneys for the District of Minnesota—first Todd Jones, a former Marine and prosecutor who was appointed by Bill Clinton, and later Tom Heffelfinger, appointed by George W. Bush. Under both U.S. attorneys, we made a substantial effort to improve the relations between our offices. Some tension between federal and local prosecutors is pretty much the norm. After all, the U.S. attorneys have the nice offices, the high-profile cases, and the gift of more time to spend on their cases. The local DA offices handle a huge volume of cases, and sometimes a major case can simply be "picked off" by the feds.

Todd was as committed as I was to improving the relationship among our prosecutors, and Tom continued that effort. The results, all for the better, meant that we conducted joint training sessions, limited jurisdictional fights, and teamed up on white-collar cases. Once Todd even held a party in their beautiful new offices for our adult prosecution division. Todd can be very funny, and after I got there but before my fellow prosecutors arrived, he got on the office's PA system and announced, "Nail down the furniture, the cousins are coming over."

Funny, Todd, funny.

Todd and I got along so well that in April 2000 I got a call from the

White House inviting me to a hate crimes conference with President Clinton. Todd was also invited. An invitation to the White House was not something that happened every day, and I remember my assistant Paula Mahnke checked the number to make sure it wasn't a hoax. It wasn't, and I quickly accepted. The hate crimes event would be my first visit to the White House since my college internship with Vice President Mondale.

By this point our office had handled a number of crimes that were motivated by hate. A church had been desecrated with hateful messages, crosses had been burned outside a Minneapolis school, and an eighteen-year-old white man had shot a fourteen-year-old African American kid at a shopping center because, in his words, he "hated black people." Later we would prosecute an employer for taking a two-by-four and hitting one of his workers over the head for speaking Spanish.

The evening I arrived in Washington, Todd and I went out for beers with some of the other U.S. attorneys. I got back to the hotel around 9:00 p.m. and was surprised to pick up several urgent messages from various White House staff members. I called one of them back and before she had a chance to say a word, I joked: "Please tell me you aren't disinviting me from the meeting with the President."

"No, ma'am," she said. "We are actually calling to ask you to introduce the President."

I didn't hesitate. "Okay, I think I can manage that. How long do you want me to talk?" I asked.

"About three minutes."

"I'll do it," I said. "And who is introducing me?"

"The Attorney General of the United States."

"Is that normal protocol?"

"No."

"Okay," I said. "I've never been much for protocol anyway."

I was about to hang up when the staffer said, "Wait a minute. You'll need to write a speech and we need to review it first."

As soon as I got off the phone, I called Ross Corson, my press secretary. We faxed some ideas back and forth, and before long I faxed the speech to the White House from the hotel.

Early the next morning I ran over to an office supply store and bought a blue plastic folder for my speech. I remember that I didn't get around to taking off the $3.99 sticker until I got to the White House. Once inside, I joined a small group of U.S. attorneys and their local and state counterparts in a meeting with the police investigators who had handled the investigation of Matthew Shepard's murder. Shepard was the gay college student who, on a cold October night in 1998, was tied to a fence in Laramie, Wyoming, beaten with the butt of a pistol, and then left for dead. The bicyclist who first discovered him initially thought he was a scarecrow. Days later, Shepard would die in a hospital. Hearing about the police investigation and the way the case had changed the Wyoming officers' views about gays and crimes motivated by hate, was deeply moving.

Then, before I knew it, I was invited into the Oval Office, where Bill Clinton's first question for me was how to pronounce my name. We talked briefly about Slovenia. I knew he had been there, and to this day Slovenians still talk about his visit in the rain to the public square in Ljubljana.

Minutes later we gathered just outside the East Room. President Clinton stood on one side of me and Attorney General Janet Reno stood on the other. Eric Holder, then Reno's deputy, stood next to Reno. The event was a big deal because the legislation the president was proposing would cover a wide range of hate crimes, including those against gays and lesbians. Given the importance of the bill, there were hundreds of people in the room.

As we waited by the door, a woman wearing headphones came up to me and said, "When you get up to the podium, there's a stool to make you taller. The president and the attorney general won't need it, but you will. You have to pull it out with your foot. If you have any problem, the president will assist you."

Just before we were due to enter the East Room, a military band began to play "Hail to the Chief." I was so fixated on not messing up the footwork I'd need to pull out the stool that as soon as the music started up I began walking into the room. After a couple of steps I felt a big hand on my shoulder and heard a kind voice with a familiar southern accent: "I know you're going to do great out there, but when they play that song, I usually go first."

That was my first official visit to the White House. The president ended up pulling out the stool for me, but the speech went great. I even spontaneously added a few comments about our meeting with the Laramie police investigators. Janet Reno said kind things about the work I was doing in Hennepin County, and with Todd Jones sitting in the front row, I noted that he and I coordinated on cases so well that we talked "nearly every day." This comment prompted Todd to call me on both Saturday and Sunday of the following weekend.

"Why are you calling me?" I asked.

"Well, you told the president of the United States that we talked every day."

The strangest sideline to the whole event was that after I introduced President Clinton, he thanked Janet Reno for her work on the Elián González case. Elián González was the Cuban boy whom the Justice Department had just taken from the home of his Cuban relatives in Miami so that he could be reunited with his Cuban father. That was the first time Clinton had publicly thanked Reno for her work on the case, and his comments got a lot of media coverage.

Because I happened to be sitting between the two of them that day at the White House hate crimes event, my name was listed in the caption of every photo, making it seem as if I'd played some role in the raid. As a result, the Hennepin County Attorney's Office got a number of angry calls and letters from Cuban exiles across the country.

Bill Clinton sent me a nice note after the event. I wrote back and told him that due to his kind words about Janet Reno's work on the González case, I had received a number of angry letters from Cuban exiles. In my reply, I jokingly told the president that I would be happy to take full responsibility for the raid.

To my surprise, the president wrote back again. "Sorry I got you in hot water. Bill Clinton."

That was a good one. Even better was the fact that the hate crimes legislation announced that day by the president—formally known as the Matthew Shepard and James Byrd, Jr. Hate Crimes Prevention Act—did eventually pass the Congress. The only hitch was that it took almost a decade. First advocated by President Clinton, then championed by Senator Ted Kennedy and Representative John Conyers, it was signed into law by President Obama in 2009.

I was there when the legislation made its public debut and I got to vote for the bill when it finally passed. With sixty votes required for "cloture" under the Senate rules, all fifty-five Democrats voted for it, and we were joined by five Republicans—Susan Collins, Lisa Murkowski, Olympia Snowe, Dick Lugar, and George Voinovich.

I always looked for ways to cooperate with others during my time as county attorney, and I still think cooperation and partnership are the keys to good governance. Getting that bill passed was a good example of the kind of cooperation that we can always use more of in Washington, D.C. Democrats and a few courageous Republicans worked together and got something really important done.

Without Fear or Favor

Tough Decisions

Deciding whether to charge a case and determining the appropriate penalty was not always easy. Our office handled about five thousand adult felony cases a year, and for the vast majority of them our prosecutors and managers would make the call. But for the trickiest cases, the biggest cases, and for those cases when things went wrong before or after we charged them, I would usually decide.

I never made these decisions in a vacuum. Cindy Jesson and Kathryn Quaintance—and later Pete Cahill, my chief deputy for six years—would meet with me and discuss especially challenging cases in detail. Sometimes we would talk with the managing attorney for the division and the prosecutor. Sometimes one of my deputies would meet with the prosecutor and come to me with a recommendation. Every so often I would reach out to the police chief or the sheriff, depending on the office investigating the case.

By the end of my second term as county attorney, Pete and I understood each other so well that he almost always knew what I would think about a certain set of facts and I could predict the same of him. But Pete never told me what I wanted to hear—he was too honest and strong-minded to be a "yes man." The same was true of all our prosecutors. They were fiercely independent, and I could always count on them to engage in open discussions about how to handle difficult cases. I learned an important lesson from Pete: make the right decision under the law and the facts, and then find a way to explain it to the public. Don't ever make the wrong decision just because it is easier to explain.

Some of the toughest cases involved victims who were not particularly appealing. Others were difficult because the defendants were so sympathetic. Sometimes when I reviewed a case I would think it through by changing the "race facts." What if the victim was white instead of a person of color? What if the defendant, instead of being an immigrant woman who couldn't speak English, was a white guy in a suit? That was always a useful gut check.

A good example of a tough decision regarding a not-so-appealing victim was a case involving a man named Amiruddin Quassim. In August 2000, Quassim—who was well known to the Minneapolis police for drinking and vagrancy problems—boarded a Metro Transit bus and stopped on the top step. Though Quassim was drunk, he wasn't belligerent or hostile. He just stood there blocking the entrance, not saying a word, seemingly deaf to the demands from the driver and the other passengers that he move.

Suddenly, shortly after 1:00 a.m., a twenty-five-year-old man who was boarding pushed Quassim down the stairs of the bus at the corner of 4th Street and Nicollet Mall. Quassim went flying off the steps backward and hit his head on the sidewalk. Too drunk to react—his blood alcohol was three times the legal limit—he'd made no move to break his fall. He died of head injuries three days later.

The police arrested the young man, who had just gotten off work at a downtown restaurant. He had no criminal record, he was from rural Minnesota, and, unlike the victim, he was white. The police certainly had good cause to arrest him: the entire incident had been recorded by a security camera on the bus. The video clearly showed that the young man had shoved the older man, causing his death.

Some in our office wondered whether the case should even be pursued, but we decided to bring a charge of manslaughter. The harder question was how to prosecute the case. A debate followed. Some of our prosecutors didn't want the case to go to trial. The defendant, they felt, would be sympathetic to a jury, whereas the victim would not. Their feeling was that we should enter a plea negotiation for probation.

I felt strongly that we could not simply capitulate and agree to no jail time at all. What if the victim had been an elderly woman with Alzheimer's who'd been lost and confused? The community would have been outraged if someone had killed her by shoving her off a bus. Prosecutors don't get to choose their victims, and Amiruddin Quassim deserved justice. I told our prosecutors to go into court the next day and refuse to take a plea to no jail time. We would take our chances at trial.

In the end, with Diane Krenz as the lead prosecutor, the defendant entered a straight guilty plea (which means there was no agreement on the prosecutor's part to a reduced sentence). The judge gave him a full year of incarceration in the workhouse, ten years of probation, and a four-year prison sentence that was stayed by the judge.

These decisions—about whether to charge and how to charge, about whether to go to trial or to negotiate a plea—must be made every day by prosecutors. As the elected county attorney, my job was to make sure that no matter what we decided, our office was always focused on "doing justice."

Kirby Puckett

One of the most challenging cases we handled during my tenure involved Kirby Puckett, the Minnesota Twins outfielder who was arguably the most beloved sports figure in Minnesota. Puckett helped lead the Twins to two World Series championships in 1987 and 1991. I went to some of those games, and no one could forget Game Six of the 1991 World Series, when Puckett not only made an unbelievable catch in left centerfield but also hit a single, a triple, and the game-winning home run in the eleventh inning, forcing a seventh game that resulted in a championship. That was magic.

In 1995, due to glaucoma and the loss of vision in one eye, Puckett was forced to retire from Major League Baseball at age thirty-five. His career batting average was .318, just short of Joe DiMaggio's lifetime average. When he left the game, his jersey number—34—was retired. The Twins hired him as an executive vice president, the club's fans continued to adore their longtime hero, and he worked with a lot of charities. In 2001 Puckett received his sport's highest honor when he was inducted into the Baseball Hall of Fame.

Then came the hard part. Within months after his Hall of Fame induction ceremony in Cooperstown, New York, I found myself in the not-so-enviable position of deciding whether to charge the Minnesota sports icon with a crime. The case came to our office from the Edina Police Department after Puckett's wife, Tonya, told the authorities that her husband had threatened her in a phone conversation. According to her report, the couple was arguing over allegations that he was having an affair when he threatened to kill her. But when we learned that the conversation had occurred when they were over a thousand miles apart—she was in Minnesota and he was in Atlantic City—we decided that there was no reasonable basis for charging a crime since there was no threat of immediate harm.

When the story went public, we had a lot of press requests and I went on TV to explain why we had declined to file charges. It wasn't really a close call under the law, and at the time, given Puckett's enormous popularity, my friends said I should have announced the decision with a bunch of Twins' World Series "Homer Hankies" strung up above me. Though all reports of domestic violence and threats must of course be taken seriously, the only thing that mattered that day was whether charges were appropriate under the law. They weren't.

But when a second Puckett case came into the office the following fall, it was a different story. This time the Eden Prairie Police Department brought in the case. A woman claimed that Puckett had sexually assaulted her, and an independent witness—albeit one who, like the victim, had had some drinks—said that he had seen Puckett pulling the woman into the men's room at a bar. The victim said Puckett had grabbed her breast in the bathroom, and she had bruises on her breast, arm, and ankle. She had called 911 after she got out of the bathroom.

Puckett denied her version of the incident—he claimed that there was a line for the women's room so he had escorted her into the men's room. No one ever came forward to say they'd been in the men's room with the two of them, but our prosecutors believed her account of what had happened. We knew that the case would never result in a lengthy incarceration. We also knew that winning a "he said, she said" case with no independent witness to the actual assault would be difficult under any circumstances, but especially when the defendant was a sports hero. But we had the victim's bruises, a witness who'd seen Puckett pull the woman into the bathroom, and a $700 bar bill from Kirby Puckett's table. Our prosecutors strongly recommended charging Puckett: they cited numerous cases in other circumstances where we had filed similar charges, and we knew that we would have brought charges if the defendant was *not* a celebrity.

In the end we decided to charge Kirby Puckett. I knew this decision would not endear me to the public, especially since the Twins had just been beaten in the playoffs. My only choice: do my best to explain the charges in a way that didn't exaggerate the circumstances while also acknowledging people's understandable adoration for Puckett.

"Like most Minnesotans," I said on the day we announced the charges, "I remember watching Mr. Puckett help the Twins win two World Series, and he's a great Hall of Fame baseball player. But that night, in that bar, he was no one's hero."

We tried to make our announcement of the charging decision as low-key as possible by conducting brief individual interviews upon request instead of holding a major press conference. So it was rather alarming when my dad called from Nepal, where he was leading an adventure trip, and told me that my quote was playing on Nepalese radio.

I thought I would get massacred on our local sports radio shows. I was wrong. Some of the hosts had their own views of Puckett and the case, and that became especially apparent when one of Puckett's lawyers commented on the charges by saying, "It seems strange to me that this is the way the county attorney thanks Kirby Puckett for all he has done for the state of Minnesota." The talk radio guys and a number of citizens thought that was over the top, and someone told me that a guy on the radio even suggested starting a contest asking listeners to guess how many career RBIs you'd have to record in order to get a thank-you card from the county attorney for grabbing a woman's breast in the bathroom.

The trial was more than a little unusual. A number of people in the jury pool were big fans of the defendant—one guy, a business owner, had previously given out Kirby Puckett rookie trading cards as gifts. When the trial began, people stood outside the courtroom doors, hoping to get Puckett's autograph. Twice in the middle of the court proceedings, the cell phone of a *St. Paul Pioneer Press* sports reporter, Aron Kahn, went off and the ring tone played "Take Me Out to the Ballgame."

We assigned Al Harris, an experienced prosecutor, to the case; Todd Jones, the former U.S. attorney, was the lead lawyer for Puckett. They both did a good job. After more than eight hours of deliberations over two days, the jury acquitted Puckett. Afterward, many of the jurors talked to the media and said they thought the case was handled professionally. One of them said he didn't believe Puckett but thought the legal standard— "beyond a reasonable doubt"—simply wasn't met. A few said "if only they had the witnesses in the bathroom." That's what I said after the trial as well, and I think that statement pretty much summed up the biggest challenge we faced (except for the fact that the defendant was Kirby Puckett).

After charging the most beloved sports figure in Minnesota with a crime and then losing the case, I was surprised when I didn't get a lot of grief from the public. The lesson? Even when you don't win a major case, if you've done the right thing for the right reasons, people can usually understand why you brought charges. But you're headed for trouble when you don't explain your decision or don't charge cases because you want to avoid doing something unpopular.

Work/Family Balance

I remember the night I got home after we lost the Puckett case. John, Abigail, and I sat down for dinner, something we hadn't done for a while. "I had a hard day at work today," I said to my daughter, now seven.

"Mom," she said, "we don't have time to talk about that. We have a really important decision to make. Should I get one hamster or two?"

That would be called putting things in perspective. After much discussion we decided on one, but in the end we ended up with eight. The hamster Abigail picked out turned out to be pregnant.

That made me smile, and so did the question I was frequently asked while I was county attorney. "How do you do it?" people would say. "How do you balance being a mom with doing your job?"

On bad days, the answer I often wanted to give was, "Not very well at all." But the answer I usually gave was the one given by so many moms (many of whom had more kids than I did, worked more jobs, had fewer resources, and had no spouse to help them out): "I do my best."

But being a prosecutor created some unique challenges. You couldn't exactly "take your daughter to work" when your work involved a grisly murder case. I will never forget the Sunday afternoon a verdict came in on a murder case after the jury had been out for a long time. It involved a Somali man who had stabbed his Somali ex-girlfriend multiple times at a local shopping mall after he saw her kiss another guy in an employee entrance to the mall. We wanted first-degree murder—second-degree would have been acceptable, but manslaughter would have been completely unfair to the victim's family. The case pitted two different Somali clans against each other, and when it went to trial the courtroom was packed.

On the Sunday the verdict came in, Abigail and I were visiting my mom at a nursing home where she was temporarily staying while she recovered from knee surgery. When I learned that the jury had made a decision, I had to run over to the courthouse because we had no idea what the verdict would be and, whatever it was, I would have to explain it. Abigail was then four years old—there was no way I could bring her to a murder verdict, and there was no time to bring her anywhere else. I asked my mom if she would just let Abigail stay in her room, even though I knew that this was completely against the nursing home rules since my mom was basically bedridden.

"No problem," my mom said.

"Now, Abigail," I said, "you know you can't leave this room, right?"

"No problem," she said, imitating my mom.

That was how I left the nursing home that day—with a pledge and a promise from my four-year-old daughter and her seventy-three-year-old grandmother, one wide-eyed at the prospects of an adventure, the other drowsy on postsurgery painkillers.

The jury came back with a verdict of not guilty on first-degree, but guilty on second-degree intentional murder. Our prosecutors had worked really hard on the case and they weren't happy with second-degree, but the good news was that the defendant was going away to prison for a long time. I explained the verdict to the press, thanked our prosecutors, and dashed back to the nursing home. When I ran into my mom's room she was lying in bed, propped up on a pillow. Abigail was nowhere to be found.

"Mom, where is she?" I asked.

"She went down the hall to get a spoon for some pudding," she said.

"Mom, she is only four years old. This is a big place."

I raced down the hall to the cafeteria and there she was, eating some pudding with a really big serving spoon and entertaining an entire table of seniors.

You do your best.

My work as county attorney was not exactly nine to five. In fact, the work never ended, even on vacations. Once we were visiting friends in New York City and Abigail was playing happily in a playground in Central Park. I was sitting on a bench watching her while talking on the phone with the office about a murder case in which the type and identity of the gun were key. John was mad at me for spending so much time on the phone for work, so he left me there on the bench. A stranger sat down, and when I finished my call the guy turned to me and said, "Ma'am, I hope you don't mind me asking you this, but are you an arms dealer?"

"No," I said, "I'm a mom on vacation."

Equally challenging was raising a child while running for office. During the hotly contested race for county attorney in 1998, I was determined to do everything possible to prevent my daughter from being warped by the experience. On Christmas morning, a little more than a month after the campaign ended, I learned the hard way that I'd fallen short. My dad gave then three-year-old Abigail the gift she had longed for—a plastic kitchen set.

Abigail loved her new kitchen and she immediately went right up to the plastic oven to "make dinner." But instead of opening the oven door and putting in the plastic roasting pan, she put her finger on the outside and pressed an imaginary button while making a pitch-perfect microwave sound.

Okay, I didn't have a lot of time to cook during that campaign.

To add insult to injury, my daughter then picked up the play phone attached to the side of the kitchen set. My dad pretended to answer.

"Who is calling?" he asked.

"Abigail," she said.

"What are you calling about?" he asked.

"Money," she said. "I am calling for money."

Quickly realizing that his granddaughter had heard me make hundreds of fundraising calls during the county attorney's race, my dad asked a follow-up: "How much money are you calling for?"

"Lots of money," she said emphatically. "Lots and lots of money."

I had some great support back then. Our families and friends made a huge difference, of course, but it also helped that I had Cindy and Kathryn as my deputies for the first few years. Among the three of us we had seven children, six of whom were under the age of ten. One time I brought in a *New Yorker* cartoon for them that showed a CEO who was clearly a mom standing at the head of a boardroom table. Men sat on either side of her, and in the middle of the long table were piles of laundry. The mom was speaking to the men and the caption read: "And I'm sure no one will mind if we fold a few clothes while we talk."

As they say, a picture is worth a thousand words.

The other godsend was John. We roughly divided up the housework—he did the dishwasher and took out the garbage, I did the laundry and threw out the old food in the refrigerator. Most important, he loved spending time with Abigail and they were quite a team while I was campaigning.

John was also a thoughtful listener whenever I talked to him about my work. Mine wasn't an easy job—it involved a lot of tough choices. One time after a series of difficult plea decisions and a long weekend of calls with the office, he was inspired to get me the Dale Carnegie book—"over six million copies sold!"—*How to Stop Worrying and Start Living*. He knew it was really a book for business people, but he thought it might provide me with some good tips.

I read the book with great interest until I got to Chapter 2, which reveals the secret to Carnegie's anti-worrying "Magic Formula." The secret basically comes down to this: figure out the worst thing that can happen if you make a bad decision, then reconcile yourself to it. By way of reassurance, the "Magic Formula" included a gentle reminder that no matter how tough the decision, in the end "no one was going to jail me or shoot me" because I had made it.

This wasn't helpful. The decisions I had to make most often involved sending someone to jail (although hopefully it wouldn't be me). As for shooting people, if some of these guys didn't go to jail, they probably wouldn't shoot me, but they could definitely shoot someone else.

I tossed the book aside after reading Carnegie's famous "Magic Formula." Worrying, I decided, was just part of the job.

Knuckleheads

The volume of work in our office was pretty crazy, but there were always a few knucklehead crime stories to get us through the day. One of my favorites was about the bank robber in Detroit who once wrote his demand note to the bank teller on the back of an envelope. Unfortunately for him, it included his name and address.

In Hennepin County we produced our fair share of stranger-than-fiction crime stories. There was the guy who claimed he was innocent of murder because he was blind. What he didn't know was that in Minnesota we record all interrogations. The suspect's defense melted away when the officer who was interviewing him stepped out of the room and the camera caught the suspect reading a piece of paper in his pocket. Or there was the murder suspect who claimed he wasn't at the crime scene but then was picked up on videotape saying, "There's blood on my shoes!"

People always did silly stuff around the holidays, and our all-time best Christmas crime even made the national news, including Chuck Shepherd's News of the Weird column. On Christmas morning in 2003, the police found a naked ex-con stuck in the chimney of a store. Dubbed the "Santa Claus burglar" by the media, he had been there for hours and was discovered when someone heard him yelling. Firefighters came on the scene and got him out with sledgehammers. The name of the place made the story even better—it was Uncle Hugo's Science Fiction & Uncle Edgar's Mystery Bookstore.

The guy claimed he went down the chimney to find his keys, but he had a record of burglary and theft convictions and he was clearly in it for the goods. Given the freezing weather, police said the thief would most likely have died if he'd been stuck there much longer. Mike Sauro, the police officer on duty, noted that the Santa Claus burglar didn't "appear to be a hard-core criminal, just stupid." He ended up getting fifteen months in prison.

My personal favorite was the story about a rich guy from the western suburbs who would rig the parking meters in Minneapolis with a paper clip just to save himself a few quarters while he was having lunch. The issue? Every time he rigged the meters he broke them, and the money required to replace the meters amounted to felony-level damage to property. The broken meters were really pissing off the traffic cops, and with our guidance they performed a sting operation and caught him in the act. When we charged him, the press called the defendant the "meter eater." Wary of copycats, and warned by the traffic cops to keep our defendant's methods secret, I refused to reveal exactly how our "meter eater" had committed the crime when announcing the charges at a press conference held next to a parking meter. For a number of days a local talk radio host kept joking about how the Chinese—recently accused of spying on America—might have gotten access to our nuclear secrets, but Amy Klobuchar wouldn't reveal the modus operandi of the meter eater.

Hey, it was better than pissing off the traffic cops.

Priorities

Since ours was the biggest county in Minnesota, we knew that how our office operated and what standards we set mattered for the rest of the state. Right from the start, we worked off one very important principle: our prosecutors were "ministers of justice," and their job was to convict the guilty and protect the innocent. We prioritized the prosecution of criminals with prior convictions, and we worked closely with the Innocence Project on DNA reviews and a new kind of eyewitness identification lineup that reduced false identifications. I debated other prosecutors, including New York's Queens DA, on the subject of videotaping interrogations. We videotaped interrogations in Minnesota and I argued that it not only protected defendants' rights, but it was better for law enforcement. I also advocated for a well-funded public defender's office as a way to guarantee more fairness in the justice system. Finally, I made sure that our office reflected the community at large. Approximately thirty percent of the new lawyers I hired were lawyers of color, a higher percentage than the county's minority population as a whole.

Another major focus of the office was upping the ante in the prosecution of repeat felony property offenders. I figured that treating these crimes seriously would give us a lot of bang for the buck. After a few months on the job it became clear to me that a small number of people were committing a disproportionately high number of the county's property crimes—everything from auto thefts to garage burglaries. A new law called the "Career Offender Statute" allowed us to seek stiffer sentences for criminals with multiple felony convictions. As a sure sign that setting goals matters, a 2001 state legislative auditor's report noted that there had been a doubling of statewide sentences for repeat property criminals "attributed to an increase in Hennepin County where a new county attorney made use of the career offender statute a priority."

Assigning prosecutors by geographic area also helped to reduce property crimes. Under the great leadership of manager Andy LeFevour, we assigned a property crimes prosecutor to each Minneapolis police precinct and then divided up the forty-four suburbs as well. Our prosecutors found the program rewarding because they got to know and appreciate both community members and law enforcement in their assigned neighborhoods. In time, our community prosecution initiative led to much better teamwork and more accountability, and we were pleased when it won a grant from the Clinton Justice Department and an additional grant and award from the Bush administration.

We also made it a priority to work closely with the county's schools. Early on I saw that truancy was a major problem in Hennepin County. Reviewing the records of some of our more serious juvenile offenders made me realize that the kids with serious rap sheets had at least one thing in common: they'd started skipping school at an early age. We knew that regular school attendance was one of the most reliable predictors of academic achievement. When speaking to skeptics about our focus on truancy, I often explained it by saying that our office may have adopted some businesslike efficiencies, but in the end we weren't really like a business because we didn't want to see repeat customers—and keeping kids in school was a good way to reduce repeat customers. When speaking to seniors, I would add that if we wanted to ensure a steady supply of workers who could pay into Social Security and thus keep them financially secure in their old age, we needed kids to graduate.

To fight the problem, we beefed up our truancy unit. We pushed judges to hear the cases sooner. We issued a report card for every secondary school in the county, listing the number and timeliness of their truancy referrals and the ultimate outcomes. We made sure parents were notified when their kids skipped school, and we confronted the truants and essentially told them, "Everybody—your parents, the principal, the police, the judge, the whole community—wants you to stay in school."

I personally visited every high school in the county, meeting with school officials and students. There was a vast difference in the kinds of questions I got from students. I remember visiting with the students at one school in north Minneapolis, where the kids had been exposed to a lot of crime. The first question that day was remarkably sophisticated: "Is there a different selection process for grand jurors than regular jurors?" But when I visited a high school in the western suburbs, the first question I got from a student was: "Is mooning still a crime?"

It's a big county.

Another major focus during my tenure was drunk driving. The issue didn't come up during my campaign, but once I started in the job I was shocked to learn how many people were killed or severely injured by people driving under the influence of alcohol or drugs. I was equally shocked by some of the lenient sentences in these cases. State sentencing guidelines called for a four-year sentence for "criminal vehicular homicide," but a number of judges gave lighter punishments.

The way I figured it, a car in the hands of a drunk was just like a gun, and we made it clear that we would push hard for tough penalties. During my tenure we got scores of guideline sentences against those who drove under the influence of drugs or alcohol. They included a case against an $11 million Powerball lottery winner who used her winnings to buy drugs and was high when she killed one friend and paralyzed another while driving under the influence. In another case, a drunk driver killed Timberwolves pro basketball player Malik Sealy when he was driving home from a birthday celebration for his friend and teammate Kevin Garnett. Because of the public attention that case and others generated, it became a lot harder for judges to issue sentences lower than the guidelines. Or, to put it more starkly, how could you explain giving a four-year sentence to a killer of a pro basketball player and not to a guy who rammed his car into a twenty-year-old woman?

We even worked to change the law. In 2002, I led the effort to pass a new law that made it possible to charge a felony crime for repeat drunk drivers. The bill basically said that anyone who received four DWI convictions within ten years would be guilty of a felony and be given prison time. Until then, repeat offenders never faced more than a gross misdemeanor and local jail time.

When we brought the felony DWI proposal to the state capitol, the resistance was strong. Some legislators said they had friends who would be considered felons under the law. Regardless of party affiliation, many legislators encountered significant opposition in Greater Minnesota, particularly on the Iron Range where my relatives lived. The controversy was similar to a later debate about changing the DWI standard from a .10 to a .08 blood alcohol level. One day my pal State Representative Tommy Rukavina, a rough-and-tumble Iron Ranger, took to the House floor and said, "Mr. Speaker, if you want to lower the limit to .08, I just have one question: how is a guy in my district supposed to get to work when he could wake up at .08?"

Still, I was convinced we would win the felony DWI fight because we had the facts on our side. Some state residents had up to twenty DWIs and were still out there driving. In advocating for the bill, I told the story of one guy, Raymond Sherman, who had more than twenty DWIs. When he got his twenty-second DWI in July 2002, he told state troopers he would not "go to treatment or quit drinking" and that he would flee the next time officers tried to pull him over. Before being arrested in Hennepin County for what became his twenty-third DWI, he was true to his word, leading officers on a 3:00 a.m. high-speed chase. "I'm glad he came into my county," I said when charges were brought, "because he was my example, and now he is going to see the effect of the new law." Sherman ended up pleading guilty and got a five-year sentence for his actions.

In the end, with the help of my intrepid prosecutor and violent crimes chief Paul Scoggin, the law passed, and within five months we had charged ninety-two felony DWI cases that otherwise would have been misdemeanors. Our triumph was especially sweet because it wasn't the first time we had pushed for a felony DWI bill. One year earlier we had fought for a similar bill, but although we had worked really hard and come close, we couldn't get it passed. I still remember the supportive words of Republican State Representative (now Hennepin County Sheriff) Rich Stanek, the lead sponsor of the bill along with Democratic State Senator Dave Johnson. After we fell short, he told me, "Don't give up. Come back next year. We'll get it done."

He was right.

White-Collar Crooks

We really pushed the envelope in one other area: white-collar crime. Local prosecutors' offices do not always have the money and personnel to take these cases, but I made sure we found the resources to pursue them. I figured that it made no difference whether a crook committed a crime with a computer or a crow bar. He was still a crook.

Soon after I took office I strengthened the Complex Crimes Unit and put veteran prosecutor Pete Connors in charge. The unit began building some major cases, and when federal prosecutors shifted a lot of their attention to national security cases after 9/11, we suddenly found ourselves taking bigger and bigger white-collar referrals—from investment swindles and contractor fraud to tax evasion and identity theft rings, including a major one involving Social Security numbers stolen from a local hospital. Sometimes we would jointly prosecute the cases with the U.S. Attorney's Office. Then U.S. attorney Tom Heffelfinger and I shared the view that victims of crime rarely cared if the case was handled by county, state, or federal prosecutors. They just wanted the job done.

But as the unit's name implied, the cases were often complex. One of the best examples of the challenges we faced in prosecuting white-collar cases involved a group of pilots. In 2002, thanks to a thorough investigation by the Minnesota Department of Revenue, we charged seven Northwest Airlines commercial pilots for evading Minnesota income taxes by falsely claiming to live in states with no personal income tax when they actually resided in Minnesota. The facts were straightforward: the pilots had homes in Minnesota, and several of them sent their kids to local Minnesota schools. Yet all seven had falsely claimed residency—by renting post office boxes, for example—in states such as Florida and Texas in order to avoid paying state taxes in Minnesota. In total they owed more than $300,000 in back taxes.

While the facts of the pilots' tax evasion may have been straightforward, the response from the pilots and their lawyers was not. First they accused our office and me of being "unpatriotic," arguing that pilots should be given special consideration after 9/11. Then, in a real low point, a lawyer who worked with the pilots called me and said that our prosecutions were putting a lot of people in danger. He stated that the charges were stressing out the pilots, who were flying planes containing hundreds of passengers.

I would have none of it. "If you are actually telling me that you have reason to believe that one of these pilots could crash a plane," I said, "you need to hang up immediately and call the Federal Aviation Administration. You have an ethical obligation to report it."

Backtracking immediately, the lawyer retracted his statement and told me that in fact no one was in any danger.

When name-calling and veiled threats didn't work, the defendants' representatives went to the state legislature and persuaded some legislators to introduce a bill that would have given the pilots retroactive immunity from criminal prosecution if they paid their taxes. The state revenue commissioner was actively opposed to the bill—in fact, he told me that ever since we'd filed the criminal cases against the pilots, many other delinquent filers were coming forward and making good on their taxes. It was a revenue boon to the state.

When I testified against the bill before a state senate committee, I said that passing this kind of targeted tax amnesty legislation when actual criminal cases were pending was unorthodox at best. (Sleazy might be the better word.) I also told several legislators that I was waiting for one of them to propose the idea of voiding criminal charges for home burglars or car thieves. I made it very clear that I would never stop haranguing them if they upended actual criminal prosecutions. I didn't care what party they were in.

At the hearing we heard from one of the more popular leaders of the state senate. He was set to retire that year, and after testifying in favor of the amnesty bill, he noted that he was going home to watch the TV show

The West Wing. After he said that, I asked to respond. "Let the record reflect," I noted with a smile, "that President Bartlet would never have supported this bill."

On a close vote the amnesty bill was defeated by the committee. Thanks to the good work of our prosecutors Pete Connors and Carrie Lennon, months later all seven defendants were convicted and all received criminal sentences. They also had to pay all of their back taxes with interest and penalties.

Here are two useful tips for anyone who is considering a tax evasion scheme. First, if you have lovers or mistresses, don't let them in on it. In the case of the tax-evading pilots, the investigation originated with a report from a spurned lover who brought the tax evasion scheme to the attention of the Minnesota Revenue Department. Second, if you plan to evade taxes, do not do it by pretending to live in a post office box, unless, of course, you are the size of Stuart Little.

Who says white-collar cases are boring?

Without Fear or Favor

The tax evasion story was plenty dramatic, but it was nothing compared to the white-collar fraud case we brought against Minnesota Court of Appeals Judge Roland Amundson. Judge Amundson not only sat on Minnesota's second-highest court, he was also well known and very well connected, particularly in the Democratic Party.

Before he became a judge, Amundson had been a lawyer in private practice. When one of his clients was dying, the man asked Amundson to take over the trust set up for his severely disabled daughter. The woman was an adult, but her mental capacity was comparable to that of a three-year-old. Living in a world of dolls and stuffed animals, she needed full-time help.

Upon becoming a judge, Amundson had to seek special permission to continue running the trust. Judges rarely act as trustees, but Amundson claimed that it was a special case given the girl's severe disabilities. Officials allowed him to continue to be responsible for the trust while serving as a judge.

In the fall of 2001, the disabled woman's caretaker contacted our office. She claimed that Judge Amundson, who'd handled the trust for years, was stealing from it and using the money for his own purposes. The allegations seemed preposterous at the time and we felt reasonably sure that simple accounting errors would prove to be the culprit. But we promised the caretaker that we would investigate her claims fully.

On Christmas Eve, our prosecutor Emery Adoradio called me from his car. Crouched down in the driver's seat, he whispered into his cell phone, "There's no way he can afford this house on a judge's salary. It's impossible."

Once we started digging deeper into the evidence, the crime became obvious. Over a period of several years, Judge Amundson had indeed been stealing money from the disabled woman's trust. He would claim he was doing work on her house when he was actually installing marble floors in his house. He would claim he was buying her a new bed and medical equipment when he was actually buying china, expensive artwork, and a bronze sculpture.

Ultimately he stole about $400,000 from the trust, and he did it while serving as a judge on the Minnesota Court of Appeals. His crime was unprecedented. For the first time our office actually assisted police officers—of the Golden Valley Police Department—in executing a search warrant at the Court of Appeals on his judicial chambers. Talk about a separation of powers issue! But it had to be done.

As it turned out, the case was fairly easy to prove, and Amundson had no choice but to plead guilty and pay back the money. But as with so many white-collar cases, the sentencing was the real fight. The judge was liked and admired by many people at his church and within our community, and after he pleaded guilty, all kinds of people came out of the woodwork and asked for leniency.

My view? As I said to the *New York Times* when a reporter for the paper interviewed me about the case, "I believe he was greedy and wanted to live a lifestyle that he didn't have the money to live." He had to go to prison.

Careful to request a sentence that would be typical in a case like this one, we asked for about five years of prison time. The sentencing hearing—held before Judge Richard Hopper—was in front of a packed courtroom filled with the defendant's supporters. Amundson showed up with more than a dozen witnesses, including the minister from the biggest Lutheran church in our state. He also persuaded another sitting judge to come to court and say good things about him. He even had a former Miss America testify on his behalf. But that didn't bother me. After all, as I said to Emery that day, I was the former "Miss Skyway News" of March of 1988!

Nearly all the witnesses argued that because of all the "good" the judge had done in the community, Amundson should not be given the sentence we had asked for. The hearing went on all day with witness after witness testifying on Amundson's behalf. Finally, by midafternoon, I couldn't stand it anymore. Stepping out of the courtroom, I sat down on a bench in the hallway and put my head in my hands.

At that moment two men walked up to me. One of them said, "Is this where that judge is getting sentenced?"

"Yeah," I said, "this is the courtroom."

The other guy spoke up. "We were just up in drug court. Can we go in?"

"Sure," I said. "Take your cap off, but you can go in."

"You know," the first guy said, "we figure we've gone to jail before, so he should go to jail, too."

You got that right, I thought.

The two men walked into the courtroom and sat right in the front row. Judge Hopper later told me that he could see them from the bench—they were the only African Americans he could see in the courtroom except for his judicial clerk. As they listened to the proceedings, they would sometimes nod or shake their heads.

After a break, the two men left. But ten minutes later they were back. I was still in the hallway and just about to return to the courtroom. Pulling me aside, one of the men said, "You know, we had something else to do, but, man—you need us in there."

In the end, despite the fervent testimony of Amundson's many witnesses, we got the sentence we asked for, and to this day I think of the two guys in the courtroom that afternoon as our guardian angels. They didn't speak a word to the judge or to the rest of those gathered that day, but their mere presence sent a clear message: When people break the law, they need to be held accountable, no matter who they are or who they know or who they hire as their lawyer. It doesn't matter if they commit crimes on a street corner or in a corner office—we can't have two systems of justice, one for the rich and powerful and one for everyone else.

Paul Wellstone

To me, those two guys in the courtroom were living proof of a wise maxim about justice. A great judge—U.S. Supreme Court Justice John Marshall Harlan—once said that in the eyes of the law, the humblest must be the peer of the most powerful. In my life this inspiring ideal was best personified by Minnesota's fiery populist senator, Paul Wellstone. In Paul's own words, "I'm here for the little fellers, not the Rockefellers."

In 2002, when Paul decided to run for a third term, I wanted to do everything I could to help him. I, too, was up for reelection that year. To my surprise, the Republicans decided not to put up a candidate, which at that point was pretty much unheard of in a race for Hennepin County Attorney. Since I had already signed a contract for billboards and John was eager to vindicate our bad billboard locations in the 1998 campaign, we had dozens of billboards. We also managed to put up three thousand lawn signs. Those signs still didn't vote, but on Election Day I pulled down 98.7 percent of the votes!

The good news was that since I had no opponent, I had the time to help Paul as well as several local candidates. That summer, Paul's multiple sclerosis—which had been publicly revealed only a few months before— was obviously painful. He had a lot of difficulty walking. It was heartbreaking to see him limp down a sidewalk, especially since so many of us remembered how in the previous decade he had literally burst onto the political scene, running from one side of the street to the other in hundreds of parades, shaking every hand in sight. Now he would simply stand next to his wife, Sheila, on the back of their famous green bus and wave. But here's what was truly amazing: as the bus slowly made its way down the parade route, so many people ran around it in their green Wellstone t-shirts that you really didn't notice that Paul wasn't running himself. His supporters were running for him.

The last time I saw Paul and Sheila was at an event close to the election at a synagogue in Minneapolis. Sheila and I were speaking to a small group of new U.S. citizens from Russia. There was no media present, and it was a sweet event where Sheila talked about her life growing up in Appalachia and about Paul's immigrant Jewish parents from Russia. I spoke about my Slovenian relatives up north.

Suddenly, in the middle of the event, Paul walked in the door. He wasn't supposed to be there but he'd caught an earlier flight from Washington. He had just taken a strong stand against the Iraq war and was the only senator up for election who had voted against the Iraqi war resolution. Sheila was so proud of him, and she lit up when he unexpectedly came into the room.

I've often thought about that night. Why did Paul bother to come to this small citizenship event only a few weeks before a major national election with no TV cameras on hand and no big crowd to speak to? Looking back, I'm certain there are two answers. First, Paul embraced immigrants and the American immigrant experience. He passionately believed that everyone who came to this country should have an opportunity to succeed, just as his parents did. The second reason? He loved Sheila. Whenever he had a chance to see her, he took it.

A few weeks later we lost them both. Almost everyone in Minnesota remembers where they were when they heard about Paul and Sheila's deaths in that tragic plane crash on October 25th, just eleven days before the election. For me the day was a series of images. The faces of a group of tough prosecutors and public defenders, all of whom cried when they heard the news at a meeting we were having in St. Paul; the blocks-long wall of cards and flowers and candles left in front of the campaign office in memory of Paul, Sheila, their daughter, Marcia, and staff members Mary McEvoy, Tom Lapic, and Will McLaughlin, who perished that day along with the two pilots; hundreds of young people sobbing in the campaign office; the stoic courage of campaign manager Jeff Blodgett as he consoled them.

When I look back on the weeks following Paul's death, those are the memories I dwell on. But for many in politics, that time of mourning got overshadowed by the memorial service at the University of Minnesota's Williams Arena, which was controversial because it turned into what many considered a Democratic pep rally. I watched the service from the upper deck and to me everything about it was just sad. The event was planned by Paul's grieving supporters who made mistakes by not vetting the words of those who were experiencing even greater grief.

The people of Minnesota have kept Paul's memory alive. His spirit is very much alive, too. Through the legacy organization Wellstone Action, more than thirty thousand volunteers and campaign workers from all fifty states have attended Camp Wellstone, an organizing and campaign training program that carries on Paul's work.

When I got to the Senate years after Paul had died, Capitol police officers, gift shop workers, and even Daryl, the tram operator, came up to me and told me how much they loved Paul. Paul treated everyone with the same respect, whether they served as a senator or worked the front office. In Washington, Paul and Sheila devoted themselves to the causes of those who couldn't afford to hire expensive lobbyists. Among other things, they stood up for the victims of domestic violence and championed the rights of people with mental illness (a cause Paul took on after growing up with a brother who suffered from schizophrenia).

And Paul's deep commitment to help those with mental illness was passed on to his sons David and Mark, who—along with Senators Ted Kennedy and Pete Domenici, and Congressmen Jim Ramstad and Patrick Kennedy—helped us pass the legislation that provides insurance parity to those with mental illnesses.

In 2012, on the tenth anniversary of the deaths of Paul, Sheila, Marcia, Tom, Mary, and Will, the families and friends of the Wellstones and the three campaign staff members reunited in a quiet, snowy forest where the plane had crashed on Minnesota's Iron Range, not far from where my dad grew up and my grandpa worked in the mines. We stood beneath the trees near a beautiful memorial, engulfed by a gentle early November snowfall.

In the middle of the ceremony a baby cried. I glanced at him for a moment—he looked so warm in his little snowsuit. The man holding the baby turned out to be David McLaughlin, the brother of Will McLaughlin, the charming twenty-three-year-old who had served as Paul's driver in that last campaign. He was the youngest person who died in the plane crash. The McLaughlins had named their new baby after Will. There he was—a tiny baby tucked inside a snuggly snowsuit with brand-new snowflakes dotting his little hat. I knew then that Paul and Sheila and Will and the others were there with us that day in the woods.

Beyond Hennepin County

Once the funerals were over and the election was behind us, I began my second term as county attorney. It was a sad time, but there was nothing else to do but get to work.

In 2002, with four years of experience as Hennepin County's chief prosecutor, I was elected president of the Minnesota County Attorneys Association. That second position allowed me to travel the state and meet my Greater Minnesota counterparts, giving me a much better understanding of the broad range of issues faced by the state's prosecutors. My statewide presidency led to meetings with reporters and newspaper editorial boards outside of the Twin Cities metropolitan area, though I would always go to these meetings accompanied by the local county attorney. I was on their turf, and if I was going to sit down with their media and discuss crime issues, I wanted their blessing, whether the county attorney was a Democrat or a Republican.

In 2004, I traveled around the state for yet another purpose: John Kerry was running for president, and I spoke to a number of Democratic Party units on behalf of his campaign. I'd had my introduction to national politics a dozen years earlier when Bill Clinton was our party's nominee, but this time I was an elected official and I could actually speak as a surrogate for the candidate.

In February 2004, a month after he won the Iowa caucuses and the New Hampshire primary, John Kerry came to St. Paul and spoke at Macalester College. The night before the event I was asked to introduce him. I wrote some brief remarks, memorized them, and within an hour or so I was ready to go.

Kerry's campaign was gaining tremendous momentum just then, and the rally that day was huge. As I took to the stage and looked out at a sea of blue Kerry campaign signs, I realized that I'd never spoken at an event anywhere near as big as this one. With John Kerry and Walter Mondale standing with me on the platform along with Minnesota Democratic powerbroker Sam Kaplan and United Steelworkers President Leo Gerard, I began my introduction with an ill-chosen sentence: "It is my honor to introduce to you the next president of the United States, John Kerry."

Assuming that this was the end of my introduction, the crowd went wild.

John Kerry was so sweet. He could have just taken the microphone and started into his speech, but instead he walked over to me and whispered, "I can tell you haven't finished, you should finish." Afterward we had a good laugh about that moment, especially when he told me I was holding the microphone so tightly that he couldn't have taken it away from me even if he'd wanted to.

Five months later the campaign asked me to speak at the Democratic National Convention in Boston. They wanted me to talk about Kerry's work as a prosecutor in Massachusetts.

There was a lot of rigmarole surrounding this speech. I had to practice it the day before on the teleprompter with the Kerry convention organizers present, and they made it clear that they were less than happy with a little dig I wanted to drop in at the end. The text in question went like this: "There's a famous Texan who once said something very profound. No, it wasn't George Bush, it was the late Congresswoman Barbara Jordan, who said what the American people want is simple, we want a nation that's as good as its promise."

It was the joke about George Bush that bothered them. They were so worried about including anything negative about Bush that they insisted I drop the line. I couldn't believe how paranoid they were, but who was I to refuse?

The morning of the speech, Walter Mondale came up to me. "Now, you've memorized your speech, right?"

"Well, there's a teleprompter," I said, "so I should be fine."

"No, that isn't fine," he said. "Remember the time at the '80 convention when Carter said 'Hubert Horatio Hornblower'?"

"I remember," I said.

"That was a teleprompter screw-up," he said. "So don't trust it. Memorize the speech."

This advice struck me as a little out-of-date, but even so, I told him I would memorize my speech, and I did.

Later in the day I turned up at the appointed hour and found myself backstage with Patrick Leahy, Chuck Schumer, and Charlie Rangel. Don't ask me why the convention's organizers put me together with that high-powered congressional crowd, but they did. It was a pretty good speaking slot and the convention hall was fairly full. Senator Leahy was up just before me. He started into his speech, but after about half a minute he stopped and looked around. The teleprompter had gone dark. He made a joke about it by suggesting that the malfunction was tied to a well-publicized fight he'd recently had with Vice President Dick Cheney. Eventually someone brought out a copy of Senator Leahy's remarks.

Oh my God, I thought. From where I stood waiting at the corner of the stage, I could see Walter Mondale: he was sitting right there in the front row. I made eye contact with him, and I've never seen a more pointed "I told you so" nod in my life. Smiling, I nodded back.

After Senator Leahy finished his remarks, I stepped up to the podium. Someone gave me a printed copy of my speech, and at some point after I launched into it the teleprompter came back to life. But I rarely looked at it and I never looked at the printed copy. Thanks to Walter Mondale, I looked only at the crowd. I added some stuff, I had some fun, and the speech went great. And—ha!—I used the Bush line.

Running for the Senate

A Surprise Announcement

By the end of 2004 I knew I probably wouldn't seek a third four-year term as county attorney. I loved the job and I was proud of the work we had done in the office, but we had pushed through a lot of the changes I hoped to make, and I wanted to explore the possibility of working at a different level. I was fairly certain that if I did choose to run for county attorney again in 2006 I would be reelected, but I was ready for a new challenge.

One job I seriously considered was Minnesota Attorney General. It would be a natural step up from Hennepin County Attorney, even though my office had a bigger staff and handled more criminal cases than the statewide position. But being the top lawyer for the entire state would involve new responsibilities and I also loved getting around Minnesota and working on consumer issues.

Mike Hatch—the state's very capable Democratic attorney general—had already signaled his intention to run for governor in 2006 against our then incumbent governor, Republican Tim Pawlenty. That meant the attorney general job would be open. As 2005 began, I started to call delegates and elected officials to gauge their support, and I was pleased by the positive response.

In early February, just as I was preparing to ramp up my efforts to line up support for a potential run for attorney general, I got a call from

Walter Mondale. He asked me to come visit him in his office at Dorsey & Whitney. The day I met him, I took a seat in one of the chairs he had brought with him from his tenure as a U.S. senator, a fact I later recalled with some amusement.

"Are you getting ready to run for attorney general?" he asked me.

"Yes," I said, "and I would like your support, especially since attorney general was your first statewide office."

"Of course," he said. "But I do have one request: don't announce anything for a month or two."

"I don't plan to," I said, not quite understanding why he was so focused on an election that was still twenty-one months away. "Is someone else going to run, or is Hatch actually considering running again for attorney general if the governor's race doesn't pan out?"

"No," he said, "Hatch is not running again for attorney general. Just don't announce."

I agreed to Mondale's request. Though I was serious about running for attorney general, I still needed to lay the groundwork for the race and I wasn't planning to announce in the next few months anyway. Given the endless tactical maneuvering that's typical in the political world, what may be most surprising is that after talking to Mondale, I simply went back to my office and continued on with my day. I didn't spend much time thinking about the conversation—I mentioned it to my husband and a few friends, but otherwise I didn't tell anyone about it. Long ago I had learned that a lot of things in life are simply out of my control. What mattered for the moment was that I trusted Walter Mondale and I had his support for attorney general. If it later turned out that for some reason I couldn't run for attorney general, I would deal with that when it happened.

Then, just a few days later, a bolt of political lightning came straight from Washington, D.C. For months, Minnesota's incumbent Democratic Senator Mark Dayton had been signaling that he planned to run for a second term—he had even set up a reelection campaign committee. But on the morning of February 9, 2005, he made a surprise announcement: he would not be seeking reelection after all.

It was no secret that Dayton—now a successful two-term governor of Minnesota—was not particularly happy in the Senate. He didn't like the Senate's hobnobbing and procedural tangles and political stalemates.

With typical candor, he explained his reasons for declining to run by saying: "I do not believe that I am the best candidate to lead the DFL Party to victory next year. I cannot stand to do the constant fundraising necessary to wage a successful campaign, and I cannot be an effective senator while also being a nearly full-time candidate."

The moment I heard Dayton's news that morning, I realized that Mondale must have told me to put off an announcement about running for attorney general because he suspected Dayton might not run and wanted me to consider running for the Senate. I also realized that I only had a short time to figure out what I would say if anyone asked me if I was considering running for the Senate job.

As it happened, I was about to spend that day conducting a series of TV and radio interviews coinciding with a law enforcement conference we had put together in the County Attorney's Office. Experts from across the country were coming to Minneapolis to discuss the topic of eyewitness identification and our new pilot program to reduce mistakes by witnesses. For most of my interviews, I would be joined by one of our guest speakers, an incredible woman from North Carolina named Jennifer Thompson-Cannino. At age twenty-two and still in college, Jennifer was the victim of a brutal rape. Her testimony—based on her mistaken eyewitness identification—sent a young man named Ronald Cotton to prison for a rape he did not commit. Eleven years later DNA evidence proved the rape was committed by another man. Remarkably, Cotton forgave her, and after he was freed they would often speak jointly about the perils of eyewitness identification.

So picture the two of us—me and this outspoken rape victim whom I had met for the first time that day—meeting with one reporter after another and being asked time and time again whether I was going to run for the U.S. Senate. After telling them that I was seriously considering a run, I would try to steer the interview back to issues involving eyewitness identification. Jennifer was so delightful and enthusiastic that by the end of our string of meetings with the press, she would say in her strong southern drawl, "And could I add that I think Amy would make a great senator for the state of Minnesota!"

Hers was my first endorsement. My second came from Keith Ellison, now a congressman but back then a state representative. The day of

Dayton's announcement, Keith ran into me in St. Paul and told me I should run for the open seat. He wrote me a $50 check on the spot, pledging to help me any way he could.

That first day everything happened so quickly that I didn't even have time to talk to John. Finally he called me in the middle of the afternoon and said, "They're saying on the news that you might run for U.S. Senate. Maybe we should talk about it first."

Another bad work/family balance moment!

Actually, John was all-in from the start. I knew the race would take a toll on our family, but John was immediately encouraging—he told me that not only did he believe I could win, he was certain I would do a good job. My parents, John's parents, and all our friends also wanted me to run.

We talked to Abigail, of course, then age nine. I vividly remember tucking her into bed one night soon after Dayton's surprise announcement. I told her I was thinking of running for the U.S. Senate and said that if I did get into the race, it would inevitably change our lives in many ways.

"Campaigns can be hard," I said. "Sometimes they run mean ads on TV, and they follow candidates around with a video camera and try to catch them making a mistake."

Her eyes got big, and she reminded me of the time around the Kirby Puckett trial when we had made an ill-timed visit to Milwaukee with my mom to see her relatives. When we checked in to our hotel, we discovered that the entire Twins baseball team and the reporters who followed them were staying in the same place. Abigail reminded me that I had wanted to avoid the media on our family get-away and that she'd helped out by walking through the hotel's lobby with her stuffed giraffe in front of her face, just in case anyone recognized her from our county attorney campaign brochures. She had clearly enjoyed the experience, and now she seemed eager to reassure me that she knew how to deal with negative campaigns and relentless Senate campaign trackers.

That's right, I thought, that'll fix those trackers—all we have to do is to pull out a few stuffed giraffes when we need to duck them.

But then Abigail turned serious. With the kind of drama in her voice that only a nine-year-old girl can muster, she asked, "Mom, do you think they'd put *me* in the mean ads?"

This was one of those mom moments that could not go wasted.

"Well," I said, "probably not, but if you don't keep practicing the piano and the video trackers come to the recital, I don't know what could happen."

I told her I was only kidding, and that was the end of the discussion.

Earl Maus's Fish House

Before I could make a final decision about whether I would run, I needed to do a lot of homework. For one thing, I wondered whether it would make sense to set up an exploratory committee. I remember having a very pointed conversation about this issue with Blanche Lincoln, the then senator from Arkansas. She gave me sage advice made all the more memorable by her colorful Arkansas twang: "In my part of the country they think an 'exploratory committee' sounds like some kind of surgery. Either you're in or you're out. Just announce."

Blanche was right about the exploratory committee, but before I announced, I wanted to talk to a number of people about what it would take to not only win the race but also to do the job well. Lots of people wanted me to run, but that wasn't reason enough to launch a Senate campaign. For one thing, I needed to evaluate the strength of the support I could expect. For another, I had to take a hard look at how much money I'd have to raise—predicted to be around $10 million—and decide whether I could pull it off. Most important, though, I knew from experience that the desire to take on the enormous challenges of public life must come from within. You have to want the job as much as or more than you've ever wanted anything. You've got to have the passion to do it well, and you've got to believe that you can make a substantial contribution.

I began to think seriously about the issues that mattered most to me. I felt strongly that bad decisions had been made in Washington that weakened our country in all sorts of ways. I did not agree with President Bush's decision to go to war in Iraq. As a prosecutor, I was horrified by the major ethical breaches that were coming out of Congress, breaking down the fundamental trust with the electorate that was so important for a functioning and effective democracy. How could the people of this country get a fair shake when—as I would learn—members of Congress were giving favors to lobbyists in exchange for golf trips to Scotland and hiding $90,000 in cash in their freezers?

I came from a middle-class background. Before becoming county attorney, I'd spent more than thirteen years in the private sector, and for the past six years I'd been running a four-hundred-person government agency. I'd seen the power of government to do enormous good—and to help people—if decisions were made for the right reasons. And in a fast-changing global economy, I felt there was a lot more that Washington could do to provide economic opportunity for Americans.

I believed I had both the passion and the qualifications for the job, but I was keenly aware that I needed to think hard about three critical issues: gender, money, and my likely opponents. From the day I publicly said I was considering the race, I had been repeatedly asked whether a woman could win a U.S. Senate seat in Minnesota. No woman had ever been elected to the U.S. Senate from our state; for that matter, no woman had ever been elected governor. At the time, men outnumbered women in the U.S. Senate by 86 to 14. And in the last two decades, Minnesota had twice rejected qualified women candidates—former Secretary of State Joan Growe in 1984 and the state's Senate Majority Leader Ann Wynia in 1994—in favor of men. Would yet another decade go by before a woman was elected to the Senate from our state? I hoped not, but I knew that if I did decide to join the race, I would seek out and depend on the support of women, but I would not run a gender-themed campaign. I would run on my record as a prosecutor and my belief that government could actually get things done.

I knew that it would be a challenge to stand out in a crowded field and that raising a significant amount of money would be crucial to my effort to do so. I also knew that I would almost certainly have several competitors for the Democratic endorsement, and that if I did survive the endorsement round, I would undoubtedly face a strong Republican opponent, most likely third-term congressman Mark Kennedy. The other Senate seat in the state was held by Republican Senator Norm Coleman, and Coleman could be counted on to lend his support to Kennedy or another Republican nominee. Many of those who told me I shouldn't run—and a number of people actively discouraged me from jumping into the race—said that I could never raise the necessary money, especially given all the competition, which was likely to include one or more millionaires who could fund their campaigns without a lot of outside help. Others pointed out that I was a woman from the metro area who had never run in a statewide race.

Run, don't run. You'll never be able to raise enough money, somehow you'll find the money. You can win, you can't win. You could be the first woman to break Minnesota's glass ceiling for U.S. Senate, you could be the third one to fail. You could run for attorney general and win, you could run for Senate and be out of a job. I remember going back and forth on all these points with John during a long drive in February of 2005 from the Twin Cities to northern Minnesota's Leech Lake. John and I had planned this trip months earlier and the day had finally come. It was a Saturday morning with only a slight chill to the air, and we were on our way to a day of ice fishing with then Cass County Attorney and now Minnesota District Court Judge Earl Maus and his wife Jean.

I had come to know Earl through the Minnesota County Attorneys Association, and he had been persistent in his quest to get John and me to visit his hometown of Walker—the biggest town on Leech Lake—for none other than the International Eelpout Festival. To get a sense of this annual festival, you need to know only three things. First, an eelpout is an eel-like, bottom-feeding fish that isn't particularly appealing to look at but is really tasty when fried. Second, calling this an "international festival" proves beyond a doubt that people in northern Minnesota think big. Third, almost the entire festival is held on a frozen lake—and yes, it's usually really cold. Minnesotans are passionate about ice fishing. Some anglers fish outdoors over holes that they've drilled in the ice; others drill within the privacy of their own "fish house," which usually looks like a small shack but can get very elaborate, with porches, mailboxes, and fancy paint jobs, mostly involving Vikings helmets.

As much as John and I were looking forward to visiting Earl and Jean on that unseasonably warm day, our excitement about the one-day road trip to the north woods was tempered by the "run, don't run" loop that was circling endlessly in my mind. I thought about one person who told me that I wouldn't have "a prayer of winning" unless I could put $3 million in the bank in the first three months. I looked over at John driving our 2001 Saturn, knowing that even a second mortgage on our $168,000 house wouldn't get us anywhere near $3 million. Absurdly, I had responded to the person who insisted that I had to raise that impossible sum in just ninety days by saying, "Oh, I'm sure I can raise that much."

Right.

Once we finally arrived at the Eelpout Festival, we met up with Earl and Jean, watched a few people take the polar plunge into the ridiculously cold water through holes in the ice, and scarfed down some fried eelpout. Then we climbed into Earl's truck and drove out to his fish house, a silver shack with the word "Maus" painted on the outside. We dropped our lines into the water. Before long, I began telling Earl about all the advice people had been giving me about whether I should run for the Senate.

In his no-nonsense northern Minnesota way, Earl listened carefully, all the while looking down at the cold, dark water through the deep holes he had cut in the frozen ice. When I got to the part about raising $3 million in three months, he stopped me. "You've done a good job as county attorney, and the other guys who are county attorneys think so, too. I'm not that political, but I think you're good." He looked at me, paused, and in his halfway-to-*Fargo* accent said: "Do you think you would be the same way in the Senate?"

"Yes," I answered.

"All right then, you should run."

"Okay, I will."

And that was it. Sitting there in Earl Maus's fish house at the International Eelpout Festival on Leech Lake, with my husband, Earl, and his wife Jean, huddled over the dark holes in the ice, I made the decision to run for the United States Senate. We'd conducted no focus groups, commissioned no polls, and hired no consultants.

There was only Earl saying, "All right then, you should run."

A little while later we walked a few yards on the frozen ice to a parked blue bus where some of Earl's friends were hanging out. The bus had a heater and his friends had a bottle of something strong in a paper bag. We all passed the bottle around and had a drink and toasted my decision.

That was how it all started.

Getting Started

I spent the next few months learning the issues, raising money, and trying to persuade people in Washington to take my candidacy seriously—or at least to pronounce my name right. Even in Minnesota there is a dispute about how to say my last name, but my position has always been that people can say it however they want.

In Ely, where my dad grew up, they've always said "claw-BUTCH-er." But my dad and a lot of people elsewhere on the Iron Range (where there's a lot of Klobuchars) say "klo-bah-CHAR." Meanwhile, most of the people in the rest of the state (including my mom when I was growing up) say "klo-bah-SHAR," which is the way I pronounce it. Whenever the pronunciation issue came up during campaigns, I would always say, "There isn't a big difference between 'CHAR' and 'SHAR,' but there is between me and my opponent. I don't care how you say it, so long as you vote for me."

But I did care about mastering the issues. Three early mornings a week, two incredibly dedicated volunteers—Cyndi Bauerly (now Minnesota's revenue commissioner, having previously worked for Chuck Schumer in Washington) and Howard Orenstein (a former St. Paul legislator)—would come to my house, sit in my living room, and go over each issue the country faced, all before we left for work.

One day it would be immigration reform, the next day taxes. One day student loans, the next energy. I would roll out of bed at 6:00 a.m., read the information Cyndi and Howard had gathered on the issue of the day, and run downstairs in my bathrobe when they rang the doorbell. My two friends never questioned my robe, but my husband was mortified every time I answered the door. For me—a working mom with a full-time job and four hundred people to manage—this was the only way to do it.

I was very focused on understanding the issues and developing detailed positions. No matter what the circumstance, I wanted to be able to hold my own in a discussion or a debate. People who recruit candidates tell me that women will often explain their decision not to run for office by saying, "I don't know enough about the issues." Men, on the other hand, rarely cite not knowing enough about policy as a disqualifying factor. By way of explanation, former Minnesota Secretary of State Joan

Growe once reminded me, "We will know we have achieved true political equality the day we start electing as many mediocre women for office as we do mediocre men."

She was kidding, guys, she was kidding.

On the other hand, why run for office if you don't know your stuff?

Looking back, I'm convinced those early months were incredibly important. At a time of wide-ranging public debate over issues such as government spending and the war in Iraq, I had thought through my positions and knew how to explain them. Our homegrown research also allowed me to avoid delivering cookie-cutter responses to important questions. We didn't just cut and paste talking points from people in Washington, D.C. We talked to experts and wrote out policy positions ourselves. Somehow it all worked, thanks to Cyndi's knowledge of the national issues combined with Howard's command of detail and my ability to review and explain the data.

But mastering farm, foreign, and forestry policy wasn't enough. There was something else I needed to upgrade before I would truly be prepared for a run for the United States Senate. That would be clothes and hair.

One evening a few weeks after I decided to run, I left my office and went down to my car in the government center parking garage. Perched on the front hood of the Saturn was a plastic container filled with multi-colored velcro hair rollers and a note: "These will help you do well in my district. Penny."

Penny Steele—the county's most conservative Republican commissioner and a true friend—was right. My hair is thick and straight, and I knew that a few rollers in the morning would do it good. I also knew that I could use some new shoes and suits, and one morning I got a phone call from Rosalie, a salesperson at the local Marshall Field's (now Macy's) who was Joan Growe's friend. The minute I heard Rosalie's voice, I knew Joan had told her to call me.

When I answered the phone that day, Rosalie got right to the point. "Rosalie calling," she said. "I hear that all the shoes you have are worn out and scuffed. It's been described to me as a 'shoe emergency.' I also hear that your pants look baggy and you need a new bra. I'm here to help."

Thanks, Joan. Thanks, Penny. Thanks, Rosalie. And thanks also to Bea, my hairdresser for thirty years, who calls every time my hair looks bad on TV and says, "When's the last time you came in for an appointment?"

Raising the Dough

Then there was the daunting task of coming up with $10 million for the campaign. To be a credible candidate, I would have to prove my fundraising prowess from the get-go. This would require raising the money one person at a time by persuading a donor to contribute $20 or $100 or $1,000 or—if I was really lucky—$2,000. Sometimes e-mail solicitations worked, and I knew they worked especially well when candidates took positions that appealed to the base with pungent, attack-dog language. But that wasn't my style, and I insisted that our e-mails and letters be more positive than those used in the average campaign.

The bulk of the money for the campaign would have to come from my phone calls and my events. Unless you are really famous (okay, that isn't me), the most effective way to raise money is to call potential donors one at a time or talk with them at a fundraising event. I raised most of my campaign contributions in Minnesota, and when it came to a national fundraising strategy, I knew I couldn't rely exclusively on events in New York and Los Angeles. I would travel all across the country and meet people in midsize cities like Milwaukee, St. Louis, and Fargo. Every trip and every minute counted: at one point we figured out that to make my $10 million goal, I would have to raise an average of $16,000 a day.

Unlike some candidates, I didn't get calls from celebrities eager to help me meet that goal—with one memorable exception. One day, out of the blue, we got a call from the songwriter Burt Bacharach, who offered to come to Minnesota to do an event. Burt was true to his word: he arrived at our fundraiser in Wayzata with his own keyboard and then wowed the audience with "Raindrops Keep Falling on My Head" and "(They Long to Be) Close to You." Years later I would tease Al Franken about that event. He might have persuaded Conan O'Brien, Jon Hamm, and Amy Poehler to help him out, but he never did get Burt Bacharach.

When I wasn't at work or traveling around the state, I spent most of my fundraising time sitting alone at our dining room table calling people on the phone. I mostly called people who could afford to give large donations, but I also called potential hosts and attendees for fundraisers, sometimes for small events or house parties. Using "call sheets," which show a donor's giving history, I would make call after call after call. Some days I would raise no more than $100 to $250 a person.

Often I made cold calls to people I'd never met. I can't tell you how hard it is to pretend to be happy when a major donor—someone listed on the call sheet with a record of giving thousands of dollars to male candidates—tells you he will give you $200. I can't tell you how embarrassing it is when someone answers her phone and then pretends she's her own assistant to avoid your ask. Or when you call someone and his widow tells you he died two years ago. Or when you call the right name but get the wrong person.

When you make fundraising calls, you've got to have a thick skin. But though you get used to rejection, you also come to appreciate people's generosity—the willingness of ordinary citizens to part with their hard-earned money to help elect someone they believe in. While making my calls, I was often impressed by how much people cared about the future of our country and touched by their confidence that I could make a difference. I learned that a whole lot of people, including those of very modest means, care deeply about this democracy of ours and are anxious to make it better.

A particular challenge for women candidates is that a donor often believes that the person calling is your assistant, not the candidate herself. Not only did that happen to me, it even happened when I insisted that I *was* the candidate. But to compensate, I came up with a few pretty effective calling techniques. One was calling before, during, or after the broadcast of the then hit show *The West Wing*. People always felt guilty that they were glued to the set watching a pretend democracy while I was trying my best to make a difference in our real one. Another unorthodox idea involved going through every old address book and Rolodex I could find. Not only did I call long-ago pals and classmates, I set an all-time and yet-to-be-beaten Senate record: I raised $17,000 from ex-boyfriends. But as my husband said at the time, it's not an expanding base.

I needed the money to pay for my campaign expenses, of course, but fairly or unfairly, the fundraising totals were also important to my credibility, especially early on in a competitive Democratic field. The media constantly focuses on how much money someone running for office raises. A Senate candidate's fundraising activities are reported on a quarterly basis, which means that a candidate faces a new reporting deadline every three months.

The first quarter of my yet-to-be-official campaign would end on March 31st, only six weeks after I'd gotten started but right before I formally announced my candidacy. I was determined to make a good showing, knowing that if I didn't establish myself as a competent fundraiser, I would never be taken seriously as a candidate. I also knew that if I didn't put up an impressive number, I would soon be out of the race altogether. Too many wealthy people were considering jumping in.

In the end, with no campaign office save my dining room table and one paid fundraiser—the charming and intrepid Tom Perron—I ended up raising $592,000 by the end of the first quarter. It was less than many U.S. Senate candidates would raise in a quarter, but the number did catch the eyes of the pundits in Washington. Suddenly I had the rabbit that every political candidate needs to pull out of her campaign hat: legitimacy, or at least political pundit legitimacy.

My Announcement

I set Sunday, April 17th, as the date for my formal announcement and chose my mom's house in Plymouth as the site for the kickoff event. I'd grown up there, and the neighborhood had great schools and a strong sense of community.

Hundreds of friends and supporters joined me on that Sunday afternoon. The weather was great, and people I'd known from all walks of life gathered in my mom's driveway in front of her garage. The crowd spilled onto her front lawn—my high school teachers, my friends from the two law firms where I'd worked, our neighbors, our church members, people from the County Attorney's Office, legislators.

"Welcome to the house I grew up in," I began, noting first that my mom had one important piece of advice for everyone: "Don't step on the tulips."

Honestly, by the look on my mom's face, it wasn't really a joke. So many more people had shown up than we'd predicted that she was having a fit. The street was filled with cars, and as my mom pointed out with some heat, "Someone parked right on Ila's grass." The way my mom saw it, keeping Ila's vote would now be a serious challenge.

With John and Abigail beside me, and my mom and dad looking on, I told the crowd: "This house, this driveway, have marked the beginning of many journeys for me." I talked about walking across the street and up the hill for my first day of kindergarten, about starting cross-country bike trips with my dad from the very spot where we were standing. I told them about the bike trip to Jackson Hole, Wyoming, when we covered eleven hundred miles in ten days with all our gear on our bikes and our backs, enduring three flat tires, five angry farm dogs, and one tornado. "Compared to that trip," I said, "this journey is going to be simple."

I then told everyone why I was running for the Senate. I explained that I wanted to make a difference for the people of Minnesota and put the good of the many ahead of the interests of the few. I spoke about my belief in hard work, fair play, and personal responsibility, as well as my intention to focus on solutions that improve people's lives instead of issues that divide us. I expressed pride in the way Minnesotans take care of their children, the elderly, and the disabled, and I promised to "bring Minnesota common sense to the halls of Congress."

I ended my speech with a litany of simple statements, one that I would repeat again and again on the campaign trail in the weeks to come:

I am the daughter of a teacher and a newspaperman.

I am a wife and a mother.

I am a prosecutor.

I am an advocate.

I am a Minnesotan. And with the help and support of the people of Minnesota, I will be your United States Senator.

The Field

In my campaign for the U.S. Senate, I knew that I would face at least three worthy opponents for the Democratic endorsement: Patty Wetterling, Kelly Doran, and Ford Bell. They were all smart and focused on the issues, and each brought a lot of energy to the race.

Patty Wetterling, a tireless advocate for missing and exploited children, had come to politics because of a personal tragedy. In 1989, her eleven-year-old son, Jacob, was abducted at gunpoint by a masked man. Jacob was riding his bicycle near his family's home in St. Joseph, Minnesota, and since that horrible day, though the search continues, he has never been found. In 2004, Patty had run for Congress against Republican U.S. Representative Mark Kennedy. I had supported Patty in that race, but her campaign against Congressman Kennedy had been unsuccessful.

The media took note of Patty's Senate candidacy from the beginning. With Representative Kennedy planning to jump into the race for the open Senate seat, too, the prospect of a Kennedy-Wetterling rematch made for a compelling story. I knew Patty would be a formidable opponent, not least because early polls showed that she enjoyed far better name identification than I did.

Real estate developer Kelly Doran—a successful businessman from Eden Prairie—was not, as he pointed out, a career politician, and I knew voters would be impressed by his entrepreneurial savvy. Kelly and I both regularly voiced serious concerns about the federal budget, and both of us also spent a lot of time talking about jobs and the economy. But Kelly had one advantage I did not: the ability to bankroll his own campaign. According to a financial disclosure form he later filed, Kelly's assets were estimated to be between $57 million and $210 million.

Because of his money and his success in business, Kelly was instantly a credible candidate. And when he retained John Wodele, former Governor Jesse Ventura's spokesman and a respected political operative, he sent a clear message that he was serious about running a good campaign.

My third Democratic opponent, Ford Bell, was a veterinarian and a philanthropist from a leading Minnesota family. The grandson of General Mills founder James Ford Bell, Ford had served on a number of nonprofit boards, including the board of the Minneapolis Institute of Arts. As chair of its "Bring Art to Life" capital campaign, he helped raise more than $100 million. Though his personal assets were estimated to be between $1 million and $5 million—far less than Kelly Doran's—I had no doubt that Ford knew how to raise large sums of money and would have the means to get his message out.

For me, getting the Democratic endorsement at the party's convention in June—and winning over rank-and-file voters—would be critical. In our state a candidate can receive an endorsement from a party convention, but challengers are still allowed to seek the support of voters in a primary. I needed the party's support and organization to win, but even then I recognized the threat that a well-financed post-convention primary challenger would bring. That challenge could come from Kelly Doran or Ford Bell or a prospective candidate such as Mike Ciresi, a prominent trial lawyer who was sending signals early on that he might enter the race. Both Patty and I had pledged to support the party's endorsed candidate from the convention, but the other, wealthier opponents did not make that pledge.

On the Republican side, Representative Kennedy—whose district included rural and suburban areas in central and western Minnesota—got off to a fast start and quickly emerged as the front-runner. Before seeking office, Kennedy had a very successful business career. In 2000, he won his first congressional race against incumbent Democratic Congressman David Minge. Two years later he won again, and in 2004 he beat back Patty Wetterling's challenge. For a brief time, former U.S. Senator Rod Grams launched an attempt to win the Republican endorsement, but around the time I formally announced my candidacy he abandoned his effort and decided to support Kennedy. From the beginning, then, I knew that the winner of the Democratic endorsement would almost certainly face Congressman Kennedy in the fall of 2006.

As the year went on, the question of electability became very important to people within our party. The four Democratic candidates—Patty, Kelly, Ford, and I—took fairly similar stands on the major issues, so before long what mattered most was who could get enough votes in the general election to beat Mark Kennedy. Meanwhile, the four of us participated in dozens of community events and candidate forums. The beauty of grassroots politics is not only that it evens the playing field but that it allows voters to make decisions based on both the issues and the relative strength of the candidates.

In September 2005, I got a big boost when I received the endorsement of EMILY's List, an organization that supports pro-choice Democratic women candidates. Ellen Malcolm—the president and founder of EMILY's List—praised Patty as "a remarkable woman," but in announcing the endorsement, Malcolm said my campaign had gotten off to a "spectacular" start. Clearly

EMILY's List didn't want to see Minnesota Democrats get dragged into an expensive primary, and the group's support meant that their supporters would be asked to donate to my campaign, even as it also sent a signal to other Democrats to rally behind me. The fact that EMILY's List was willing to choose between two women candidates and gave me their endorsement was hugely helpful to me.

The support I built was strongly grounded in my two terms as county attorney, and by the fall of 2005 my campaign was really beginning to take off. With the help of friends and neighbors, state legislators and local officials, law firm colleagues and clients, labor unions, and business owners, I assembled a strong grassroots operation. Over time our campaign created so much momentum that the other Democrats left the race.

Kelly Doran left the Senate race in September 2005 when he announced that he would be running for governor instead. In early 2006, Patty Wetterling decided to run for something else, too. Congressman Kennedy's decision to run for the Senate seat created an opening in his Sixth District House seat, and one day in January Patty called me to let me know that she was pulling out of the Senate race and would run for Congress instead. She was also kind enough to publicly pledge her support to me. Eventually Patty would square off against Michele Bachmann—then a Republican state legislator—and though Patty ran a hard-fought campaign, in November Michele came away with the victory.

On February 7, 2006, Mike Ciresi—who'd run for the Senate before, challenging Mark Dayton in the 2000 primary—announced that he had decided not to run again. That left Ford Bell and me to duke it out for quite a while longer, although straw polls after the precinct caucuses in March showed that I had over 75 percent of the delegates' votes. Finally, in July 2006, Ford announced that he was pulling out of the race, allowing me to focus all of my energies on the general election.

At the DFL convention that June, I easily won the Democratic endorsement. By then I had been campaigning for almost a year and a half, and the election was still five months off. But I had come a long way since our visit with Earl Maus at the Eelpout Festival, and I was thrilled to know that I had so many people supporting what had once been such a long-shot effort to win the Senate seat. I also knew that my opponents for the

Democratic endorsement had made me a better candidate—throughout the process, they had shown real gumption and had respectfully aired their views. I still admire all of them, not only for how they handled themselves during the campaign but for the good work they've done since.

On the Trail

Throughout the second half of 2005 and 2006, our campaign was all about getting around the state. Grassroots campaigning at parades, picnics, and county fairs was essential to everything we did because, just like in my first county attorney's race, I was going to be the underdog in terms of money. Our fundraising efforts were in full swing, but everyone involved with the campaign knew the score: there was no way we were going to buy our way to victory over Congressman Kennedy.

Our campaign exuded youth and energy, and that persuaded a lot of students and volunteers to help us. On the Fourth of July in both 2005 and 2006, we covered hundreds of parades with our network of high school and college interns and volunteers. Our parade units featured kids sweeping brooms with signs that said "Bring Sweeping Change to Washington." The students would dance with the brooms and come up with all kinds of clever ways to synchronize them.

I'd grown up and worked in the Twin Cities, so I was eager to spend a lot of time in Minnesota's rural areas. In 2006 I visited all eighty-seven of the state's counties, and during the campaign I promised that once I got into office, I would make a point of visiting each of those counties every year I served in the Senate. Nine years later I've continued to keep that promise.

As the support for my candidacy grew, my campaign staff grew as well. By the summer of 2006, between the campaign and my work as county attorney, I rarely controlled my own schedule. But sometimes I would rebel against the campaign's senior staff, who of course wanted me to do the prudent thing and spend most of my free time raising money. Some weekends I would get in the car with just one staffer and we'd drive as far as we could go to whatever festival or fair I could find on the schedule. I figured that as long as I raised money while out on the road, how could anyone complain? As we drove, I would sit in the passenger seat with my cell phone and the call sheets. Before long I got to know every area of bad cell phone service on every highway in the state.

One day I enlisted my aide Jessica Wright to escape with me and drive four hours to a farm picnic in the two-hundred-person town of Flom, Minnesota, not too far from the North Dakota border. Not until Jessica and I were on our way did I tell our campaign management that we were headed to Flom, and when they asked for the address of our destination I told them, "They don't have any addresses in Flom." I raised money the whole way there, and the western Minnesota farmers will never forget I came. Going off the grid and driving to Flom with Jessica was so much fun that I never got to do it again.

Whether meeting farmers in Flom or students in St. Cloud or steel-workers on the Iron Range, I just loved grassroots campaigning. I loved the parades, the festivals, the county fairs, and even the supermarket lines. As I learned from Paul Wellstone, person-to-person campaigning is a great way to find out what's really on people's minds. Minnesotans are famously polite—we like to call it Minnesota Nice—and many of them won't call an elected official to complain. But if you make the effort to meet them in person, whether in a shopping mall or on a parade route, they're more than willing to tell you what they think about an issue or express their views about something you've done. Besides, you can't solve a prob-lem if you don't know about it. I've fixed a lot of problems just by show-ing up at a grocery store.

My family also enjoyed grassroots campaigning. John and Abigail did great work at the local festivals—judging a chili-tasting contest in Meeker County, hanging out with the hunting dogs at Game Fair, sampling squirrel booya in South St. Paul, and playing bingo while munching on fried cheese curds at county fairs throughout the state. And everywhere they traveled, they'd look for our bumper stickers on passing cars. John got so obsessed with making sure that our bumper stickers were affixed to our supporters' vehicles that I promised people at events that if they put one on their bumper, he would personally come out after the campaign was over and peel the sticker off with a blow-dryer.

As in previous campaigns, we had special t-shirts made for family members, including ones for my in-laws that said "I'm Amy's Mother-in-Law" and "I'm Amy's Father-in-Law." I always found it pretty amusing when people would come up to me and say, "I think it's cool that you have your mother-in-law's support." Really? Who else was she going to support?

In parades my mom would carry a sign that read, "Hi, I'm Amy's Mom." Once in the Robbinsdale Whiz Bang Days parade someone actually asked me if she was my real mom. "Okay, you guys," I joked with the curbside crowd, "do you think things have gotten so cynical that politicians rent out fake moms and put signs in their hands?" Everyone laughed.

Then there was the time my dad heard a guy yell at him from the side of the road as he was walking down the parade route with my stickers. "Hey, Jim," the guy bellowed, "I can't believe you're here. I had no idea you were still alive."

The crowd gasped, but my dad grinned and then went over and shook the guy's hand to show him just how alive he was.

The race was such a family affair that Al Franken—who became my U.S. Senate colleague two years later—would recall that he learned how to campaign by watching our family. One of my favorite stories Al tells is about how our family would show up at nearly every event in the state. If there were sixty festivals or picnics or bean feeds, he remembered, "Amy was at forty of them. And if Amy wasn't there, her husband John was there with their daughter Abigail. And if John and Abigail weren't there, Amy's dad Jim would be there. And if none of them were there, I would always ask myself, 'Why am I here?'"

The A Team

To manage a big campaign and raise the necessary funds, we needed a devoted staff willing to work long hours. I'm pretty good at spotting talent, and I have high expectations for the people who work for me. I figure that if they work really hard and do a good job on one of my campaigns or in my office, that experience will serve them well later on. I'm proud of how often it's worked that way: over the years we've helped a lot of people to launch their own successful careers.

My first hire for the Senate race was Justin Buoen, who started with parades in 2005 and went on to be our in-state fundraiser in the 2006 campaign. Justin and I worked together for the next six years and in 2012 he stepped into the top job and managed my reelection campaign. Justin has a can-do attitude and loves his work. His story of going from holding up "Meet Amy" signs in parades to managing a U.S. Senate race is inspirational to every college kid who wants to get into politics.

In June 2005 I brought on Jessica Vanden Berg as my campaign manager, and by mid-August she had amassed thousands of volunteers throughout the state. We held weekly strategy sessions with Wellstone alums Jeff Blodgett and Dan Cramer, and soon those sessions included media guru Mandy Grunwald and strategist Al Quinlan. We were right in the thick of the endorsement race against Patty Wetterling, and I knew Mandy had done great work for Paul Wellstone, Hillary Clinton, and Ken Salazar. Before hiring Mandy, I called her and explained why having Patty as an opponent posed some unique challenges. As I put it to Mandy that day: "It's kind of like running against Mother Teresa, and meanness is not in our playbook. Can you deal with it?"

Over time we would add lots of terrific staff members, and many of them would go on to accomplish great things. In early 2006, Jessica left to manage Jim Webb's successful campaign for the Senate in Virginia. To replace her, I hired Ben Goldfarb, a mentee of Jeff Blodgett's, to be our campaign manager. He did a wonderful job—a local magazine called him "The Natural"—and he now heads up Wellstone Action, an activist non-profit group. Sara Grewing, who was originally hired as our political director, soon became my state director; later she became the St. Paul city attorney and is now a judge. Rose Baumann, a young volunteer from Gustavus College, worked her way up the ladder in our office and eight years later became my stellar chief of staff. Our field director, Zach Rodvold, would go on to be my state director and then the manager of campaigns across the state; staffer Charlie Poster is now assistant commissioner at the Minnesota Department of Agriculture; and fellow staffer Jake Spano now serves as a local elected official himself.

Nine key people in the campaign went on to great jobs in the Obama White House or on the president's campaigns. My scheduler Franny Starkey became Michelle Obama's scheduler, and my press secretary Semonti Mustaphi was her Deputy Communications Director; Andrea Mokros went from our campaign to my deputy chief of staff to several leadership positions in the White House; Jessica Wright, who started working for me right out of college, became the President's Director of Scheduling, and Lizzie Nelson a top scheduler; Joe Paulsen, who spent his first two years in politics on my campaign, is now the president's Traveling Aide and one of the chosen few to make the president's golf foursomes; Mitch Stewart, who helped with our field operation, served as national director for Obama's grassroots organization, Obama for America; Tara McGuinness became a senior White House and Office of Management and Budget adviser; and Tom Sullivan, our campaign photographer, worked his way up the ranks of my office to deputy chief of staff, and after five years with me became John Kerry's deputy chief of staff at the State Department.

And then there was Tom's brother, Jake Sullivan, a Rhodes Scholar who had clerked for Supreme Court Justice Stephen Breyer. Jake joined us for the last four months of the campaign to help Sara Grewing with my debate prep, and he would later come to Washington to work as my counsel. But that was just the beginning: in 2008 Jake headed up Hillary Clinton's debate team during her presidential campaign, and he later joined her staff as policy adviser when she became U.S. Secretary of State. When Secretary Clinton left the State Department, Jake became Vice President Biden's top security aide.

I still remember Sara Grewing calling Mandy during the campaign and telling her that she wanted to bring a "new guy" out with us to Washington for an important debate prep. Mandy was alarmed. "Why would you want to do that? How do you even know this guy?"

Sara, without missing a beat, simply said, "I don't know, he's on my husband's curling team"—true fact—"and he wanted to leave his job at his law firm and help Amy."

Jake did a great job, and of course Mandy was impressed. She later told Hillary Clinton about him, and the rest, shall we say, is history. Sara's husband is still holding that spot for Jake on the curling team.

Those are just a few of the examples of the great staff we had that year. It was an A-team campaign, and it showed.

The Race

In 2006, Republicans held fifty-five of the one hundred U.S. Senate seats. Going into the midterm elections, President Bush's popularity was slipping, so the Republican Party knew it would have to fight tooth and nail to retain control of the Senate. The state of Minnesota was seen as a pickup opportunity for their party: in April 2005, political analyst Charlie Cook—writing for the *National Journal*—rated the Minnesota Senate seat as "in the toss-up column." I could have been discouraged by that news, but instead I used it to motivate me and everyone on our team.

Minnesota already had one Republican senator, Norm Coleman. And although the state had voted Democratic in many presidential elections, it often voted for Republicans in state and local races. The governor was Republican, as were two of the three other state constitutional officers. The state legislature was split, with the state senate controlled by the Democrats and the state house of representatives by the Republicans. The big Republican footprint in Minnesota was one reason why so many people in Washington initially saw Congressman Kennedy as the favorite in the U.S. Senate race, with Patty Wetterling as his likely opponent.

Though I continued to build a strong grassroots campaign and post good fundraising numbers as 2005 went on, at the start my candidacy was pretty much ignored by the national media. Early on, I always attributed the lack of attention my name got in Washington to the simple fact that so many people couldn't pronounce it. But I also thought it wasn't necessarily a bad thing to stay off the political radar screen while I built support in the state.

By the time of the Republican and Democratic endorsing conventions in June 2006, all that had changed. Many thought Mark Kennedy would still win, but people in Washington were beginning to realize that I posed a serious threat. I used my endorsement speech to draw some sharp distinctions between my positions and Congressman Kennedy's. I also spoke out against the "incompetence, cronyism, and corporate greed" in Washington. I went after policies that were not just "fiscally bankrupt" but also "morally bankrupt." In a not-so-subtle jab at President Bush's policies, I said, "When I'm your next U.S. senator, I won't follow the Lone Star—I'll follow the North Star."

I spoke to "changing the course in Iraq, not staying the course." Calling for a national renewable energy standard and higher gas mileage standards, I asked that we "invest, not in the oil cartels of the Mideast, but in the farmers and workers of the Midwest." I called for properly equipping our soldiers and first responders and giving tax relief "to the many, not the few." I talked about the rising cost of college and prescription drugs and the need for the government to negotiate prices on drugs under Medicare Part D.

I appealed directly to independents and moderate Republicans, as I would continue to do throughout the campaign. And then I did something pretty much unheard of at a Democratic convention—I went out of my way to praise some state Republican leaders, showing a willingness to give credit where credit was due. Former Minnesota Governors Elmer Anderson and Arne Carlson had done some good things for our state, and U.S. Senator Dave Durenberger had long worked on the issue of trying to make health care more affordable.

At the Republican endorsing convention, Congressman Kennedy told delegates that "a Senate seat is a terrible thing to waste." He focused on his business background and the need to bring down taxes, and in his speech he advocated "common sense solutions that would reflect our Minnesota values." He made only one reference to me—as one of the state's newspapers put it that day: "Speaking about Democrats who wanted to raise taxes, Kennedy whispered to delegates, 'Amy Klobuchar.'"

Kennedy never mentioned George Bush in his speech, and in fact the president was a problem for him. In mid-2006, Bush's approval ratings in Minnesota were below 40 percent, and Governor Tim Pawlenty, a Republican, conceded that "the president continues to struggle here." Even so, Kennedy raised lots of money with the help of President Bush, First Lady Laura Bush, Vice President Dick Cheney, and many other Republicans in Washington, including President Bush's key political strategist, Karl Rove. When reporters asked me about Bush and all the Bush administration people who were helping Kennedy at the time, my response was far from subtle. "I hope they keep it up," I would say. "Every time one of them comes to Minnesota, I go up in the polls."

That statement was admittedly hard to quantify, but it made the point.

The Ad Wars

Kennedy and I broadcast our first TV ads in July 2006, months after political ads had already started running in other states. My first ad, a thirty-second spot about my time as Hennepin County Attorney, noted that I'd gone after offenders like Democratic appointee Judge Amundson "without fear or favor." I remember I had a cold when I recorded the ad, and years later I can still hear it in my voice. Lesson for all: the campaign schedule never adjusts to real life.

In late July, we launched our second ad, another positive one about my role in helping to pass the 1996 Minnesota law requiring hospitals to offer new moms and their babies a minimum forty-eight-hour stay. Political ads nearly always end with that familiar message from the candidate: "I approve this message." But for this commercial we added a new feature to the boilerplate closing: our smiling daughter. Abigail, who had just celebrated her tenth birthday, was shown in several shots twirling around as she walked down the street. At the end of the ad's filming, she spontaneously held up her two thumbs as I said, "I'm Amy Klobuchar and I approve this message." The image became her trademark.

At the end of July, Congressman Kennedy launched his first ad, a light-hearted spot emphasizing what the *StarTribune* called his "softer side." As the newspaper described it: "GOP Senate candidate Mark Kennedy wants you to know a few things about him: He likes plaid shirts, met his wife at a 4-H booth at the State Fair and grew up sleeping in the same room with three brothers who like to rib him." But by August, Kennedy had begun falling behind in the polls, and his ads got more and more negative. I would joke that thanks to all of our positive ads and all of Kennedy's negative ones, my face (or at least my name) was on TV twenty-four hours a day.

Among other things, Kennedy used his large ad buys to attack my record as a crime fighter—in fact, he spent hundreds of thousands of dollars on ads that tried to demonstrate that as Hennepin County Attorney I'd been ineffective in reducing crime. But I'd delivered some good results while in office, and those attacks pretty much stopped after we ran what I considered to be our best ad of the campaign. It featured three people whose family members were crime victims. First, a man whose dad had been a victim of identity theft showed a picture of his dad fishing and said, "Amy made sure that the perpetrators went to jail." Second, Jon Cummings of Minnesotans for Safe Driving appeared on the screen with a picture of his son Phillip and said, "My son was killed by a drunk driver and Amy Klobuchar cared enough to do something about it."

Finally, and most touching, Linda Longino and her husband, Leonard Winborn, spoke about Linda's eleven-year-old daughter, Tyesha, who had been killed in a gang shoot-out in south Minneapolis. The facts of the case were tragic, and many people watching the ad remembered them: Tyesha and her sister were sitting at their dining room table doing their homework when a gangster's bullet tore through the wall and pierced Tyesha's heart. Near the end of the ad Linda looked right at the camera and said, "When our little girl Tyesha was murdered, Amy made sure that those gang members went away."

The ad closed with a powerful moment. After an announcer noted that the police had endorsed me, he said, "Trust their word, not Mark Kennedy's attacks." Then Linda appeared again and said my opponent should be ashamed about the attack ads.

I didn't know what the people of Minnesota would think of a grieving mom saying that about a congressman. Yet Minnesotans had clearly become disenchanted with negative ads—a late poll showed that when voters were asked "what else was on their mind," a surprising number of them responded that Kennedy should be "ashamed" about all the attacks.

But the negative ads continued on other fronts, and among other things Kennedy went after my support for comprehensive immigration reform. He also criticized my proposal to allow Medicare to negotiate on the prices for prescription drugs for seniors, something any private business would be allowed to do. In one ad, Kennedy claimed that this kind of negotiation would stop Medicare recipients from getting access to Lipitor, the drug used to reduce high cholesterol.

I responded with an ad showing me standing in a courtroom. "When somebody fabricates evidence the judge can throw it out," I noted. "That's what I hope you will do with the charges Mark Kennedy has fabricated against me." After a pause, I said, "Rationing Lipitor for seniors? That's ridiculous." And then came the kicker: a smiling photo of my mom standing next to Abigail and me. "My mom takes Lipitor," I said.

This ad accomplished several things: it was effective in responding to the Kennedy campaign in a lighthearted way, it reminded people of my prosecutorial credentials, and it made my mom really, really happy. She got her picture in a TV ad—even if it was about her taking a cholesterol drug!

Farmfest

During 2006 Mark Kennedy and I would take part in many debates. Each debate had its moments, but three stand out.

The first was held at Farmfest in August. Minnesota is one of the biggest states in the country when it comes to agriculture, and Farmfest is the state's largest farm-focused gathering. It features the latest farm machinery, booths sponsored by groups such as the Minnesota Farmers Union and Future Farmers of America, and, thanks to the Minnesota Farm Bureau and our pork producers, some of the best pork chops on a stick you'll ever eat. But it's also the site of the annual Farmfest political candidate forum, which is held under the big tent amid bales of straw. In rural Minnesota, that's where candidates are made or broken.

Farmfest would be a major test of my ability to win strong support in farm country, but I knew that passing the test wouldn't be easy. For one thing, Congressman Kennedy had grown up in a rural area and had been on the House Agriculture Committee for two years. Unfortunately for him, the political value of that experience was somewhat tempered by the fact that he'd left the Agriculture Committee to join the Banking Committee, thereby incurring the wrath of one of my strongest supporters, agricultural leader and western Minnesota Congressman Collin Peterson.

I was glad to have Collin's help and a growing base of rural support, but I did have a major problem as I headed into Farmfest: my right hip. I'd had it replaced only seven days before the debate—and it was the second time I'd had it replaced.

I had long suffered from what's known as dysplasia, which meant that one of my hip sockets was not in the correct position. Over time, the cartilage around my right hip had grown thin; the hip became painful, causing me to limp. In April 2006, right in the middle of the campaign, I'd finally had it replaced. Unfortunately, the surgery was botched and my hip had grown more and more painful as the months went on. By June I was taking ten to fifteen Advil a day. And by the Fourth of July I could hardly walk in the parades. No one who saw me during those weeks understood that what appeared to be a loving, hand-holding walk with my husband along the parade route was actually nothing of the sort. I was using John as a crutch, leaning hard on his hand so I wouldn't limp.

For years people would come up to me and say, "You and your husband always looked so sweet in those parades."

"It wasn't exactly love," I would reply.

In mid-July, doctors at the Mayo Clinic (which had not performed the original surgery) told me that my initial hip replacement needed to be completely redone, and soon. The surgery—to be performed by Mayo's Dr. Robert Trousdale—was scheduled for August, just a week before the Farmfest debate and a little over three months before the election.

The surgery went smoothly, but toward the end I woke up while I was still on the operating table. "Is Dr. Trousdale a Republican?" I asked the shocked surgical team.

A few hours later I woke up again, this time in the hospital room. Dr. Trousdale was standing over me. "I'm an independent," he said, kindly failing to point out that perhaps I should have asked about his political affiliation earlier if it was of such concern to me. (It wasn't; it must've been an anesthetic-induced curiosity.)

Though the surgery was a success, my low blood count prompted the doctors to give me a blood transfusion two days later. I finally left the hospital four days before the Farmfest debate, but for two more days I was still on painkillers. I had to use crutches, and my right leg was so swollen and painful that I had to buy new pants.

When I arrived at the debate and took my place on the stage under the big tent, I looked so white and pasty that someone asked me if I was still on drugs. Hundreds of people were there and my supporters looked really nervous. But I wasn't nervous at all, maybe because I was in too much pain.

Over the past year, I had listened to a lot of farmers talk about what mattered in farm country. I also had great teachers in Congressman Peterson and former Farmers Union National President Dave Frederickson, who would later become my agriculture staffer and then Minnesota's Agriculture Commissioner. And despite the surgery, I had read a lot of useful briefing materials over the previous week thanks to Sara Grewing and her team. I was prepared, even if I had done most of my prep work with an IV in my arm.

During the debate, Congressman Kennedy and I got questions about renewable fuels, rural development, dairy and crop programs. But the most memorable part of the debate focused on—of all things—manure.

At one point Kennedy tried to be folksy. "I got a red ribbon at the State Fair for a heifer I raised," he told the crowd, adding, "All our kids took sheep to the county fair." But beneath that pleasant veneer lay a fierce competitor. He was behind in the polls, and he needed to try to shake things up. As the *Owatonna People's Press* reported: "Kennedy came out swinging first, telling the crowd that Klobuchar is supported by an interest group—the League of Conservation Voters, which he never named from the stage—that considers manure a toxic waste."

"I don't want to get into the manure here," I shot back, "but I don't think manure is a toxic waste."

After the debate, I quipped: "If he wants to go down into the manure, I will go down with him."

The media, of course, couldn't help but take it from there. "Politicians spread manure at Farmfest," the headline in the *Mankato Free Press* reported after the debate. "Kennedy's manure spin just doesn't pass the smell test," Willmar's *West Central Tribune* chimed in.

I couldn't have said it better myself.

Meet the Fairgoers

From the Farmfest debate, it was on to an even bigger stage at the Minnesota State Fair, where Congressman Kennedy and twenty-nine-year-old Independence Party candidate Robert Fitzgerald and I would debate before nearly one thousand people. The State Fair is not only a Minnesota phenomenon; it's also the biggest state fair in the country. (In 2014, 1.8 million people came to the fair over the course of twelve days. The Texas State Fair attracted more fairgoers, but it's open for nearly a month, so in Minnesota we don't count it. They do count it in Texas.)

Famous traditions at our State Fair include all kinds of food on a stick, from chocolate-covered bacon to chocolate-covered bananas; the Mighty Midway; roasted corn and enormous crowds; and plenty of beer. A major highlight is the all-day butter-carvings of Princess Kay of the Milky Way and her court, in which a down-coated woman in a revolving, glassed-in, refrigerated booth carves a new princess butter bust every day as fairgoers watch her and the tiara-wearing princesses from all sides. Once I asked a princess what she would do with her butter bust when the fair was over. "Oh," she said, "we'll put it in my mom's freezer, but since the features degrade over time, we plan to set it out at the annual town corn fest and everyone will dig in with their ears of corn." Yum.

One of my favorite State Fair events is the "Ladies' Sheep Lead," which movie director Jonathan Demme fell in love with when he visited our fair. This event features women sheep farmers in predominantly wool outfits parading their sheep around the ring in front of an adoring crowd. The contestants get extra points if their garments come from wool sheared on their own farms.

But nothing at the State Fair—aside from the Tiny Tim Donuts, the Giant Slide, and, according to my husband, about a hundred other things—is better than the politics. Each candidate has a booth. In 2006, Mark Kennedy's booth evoked a rustic bait shop, while ours was a twelve-by-ten-foot blue-and-white house with a front porch, complete with an address of "2006." Located next to Bob's Snake Zoo and across the street from the Haunted House, our booth became a gathering place for our campaign supporters. Using a portable microphone, I'd speak about the issues from the front porch.

The State Fair debate took place on September 1st, and an enormous parade of supporters accompanied me from the booth to the debate and back. At the debate, Congressman Kennedy immediately attacked me as "another lawyer-lobbyist" and asked voters to send him to the Senate because of his record as a certified public accountant.

I was ready for that line. During the campaign, I had laid out a plan to reduce the debt that included both spending cuts and a proposal to roll back the Bush tax cuts for the top 1 percent of the nation's earners. Kennedy would not agree to any changes in the tax rates, even for the very wealthy.

I hit back. Noting that I had just visited the State Fair's beer garden, where I'd heard one student tell another that the beer they'd been drinking was "all foam and no beer," I turned to Kennedy and said, "That's your economic plan, Congressman. It's all foam and no beer."

That got the crowd going, and the line played almost constantly on radio and TV for the next twenty-four hours.

Meet the Press

Of all our debates, the most important one from a national perspective was scheduled for October 15th, when Congressman Kennedy and I were due to appear in Washington, D.C., on NBC's *Meet the Press*. The debate, moderated by legendary host Tim Russert, had been booked weeks in advance. It generated a lot of hype: in late August, the *StarTribune* billed it "as part of a debate series on the half-dozen hottest Senate races in the country."

Labor Day came and went, and my race continued to go well. By this point I was enjoying a twenty-plus-point lead over my opponent, and some pundits were predicting a wave of Democratic victories across the country. Perversely, my strong position only increased the amount of pressure I was feeling—the last thing I wanted was to blow my lead with some kind of gaffe or misstatement.

Since mine was one of the last debates in the series dedicated to the Senate races, John and I dutifully prepared by watching the earlier *Meet the Press* debates on our VCR. The debates showcased the Ohio and Missouri candidates, and the lead-in music itself was enough to make your pulse quicken. Each of the debates began with a dramatic opening line: "The Democrats must gain six seats to take control of the U.S. Senate." Then, accompanied by the rising crescendo of the show's lead-in music, the introduction continued with details about the candidates who would debate on the show and comments about how the races were too close to call. In most cases, the polls made it clear that the candidates were locked in extremely tight races, so the stakes were very high. But since it would be harder to hype our appearance given my big lead, John jokingly claimed that during our introduction, just as the *Meet the Press* music was at its most dramatic, Tim Russert would look into the camera and ask his producers, "Why did we book this?"

Before the debate, I flew to Washington accompanied by my young and eager debate team: campaign manager Ben Goldfarb, political director Sara Grewing, and debate adviser Jake Sullivan. (Not one of them was even thirty yet.) Two days later, as we entered the historic studio on the morning of the debate, an intern met us at the door. He told us that after the debate ended I could leave the studio in one of two ways. I could walk out the front door and speak to the waiting media about the debate. "Or," he added, "if it goes really badly, I can show you a way out the back."

Now there's a confidence builder.

As we entered the studio itself, the intern told us all kinds of interesting historical facts. "This is the famous studio," he said, "where Nixon and Kennedy debated. If you recall, Nixon was well ahead before the debate began, but he was recovering from the flu and he looked so bad on TV that the debate gave Kennedy a big lift, and that was pretty much the end of Nixon's campaign."

Okay, kid, we get the message.

Fortunately, none of these ominous warnings meant anything—the debate went well. We first discussed North Korea and then spent a lot of time talking about the war in Iraq. Kennedy called the war the "number one issue in this race" and repeated his position that although we had made some mistakes, we should stay the course. I noted that we had already spent $300 billion on the war and that while we should not suddenly pull out, we needed to turn the governing of the country over to the Iraqis and over time withdraw our troops. When I was given a chance to ask Kennedy a question, I asked him if he believed he was wrong to vote for the war in Iraq. He said he wasn't.

In the end I felt good about my performance. But maybe some of the credit should go to my lucky red suit coat, which had been given to me by the wife of a moderate Minnesota Republican legislator. I'd seen her wearing the coat at an event, and afterward I'd told her that I liked it and asked where she got it. Then and there she took off the coat and handed it to me, saying, "It's really old and worn out and I don't want it anymore—take it." So study up, NBC tour guide interns past and present: I may have been the first United States Senate candidate to wear a hand-me-down on *Meet the Press*.

My fondest memory of the debate was meeting Tim Russert. After the debate, I had a chance to talk with him about my dad's newspaper coverage of a famous Bills/Vikings game that took place in the middle of a blizzard in Buffalo in 1975. I asked Russert, a die-hard Buffalo Bills fan, if he remembered that as the Vikings' lead got bigger and bigger, the Bills' fans got madder and madder. Soon the fans started throwing snowballs at the visiting team, and one of them hit the Vikings' star running back, Chuck Foreman, in the eye. "Do I remember that game?" Russert said. "*Remember it?* Your dad might have been there covering the game, but I was there throwing the snowballs."

The Homestretch and Election Night

The last stretch of our campaign was heady stuff. I would liken it to the fourth quarter of a football game—even if you're way ahead, a few fumbles or an interception could quickly change the game. President Clinton came to town and spoke at a big event, which meant a lot to me, especially when he praised the kind of campaign we'd been running. We also got a tremendous boost from then Senator Hillary Clinton, who came to Minnesota along with Senators Patty Murray and Blanche Lincoln. I still have a wonderful photo of my mom and Hillary at that event. And in the final weeks of the campaign we got a visit from Senator Barack Obama—his third, actually. He was a big draw after his Democratic National Convention speech in 2004, and there were already rumors that he, along with Hillary, might run for president in 2008.

Obama's first visit to Minnesota was the most memorable, at least from a family standpoint. He had joined us for a rally in St. Louis Park, and at some point in his speech he declared that I would bring "decency" to the U.S. Senate. Abigail was standing nearby, and she immediately looked at me and vigorously shook her head "no" while mouthing the words "the movie, the movie."

For days my daughter had been ribbing me for allowing her to watch *Broadcast News*, a movie I had remembered fondly. Before renting it and showing it to a ten-year-old, I had forgotten (1) the sex scenes and (2) the scene where Holly Hunter gets caught with condoms in the metal detector at the White House Correspondents' Dinner. "What are those?" Abigail had asked. "Cigarettes," I improvised, "cigarettes."

But when I covered up her eyes for the sex scene, she knew she had me. The next day I came home to Post-it notes around the room that said, "Mom who shows R-rated movies lives here." This was all in good fun until she threatened to go public with the story in front of thousands of people.

Barack Obama said I would bring "decency" to Washington? Abigail knew what that word meant, and she wasn't going to let it go. If John hadn't given her his sternest of stern looks—a rare occurrence—we're convinced she would have kept it up throughout Obama's speech, mouthing the words "the movie, the movie" over and over. Fortunately our future president never seemed to notice the family drama taking place right behind him on the stage.

For the last week of the campaign we traveled around the state on a bus tour. Former Vice President Al Gore and North Dakota Senator Byron Dorgan joined me for the tour kickoff at the University of Minnesota. When we got on the campaign bus after an exuberant rally—which featured volunteer students in maroon and gold playing the school's fight song, along with Paul Simon's "You Can Call Me Al" in honor of the vice president—we were impressed to find that the bus was fully equipped and even included a kitchenette. That's when Senator Dorgan put it all in perspective: "Four months from now, when you're sitting at your desk by yourself in the Senate, eating a tuna fish sandwich and trying to understand an obscure legislative provision, remember this moment. It will never be this exciting again."

Sobering advice, but welcome nonetheless.

As Election Day approached, we continued to feel optimistic about our chances of winning. But we were hardly overconfident: no one in the campaign had forgotten that the Republican Party had targeted the open Minnesota seat as its number one opportunity for a switch-over, which was why the Democratic Senatorial Campaign Committee had originally budgeted $3 million to be spent in Minnesota. Meanwhile, it was exciting to know that the country's other Senate races were also going well for the Democrats, though several of those races were much tighter than mine.

And, as it turned out, I inadvertently helped my soon-to-be colleagues simply by being ahead in the polls.

One Sunday morning I was stuck in a small airport in Massachusetts after taking part in a Democratic Senate Campaign fundraising event the night before. The fog was so thick that the plane couldn't take off. I was sitting with John on a bench, glumly insisting that I could never win my race if I missed the Hopkins Raspberry Festival parade, which was certainly going to happen if our flight was delayed much longer. At that moment the phone rang. It was Ben Goldfarb, calling to tell me that an independent poll had just been done showing me nineteen points ahead.

Eager to pass on the good news, I raced through the airport looking for New York Senator Chuck Schumer, the indefatigable Democratic Senate campaign chair. But first I ran into his wife Iris. "Iris," I said breathlessly, "a poll just came out showing me nineteen points ahead."

She grabbed my shoulders, looked me in the eyes, and said, "Great. But don't tell Chuck. He'll cut you off. He'll cut you off today."

Iris was both wrong and right: it didn't happen that morning, but three days later we learned that our state wouldn't be getting that $3 million. Instead the money went to Missouri, where it helped Claire McCaskill; Montana, where it helped Jon Tester; and Virginia, where it helped put Jim Webb over the top.

It was good to know I had helped my friends.

On Election Night my family and friends and supporters gathered in a big ballroom at the Crowne Plaza Hotel in St. Paul. The mood in the room was electric: after so much work, people could feel that a victory was at last within reach. The polls closed at 8:00 p.m., and just minutes later I was declared the projected winner. When all of the votes were counted, I ended up getting 58 percent of the vote to 38 percent for Congressman Kennedy.

In hindsight it was clear that Congressman Kennedy faced an uphill battle from the very beginning because of the anti-Bush wave across the country. Exit polling also showed that independent voters overwhelmingly broke my way and that I had done much better in Greater Minnesota than many Democrats in other races. In a tough loss, Mike Hatch, the Democratic candidate for governor, failed by a very thin margin to unseat the incumbent, Republican Tim Pawlenty. But fortunately for our party,

Democrats would win all three other state constitutional officer races and take back the Minnesota House of Representatives.

I was particularly pleased to learn that I had done well on Minnesota's Iron Range, where my dad was from. There weren't many women legislators in that part of the state, and initially I had encountered some resistance from people up north to the idea that a woman could serve as their U.S. senator. I will never forget a meeting of retired steelworkers and their families in northern Minnesota. At one point an older woman stood up and said, "I have never voted for a woman before. I think they should be home with their kids. But in your case I have decided to make an exception." That woman was Rose Bradovich of Chisholm, and after that meeting she and her husband sent me several small checks. The steelworkers up north were one of the first groups to endorse me in the state. Especially since my grandpa gave practically his whole life to the mines, that meant a lot to me.

I also took joy in the knowledge that after the heartbreaking losses of my friends Joan Growe and Ann Wynia in their U.S. Senate races in '84 and '94, I had taken up their torch and carried it to the finish line. In her postelection analysis, Pat Lopez, now political editor for the *StarTribune*, noted that although Minnesota had never before elected a woman to the Senate, and only thirty-four women in history had served in that capacity, I "never highlighted gender" in the race. In an interview, I told her that I had decided to downplay gender right from the start, in part because the campaigns of the two worthy women who ran before me had both emphasized it.

But if anyone did want to speak about my gender, I was glad to have shown the state that a woman could win by running tough and being unafraid to mix it up in debates. In 1998, during my first campaign for Hennepin County Attorney, I was once accused by my opponent of being "nothing but a street fighter from the Iron Range." All I said in response: "Thank you." During the Senate campaign, I fought back whenever I was attacked. I suppose it's fair to say that sometimes I campaigned like a street fighter, but that's very different from taking the low road and being relentlessly negative.

The state—and the country—needed optimism and a positive path forward, and my election night speech reflected that. I said nice things about Congressman Kennedy, who deserved credit for working very hard, running a good race, and serving our democracy (something he still does as head of George Washington University's Graduate School of Political Management and as the chair of the nonpartisan Economic Club of Minnesota). I also thanked my supporters, my excellent staff, and of course my family. Among other things, I mentioned that whenever Abigail had asked for something during the past two years I had so often said that we would "deal with it after the election" that she had started writing down every promise I made. By Election Day she had compiled a list of twenty-seven promises I'd made to her during the campaign, some of which I revealed to the crowd. They included "buy her a new dress" (done on Election Day), go to Disneyland (we eventually got there), go to IKEA (done, even though we are the state of Target), and buy her another hamster (somehow avoided or forgotten).

As important as the mom list was, another list would define my work over the next few years. It was the list of things I wanted to accomplish in Washington, including pushing through ethics and immigration reform, bringing the troops home from Iraq, and rolling back the Bush tax cuts for the top 1 percent. But as I stood up there on that stage in St. Paul, I had no idea just how hard it would be. Yes, the good people of Minnesota wanted action and they yearned for compromise. To them, gridlock was something that happened in traffic, and filibustering was always done for a good cause, like in the movies.

I believed that, too. And then I got to Washington . . .

Under the Capitol Dome

Blue Sky

In late December 2006, with the campaign and the holidays behind us, John, Abigail, and I made final preparations for the eleven-hundred-mile drive to Washington, D.C., in our family car, the 2001 Saturn. Our destination? Rosslyn, Virginia—a place described by its own county of Arlington as an "urban village," consisting of a whole lot of high-rise apartments (over six thousand units) and layers of corporate offices (over eight million square feet). But our apartment building would be right on the Metro line and within walking distance of the Iwo Jima Memorial and Arlington National Cemetery.

From our family's point of view, what mattered most was that Rosslyn was part of the Arlington school district, a great public school system that had been highly recommended to us by Arkansas Senator Blanche Lincoln. Every morning eleven-year-old Abigail would be taking the long bus ride from Rosslyn to Williamsburg Middle School in Arlington. Joining a new school halfway through the year would be hard enough, but arriving smack in the middle of the Revolutionary War battlefield unit— taught by the formidable sixth-grade history teacher Mrs. Churchill—was certainly a bigger challenge than any senator's first vote.

Our eighteenth-floor, twelve-hundred-square-foot apartment with one parking space would cost us three times more per month than what we'd been paying for our mortgage in Minnesota, so the last thing I wanted to do was shell out even more money for new furniture when we already had a houseful in Minnesota. But as John reminded me more than once, Abigail did need a desk to do her homework, and we needed a kitchen table and, yes, a bed.

Maintaining two households would not be easy or cheap, so I scavenged through our Minnesota house and my mom's and John's parents' basements for old furnishings, cookware, and bedding to bring with us to Washington. I even found my twenty-five-year-old white wicker trunk and chest of drawers (dubbed by John as the "Pier One college dorm bedroom set") and lugged them out of the basement. I had paid for my own furniture in the County Attorney's Office, so the mustard-colored leather couch and chairs, and the faux-Oriental office rug and end tables, would soon become our living room décor in Virginia. After loading up the moving van with the office furniture, the wicker bedroom set, and every hand-me-down kitchen item I could find, I stuffed our car with spillover items like my grandma's Crock-Pot, the dishes from John's bachelor days, and my mom's old silverware.

Over a hundred friends and relatives bid us farewell as we crammed into the car in front of our house in Minneapolis. And then, with Abigail far from happy about her corner-of-the-backseat space—surrounded as she was by throw pillows and cardboard boxes—we began our long journey to Washington, stopping first to greet supporters at Daube's Bakery in Rochester, and then heading east through Wisconsin, Illinois, Indiana, Ohio, Pennsylvania, Maryland, and Virginia. Our daughter would later describe the trip as "the three-day drive that I had long dreaded, due to the fact that I was stuck for a long time with my parents in a tiny car." But somehow she survived, and soon after arriving in Virginia we unpacked everything and set up the apartment, complete with new mattresses from Sleepy's, floor lamps from Target, and, of course, bookshelves courtesy of IKEA.

On a bright, sunny January day a week after we arrived, I was officially sworn in. Many, many Minnesotans joined us for the ceremony and the parties leading up to it. I shared their enthusiasm—I was full of optimism about the new Congress and the years ahead. As I wrote in my personal notes on January 4, 2007:

It was a beautiful day with a bright blue sky. No coats in January! The Minnesotans went crazy. It was like a bright blue breath of fresh air whooshed through the Capitol as the freshman class of 2006 made it official!

Okay, that was supersized optimism.

That morning I was beaming as my three escorts—Norm Coleman, Mark Dayton, and Vice President Mondale—walked me down the "Senate aisle" to my swearing-in in the Senate chamber. Joe Lieberman would later joke that I must have been unusually popular, as he had never seen a new senator come to the ceremony with three Senate escorts. But each of the three meant something special to me: Norm, the hope of bipartisanship and a future friend and colleague; Mark, my immediate predecessor and a public servant with a strong moral compass; and Walter Mondale, my friend and mentor and a beloved former member of the Senate.

I had passed out about two dozen tickets to friends and relatives for the swearing-in, and hundreds of other guests watched the ceremony on closed-circuit TV in our reception room. After the swearing-in, I spoke to the crowd of supporters about the challenges facing our country—from bringing the troops home from Iraq to helping the middle class.

Noting the legacy of Hubert Humphrey's joyful approach to his work in the Senate, I said, "Starting out in the 110th Congress, I, too, remain an optimist. I am an optimist because of the faith the people of my state—from across the political spectrum—put in me to do the right thing."

Our new class of senators also filled me with hope that day. Elected with me were Sherrod Brown of Ohio, Ben Cardin of Maryland, Bob Casey of Pennsylvania, Bob Corker of Tennessee, Claire McCaskill of Missouri, Bernie Sanders of Vermont, Jon Tester of Montana, Sheldon Whitehouse of Rhode Island, and Jim Webb of Virginia. They all brought wisdom and new ideas to Washington, not to mention some wit and good humor. The bond we formed leading up to the election and afterward remains with us today.

I have a lot of happy memories from that magical first week: the two beautiful parties held for me at the homes of Washingtonians Elizabeth and Smith Bagley and Dan and Sunita Leeds, and their good-natured acceptance of the large number of Minnesotans who, expecting cold weather, turned up in their snow boots; the joy on my mom and dad's faces as I was sworn in; Vice President Dick Cheney performing the official swearing-in and joining us for a picture-taking session as I hoped against hope that my eighty-year-old mom didn't use the opportunity to "say what was on her mind" (she was doing a lot of that at the time); my dad getting to meet Ted Kennedy and recounting to Ted that day in 1960 when, as a young reporter, he called the presidential election for his brother; misplacing my official Senate pin on the very first morning; and getting lost numerous times in the labyrinth of the Capitol corridors as we pushed my mom in her post–knee surgery wheelchair as fast as we could.

"Be careful, you're going to lose me!" she would yell from her rolling perch.

"We can't lose you!" I'd shoot back. "We are pushing you in a wheelchair!"

But my most vivid memory of that first day was walking under the cloudless blue sky to the gleaming white, cast-iron Capitol dome. That flawless sky truly made me believe that anything and everything was possible. It was a new beginning for me and for our country. I was the senator for the state of Minnesota.

Transitions

Within the first few months it became clear to John and me that of the three of us, Abigail made the easiest transition. From the first day—when I dropped her off at her new middle school and watched her trip on her seat belt, fall to the sidewalk, and spill her perfectly stacked sixth-grade notebooks and highlighters right in front of a line of kids standing out in front of the school—I knew she would survive the move. Why? She picked herself up, gathered her books and supplies, and turned to me in the car, where I had watched it all unfold while trying to pretend that nothing had happened. With calm assurance she said, "Don't worry about it, Mom. Most of those kids look like eighth graders, so I won't be in classes with them anyway."

That was when I knew she was going to make it in Washington.

Abigail adjusted quickly. She made lots of new friends, learned all the names of the Revolutionary and Civil War generals and battlefields, and repeatedly showed off our apartment building's trash chute to visitors by dropping various items down the steel enclosure and listening to them clank floor by floor down to the bottom. The dad of one of her friends was the commander of a nuclear submarine. We were a long way from Minnesota.

The fact was that not many kids at her middle school—and later at her high school—even knew that her mom was a senator. That was all right by Abigail. As she wrote at the time: "It's not very different having your mom as a Senator. What is unique, though, is that if I want to know what my mom is doing, I just have to turn on C-SPAN."

I tried my best to make it to every dance and piano recital and school conference, but sometimes the Senate vote schedule won out. It helped that Abigail and John were best pals, but sometimes hanging out with dad wasn't quite the same as hanging out with mom—like the time she called me just as I was about to walk into the Senate chamber for a national security vote. The phone vibrated in a maddeningly "don't forget your family" way, and John's name flashed on the phone screen. Since no phone calls are allowed on the Senate floor, I stopped in my tracks as the young pages held open the heavy ornate doors that led to the Senate chamber.

It turned out that Abigail and her dad were at Target shopping for a swimming suit for the end-of-the-year middle school pool party. The invitation specifically said that while bikinis would not be allowed at the party, tankinis were okay. With much emotion Abigail described in ferocious detail how her dad had taken a hard line on any two-piece bathing suit, thereby forbidding her from using the school invitation's tankini loophole.

My daughter needed to right the wrong. That was why she called her mom.

Listening impatiently, I quickly realized the problem—her dad clearly did not understand the crucial difference between a bikini and a tankini.

"Get him on the phone, now," I said to Abigail. "I need to vote."

"Listen," I said to John, "give her a break. Bikinis are banned but tankinis are not."

"What's the difference?" he said. "They all look the same." The Senate pages, still holding open the doors, looked down and tried not to laugh.

"Trust me, there is a difference and it has to do with the amount of fabric covering her stomach. Just let her pick one out."

At the moment I uttered those words, Senator Lindsey Graham came bounding out of the Senate. I almost knocked him down as I tried to dodge to the side.

By now the vote was almost over. "Don't argue with me," I said. "Put your Catholic school memories behind you and buy the tankini."

He relented, she bought the swimsuit, and I made the vote.

Abigail loved to contrast her life with her Arlington classmates by regaling me with stories of all the "helicopter moms" at her school. According to my daughter, they were always "there" for their kids—reviewing their homework, setting their curfews, and picking out their swimsuits in the Target dressing rooms.

She knew that the helicopter-mom label didn't fit me, but one day she finally came up with the right one. "You," she said with great glee, "are a submarine mom."

"What's that?" I asked. "It sounds tough and cool."

"Not really," she said. "It means you lurk beneath the surface and come up unexpectedly from time to time. That's you."

Nice.

For John the transition was the hardest. For one thing, he spent a lot of time on his own, especially since I went home to Minnesota almost every weekend. For another, he spent the first six months—before he started teaching law at George Washington University, and then later at Georgetown and as a professor at the University of Baltimore law school—working for his old law firm in Minneapolis out of our Rosslyn apartment.

It was a lonely beginning, but it did give him time to get involved in a few new activities, including the Spouses of the Senate. He was the first male Senate spouse to truly get involved in the club, so much so that he was put on the hospitality committee and helped plan the club's annual First Lady's luncheon. He did such a good job that when the lunch was held at the United States Botanic Garden, he was seated at the same table as First Lady Laura Bush.

I knew things were getting a bit out of hand with the spouses' club the day Claire McCaskill and I were driving out of the Capitol together to go to an event. Claire spotted John walking across the Capitol lawn and said, "What is John doing walking across the lawn with a box wrapped all in pink paper?"

I yelled out the car window to him: "Where are you going with that pink box?"

"It's a Senate Spouses club event," he yelled back. "I'm going to Jim Webb's wife's baby shower."

Claire and I high-fived, rejoicing in the knowledge that we were witnessing a milestone in Senate spousal history. Rolling down the window, Claire called out to him, "John, that's one of the sexiest things I've ever seen."

Not many members of Congress bring their families with them to Washington anymore, but for me it was a "family first" decision. I wanted John to be part of this new life. I wanted to know Abigail's school and her teachers and her friends. I wanted to be there for the science fairs and the parent nights. But I also didn't want to shortchange my state, which meant that about three weekends out of four I would fly to Minnesota by myself. Sometimes I would get back to my family on Sunday; sometimes I would stretch it to Monday. And for each school break and every summer, John and Abigail would join me at our home in Minneapolis.

That's how we juggled it for years. I always figured it was nothing compared to what most families do every day, with many parents working two or even three jobs just to pay the mortgage or rent. But if John hadn't been such a good sport and such a good dad, it never would have worked. As my colleague Al Franken says about his marriage and the Senate, "Franni and I always like to say that 'we' ran for the Senate, but the truth was that, in the end, only one of us could be senator."

To this day, I know that John made the biggest sacrifice.

How Did I Get Here?

I had to make a big adjustment of my own, of course. Every hour was scheduled, and every day brought a new adventure, a new challenge, and a new hazard. Passing my first bill, going to the White House, seeing the original Declaration of Independence? Those were all big thrills. And getting a call from then Senator Joe Biden and hearing him say he really liked my speech on the floor of the Senate when I thought no one was watching? That was cool, too.

But how did I end up bringing a strawberry yogurt and a plastic spoon on the Senate bus to Gerald Ford's funeral? How did my new classmate and knight in shining armor, Senator Bob Casey, end up carrying that yogurt in his coat pocket into the National Cathedral?

Well, that happened.

And how did I end up going to a meeting with President Bush in the Oval Office and sitting on a big gold pillow on an ornate couch looking like Little Miss Muffet? The president's staff had nicely suggested that I might want to "use a pillow" because I was short and the couch was so deep, but instead of placing the pillow behind my back, as they intended I do, I put it flat on his couch and sat on it.

Well, that happened, too. And I didn't just sit on the pillow for a few minutes—I sat on it for nearly an hour. I realized my error within five minutes but then I just decided to own it.

Sometimes as I entered the Capitol building I would mouth the words of "Once in a Lifetime," the Talking Heads song that starts:

And you may find yourself living in a shotgun shack
And you may find yourself in another part of the world
And you may find yourself behind the wheel of a large automobile
And you may find yourself in a beautiful house, with a beautiful wife
And you may ask yourself
Well . . . How did I get here?

The joke around the Senate is that new senators spend the first few months on the job wandering around the Capitol with their eyes wide open asking exactly that question—"How did I get here?" But then, after dealing with certain of their colleagues in Congress, they spend the rest of their time in office muttering to themselves, "How did *they* get here?"

I still remember my first fancy lunch in the Capitol. My Democratic Senate colleagues and I were seated in the Lyndon Baines Johnson Room at five round tables, and I was awed to be surrounded by icons—Robert

Byrd, Ted Kennedy, Danny Inouye. A huge portrait of LBJ—the former president, vice president, and, most important for our purposes, Senate majority leader—loomed above us. Soon after the lunch began, I walked over to the buffet table and got a salad and what I thought was a bowl of soup.

Just as I was about to dig in, with my soup spoon full of what looked like the creamiest, most delectable soup ever created, Senator Patty Murray ran around the table and grabbed my arm. "Amy," she said, "you just took the entire bowl of Thousand Island dressing and you're about to eat it."

My spoon still suspended in midair, I looked at her confidently and said: "That's what we do in Minnesota. We eat the Thousand Island dressing."

Senate table etiquette was far from my only problem. For starters, my work as county attorney had nothing to do with Congress. I didn't know Washington. I didn't know the people who made it run. I didn't have a group of staff members to "bring over" from the House. But my biggest challenge was that I didn't know the Senate rules. During our first week on the job, all of the new senators began taking turns presiding over the Senate for at least three hours per week. Of course, every one of us made some rookie mistakes when we served as the official "president" of the Senate those first few months, but mine was there for the world to see, or at least the part of the world that watches C-SPAN.

On January 31, 2007, Dick Durbin, the chief whip, approached me at the presiding desk and told me that a certain senator—I no longer remember who it was—might try to put an amendment in. If that happened, no one else would be there to object so I should simply say, "In my capacity as the senator from Minnesota, I object."

"No problem," I said.

Thinking I had all kinds of new powers as a result of Dick's request, I soon saw an opportunity to use them. Senators David Vitter and Mary Landrieu of Louisiana had made a wager on the National Football Conference playoff game between the New Orleans Saints and the Chicago Bears. Their team had lost, and as part of their bet with the Illinois senators, they had agreed to come to the Senate floor that day to speak about the game and congratulate the Chicago Bears on their victory. As soon as the Louisiana senators had satisfied the conditions of their wager, I got my chance to deploy my new procedural trick.

"Speaking in my capacity as a senator from Minnesota," I said audaciously from the elevated presiding dais, gavel close at hand, "I will say that our team, the Vikings, went four times and never won the Super Bowl, so there is always hope."

Suddenly phones were ringing and red lights were going off. One of the Senate parliamentarian's staff members ran over and said, "What are you doing? As Senator Durbin told you, when you're presiding the only thing you can say in your capacity as the senator from Minnesota are the words 'I object.' You can't talk about football teams and Super Bowls. This is a complete breach of Senate protocol."

It was bad enough to hear this reproach and see the ashen faces of the entire floor staff, but then another staffer came running in from the cloakroom and said, "There's a rumor that Senator Byrd is on his way to the floor to talk to you."

This would be the end of me, I thought. West Virginia Senator Robert Byrd was the president pro tempore of the U.S. Senate. After forty-eight years in office, his encyclopedic knowledge of the arcane Senate rules was legendary. He was known for outmaneuvering the savviest of opponents with a single objection or by citing a century-old precedent. Most of all, he was known for zero tolerance when it came to protocol breaches and rules violations.

To say this wasn't a good way to start my congressional career was the senatorial understatement of the century, or at least of the year.

But then something happened, or maybe *someone* happened. I never got a visit—or even a note—from Senator Byrd about the incident.

After that I painstakingly memorized the presiding rules and was careful to follow them to a T. So careful, in fact, that months of presiding would pass without another breach of protocol. But when it happened again, the breach was just as memorable.

One sleepy Thursday afternoon, while presiding over an empty Senate chamber, I got an anonymous note passed through a Senate page that read, "Senator Klobuchar, pull up your shirt, your cleavage is showing."

I bet *that* never happened to Mike Mansfield or Everett Dirksen. (Although for the record, cleavage historians should note that in July of

2007 Hillary Clinton was called out for the same thing when she gave a speech on the Senate floor. At least I wasn't alone.)

I never did figure out who gave me that oh-so-helpful tip. But since the chamber was empty, it must have been someone who was watching the C-SPAN feed. My Senate classmates would laugh at that story for years, and Jon Tester (who did not send me the note) particularly enjoyed ribbing me about it. For months, he would send me "anonymous" notes every time I presided. In bold print they would say things like, "YOUR EARRINGS DON'T MATCH" or "YOUR SHIRT IS WRINKLED, IRON IT."

My learning curve in the Senate was not limited to floor decorum and obscure procedural rules. Early on, I asked for a bunch of committee assignments, each time trying my best to sell my virtues to Majority Leader Harry Reid. In the end, Harry—a master at juggling all such requests— placed me on Agriculture and Forestry, a very important committee for my state. (After all, Minnesota is tenth nationally in forest products, fifth in agriculture, third in soybeans, second in sweet corn and hogs, and first in turkeys.) In time, I would also be given seats on the Commerce Committee, the Judiciary Committee, the Joint Economic Committee, and the Rules Committee. And, in addition to being placed on committees, I was assigned to multiple subcommittees on each of my committees. On the Commerce Committee, for example, I was placed on the Oceans Subcommittee.

Okay, let's be honest here: I'm from Minnesota, and we don't exactly have an ocean.

When I went to my first Oceans Subcommittee hearing, I looked around and realized that every senator on the subcommittee had an ocean except me. I saw Olympia Snowe of Maine, John Kerry of Massachusetts, Trent Lott of Mississippi, Maria Cantwell of Washington State, Bill Nelson of Florida, and Barbara Boxer of California. I finally passed a note to Frank Lautenberg, the senior senator from New Jersey, who was seated next to me.

"I am the only senator on the Oceans Subcommittee who doesn't have an ocean," I wrote.

"No problem," he wrote back, "just come back next year and ask for one."

Welcome to Washington.

Robes in the Russell Courtyard

Our entire class had run their elections on change in Washington, including calling for significant reform to our congressional ethics rules—from limiting corporate charter flights, to establishing gift limits, to making changes to the campaign finance laws and earmark rules. Senator Barack Obama of Illinois, who had been elected only two years before, was also a big proponent of changes, as was long-standing campaign finance reformer Russ Feingold of Wisconsin. Harry Reid, the new majority leader, was well aware that our class of Democratic senators had—as I said in my notes the day of the swearing-in—"whooshed" into Washington under that clear blue sky on a platform of change.

The American people were clearly fed up, and no wonder: the flagrant and well-publicized violations—from lobbyists paying for overseas trips to bundles of cash in a congressional freezer—would drive anyone to vote for change. In many of the congressional races, these kinds of violations—as well as the decision to go to war in Iraq—led to a deep mistrust of incumbents and ultimately led to a Democratic takeover in both the House and the Senate. As new members of Congress, we were as impatient as the public: we wanted to pass reform laws right away. In fact, even as John, Abigail, and I were on that three-day December road trip from Minnesota to Washington, our freshman class and Senator Obama held conference calls on ethics reform legislation. And shortly after the new Congress was seated, our class members held a press conference with Majority Leader Reid and Senator Obama calling for aggressive reform.

Early on I decided I wanted my first Senate speech to be about ethics reform. Traditionally your first speech is a big deal. In the old days—in fact, pretty much up to the time when our class started—the common practice for a new senator was to wait for months and sometimes a year before taking to the floor for a speech. The idea was that new senators should listen and not speak. But that approach didn't suit Sherrod Brown or Claire McCaskill or me, not to mention Bernie Sanders.

With Jon Tester there for moral support, I gave my first floor speech on January 12th, only eight days after being sworn in. After describing the glaring congressional ethics problems and discussing potential solutions, I turned to what I saw as the core issue: decision-making in

Congress was less than honest. Calling for a change to the "business as usual" ways of Washington, I said that we could no longer tolerate a playing field tilted toward special interests and against the middle class. Ethics violations not only eroded the public's trust, they were also at the root of too many public policy decisions that hurt regular people.

Although most senators were in some way supportive of reform, there was an undercurrent of resistance from some of the more senior members of the Senate. They argued that if we weren't careful, the bill could set senators up for inadvertent ethical violations and even jail time. They were also worried that limits on such things as trips, planes, and dinners could end up hurting senators of more modest means—a group that included me and a couple dozen others—since we could not afford the pricey dinners and chartered flights. The wealthy senators, they argued, would not be affected because they could pay for everything.

I particularly remember an amusing note of caution expressed early in the debate by Senator Trent Lott, the Republican whip. Lott was in the Senate chamber the morning I came to the floor to hear Jon Tester deliver his maiden speech on January 9th. When Tester finished, Lott stood up and made extemporaneous remarks while Tester and I sat at our desks. Even as he addressed the presiding officer, Lott often looked in our direction, and at one point he went so far as to mention our states by name. Though he was for the most part positive about the reform bill—and made some good points I agreed with about reforming but not eliminating earmarks—the most memorable part of the speech was the image he conjured up about the century-old Russell Senate Office Building, where many senators have their offices.

"If the bill went too far," he said, "if we start trying to satisfy certain media people, certain ethics groups, there's no limit." If we weren't careful, he warned, all of us in the Senate might ultimately find ourselves "living in robes in the Russell courtyard with no access to the outside."

That vision of a harsh future made me smile, since at the time our entire office staff and I were temporarily working out of a warren of cubicles in a double-wide trailer in the Russell Building courtyard. The trailer was not only a stark contrast to the beautiful public spaces found in the Capitol, it was also really hot. Not until Jim Webb—who started out in a trailer connected to ours—moved to his permanent space did we realize that his trailer housed the temperature control that set our heat. But hey, they were from Virginia and used to hotter climates. We were boiling.

Jon Tester's office was similarly low-glamour. Ranked number 100 in seniority—that would be last—he had been put in the basement of the Dirksen Senate Office Building. He didn't even have a window. I figured he could handle it, though: as a farmer from Montana who had lost three fingers in a meat grinder at age nine, he didn't require a lot of cushy sofas or fancy paintings.

Trent Lott, a well-respected Republican leader who'd served in Congress for thirty-four years, had more than a modicum of clout over Tester and me as we listened from our desks that day. Looking back, however, I now realize that he wasn't being partisan. He just didn't think we quite understood what we were getting ourselves into with our zeal for reform.

As Tester and I sat in one of the back rows of the Senate chamber, surrounded by the ornate balconies and time-worn wooden desks carved with names like "John F. Kennedy," "Daniel Webster," and "Henry Clay," I wrote my classmate a note in response to Lott's comment about ending up in the Russell courtyard in our robes. My trailer is so hot, I told Tester, that I might start wearing a robe anyway, and since I am already working out of a double-wide in the Russell courtyard, I don't have much to lose. Tester, smiling, gave me one of his knowing, crew-cutted nods and winked.

One thing we knew for sure. Even if we were housed in a trailer in the Russell courtyard and a dingy basement office, we were still in the United States Senate. We were a force to be reckoned with—or at least Trent Lott seemed to think so.

A week later, our Senate Democratic class, with the blessing of our leadership and a number of Republican reformers as well, passed the first bill introduced that session: Senate Bill 1, the Honest Leadership and Open Government Act of 2007. In the end it included amendments that we had sponsored to make the original bill even stronger. Later that summer the final bill would go to President Bush and he would sign it into law.

Iraq and Our Troops

In addition to ethics reform, the other public mandate coming out of the 2006 election was to change the course of the war in Iraq. From 2003 to

2006, we had lost more than three thousand U.S. military men and women in the war, forty-five of them Minnesotans. And besides the tragic loss of American and Iraqi lives in the military effort, our country had already spent more than $300 billion on the war.

After my election to the Senate, I wanted to do everything in my power to help end the war. A homily delivered by a Minnesota priest at a funeral held in the Cathedral of St. Paul for a young soldier who died in the war has always stuck with me. At the December 12, 2006, service for Sergeant Bryan McDonough, a twenty-two-year-old National Guard member from Maplewood killed by a roadside bomb near Fallujah, the Catholic priest had looked straight at all the politicians sitting in the front pew (including me) and said: "We are asking our young people to make tremendous sacrifices in Iraq and Afghanistan and other places, at home and abroad. But if we are asking such things from our children, what kind of people must we be?" Reflecting on the parents' painful loss of their child, a 2002 high school graduate who'd studied at St. Cloud Technical College, the priest spoke of Bryan's heroism and sacrifice and how "it takes an eight-foot parent to raise a six-foot child." His central message: "it takes eight-foot-tall parents and leaders and friends to ask our children to stand up to their full stature." He was not so subtly telling us that, as elected officials, we had to rise to the challenges before us like the young men and women sent off to war—and to make the right decisions.

In March 2007, just months after Sergeant McDonough's funeral, Senators Sheldon Whitehouse, Lisa Murkowski, John Sununu, and I flew to Iraq. We traveled to Baghdad and Fallujah, and we met with General David Petraeus, General Ray Odierno, Iraqi officials, and other military commanders throughout the region. Every place we went I sought out our Minnesota soldiers and gave them Twins baseball caps. Later, after we returned home, I called their moms and dads and husbands and wives to tell them how they were doing. We had almost three thousand Minnesota Guard and Reserve troops in Iraq. Many of them had been told they would come home months before, but they kept getting redeployed.

My most enduring memory from our trip to Iraq came near the end as I stood waiting on the tarmac of the Baghdad airport. I was called over by nine firefighters, all proud service members from Duluth who were taking part in a formal ceremony. A few minutes later, six caskets, each draped in the American flag, were carried onto a plane, one after the other. The firefighters didn't know the soldiers who had died. But they stood tall and saluted each casket as the fallen soldiers began their final journey home.

A few weeks after I returned from Iraq I was tapped to give the national response to President Bush's weekly radio address. After describing my trip to Iraq, I spoke about our soldiers' bravery and commitment but also about the need to withdraw our combat forces on a sensible timetable, train the Iraqi police, and transition to Iraqi governance. I also discussed a meeting the four senators had had about our trip with President Bush when we returned. "I appreciated the time he took to honestly discuss our points of agreement and disagreement on the war," I said. "I told him that now is the time to forge cooperation with our Democrats in Congress." Joining many of my Senate colleagues, I voted numerous times to bring our soldiers home on a measured timetable.

But our work was far from done. Between the Gulf War in the early 1990s and our invasions of Iraq and Afghanistan, our country had spawned a generation of young veterans with unique needs. All too often they had traumatic brain injuries (the signature injury coming out of these wars) or mental health issues or a lack of gainful employment when they returned home. As I said at dozens of deployment and welcome home ceremonies, we owed it to our troops to do the right thing—despite major disagreements about the policy in Iraq, our nation simply could not make the same mistake that so many made during the war in Vietnam. This time, we would agree to disagree about the war but still respect and support the warriors.

"When our troops signed up to serve our country there wasn't a waiting line," I would say, "and when they come home to our country and they need a job or a house or health care or an education, there should never be a waiting line in the United States of America."

Words are fine, but actions are more important. The month after I was sworn in, we learned about the unacceptably low level of care at Walter Reed Army Medical Center. The Senate later voted to dramatically increase funding for veterans' health care, including support for caregivers. And under Senator Jim Webb's leadership, we passed the 21st

Century GI Bill of Rights, which ensures that our soldiers and National Guard members get the educational benefits they deserve.

At the same time, Norm Coleman and I worked together to expand Minnesota's groundbreaking "Beyond the Yellow Ribbon" initiative (started by Governor Tim Pawlenty and championed by my Senate predecessor, Mark Dayton) to other states. The idea behind the program was to make sure that those service members who didn't have an active-duty base—like Guard members and Reservists—would have a support network when they returned from the war. I also paired up with our two Minnesota veterans in Congress—Republican John Kline and Democrat Tim Walz—to pass legislation focused on everything from preserving soldiers' benefits to helping our vets get housing and mental health services.

But for me, the most rewarding work was helping individual veterans like Staff Sergeant Ryan Hallberg of Coon Rapids, Minnesota, who lost his leg to a roadside bomb in Iraq. Despite earning a Purple Heart for his injuries, he was twice denied his benefits, purportedly because there was "not enough medical information" to support his claim—which turned out to mean that his medical records were lost by Walter Reed hospital. All you had to do was look at Ryan's amputated leg to know that, as Ryan put it, he'd donated his limb to his country. But his country owed him a lot more than a dysfunctional bureaucracy, and I fought to get him the benefits he was owed by personally calling government officials. The day he got the check we celebrated with his family and friends.

Whatever their war, our veterans deserve to be treated with respect and dignity. I often remind the hardworking veterans' caseworkers on my staff of the night I met one of the World War II honor flights that had just returned to Minneapolis from Washington, D.C. On the flight were more than one hundred Minnesota vets who'd visited the World War II Memorial on the National Mall. For many of them, this was the first and last time they'd see the memorial. Late that evening, when they landed back in Minnesota their families greeted them at the airport. When the World War II heroes got off the plane, many of them were using wheelchairs or walkers. Tears streamed down their cheeks as they were cheered on by their families, all holding up balloons and signs with their names.

A festive polka band was playing near the luggage area. Near the end of the event, one of the vets approached me and asked me to dance. But the band chose precisely that moment to stop playing, so I told him, "I am so sorry, sir, the music just ended."

"Oh," he said, "that doesn't matter. I have a really good voice."

He did indeed, and so as he sang the old Frankie Valli song that goes *"You're just too good to be true / Can't take my eyes off of you,"* we danced around that airport, the eighty-plus-year-old veteran and me. Yes, I thought to myself, this is how all our veterans should be treated, whether they fought in World War II or Korea or Vietnam or Iraq or Afghanistan. They should be greeted with signs and balloons. They should be cheered and saluted. They should be dancing with senators at the airport.

A Bridge Just Shouldn't Fall Down

Late in the day on August 1, 2007, I was leaving the U.S. Capitol to go to an event, trying over and over to call Keith Ellison, our Minneapolis congressman, about a pending bill. "Keith gets too many messages and his phone goes on overload," I said to one of my staff members. "Now I can't even connect."

Well, I was wrong. The reason Keith didn't answer was that the phone system in the 612 area code was overwhelmed by people calling to check on friends and loved ones. A major bridge in Minneapolis, the I-35W Mississippi River Bridge, had collapsed during the evening rush hour. But it wasn't just a bridge: it was a big chunk of an eight-lane highway, one of the main arteries north out of Minneapolis and one of the busiest bridges in our state, carrying an average of 140,000 vehicles a day. And it was eight blocks from my house.

Immediate reports from the scene were sketchy, but it was already clear that a number of people had died. A thousand-foot section of the bridge had collapsed, with the bridge's main span falling more than one hundred feet into the murky, fifteen-foot-deep Mississippi River below. Cars and trucks were submerged in the river, ambulances were rushing survivors to nearby hospitals, and a school bus was perched precariously on the broken bridge's edge. Minnesota Governor Tim Pawlenty accurately described it as "a catastrophe of historic proportions."

Within an hour Norm Coleman and I had talked on the phone. By then we'd learned that President Bush's transportation secretary, Mary Peters, would be flying to Minneapolis in the morning and that she had invited the two of us to accompany her to the scene. Despite some votes scheduled for the next day, Norm and I immediately decided to go. Fixing the bridge would be a federal responsibility and we knew it would be our job to get the funding through the Senate.

Many more grim details emerged by the next morning. Security camera footage from the Army Corps of Engineers had captured the bridge's horrifying collapse. One hundred and eleven vehicles were involved, and a number of the cars and trucks, along with their occupants, had fallen as much as 115 feet into the river. The security video showed the bridge and the dozens of vehicles on it free-falling into the water and onto the riverbank and rail yard below. Later we would learn that thirteen people lost their lives that tragic day, and well over one hundred others were injured. Given that so many cars ended up submerged in the Mississippi River, it was a near miracle that more lives weren't lost.

Our first responders and 911 system operators had planned and rehearsed for disasters for years, and it made a big difference that many first-rate hospitals were located nearby. Quick and capable responses by state and local officials, led by Minneapolis Mayor R. T. Rybak, made a difference, too. But what mattered most was the courage and bravery of ordinary citizens. Under unimaginably difficult circumstances, true heroes emerged.

Who could forget the image of the off-duty Minneapolis firefighter—a woman named Shannon Hanson—diving in and out of the water searching for survivors up and down the river? Or Paul Eickstadt, the fifty-one-year-old driver of a Taystee semi-truck, who burned to death in a crash after veering to give a school bus full of young kids space as the bridge collapsed? Or a youth worker named Jeremy Hernandez, who, after that school bus had fallen thirty feet and was resting by the burning truck and alongside the guardrail of the broken bridge, had the presence of mind to kick open the emergency door and one by one hand fifty-two frightened schoolkids out the back of the bus to other survivors?

Instead of running away from the disaster, so many men and women ran toward it. We owed it to them, as well as to the survivors and the families of those who had been killed, not only to find out what had caused

the tragedy but also to rebuild the bridge. As I said the day after the collapse, a bridge just shouldn't fall down in the middle of America. Not a
bridge that's a few blocks from my house, not an eight-lane highway, not
a bridge that I drive over every day with my husband and my daughter.
But that's what happened that sunny summer evening in Minneapolis.

I had been in the Senate for only seven months, but I knew this was
my first real test of leadership. I had two major responsibilities. First, I
had to secure the money in the Senate for a bridge replacement as soon as
possible. Beyond the obvious tragedy, the lack of a bridge that carried tens
of thousands of vehicles each day was a major impediment for commut-
ers and commerce, costing our state an estimated $400,000 per day. Sec-
ond, I had to make sure the federal government—working through the
National Transportation Safety Board—got to the bottom of how this
disaster had happened as quickly and as thoroughly as possible.

Back in Washington, Norm and I worked with our Minnesota House
colleagues Congressman Jim Oberstar (my Iron Range ally and the powerful chair of the House Transportation Committee) and Congressman
Keith Ellison. The four of us quickly agreed to introduce a bill that would
waive the $100 million federal cap so that Minnesota could receive suffi-
cient funds to rebuild the bridge from the U.S. Government's Emergency
Relief Program.

Norm and I passed that bill in the Senate two days after the collapse
and before the last victim had even been recovered from the river. Jim and
Keith went on to pass it in the House. But our work was not done. The
initial action had simply waived the cap and authorized the spending.
Now we needed to get the actual money.

A month later, the Senate began debating a major bill that would provide infrastructure funding for such projects as bridges, highways, and
airports. The bill had long been in the works, but the collapsed bridge provided a powerful argument for its passage. In speeches, numerous senators on both sides of the aisle made impassioned calls to action using our
broken bridge as the reason to pass the legislation. The only problem? The
legislation divvied up the infrastructure money among the states under
a preexisting formula—and the extra funding needed for our bridge wasn't
in the bill.

The weekend before the vote on the legislation, I called Senator Reid,

Senator Durbin, and Senator Murray, the chair of the Transportation Sub-committee of Appropriations, about getting an amendment added to the bill to include our funding. They all pledged to help, but it wasn't clear how this could work and there was a lot of talk about taking care of the funding in a later bill. I was also told by some senators that by amending the bill, I would prompt other senators to add their own provisions for extra funding in their states, which could bring down the entire legislation.

None of that talk made any sense to me. Our bridge had actually *fallen down*, so I prepared an amendment to add the funding to fix it. As I told my colleagues at the Democratic caucus lunch that week, it was hypocritical for any senator to be using the I-35W bridge as the justification for passing the infrastructure bill if the legislation didn't provide the funding to fix our bridge. The fact that the bill lacked the necessary funding was a surprise to many of them and they all vowed to help. To make my case, I also said the same thing to the press.

Then, on the morning of Tuesday, September 11, 2007, the anniversary of 9/11, I walked into the Senate chamber and sat at my desk before the Senate opened for business. The previous night, I'd decided that as a brand-new senator I didn't seem to have the clout to get the money through the normal channels, so I devised a protest strategy. My plan? I wouldn't leave my seat in the chamber until my funding amendment was included in the larger legislation, no matter how long it took. Given that I was only a freshman member of the Senate, I couldn't think of any other way to call the public's attention to the extreme hypocrisy of the situation.

When the Senate opened I was the only senator in the chamber except for the presiding officer and the leaders. As was the customary practice, Chaplain Barry Black opened the Senate with a prayer. The next thing I knew, Senator Durbin, the chief whip, came over and sat down next to me.

"Somehow I think you're here to do more than pray," he said.

"Yes," I said, "I need my funding. I don't want to hear another senator talk the talk about our bridge and not put up the money to fix it."

"I'll help you," he said.

As the morning got under way he suggested I ask Senator John Cornyn of Texas to "yield" some of his speaking time to allow me to call up my amendment. He said he thought Cornyn could pause in his speech about another amendment and then allow me to make the procedural motion.

At an appropriate moment, addressing the Senate's presiding officer, I asked, "Mr. President, will the Senator yield for one minute?"

"Mr. President," answered Senator Cornyn, "I will not yield at this time, although after I get through speaking I am happy to yield to my colleague."

Turning to the chief whip, I said, "Okay, Durbin, that didn't go too well."

After more speeches by other senators, and more strategic planning with Senator Durbin, I got a break when Senator Murray addressed the chamber and noted that "the senator from Minnesota has been waiting for some time." She then asked that I be given the opportunity to speak. This time Senator Cornyn, who later became a frequent partner of mine on a range of bills, extended his senatorial courtesy and did not object.

Ultimately the amendment—cosponsored by Senator Coleman—was included in the Senate bill, which passed two days later. And, by the end of the year, after negotiations with the House, the infrastructure legislation, including the bridge funding, was signed into law by President Bush.

The new bridge was built in record time, taking only 339 days from start to finish. It opened for business on September 18, 2008, a little more than thirteen months after the collapse. A short while later, the National Transportation Safety Board completed its investigation into the disaster. The NTSB announced that the primary cause of the collapse of the 1960s-era bridge was an inadequate load capacity due to a design flaw involving the large steel gusset plates that connected the bridge's girders. On the day of the collapse, there were heavy construction vehicles and hundreds of thousands of pounds of sand and gravel on the bridge, and its gusset plates—already bowed and too thin to handle the load— fractured, leading to the bridge's catastrophic failure at 6:05 p.m. during the August 1st rush hour. The NTSB's report also pointed to a lack of appropriate inspection of the poorly designed gusset plates and the lack of construction repair guidance as additional issues.

The rebuilding of the I-35W bridge was a federal project, and President Bush and his transportation secretary, Mary Peters, were an enormous help. They promised they would expedite the federal funds and approvals for a new bridge and they did. President Bush personally visited the site three days after the collapse, and he invited Norm and me and members of our congressional delegation, including Representatives Ellison, Kline, and Bachmann, to accompany him on Air Force One. Before inviting the House members to join him in his private office on the plane, President Bush asked Norm and me to meet with him and Karl Rove and his chief of staff, Andy Card.

The president was pleasant and engaging. After talking at length about the bridge, we turned to a lighter subject. I reminded him that after his last State of the Union address, one current occupant of the plane—Representative Michele Bachmann—had him in her grasp for a significant amount of time in the House chamber in front of all the cameras. The TV networks had clocked her clutch at thirty seconds, with video footage recording the newly elected congresswoman embracing him, kissing the president's cheek, and collecting two autographs.

The president was quite amused by my mention of the story and kept teasing me about it. When we landed he called me over after a police officer I knew gave me a hug. President Bush jokingly told me I should be careful about setting the kind of precedent he'd unwittingly set with Representative Bachmann after the State of the Union.

"Oh," I said, "I can hug the cop. You just can't kiss Representative Bachmann again because the stopwatches will start running."

Though I had been in office for less than a year, the Air Force One meeting was the second time I had met with President Bush. The first was a lengthy conversation in the Oval Office with my three colleagues in the Senate after we returned from Iraq. At that meeting I had told the president that our Minnesota National Guard Red Bulls were the longest-serving National Guard unit in Iraq, and I hoped that they would be brought home as soon as possible and not given another extension. During our meeting on his plane four months later, the president brought up the Red Bulls and mentioned that the unit had indeed come home. I was surprised that Bush remembered all the details of our previous conversation. Though he never implied that our conversation made a difference in the timing of their return, since they were slotted to come home then anyway, the fact that the president had clearly looked into the situation and followed up with me was impressive.

As much as I disagreed with President Bush about the invasion of Iraq and a number of his economic policies, I truly appreciated how he treated me during his last two years in office. After surveying the I-35W bridge site, he offered his prayers on behalf of the American people, thanked the first responders and all of Minnesota's elected officials for "working in a coordinated way to respond to this tragedy," and solemnly pledged "to get this bridge rebuilt."

For me, demonizing George Bush wasn't the answer. That wouldn't bring the Red Bulls home any sooner or fix the bridge any faster. What really mattered was that President Bush had followed up on my question about the Red Bulls and delivered on the bridge.

Putting People First

Getting the money to rebuild a major bridge and working on Minnesota National Guard issues were important constituent causes, but sometimes the work of a senator is not nearly so visible. Sometimes, in fact, the work affects only one life, one person's cause.

I figure that if my job and my title can solve a problem when nothing else can, I should do something about it. Besides, helping one person or one family can often result in a solution that helps many others. As Bill Clinton often said during his 1992 presidential campaign, "putting people first" is a good priority for any elected official.

My consumer work in the Senate started with a little girl in a swimming pool. I first met Abbey Taylor, a six-year-old with beautiful brown eyes and a big smile, in Children's Hospital in Minneapolis. In June of 2007, she had been horribly injured in a kids' wading pool in a suburban country club. Abbey was sitting on the floor of the children's pool when, due to the faulty design and installation of a drain cover, the pool drain literally sucked out her intestines.

When I saw the story about Abbey in our local newspaper, I had to stop reading it because the details were so disturbing. I thought it must have been a freak accident. But after receiving a call from Congressman Jim Ramstad, I soon learned that these types of drain covers had failed to protect children many times, causing dozens of deaths and lots of serious injuries. The drain cover defect even had a name: pool entrapment. I also learned that legislation designed to make pools safer—the Virginia Graeme Baker Pool and Spa Safety Act, named after former U.S.

Secretary of State James Baker's granddaughter, who had drowned in a pool due to a defective drain—had been languishing in Congress for years.

A few weeks after this tragic accident, Abbey's parents, Scott and Katey Taylor, invited me to meet their daughter in her hospital room. Looking up from her coloring book, the little girl told me that she didn't want this to happen to any other boy or girl ever again and she wanted me to fix it. Her parents said the same.

What was I going to tell them? That the common wisdom in Washington was that after its last defeat, the bill aimed at reducing pool deaths was going nowhere?

I didn't tell them that. Instead, I went to work. I started by talking with Commerce Committee Chairman Dan Inouye and Republican ranking member Ted Stevens (two World War II vets who were best friends and knew how to get things done). They pledged to help. I then met with Mark Pryor of Arkansas—a kind and devoted senator whom I already knew from our weekly prayer breakfast meetings—who was the head of the Consumer Subcommittee of Commerce and the stalled bill's chief author. Mark went out of his way to meet with Abbey and her dad and me in Minneapolis during a period when Abbey was in between surgeries and out of the hospital. I will never forget the sight of the little girl with her beaded pink purse meeting with two senators at the fancy downtown Minneapolis Club.

Sadly, the draft bill had been weakened over time so that it would only require better drains on pools yet to be built. That made no sense. With the help of Senator Stevens and Representative Debbie Wasserman Schultz in the House, I worked to significantly strengthen the bill so that it required anti-entrapment drain covers for all existing public pools. I still remember Ted Stevens's reaction when I called him at home one day and asked for his support to improve the bill: "Sure I'll help you. I used to be a lifeguard so I get it. Besides, we don't have a lot of pools in Alaska anyway!"

Back in Minnesota, Scott, Katey, and Abbey Taylor always believed the bill would pass. And with Abbey's health deteriorating, her parents knew this bill could be her legacy, her gift to other children. While I was working on the bill, Scott called me every single week to get an update and encourage me to move forward. He even offered to come to Washington if I thought it would help.

Sometimes I had good news for Scott when he called. I remember being especially happy when I told him that we had succeeded in getting the stronger version of the bill through the Commerce Committee. Other calls weren't nearly as upbeat, such as the time I had to tell Scott that Senator Tom Coburn, a regulatory and fiscal watchdog, had an issue with the bill. Senator Coburn was blocking the bill from being voted on before the full Senate, and the Senate's rules made it all too easy for him to do that.

A bill can move through the Senate in one of three ways: it can pass unanimously; it can pass as an amendment to a bigger bill; or, as was the case with our pool safety bill, it can be left on its own for a vote, which means that any individual member can hold up the bill for final passage for an entire week, during which time no other bills can be considered. The rules allow one senator to do that, even if the vote on the legislation is ultimately 99–1.

While safety groups pushed to get Senator Coburn to change his mind, I negotiated with him in good faith for a couple of weeks to try to address his concerns. I also started giving floor speeches about the fact that the bill was being blocked. Looking for a way out of the impasse, Harry Reid and Trent Lott worked to attach the pool safety bill to an unrelated energy bill, the Energy Independence and Security Act of 2007. In the end our bill got attached to the bigger bill, passed the Senate on December 13th, and was signed into law by President Bush on December 19th.

Against all odds, the Taylors had won.

Calling Scott Taylor from the Senate cloakroom and telling him that we had passed the bill is still one of my best moments in the Senate. He had never given up hope, and neither had Katey or Abbey. Sadly, Abbey would not live much longer. She died the following March after braving the last of her sixteen surgeries, this time a triple organ transplant. Although Abbey did not survive, her fighting spirit, her big smile, and her parents' willingness to tell her story to the world made all the difference. And since the bill's passage, deaths from public swimming pool entrapments have been significantly reduced.

After that experience I knew that my seat on the Commerce Committee—and later the Judiciary Committee—put me in a strong position to pass consumer protection bills. I also realized that if my previous job as a prosecutor didn't immediately equip me to deal with the ways of Washington, it did provide me with the skills I needed to work on consumer safety issues. And because my work had been nonpartisan for such a long time, I came into the Senate with a problem-solving mind-set that probably made it easier for me to partner with Republicans to put my ideas into action.

My other advantage? I had constituents who were never shy to tell me when things were messed up. Minnesota has one of the highest voter turnouts in the nation, and the people of our state—even when they don't agree with you or have always voted for the other party—still believe that individual citizens should be able to influence policy decisions. Scott Taylor is a Republican, as are many of the other constituents I've helped over the years. As the senator from Minnesota, my job is to help people, no matter who they are, or where they come from, or who they voted for.

Not All Angels Fly

When our daughter was four she was in the Christmas nativity play at our church. Her assignment was to play the part of the guardian angel. One day, as we sat in a pew during the rehearsal, she told me she didn't want to play her part. She was all decked out in her angel costume, her giant wings rising up on each side, but she was miserable.

"Why won't you go up and practice?" I asked.

"I want to be the donkey," she said.

"You can't be the donkey," I said, eyeing the two teenage boys huddling and sweating in their donkey costume. "Those boys are the donkey."

"I want to be Mary," she offered.

"You can't be Mary—you're too young to be Mary. Why don't you want to be the angel? You get to go out at the end and spread your wings. It's the best part."

Pausing, she looked up dramatically to the top of the vaulted ceiling above us. Then she leaned over and whispered in my ear. "Mom, I don't know how to tell them. I can't be the angel. I don't know how to fly!"

I looked up at the ceiling for a moment and whispered back: "That's okay, honey, you can still do the part. Not all angels fly."

Not all angels fly.

To this day I think of Scott, Katey, and Abbey Taylor—and all the people who put their faith in our imperfect democracy—as our guardian angels. They are guardian angels for our politics in that they believe that citizen advocacy matters. They are guardian angels for their fellow citizens because their actions often make a difference for people they will never meet and never know. Through their work, they give other people the wings to fly.

The Taylors weren't my only guardian angels.

There was Axel Zirbes and his parents. A young boy with leukemia, Axel was going to have to travel to Canada to receive the cancer treatments he needed because his prescribed drugs were suddenly unavailable in our country. Axel's family, along with several Minnesota pharmacists and doctors, urged me to lead an effort to set up a better process for reducing prescription drug shortages. When I first began working on the legislation, only my pals, Senators Bob Casey and Susan Collins, would sign on. But as the drug shortages grew, and after CBS News' chief medical correspondent Dr. Jon LaPook did an Emmy Award–winning segment on the issue, more senators joined me on the bill. Ultimately the legislation passed the Senate by a vote of 96–1 and the House by a vote of 387–5. The bill—which started with Axel, his parents, and a few pharmacists and doctors in my state—has now become the law of the land.

Time and time again, my constituents have guided my work in the Senate. At the urging of Cheryl Burt, a Minnesota mom whose two young children, Nicholas and Zachary, died of carbon monoxide poisoning, I introduced a bill to incentivize the installation of carbon monoxide detectors. After three Minnesota nursing home residents perished from eating contaminated peanut butter, I worked with Republican Senator Saxby Chambliss of Georgia to pass a bill establishing Food Safety Centers of Excellence, and the University of Minnesota is one of them.

Then there was Jarnell Brown, the four-year-old boy who died from accidentally swallowing a free charm that had come with a pair of tennis shoes. Jarnell didn't die from choking on the charm—he died because the charm was 99 percent lead. In 2007 and 2008, with unprecedented recalls of millions of toys under way, senators on the Commerce Committee began introducing bills to bolster the ability of the Consumer Product Safety Commission to regulate and monitor children's products, particularly those from foreign countries. With the help of our superb staff members Tamara Fucile and Kate Nilan I wrote the lead standard that became a major part of the Consumer Product Safety Improvement Act of 2008, and with a strong coalition of safety advocates and businesses behind us, the legislation passed the Senate on a 79–13 bipartisan vote.

While there are many other stories of legislative successes based on the good hearts and good will of my constituents, my favorite involves the Merkouris family of Cambridge, Minnesota, who had the unimaginable dream of adopting nine sisters and brothers from the Philippines. Tim and Renee Merkouris had fallen in love with the nine children when they visited them in a Philippine orphanage. The kids' story was tragic: their mom had died, and all nine children were put in an orphanage. The family wanted to stay together, but when the two oldest children turned sixteen and seventeen, they became ineligible for adoption in the United States.

Tim and Renee, already parents to three biological children and two adopted ones, were ready for these nine kids. They had expanded their farmhouse and added more sleeping space, a bigger basement, and of course a bigger laundry room. But the law was inflexible and it required the Merkourises to make a painful decision: Should they leave behind the two older kids—Jeneviev and Nino—who were no longer eligible for adoption under U.S. law and adopt the other seven children? Or should they wait and try to find a way to keep the family together and bring home all nine kids? It was a Sophie's choice, but the Merkourises, strong Christians that they are, believed that God would not have wanted a restrictive legal standard to get in the way of keeping the family together. There was only one solution: the law had to be changed. They brought their case to me.

I led the bill to change the adoption restriction, and along the way I got the help of Senator Mary Landrieu (my mentor and a longtime adoption leader), Senator Jeff Sessions (who made some critical calls at just the right time), Senator Jim Inhofe, as well as several House members, including Representative Zoe Lofgren of California. It took more than seventeen months, but in the end (with great staff work by Marian Grove) we were able to pass legislation that allows sixteen- and seventeen-year-old kids from other countries to be adopted if they have a younger sibling who is also being adopted. The International Adoption Simplification Act meant that after years of waiting, thousands of kids, including the children the Merkouris family adopted, would be able to come to the United States to loving parents.

Tim and Renee Merkouris were our true heroes. They didn't just help their children, they helped so many other children. When we met resistance in the House and the Senate, the Merkourises volunteered to come to Washington to help. They went from office to office, showing staffers of recalcitrant members a heart-wrenching video of the nine children in the Philippine orphanage. Sometimes staff members would call our office in tears and promise to get their senator or representative to stop objecting to the bill.

After the legislation was signed into law, it was such a joy to visit the Merkourises and meet all nine of their adopted children. Seeing them smiling and buoyant in their new home, I felt as if I'd suddenly landed in a Minnesota/Philippines production of *The Sound of Music*. The kids had come to Minnesota from the Philippines in the middle of the winter, yet they were as happy and as warm as could be because they were home with a family who loved them.

At an event celebrating the Merkourises' adoption at Minnesota's Bethel College, one speaker called the passage of the bill allowing the children to be adopted "a miracle." In these days of legislative gridlock, I suppose that's an understandable response. But to me it's the Merkourises— and all the citizens I've worked with over the years who never give up faith that government can work for them—who are the true miracles. They have been my guardian angels.

10

Governing

Governing by Crisis

As I learned during my first few years in the Senate, governing is in large part about taking on the concerns—both big and small—of the people of this country. It means listening to a wide range of voices and figuring out how to solve difficult problems. It means describing those solutions clearly and then coming up with creative ways to get people and politicians behind them. That's governing.

But the part of governing that seems to have eluded our country so far in this century has been governing for the long term. We have found it increasingly hard to anticipate both our problems and our opportunities. Instead we have been governing by crisis.

There is no better example of this than America's 2008 financial collapse.

During the summer of 2008 I started to get more and more constituent calls and visits about financial issues, job losses, and mortgage defaults. Soon it became clear that years of easy credit, lax financial regulations, and regulatory loopholes had allowed certain investment banks and mortgage lenders to make a lot of money at the expense of ordinary citizens. Predatory lending and poor underwriting practices, coupled with the sale of opaque, complex securities, had dramatically increased financial risk at the expense of the country's long-term economic stability.

Then came disaster: when the housing and global credit markets collapsed—when the financial industry's house of cards fell and its fancy financial instruments turned out to be worth less than the paper they were printed on—millions of regular people who had had nothing to do with those high-flying banks or lenders were badly hurt. Home values tumbled, the assets in 401(k) plans and pensions tanked, and people's life savings were lost or put at risk. Because of bad decision-making by credit-rating agencies and regulators—as well as in the housing, banking, and financial services industries—a chain reaction was set in motion. It was brought about by a dizzying array of forces, including poor accounting practices, lies and misrepresentations, and downright greed, but it sent financial markets into a panic not seen since the Stock Market Crash of 1929.

It happened all too fast, putting homeowners underwater and businesses into bankruptcy. On September 7, 2008, the U.S. government took over mortgage giants Fannie Mae and Freddie Mac. On September 15th, Lehman Brothers—a once well-respected investment bank—filed for bankruptcy, sending shock waves throughout the entire financial system, both at home and abroad. The next day, AIG, the world's biggest insurer, took an $85 billion federal bailout.

On Friday, September 19th we held an emergency senators' conference call with Treasury Secretary Hank Paulson and Federal Reserve Chairman Ben Bernanke. Describing the even more devastating financial consequences they thought would result from government inaction, they made their case for immediate, aggressive legislation that would allow the government to loan money to banks and to mortgage and insurance businesses, which would in turn prevent more bankruptcies and stabilize the financial markets.

That conference call would soon be followed by a number of meetings with Paulson, Bernanke, and other Bush administration officials. Perhaps the starkest warning came from Federal Reserve Chairman Bernanke himself. The day before the conference call he had warned that if Congress did nothing, "we may not have an economy on Monday."

The underlying premise—that the government would have to help out predominately East Coast investment banks that had been making enormous amounts of money for years—was tough to swallow. The idea that the taxpayers could ultimately foot the bill for their folly was even worse. It was especially galling for a senator from Minnesota because the vast majority of our banks, including our many community banks, midsize TCF Bank, and Minnesota-based U.S. Bank (now the sixth-largest bank in the country), had not gotten themselves into Wall Street–sized trouble. The reason was obvious: our banks had not engaged in the same risky behavior. The executives running our banks may have made less money than high-rolling financiers over the years, but their prudence would not be rewarded in a world where investment firms could simply run to the government and get bailed out whenever they got into trouble.

The infuriating part was that the crisis could have been prevented. People like Sheila Bair, the chair of the Federal Deposit Insurance Corporation, had long been voicing concerns to the Bush administration about the threat of subprime mortgages to the economy. As I said in a Senate floor speech in September, "During the past eight years, the financial and economic policies of this administration have been off course. . . . It permitted the large financial institutions to run amok, to turn the economy into a gambling hall playing with funny money. Finally, in the eleventh hour, the house managers, Bernanke and Paulson, have been asked to step in to shut down the game."

The original Troubled Asset Relief Program bill—authorizing $700 billion to be spent on buying distressed mortgage-related assets—was presented to Congress overnight on September 20th as a three-page document. It would be a considerable understatement to say that the reaction among senators (including myself) was negative. I still remember Bernie Sanders yelling at Hank Paulson, complaining about the "huge" (with his Brooklyn-accented dropped "h") amount of money they wanted us to fork over. As Bernie noted, they were expecting us to give them $700 billion on the promise of a three-page bill that contained no real checks on their authority and included no relief for individual home owners. I had signed car loans and credit applications that were longer.

The bill was eventually redrafted, and the new version came in at 169 pages. Some congressional oversight was added, along with a requirement that the government be reasonably transparent about its actions. Even so, the essential purpose of the legislation was to stabilize the economy by keeping the large financial institutions afloat.

So much more needed to be done. I pledged that after we stabilized the financial system, our next major bill would have to provide help for people on Main Street. We also needed to tighten our financial regulations so that this couldn't happen again. But right then—in September of 2008, less than two months before a presidential election—I had to decide how to respond to the immediate crisis. At some point you don't have the luxury to "change the bill" or "add more provisions."

The urgent question was this: Did I believe these loans and asset purchases were necessary? Furthermore, did I believe that if we did nothing the consequences for regular people would be worse? In the end, along with seventy-three other Democratic and Republican members of the Senate, including presidential candidates Senators Obama and McCain, I came down on the side of yes and voted for the bill. After some up-and-down votes in the House, with the stock market plunging further with each negative vote, the TARP bill was signed into law by President Bush on October 3, 2008.

Governing by Crisis—Part II

The financial industry's near collapse soon led to another crisis that hit much closer to home: long-term job losses all across the country. As soon as President Obama took office the following January, congressional debate turned to stimulus funding. I supported the idea of public investment as a way to bolster our economy.

By this point our country was shedding jobs at an alarming rate. In January 2009 alone, the United States lost more jobs than there were people in the state of Vermont. I was getting countless calls and letters from people who were hurting. One woman wrote to say that she had planned to use the money she'd inherited to help pay for her daughter's wedding but then lost it in the stock market. I met another woman in a Litchfield, Minnesota, cafe who said she was working three jobs just so she could get her kids Christmas presents. Then there was the man who wrote that after he and his wife put their daughters to bed at night, they would sit at their kitchen table and put their heads in their hands because they didn't know how they could make ends meet.

The battle over stimulus funding raged on through February. I had initially believed that our bill would focus on investing in infrastructure, energy, and broadband Internet services. I thought those investments would plow money into the economy quickly and provide help in areas such as construction and manufacturing, both of which were experiencing enormous job losses. The final legislation did some of that, but it also divvied up the money among way too many programs. I would have preferred a more targeted bill, but as with the TARP bill, at some point I didn't have the luxury of making the perfect the enemy of the good. Hundreds of thousands of jobs were being lost and a lot of people were suffering. In the end, we passed the Democratic bill and on February 17, 2009, President Obama signed it into law.

The rest, as they say, is history. By many accounts, both responses to the crisis—the bipartisan TARP bill and the Democratic/Obama stimulus bill—helped to stabilize our economy along with Chairman Bernanke's even hand at the Federal Reserve. (By contrast, many European countries that were hit hard by the downturn responded by implementing austerity programs, and their economies did not recover at the same pace as ours.) While neither of these bills was what I would have drafted from the get-go, when accounting for interest earned by the government, most of the TARP money was paid back, and the stimulus helped at a time when we needed it most.

But the work of managing the crisis and cleaning up after the downturn still wasn't done. The American auto industry was in deep trouble—Chrysler filed for bankruptcy protection in April 2009, with GM following suit on June 1st—and the big car companies were threatening to close thousands of dealerships, often indiscriminately. Through my position on the Commerce Committee and with legislation and advocacy, and with the help of James Ahn of our staff, I fervently made the case for my state's dealerships and their employees, and, along with many others, helped to save more than twenty businesses. As a young girl I never would have guessed that I would one day be named the Minnesota Auto Dealers' "Legislator of the Year," but it happened.

It was also clear that financial regulatory reform was needed. In the months after the collapse, Chris Dodd, the head of the Senate Banking Committee, along with Barney Frank, the House banking chair, began putting together a package of provisions aimed at reforming our financial system. Consumers had to be protected from predatory and unscrupulous practices. People were being duped into signing contracts full of unintelligible fine print that put them into debt for the rest of their lives. That's why we ultimately tightened the financial regulations and set up the Consumer Financial Protection Bureau, first led so capably by now Senator Elizabeth Warren and later by my fellow University of Chicago Law School alum Richard Cordray.

I worked on several consumer provisions in the Dodd-Frank bill, but I also tried to get some exceptions for small banks. Minnesota has one of the highest percentages of community banks in the country. These banks did not cause the financial crisis, and along with Kay Bailey Hutchison, the then Republican senator of Texas, I worked hard to address their issues. In February 2009, in an op-ed for the *Washington Post*, I wrote about the many small businesses and banks that had suffered as a result of bad business products and practices they'd never peddled or used. In that piece, titled "Banks That Had a Brain," I conjured up the illusory world of Oz and the image of a midwestern banker, sensible briefcase in hand, the debris of credit default swaps swirling around his head. As he tries to keep his feet firmly planted in the heartland, he says, "Toto, we're not in Kansas anymore."

For every American who struggled to recover from the financial excesses of a few, I thought that bewildered banker's sentiment pretty much summed things up: "Toto, we're not in Kansas anymore."

The Only Senator

During the worst of the financial crisis, our state experienced its own political crisis: the Franken/Coleman U.S. Senate recount.

The election in November 2008 between incumbent Republican Senator Norm Coleman and Democratic author, radio host, and former *Saturday Night Live* star Al Franken was so close—the initial margin was 215 votes out of more than 2.9 million cast—that it led to eight months of legal battles, extended vote counts, and court decisions. As the economy

plummeted during the first half of 2009, Minnesota was the only state in
the Union with just one senator, a situation that generated more than a few
late-night TV jokes. In fact, one evening well into the recount I was alone
at home in Minnesota, propped up in bed eating popcorn, reading legislative memos, and half-watching the *Late Show with David Letterman*. Out
of the blue Letterman started talking about the Minnesota Senate recount
and then made a joke about that "poor woman" from Minnesota who was
still, after months and months of counting, the only senator for the state.

"That's me," I thought, "that's me."

Those eight months were wild. A new president was inaugurated. The
country was in the worst downturn since the Great Depression. We saw
our office's casework double and our calls increase fivefold over the year
before. Much of the increase was because of the recession; some of it was
due to the fact that we'd taken over hundreds of the Coleman office's constituent cases. And then there were the callers who had heard I was the
only senator and admitted, "I was just calling to see if you guys answered."

During the long wait for a winner to be declared, my first goal was to
be publicly calm about the situation. It was what it was. The votes needed
to be manually recounted and the process would take a while. While I was
clearly supporting Al, Norm and I had worked well together in the Senate
and, given how close the vote was, I never criticized his decision to go
forward with legal appeals.

My second goal was to make sure that Minnesota's interests were fully
represented while we only had one senator. I was especially concerned
about appropriations requests for the funding of state projects, better
known as earmarks. The circumstance certainly called for a creative strategy. After calling all of the Senate Appropriations Subcommittee chairs to
highlight the unique challenge we faced, I submitted two sets of Minnesota appropriations requests: one from me and one from a mythical
"Senator B," whose requests, of course, identically matched mine. Thanks
to my amazing staff at the time, which included Lee Sheehy, Marjorie Duske,
Travis Talvitie, Andrea Mokros, Jonathan Becker, and Moira Campion, we
ended up faring well during the appropriations process despite operating
with half the usual engine power.

The other area that concerned me was legislative. If I didn't look out
for our state on the floor, who would? Language matters in the Senate.

Does legislative wording about unemployment benefits phasing out at a certain level help Wisconsin residents and hurt Minnesotans across the border? On one amendment, I made the strong case that this wasn't fair and won. And what if a stimulus provision is written in a way that helps a window company in one state but hurts Marvin or Anderson Windows in my state? We needed provisions that encouraged all American companies to build energy-efficient windows. I repeatedly made the case for fair treatment of our state and came away feeling good about the outcomes.

With the economy in near free fall, we spent a lot of time helping people who were out of work, not only with unemployment benefits but also with workforce training. I also did everything I could to help our unions and businesses weather the financial storm. In my first two years, with Bush as president, Norm Coleman had taken the lead in working with our companies on various issues in Washington. Now that responsibility fell to me. No one else in Washington who'd been elected statewide could do it. In fact, there *was* no other Minnesota statewide elected official in Washington!

I truly enjoy working with our businesses. Minnesota consistently has one of the lowest unemployment rates in the country. With companies such as 3M, UnitedHealthcare, U.S. Bank, Ecolab, General Mills, and Cargill, as well as all of our medical device manufacturers (Medtronic, St. Jude, and a major Boston Scientific presence), retail and service companies (Target, Best Buy, Carlson Companies), and food producers, we have a truly diverse economy. We are also fortunate that many successful employers have large presences in Greater Minnesota—Mayo Clinic, Schwan's, Land O'Lakes, Polaris, Arctic Cat, Cirrus, and Digi-Key, to name a few. And don't forget Hormel in Austin, Minnesota, home to the world's only museum devoted entirely to Spam, or as we like to call it, the Guggenham.

Not many states are both in the top five for agriculture and in the top five per capita for Fortune 500 companies. And though I will never agree with our companies' positions on all of the issues, policies that are generally fair to them *and* their employees are good for our state and our country. I would rather have the jobs in St. Paul than Shanghai; I would rather see the growth in Duluth than Dubai. I took care in my letters and

Senate speeches to differentiate between the work that needed to be done on financial regulatory reform and the general work of our businesses.

On June 30, 2009, Al Franken was declared the victor in the recount by a razor-thin margin of 312 votes. After the Minnesota Supreme Court's unanimous ruling that day, Norm Coleman made the decision not to pursue further legal action. It had been a brutal eight months of legal wrangling, and I knew that the continuation of the trust Minnesotans historically placed in both our state's election system and elected officials depended on whether they'd accept the outcome. Norm helped ensure a smooth transition with his gracious words and actions when he conceded. Al helped by how he did his job. Like an expectant mother, his wife, Franni, had kept a packed suitcase by their bed in case her husband was suddenly declared the victor and had to go to Washington on short notice. And when the time came at last, almost eight months after the actual election, they were ready.

Al was ready not just because he has the mind and the ability to do the job, but also because he has the heart to do the work. From the very beginning he proved to be a serious legislator, distinguishing himself especially for his work on technology, privacy rights, and health care. He focuses on the details of proposed policies and how they affect Minnesota. He cares deeply for his staff and his family. We sit together on the Judiciary Committee and he's always got the latest picture of his grandson Joe ready to show me. And one last thing that comes to mind about Al? He can't talk about Paul Wellstone, the man whose Senate seat he now holds, without shedding a few tears.

Once Al finally took the oath of office on July 7th, I had to get used to the fact that the other senator from my state was a celebrity. Not long after he arrived, in fact, Chuck Schumer and Dick Durbin sat me down to explain their own experiences—Schumer with Hillary Clinton, Durbin with Barack Obama—of having a famous person as their Senate colleague. Sometimes Al and I would be attending the same event and strangers would ask me to take their picture with him. On several occasions people who knew who I was asked me if I could set up a meeting with Al or give them his phone number.

Those encounters were memorable, but the best moment came one evening when Al and I got on a Minnesota-bound plane, one that happened to be filled with people from our state. Soon after we boarded, the flight attendant—who, with her strong southern accent, was decidedly not from Minnesota—declared quite loudly, "Well look, we have some celebrities on the plane, Mr. and Mrs. Al Franken."

Everyone started laughing. "No, no," Al said, "she's the other senator from Minnesota."

"Oh my," she said. "How cool is that—husband and wife senators."

More laughter.

"No," I said, "I am not Mrs. Franken. I'm the other senator."

"Oh," she said, seeming a little disappointed. "Well, then I think I'll go back and get Senator Franken's autograph."

Soon I noticed that my suitcase, which the flight attendant had earlier promised to take up to the front of the plane when she thought I was Mrs. Franken, was still sitting precariously on an empty seat. Since the plane's doors had been shut and the flight crew had told us we could no longer get up from our seats, I reminded the attendant about the stranded suitcase. "I would do it myself," I said, "but now I can't."

"Oh no," she said, "I'm not sure what to do about that now."

After pausing for a moment, she did take my suitcase, but at the time I didn't know where it ended up.

A few minutes later, as the plane was taking off, there was a bump on the runway. Two nearby passengers simultaneously turned back to me and yelled out with great amusement, "Senator, that was your luggage!"

In any case, I got my suitcase back, the flight attendant got her autograph, Al and I had a good laugh, and a plane full of people had a funny story to tell when they got home.

Governing for the Long Term

With the only/lonely senator year of 2009 behind me, and our economy having at least stabilized after the collapse, it was time for our government to stop governing by crisis. We needed to get back to governing for the long term. But what was often referred to as the Great Recession continued to take its toll for years. Even in 2012, when I was running for reelection, many people in our state were still struggling to find work and get back to their pre-recession salary levels. More than ever, I was convinced that our immediate economic challenges could only be met by both short-term and long-term strategies.

It would ultimately take more than six years to dig our country out of the hole we put ourselves in, and even then the recession meant that major legislative initiatives that were important to our country's long-term economics were delayed. As the years went by and we continued to struggle to respond to the 2008 financial crisis, legislation on issues as critical as infrastructure, immigration reform, energy and climate change, tax reform, and education fell by the wayside.

As the Hennepin County Attorney I spent eight years in what I now consider a "normal" government management job—one where we were expected to draft a budget, present it to the public, and report to the county board and the general public on our results. As a U.S. senator, however, I've encountered a completely different approach to fiscal matters and long-term goals, a tumultuous wait-and-then-hurry-and-then-duck form of governing, complete with 3:00 a.m. votes and constant threats of shutdowns and other calamities. Almost every time we close in on an opportunity for some productive, long-term fixes, a lot of good work is scuttled in favor of a short-term band-aid.

That all became crystal clear to me on December 31, 2012, during the so-called fiscal cliff vote. The Senate worked all that evening and into the early hours of New Year's Day to stop tax rates from going up for all Americans. Ultimately, Congress allowed the tax rates for only those households with annual incomes of more than $450,000 to go back to the levels established during President Clinton's tenure.

That was one of my most memorable sessions as a U.S. senator. Just before midnight on New Year's Eve—that magical, romantic moment when the clock strikes twelve—there I was, still on the Senate floor. I looked to my left and saw Harry Reid. I looked to my right and saw Mitch McConnell. It was New Year's Eve. Every girl's dream.

Yes, we got the bill done. But it was another long-term opportunity squandered. We lost an opportunity for tax reform that would close the loopholes and simplify the system, an opportunity to reduce our debt with both spending cuts and additional revenue, and an opportunity to establish a pathway to legislative sanity.

Over the past few years it's become apparent to me that the senators who seem to have the most difficult time adjusting to the congressional gridlock and lack of strategic planning—the ones who get the most frustrated by the stop-everything-in-its-tracks mentality—tend to be those who used to run something. They once knew the thrill and reward of making a decision, implementing it, and measuring the results over the long term. This group includes former governors such as Jeanne Shaheen, Lamar Alexander, Tom Carper, Mark Warner, Tim Kaine, Joe Manchin, Mike Johanns, John Hoeven, Jim Risch, Mike Rounds, and Angus King. It also includes former mayors like Cory Booker, Mark Begich and Bob Corker and those of us who've managed major agencies or departments, whether as attorneys general or chief prosecutors, or those who've run a company.

One day you are solving problems and writing your own annual budget and long-term goals, and the next you are thrust into an environment where outdated laws are left unchanged, repeated short-term extensions are commonplace, and the real issues are relegated either to bills that are introduced but killed in committee or studies that are left to collect dust on a shelf. Plenty of reports and proposals are highly lauded but never implemented. That happened with the good work of the bipartisan National Commission on Fiscal Responsibility and Reform chaired by Erskine Bowles and Alan Simpson. It also happened with the work done by the "Gang of Six," consisting of Senators Dick Durbin, Kent Conrad, Mark Warner, Saxby Chambliss, Mike Crapo, and Tom Coburn. Both efforts were aimed at restoring fiscal discipline in Washington, D.C. While I may not have agreed with every element of the plans, we never truly got an opportunity to debate them. They never made it to the Senate floor.

For those of us who've managed major state or local offices, it seems as if everything we learned about good management—the importance of goals, planning, time management—disappears like ether in the rarified atmosphere of the Capitol rotunda. Time and time again we are told that the best way to strike a deal is to "wait to the very end" (when the stock market is tanking or taxes will go up or the military will be defunded). Then and only then will intransigent people risk the vote or make the deal. But the way I see it, this approach almost always leads to short-term thinking, bad deals, and more legislative messes, which then cause the public to distrust the government even more.

A good way of analyzing these governing problems is to use what are sometimes called the four quadrants of decision-making—a management matrix originally used by President Eisenhower and later popularized by Stephen Covey, of *The Seven Habits of Highly Effective People* fame. This technique was passed on to me by Chuck Schumer, who told me that his mentor, New York Assemblyman Anthony Genovesi, also used the quadrants.

Here's how it works: Along the top of a square box of four quadrants is the word "Important." On the bottom of the box is the word "Unimportant." The left side is labeled "Urgent" and the right side "Not Urgent." I've found this matrix useful when thinking about how best to govern, but it's also a useful tool for life in general.

Congress understandably spends most of its time dealing with issues in the top left quadrant—the "Urgent, Important" quadrant—for crises like Hurricane Katrina, Superstorm Sandy, and the financial collapse. The problem is that—with the exception of unforeseeable natural disasters—we often put ourselves into that box by not spending enough time on the top, right-hand quadrant, "Important, Not Urgent." If Washington had been willing to increase our federal investment in infrastructure, for example, we would not have seen some of the rail, highway, and lock and dam problems we've sadly had to deal with in recent decades. If previous Congresses had passed tougher financial regulations (and the Bush administration had advocated for them), we might not have seen the 2008 economic collapse. In both cases, early warning signs were ignored.

As for the other two quadrants? Like most people, we don't spend a lot of time on the right bottom quadrant, "Unimportant, Not Urgent." That's okay, but we also spend way too much time on the left-bottom quadrant, "Urgent, Unimportant." Year after year, we respond with frenetic energy to endless contrived and manufactured partisan crises and media-generated hooplas.

Throughout his presidency, Barack Obama has valiantly tried to stay focused on the long-term work in the top right quadrant. And during my first year in office, when Ted Kennedy invited Sheldon Whitehouse and me to be part of the bipartisan immigration reform group, I saw first-hand President Bush's top-right-quadrant effort to change the country's approach to immigration. President Clinton was able to keep the majority of the public with him for years by focusing his efforts on that "Important, Not Urgent" quadrant, even while nearly always responding effectively to urgent matters as well. Clinton's constant focus on the economy delivered a huge payoff: during his tenure, the country saw more than twenty-two million new jobs created and witnessed the longest economic expansion in American history.

President Obama has been successful with a number of long-term initiatives—the stabilization and improvement of our economy, the Affordable Care Act, increased gas-mileage standards, increased exports and trade, the negotiation of international climate change agreements, and the promotion of marriage equality. But with other efforts—a long-term debt reduction deal, tax reform, domestic climate legislation, a reauthorization of the Voting Rights Act, and immigration reform—he has been thwarted by all kinds of factions and special interests. Stirring up negative news stories and airing vitriolic TV ads is easy to do when you want to prevent the president or Congress from accomplishing anything. Meanwhile, serious problems turn into real crises that remain unaddressed.

Of course, elected officials and government employees do make mistakes, and sometimes they needlessly antagonize the public by minimizing something important, even when they actually know it is important. Bush's decision to "fly over" New Orleans and his statements about the post–Hurricane Katrina performance of "Brownie" (a reference to his then FEMA director Michael Brown) come to mind. Other times, major ill-advised governing decisions with long-term consequences are made without regard to the facts or circumstances, such as the Obama administration's botched launch of the inadequately tested Affordable Care Act website or President Bush's decision to invade Iraq.

But do mistakes (both big and small) mean that we should turn our backs on long-term governing issues? Do they mean we should limit our roles as citizens and elected officials to armchair critics who are never happy with the outcomes, always eager to tear down, and never ready to build up? I don't think so. Just ask the people of Moorhead, Minnesota, and Fargo, North Dakota, who nearly lost their towns to a raging river. Just ask the sons and daughters of Alzheimer's patients who come to the Capitol in their purple shirts every year asking for more investment to find a cure.

And just ask Tiffany Kirk, the single mother I met from Houston, Texas, who came to Washington, D.C., to push for a higher minimum wage. She earned $2.13 an hour, plus tips, at the Howl at the Moon piano bar. She's one of more than 3 million tipped workers who earn that amount.

None of these citizens has time for armchair critics. They just want their government to look out for them.

As people from across the political spectrum debate the role of government, it's also important to acknowledge that sometimes it functions exactly as it should. I can think of several times during my years in the Senate when we worked successfully on important, long-term issues. They took a lot of work and victory was never certain. In 2007, for example, we increased the gas-mileage standards for the first time since 1984. I was part of the bipartisan group that worked to change those standards, and it was a great moment when we succeeded. (Okay, except for the part when I stood at a press conference and said that the gas-mileage standards had not been increased since I was still in school. I was followed by Barbara Mikulski, who said she'd been *in* Congress when they'd last been increased.) Debating and finally passing the Affordable Care Act was another success. The final bill was far from perfect, but I believe that the bulk of the ACA's policies are sound and that history will judge the legislation more kindly than it is being judged today.

Another example? As much as people like to growl about the farm bill, we have consistently come together to legislate five-year rules of the road for agriculture and rural America. As a member of the Agriculture Committee, I have been proud to be a part of those efforts and work with Minnesota Representative Collin Peterson and Senators Debbie Stabenow, Thad Cochran, Saxby Chambliss, and Tom Harkin. Imagine if we could put a five-year plan in place for renewable energy or manufacturing, instead of playing the on-again, off-again game that hobbles so many of our tax incentives. Since the regulations keep changing from one year to the next and the tax incentives keep expiring, nobody can even hope to play by predictable rules.

The Senate immigration bill of 2013? That was a great example of top-right-quadrant, long-term bipartisan work. And while it was stymied by Republicans in the House of Representatives, I still believe it will be the blueprint for what will eventually become the law of the land.

As the country moves forward in a time of political stalemate and radioactive politics, we would be much better off if our citizenry demanded a commitment to long-term governing in the areas of middle-class issues (student loans, mortgages, workforce training, family/medical leave, wages), tax reform, infrastructure and scientific/medical research financing, energy and climate change, immigration, and education. There's no question that we still have a lot of work to do on individual bills and individual causes—that must continue or the public will feel they aren't being heard. But the most challenging issues we face aren't going away, and one by one we've got to come together and take them on no matter how much the interest groups spend, fight, or want.

As I've learned from working with the tribes in my state, there is a stewardship principle in Native American cultures that guides tribal members in thinking about the planet Earth and all of its humanity. It advises us to keep in mind the impact and repercussions of our decisions for seven generations to come. If America's political leaders thought more about the seventh generation instead of their next elections, we'd all be better off.

The Wider World

There is no better example of long-term governing than foreign policy. Oftentimes the victories are quiet ones, like the closed-door diplomacy that helps to keep a country out of a civil war. The mistakes and defeats, however, are there for the world to see.

What I learned pretty quickly in the Senate is that even if you want to isolate yourself from the rest of the world (which, of course, was not my goal), the rest of the world doesn't let you. Eventually international problems—and opportunities—come knocking at your door. They come with a phone call from a scared dad whose daughter's high school group is marooned in Guatemala by a mudslide. They come during a meeting with local steelworkers who are understandably irate over the illegal dumping of steel from South Korea.

And they come with anguished pleas to help citizens detained or left behind in foreign lands—babies awaiting adoption in storm-ravaged

Haitian orphanages; a law professor arrested in Rwanda; a University of Minnesota student imprisoned for nine months in the United Arab Emirates for posting a satirical YouTube video; and three hikers, including a Minnesota native, freelance journalist Shane Bauer, imprisoned for wandering into Iranian territory while trekking in the mountains of Iraq's Kurdish region. Each of those cases involved a lot of late-night phone calls, early morning e-mails, and patience, but in every case, our Minnesotans came home.

Like many of its midwestern neighbors, Minnesota went through a major isolationist phase decades ago when the state's congressional delegation included Congressman Harold Knutson (who notoriously said that "Europe should paddle its own canoe" after World War II) and U.S. Senator Henrik Shipstead (one of only two senators to vote against the UN Charter). But the 1960s and beyond ushered in a much more international-leaning set of Minnesota political leaders on both sides of the aisle, such as Walter Mondale, Hubert Humphrey, Senators Eugene McCarthy and Rudy Boschwitz, and Representatives Don Fraser, Bill Frenzel, Jim Oberstar, Keith Ellison, and Betty McCollum. Their interests ranged from human rights and diplomacy to Israel and Middle East peace, from the promotion of American exports and trade to the building of the infrastructure necessary to bring our goods to foreign markets.

As was the case in so many other parts of the country, our state's political environment changed in sync with the growth of our international businesses, increased international outreach by religious and nonprofit organizations, a rising number of international adoptions, increased international travel, immigration, and the arrival of refugees from the world over. I am proud that our state has the largest Somali population in the nation as well as a large Hmong population.

But in the first decade and a half of this century, the American interconnection to the rest of the world (in the form of new immigrants, exports, and shared international security interests) that has been so key to our country's success has been slowly but surely unraveling. The tragedy of 9/11, the recession, the public's understandable disillusionment with the war in Iraq, and the failure to pass sensible immigration reform that could have set up a better system for legal immigration while clamping down on illegal immigration all have contributed to an increasingly isolationist view. And the increasing partisanship associated with foreign policy also contributes to the public's cynicism and a feeling that arguments about policy are all about political posturing and not the national interest.

Little wonder that it's tempting for citizens—and even more for the politicians who represent them—to come down on the side of international isolationism by making the case that the rest of our problems will go away if the rest of the world goes away. But we know it just isn't so. Terrorists schooled abroad show no mercy in attacking our cities and our citizens. Decisions about oil production in foreign countries affect the price of gas in Pittsburgh, bad agricultural practices in lands far away from home make people sick in Wisconsin, and viruses in remote villages in Africa will eventually cross the ocean to Texas.

In my time in the Senate I have learned that closing our eyes to all of this is not the answer. But shouldering all the world's problems is also not the answer. The answer, as with so many things in politics, is somewhere in the middle, not only of the foreign policy spectrum, but also of our country, at least if history is any guide.

In February 2014 David Ignatius of the *Washington Post* wrote a column entitled "The Internationalism of the Heartland," in which he talked about the fact that some of the defining voices of global commitment over the past half-century have come from America's middle: Senator Howard Baker of Tennessee; Senator J. William Fulbright of Arkansas; Representative Lee Hamilton of Indiana; Senator Walter Mondale of Minnesota; Senator Mike Mansfield of Montana.

When Ignatius interviewed me for that column, I told him that as a senator from the Midwest, I believed we needed to "embrace" rather than "tolerate" internationalism, and he summarized my comments by saying that "after a difficult decade . . . the United States needs a refreshed internationalism that recognizes its stake in the world, even as it avoids costly military commitments where possible." Ignatius called that balanced approach "internationalism of the heartland" because "it sustains the deep links forged by heartland Democrats such as Hamilton, Mondale and Mansfield."

To my mind, a principal goal of U.S. internationalism should be to increase American jobs through exporting our goods to international markets where trade agreements are fair and actually enforced. (I have testified several times in front of the United States International Trade Commission for stringent enforcement of laws when foreign companies have illegally dumped their products—primarily steel—on our shores.) While I've voted for some trade agreements, I've voted against others based on my concerns about the impact on Minnesota workers and businesses.

During the worst of the economic downturn, I became convinced that the key to digging ourselves out was exports. The relatively inexpensive cost of expanding natural gas reserves, the value of the dollar on the international market, and the eventual decrease in the price of oil— due in part to increased domestic supplies, higher gas mileage standards, and competitive biofuels—meant lower input costs for manufacturing. A rising middle class in countries like China and India meant more people wanted to buy our goods, fly in our planes, and visit our country. When I chaired the Senate Subcommittee on Competitiveness, Innovation, and Export Promotion, increasing exports was my focus.

One of the benefits of my commitment to visit each of Minnesota's eighty-seven counties every year is that I've been able to visit a lot of businesses, big and small. I've seen a lot of successes, from companies like southern Minnesota's Akkerman Inc.—which got the little-known honor of being named the "Trenchless Digger of the Year" due to the growth of its underground piping exports to China and India—to Mattracks, of Karlstad, Minnesota, a town near the Canadian border known as the "Moose Capital of the North." Mattracks grew from two to thirty employees by selling its tanklike attachable truck tracks around the world.

From my position on the Commerce Committee and on the President's Export Council, I've worked hard on a number on export issues. But two stand out: working with Republican Senator Roy Blunt to reauthorize the Travel Promotion Act, which allows America to compete with foreign countries by advertising U.S. tourist destinations abroad; and supporting and expanding the U.S. and Foreign Commercial Service—the part of the Commerce Department that works at home and in our embassies across the world to promote American products overseas. The way I see it, the more people visit our country, and the more people in other countries who buy American-made goods, the more jobs there will be in America.

One example of a major trading partner that I've worked with extensively is Canada. Early on in my Senate career, Harry Reid asked me to head up the Canada–United States Inter-Parliamentary Group, along with Idaho Republican Senator Mike Crapo. Through our many laborious but helpful meetings over the years, we've worked with our Canadian counterparts to hash out issues from border crossings and ballast water to timber and wood pulp, beef, and energy. Many times I've reminded my colleagues that Canada is America's biggest trading partner and that only the embassy of Canada (which I appear to be the only senator in recent history to choose as the site for my Senate reelection swearing-in party) would drape itself with signs that say "friends, neighbors, partners, allies."

Another very different economic opportunity lies just ninety miles off the coast of Florida: Cuba. In December 2014, President Obama announced a major foreign policy shift toward Cuba, and not long afterward I had the chance to travel there. I met Cuban entrepreneurs who are ready for change, ready for a shift from a state-controlled economy to a market-based one. I'm leading the bipartisan bill with Jeff Flake, Mike Enzi, Patrick Leahy, and others, to lift the fifty-three-year-old trade embargo because I believe that normalizing relations will bring economic opportunities—and increased prosperity—for the people of both countries.

Of course, internationalism is about more than economics. American internationalism should also include humanitarian policies—and an abiding concern for human rights—grounded in our democratic values and our faith and moral purpose. On the first all-women senators' trip to Africa with Senators Debbie Stabenow, Maria Cantwell, Heidi Heitkamp, and Mazie Hirono, I saw firsthand the way our government's USAID (then under the able leadership of my friend Rajiv Shah) has taken smart, pragmatic economic- and health-focused approaches to foreign aid. Foreign aid is a much less expensive way of engaging with the rest of the world than foreign military involvement. I will never forget Bill Clinton's story of once visiting a shirt-making factory in Africa after he'd left the presidency. U.S. economic aid had helped build the factory, which had brought a lot of jobs to an impoverished area. Clinton brought some of the shirts home with him and hung them in his closet. Every time he looked at them he thought to himself: "They don't hate us. They don't hate us."

A major part of our humanitarian and government work must be to promote the status of women across the world. As Nicholas Kristof and his wife Sheryl WuDunn write in their book *Half the Sky*, the world can no longer afford to lose "half the sky" by treating women as second-class citizens, including selling them off as sex slaves. I led a trip to Mexico City in 2014 with my friend and nonprofit leader Cindy McCain, wife of my colleague John McCain, and Senator Heidi Heitkamp of North Dakota to focus on our partnership with Mexico in combating sex-trafficking rings. One of the most memorable moments on that trip was meeting a young sex-trafficking victim named Paloma. Unlike the other girls in the shelter, she wouldn't speak to her foreign guests; she would only cry. I was reminded of a conversation I'd once had with a Syrian refugee in Jordan; she had told me that what she'd seen would "make stones cry." Through her silence, I know that's what Paloma was telling us, too.

Finally, internationalism involves security policies that will protect our country's citizens in an unstable, increasingly volatile world. This means providing our military with adequate funding. It means tackling the pure evil of terrorist groups like Al-Qaeda and ISIS, but doing so whenever possible with other partners. It means standing up for Israel—a beacon of democracy in the Middle East—while working toward a two-state solution, one that will ensure the long-term security of Israelis and Palestinians who yearn for peace. And it means knowing that our country cannot abandon innocent people on a mountaintop—in 2014, Minnesota airmen airlifted food and water to Yazidis and Christians forced from their homes and trapped by ISIS militants on Mount Sinjar in northern Iraq—or put our heads in the sand in the face of Vladimir Putin's aggression.

America's international engagement—and our portrayal of it to the rest of the world—is a key part of our ongoing effort to fight terrorism and extremism and reduce the global poverty that, in so many cases, breeds it. And although the U.S. military has a significant role to play in fighting the scourge of terrorism, we must also remember that avoiding unnecessary wars and military entanglements is a critical part of what good diplomats—and good political leaders—do.

America must and ultimately will win the war of ideas—between tolerance and America-style capitalism, on the one hand, and terrorism and radical extremism, on the other—that is being waged around the globe. Through economic engagement and shared prosperity, as well as strategic humanitarian and targeted military operations overseas to fight the evil of terrorism, we should also be able to win back the American people to a new internationalism—one grounded in the pragmatism, patriotism, and faith of our nation's heartland.

Republicans and Dems I've Loved (to Work With)

To get the long-term work of governing done—whether on the domestic or international fronts—our country needs representatives who will stand up for their principles but also, whenever possible, find the good will to work together when there is common ground. When I worked as county attorney, nearly half of my commissioners were Republicans; when I came to the Senate I entered a parallel partisan universe in which members of the two parties segregate themselves for caucus lunches, for meetings, and even at committee hearings. As a prosecutor, it was my job to keep politics *out* of my work. Now it was blatantly *in* my work on a daily basis.

From the beginning I've never been comfortable with the "two teams fight it out every day" model of governing. I have a real issue with extremism on the right that so often blocks progress and reasonable compromise. And members of both parties sometimes reflexively reject new ideas. Like many of my colleagues, I like working together to get things done. I am proud to be a Democrat, and yes, you stand your ground. But you also look for ways to come together.

America's legal system is, properly, an adversarial one, but America's politicians—as President George Washington warned in his famous Farewell Address—should beware of "faction" and "the baneful effects of the spirit of party generally." And if Washington were here to give that same address today, I have no doubt he would have added Super PACs, billionaire funding, and outside independent expenditures to his list of "baneful" sources of trouble.

When I came to the Senate, I was determined not to fall into the trap of bitter partisanship. And in my quest to find common ground with my colleagues, I had a couple of things going for me. First, however frustrating it is, the labyrinth of the Senate's archaic rules and procedural roadblocks forces people to work together. Because of the filibuster rules, you need 60 out of 100 votes to get anything passed. You really have no choice: your work must be bipartisan. Second, the American people, and especially the people in my state, are sick and tired of the fighting in Congress. They want to see peace and progress, which means that at least some senators feel a growing responsibility to work together.

I realize that people find it hard to understand why it's so difficult for representatives to compromise in Congress. A lot of it has to do with the pressure that comes from their own parties and the interest groups whose powers grow with each new outside expenditure. Compromisers get hit from both sides, but it's the criticism from their own side, from their own base, that's really punishing. Just ask Senator Lindsey Graham how he got treated on some right-leaning shows when he came out for Supreme Court nominees Sonia Sotomayor and Elena Kagan, or how any moderate fares when appearing on either Fox News or MSNBC on a political hot-button issue of the day. It can be pretty brutal. Money in politics—in particular the expanding role of outside money after *Citizens United* and other U.S. Supreme Court decisions—is also a major polarizing force. And social media, which can be such a powerful and positive political force thanks to an incredibly active American Internet citizenry, can also be used to deliberately mischaracterize positions and votes. It can also spread distrust and disdain for elected officials who embrace positions that are not 100 percent with their own base.

During my first years in the Senate, I learned the art of bipartisanship by watching Ted Kennedy. I saw him work successfully with people like Orrin Hatch and Mike Enzi and Pete Domenici. During the immigration debate in 2007, Sheldon Whitehouse and I were lucky enough to be in the room when he worked with the Bush administration and Republicans such as Lindsey Graham and John McCain to try to pass that bill. And Senator Kennedy was a great mentor. He'd invite a small group of new senators to his hideaway in the Capitol during late-night votes and regale us with stories. What always came through was his genuine affection for those he worked with (both Democrats *and* Republicans), his love of legislating, and his love for his country.

After Senator Kennedy was diagnosed with a malignant brain tumor, Senator Mike Enzi—a conservative Republican from Wyoming—spoke movingly about his friend on the Senate floor. "Many find it hard to believe," Enzi said, "that Senator Kennedy, the third most liberal Senator in the Senate, and I, the fourth most conservative Senator in this body, could get along or actually enjoy each other's company. But we do." While chairing the Committee on Health, Education, Labor, and Pensions, Enzi pointed out, he always worked under what he called his "80 percent rule" when dealing with his friend. As Enzi put it: "I always believed we could agree on 80 percent of the issues and on 80 percent of each issue, and that if we focus on the 80 percent, we can do great things for the American people."

Eighty percent gives you a lot of room for agreement, and in my time as a senator I've found plenty of people to work with. Utah conservative Orrin Hatch and I have teamed up on many bills, including medical device issues and an immigration-related bill where we were joined by Democrats Chris Coons and Dick Blumenthal, as well as Republicans Marco Rubio and Jeff Flake. Despite our obvious age and party differences, Senator Hatch and I do have one major thing in common: the *Washingtonian* magazine once voted us the two senators least likely to get into a scandal (which, we're always quick to point out, includes with each other). Missouri Senator Roy Blunt and I are leading the Congressional Coalition on Adoption in the Senate, and the two of us, with the assistance of Democratic leader Harry Reid, have passed several critical bills to increase tourism in our country.

Susan Collins is always a bright, bipartisan light in the Senate. Not only did I work with her on ending the government shutdown, but she and I, along with my pal Senator Bob Casey of Pennsylvania, successfully passed the prescription drug shortage legislation. Her former Maine colleague Olympia Snowe was my Republican mentor and cosponsored my first bill.

My Minnesota Democratic and Republican colleagues in the House have worked with me on numerous issues, from veterans' bills to a Mississippi River lock closure to prevent the spread of invasive carp to building a bridge from Minnesota to Wisconsin. And I have many buddies on our borders: Senator John Thune and I have introduced multiple rural-focused bills together; Iowa Senator Chuck Grassley has worked with me on several health care–related bills, including legislation to stop the costly practice of pharmaceutical companies paying generic drug companies to delay bringing their competitive products to market; Chuck Grassley, former Senator Tom Harkin, and I worked together with many others on ethanol; Wisconsin Senator Tammy Baldwin and I (along with Senators Stabenow, Durbin, Franken, Portman, and Kirk) work together on Great Lakes issues; and Heidi Heitkamp of North Dakota and I (along with Minnesota Republican House member Erik Paulsen) have teamed up to combat sex trafficking.

Then there's my neighbor, North Dakota Republican Senator John Hoeven. Hoeven took me to visit the oil-drilling operations in Williston and was with me when—as a sitting U.S. senator—I got carded in a bar (yeah!). He and I have worked together so often on so many bills that the *Grand Forks Herald* once declared that we should take over the leadership of the Senate. Luckily, Mitch McConnell and Harry Reid do not subscribe to the *Grand Forks Herald*, though they should! I knew things were going a bit too far on the Klobuchar/Hoeven bipartisan scale when at one recent distracted-driving event in Minnesota, we were asked to tie "friendship bracelets" on each other's wrists and pledge to take care of each other for the rest of our lives. We did it.

Through the weekly Senate prayer breakfast I have formed many lasting friendships across party lines: Georgia Senator Johnny Isakson and I chaired the group for two years, which included heading up the three-thousand-plus-person National Prayer Breakfast. Oklahoma's Jim Inhofe, a staunch conservative, worked with former Louisiana Senator Mary Landrieu and me on a number of adoption bills. I will never forget being asked to speak at the weekly prayer breakfast shortly after Jim's son, an orthopedic surgeon, died in a tragic plane crash near Tulsa. Jim had been designated to introduce me that morning. Just days after his son died, Jim still came and did a beautiful introduction. The night before I scrambled to change the focus of my talk so I could try to provide some comfort to Jim (also an avid pilot and the only member of Congress to fly an airplane around the world). I decided to talk about the religious value of curiosity and adventure and not being afraid to test the limits. I spoke about my dad's many adventures and quoted scripture: "For God did not give us a spirit of timidity, but a spirit of power" (2 Timothy 1:7); "So we fix our eyes not on what is seen but what is unseen" (2 Corinthians 4:18).

I remember I was a bit off when I quoted one of the Biblical verses, but only Barry Black, the chaplain, knew. And Chaplain Black only told me of the error after I asked him how I did. "Are you saying you know more than Google?" I joked with him after the fact.

My classmates who came into the Senate when I did, as well as many of the other senators I've gotten to know, have become my friends. In addition, many of the senators have given great support to me—and my family. Lisa Murkowski of Alaska allowed my daughter and her friend to interview her at length for a school project. Both New Hampshire senators—Democrat Jeanne Shaheen (whom we love to visit every time we go to her state) and Republican Kelly Ayotte—are always good ones for swapping mother/daughter stories. I was honored when Deb Fischer of Nebraska not only asked me to be her Democratic mentor, but also took my advice and actually moved into our apartment building for a while. And many of my colleagues—Democrats, Republicans, and independents alike—have hosted us in their states or hometowns, sometimes even inviting us into their own homes. Over the last eight years, we've visited St. Louis and Claire McCaskill's home, eating Sunday grits in the morning with her husband and her mom; Mark Warner's Virginia farm; Maria Cantwell's loft; Angus King's rustic Maine cabin; and Michael Bennet's house in Colorado, where I was serenaded by his three darling daughters. It's been particularly fun getting to know New York Senator Kirsten Gillibrand through the annual Congressional Women's Softball Game, a charity event pitting members of Congress against the D.C. press corps that raises money for breast cancer research and survivors. (Kirsten pitches; I provide the color commentary and do the play-by-play with NBC's Andrea Mitchell and CNN's Dana Bash.)

I've come to know many Republicans through our bipartisan legislative and committee efforts. John Cornyn and I passed a good bill on prescription drug take-backs as well as bills focused on combatting sex trafficking. Mike Lee and I have teamed up to chair the Judiciary Committee's Antitrust Subcommittee, and nearly every letter and announcement we've produced on that important subcommittee has been the result of collaboration, no matter which party was in charge. Jeff Sessions (my regular State of the Union "date") and I have passed bills on adoption and judicial procedure; Lamar Alexander and Chuck Schumer continue to lead Senate reform efforts, and I'm glad to be a part of them; Mike Crapo and I lead the Canada–U.S. Inter-Parliamentary Group, and he's been incredibly pleasant to work with; Senator John McCain and I have introduced an important bill to bring down drug costs by allowing the reimportation of prescription drugs from Canada.

When I look back, it was John McCain who, through his example, taught me a lot about how to value my colleagues. In 2009, he and his best friend, Lindsey Graham, invited me to go with them on a trip to Asia focused on trade and national security issues. McCain had just lost the presidential election and President Obama's popularity was at its height. Somehow McCain still had his sense of humor: at one breakfast in Tokyo, he opened up the *International Herald Tribune* and said with a wink and a nod, "Ah, the Obamas have bought a dog."

Lindsey was a lot of fun to travel with and McCain was, well, McCain: always reading, thinking, and full of energy. He was also very kind to me. Nearly all of our official meetings—from Hong Kong to China to Japan to Vietnam—were with lots of middle-aged and older men, and at every stop he would make sure that these leaders understood that even though I was new in the Senate and looked fairly young, I was in fact the Democratic leader on the trip and should be treated as such by them.

In Japan we visited the U.S.S. *John S. McCain*, the U.S. Navy ship named after McCain's dad and grandfather, both admirals in the Navy. But nothing compared to our visit to the Vietnamese prison in Hanoi where McCain, a former naval aviator, had been kept as a prisoner of war from 1967 until 1973. Standing next to him and seeing the small cell in which he had been held for so long was heartbreaking. It was also a deeply patriotic moment, especially when I considered how he'd once rejected the opportunity for release so that he wouldn't be treated differently than the other prisoners. After seeing that cell and hearing his story of courage in the face of long-term imprisonment and torture, I was all the more proud to hear his speech in 2014 in support of the release of Dianne Feinstein's report chronicling our country's use of torture since 9/11 against terrorism detainees.

The most surprising incident on that trip occurred when the Vietnamese guides, followed by a crowd of media, showed us a new exhibit of McCain's "flight suit," featuring a pristine-looking artifact standing upright in a glass box with his name embroidered on the pocket.

"Very nice," McCain said good-naturedly.

"I don't think that was my flight suit," he later whispered to me. "It got all torn up when I was shot down. Believe me, I remember."

But walking around with Senator McCain was the best part of our visit to Vietnam. Young Vietnamese would embrace him on the streets and beg for his autograph and a photo. Despite his years of imprisonment, McCain has returned to Vietnam many times, working to improve the country and advocate for our soldiers who remain missing in action. To these young people, he is a true hero. And every time he goes back he receives—and deserves—a hero's welcome.

The Sisters in the Brotherhood

When it comes to getting things done in the Senate, I quickly realized that the key to many of our legislative successes are the women senators. We may be relatively small in number, but we know how to legislate.

Some of our power comes from winning elections. We work in a seniority system, so winning successive elections allows us to rise to the top and chair committees. Another source of power comes from working across the aisle and standing up for one another. But a lot of our influence can be traced to the individuals involved; I work with a group of incredibly talented women who have overcome long odds to get to where they are today.

In January 2015 I spoke to a group of four hundred women carpenters from across the country. They were gathered in Las Vegas at the United Brotherhood of Carpenters's national training center, a state-of-the-art facility perfectly suited to providing the kind of complex skill training our new manufacturing economy demands. Twenty years ago—even ten years ago—you would not expect to find a gathering of four hundred women at a facility like this one. One of their leaders told me that a few years back the women carpenters met to figure out what they would call their group. She said the group of women kept staring at the carpenters' logo, "United Brotherhood of Carpenters." This, they recognized, created something of a marketing problem for their group. Then someone piped up, "Why don't we call ourselves the 'Sisters in the Brotherhood'?" It was one of those "Aha!" moments when everyone in the room knew the name was exactly right.

I liked the name, too. And as I said in my speech, it could also apply to the U.S. Senate.

Here's a pretty amazing statistic about the Senate: in its entire history, from 1789 to the present, there have been 1,917 men but only forty-six women who've served. In fact, not until about thirty-five years ago was the first woman elected to the Senate who did not initially fill out the congressional term of her deceased husband. That's a lot of catching up to do.

I was reminded of this during Elena Kagan's 2010 Supreme Court confirmation hearing when I followed Senator Coburn during a second round of questioning. Kagan, then the country's solicitor general, had spent hours being grilled by a group of seventeen men and two women and was more than holding her own. During his questioning, Senator Coburn had gone off on the topic of "freedom," claiming that Americans were "losing freedom" and "losing liberty" and were freer thirty years ago. On its face his diatribe about "freedom" had nothing to do with "freedom" with respect to women seeking office or holding positions of power. But when I heard him glorifying the 1980s, all I could think about were those little bow ties I had to wear at my law firm to fit in and how few women lawyers there were back then.

I had just a few minutes before Senator Coburn finished to throw out my existing questions and come up with some new ones. With the help of the BlackBerry and my great judiciary counsel, Paige Herwig, I was ready to go when Senator Coburn's time was up.

I began by pointing out that, in 1980, the top songs were "Call Me" by

Blondie and "Another One Bites the Dust" by Queen. "Do you know, Solicitor General," I then asked, "how many women were on the U.S. Supreme Court in 1980?"

"I guess none," Solicitor General Kagan replied.

"That would be correct," I said. "There were no women on the Supreme Court." Justice Sandra Day O'Connor, appointed by President Reagan, would not join the Court until 1981.

"Do you know how many women were sitting up here thirty years ago in 1980?" I asked her next. Again, the answer was none. Senator Dianne Feinstein was the first female senator to serve on the Senate Judiciary Committee, joining the committee in 1993.

"Do you know how many women were in the U.S. Senate in 1980, thirty years ago?" I asked next.

The answer was one—Nancy Landon Kassebaum of Kansas, the first woman elected to the Senate without her husband having previously served in Congress. The daughter of Kansas Governor Alf Landon, she'd first gotten elected in 1978 and served in the Senate until 1997.

Freedom, I concluded that day, is "all in the eyes of the beholder."

It never ceases to amaze me how slow change can be, though much progress has been made. In 1958, Minnesota's first congresswoman, Coya Knutson, was defeated in her reelection bid after her opponents got her husband drunk and cajoled him into signing a letter to his wife telling her he needed her at home to basically cook and clean. The local newspaper got the letter and ran it with the headline "Coya, Come Home." She would go on to lose to six-foot-four-inch Odin Langen, whose campaign slogan was "A Big Man for a Man-sized Job."

It was not until the year 2000, with the election of Congresswoman Betty McCollum, that Minnesotans would send the next woman to the U.S. House of Representatives.

Sadly, variations on Coya Knutson's story have been around for decades, though the outcomes are changing. In the 1980s, as noted earlier, Patty Murray was told by a legislator that she couldn't make a difference because she was just a "mom in tennis shoes." But she ran for office, used it as a campaign slogan, and won. In 2012, Claire McCaskill's U.S. Senate opponent, Republican Todd Akin, spoke of "legitimate rape," claiming that if a woman was raped, "the female body has ways to try to shut that whole thing down." Claire used Akin's ill-informed views against him and pulled out a victory in her 2012 Missouri reelection campaign.

In the twenty-first century, the use of sexist or demeaning comments may actually no longer work against women candidates; in fact, they can backfire. In 2012, my Republican opponent's campaign manager called me "Daddy's little girl" and a "prom queen" in press releases. My actual Republican opponent, Kurt Bills, quickly disavowed those statements, saying he'd never approved them and that his campaign staff needed to be more respectful. I went on to win that race by a spread of 35 percentage points, though I don't honestly believe that those isolated comments (which I simply ignored)—or being characterized as "Miss Congeniality" at another point in the race—affected the election's outcome in any way.

Although women in politics have made great strides, I feel strongly that we must never rest on our laurels. We need a forward-looking strategy to add to our numbers. First up, we must make sure women are in positions that involve actual decision-making authority. That alone inspires other young women to achieve the same goals. Our country has always thrived on a competitive spirit—in both business and government—so shutting out half the population from governing and competing at the top levels is simply not a good idea.

Hillary Clinton, Condoleezza Rice, Madeleine Albright as U.S. Secretary of State? Girls all around the world saw those three women serve in one of the country's most important jobs. Janet Napolitano as Homeland Security Secretary and Sylvia Burwell as the Director of the Office of Management and Budget and, like Kathleen Sebelius before her, Secretary of Health and Human Services? Susan Rice and Samantha Power as National Security Adviser and UN Ambassador? Elaine Chao and Hilda Solis as Secretaries of Labor? Penny Pritzker as Secretary of Commerce? Elizabeth Dole and Mary Peters as Transportation Secretaries? Janet Reno and Loretta Lynch as Attorneys General? Nancy Pelosi as Speaker of the House? These were once traditionally male jobs and these women have shown how they are more than qualified to do them.

One of my favorite moments in the last few years was helping Sonia Sotomayor get confirmed as a U.S. Supreme Court Justice. I watched as young girls clasped her hands and flocked around her, a sight that would bring tears to anyone's eyes. Every time a woman gets elected governor or mayor or is appointed police chief, she provides one more role model for one more little girl. One example from the home front? In 2015, our nineteen-year-old daughter was so excited to get her photo taken with the "Notorious RBG" (a.k.a. Justice Ruth Bader Ginsburg) that she agreed to go to a formal dinner with me just for that purpose. But before posting the photo on Facebook, she put the moment all in perspective. "Mom," she said, "I hope you're okay with this; I cropped you out of the picture."

As for the Senate, when I came in there were only sixteen of us, and now there are twenty. At least no one can ever refer to us again as the "Sweet Sixteen." As I noted in a tweet the month we reached twenty, "W/ 20 women we had our first-ever in U.S. history traffic jam in women senators' restroom. #somerecordsmustbebroken."

In addition to increasing our numbers and inspiring more women to run by creating more role models, the second way to ensure more women will win top jobs in government and business is to admit that women still face barriers when they try to seek power. The barriers may not be the same as they were in the past, but they still exist. Facebook executive Sheryl Sandberg has done a good job of taking this on in the business context, both in her much-read book *Lean In* and in subsequent newspaper columns.

My first few months in the Senate reminded me oddly of my first months at the law firm back in 1985. There were a lot of guys around and they seemed to accept me but every so often I wished I had more people that could relate to me like they seemed to relate to each other. It was just a feeling, but it was there.

I've heard people tell stories about blatant sexual harassment in the Senate in decades past, and I believe them. But in my view that era is fading with every passing year. I just don't see that when I go to work. But as a woman in the Senate, it still has not reached the point where I don't feel like a minority. With women comprising only 20 percent of the Senate, we still are very much in the minority, a situation that holds true—only to differing degrees—for female state legislators and local officials around the country. And there are still times in politics when I ask myself: "Would that have happened to me if I was a man?"

From the outside looking in, it may seem almost absurd that I would even think this way as I have risen up in seniority in the Senate. After the last election, I was appointed to a Democratic leadership position as head of Steering and Outreach. But just like so many women and racial and ethnic minorities do every day, I still ask myself from time to time if I was treated one way or another simply because I am different than most of the other people in my profession. I'm pretty sure I know the answer: sometimes I am, sometimes I'm not, and most of the time I will never know.

That brings me to the third way to fix the system, which is to show the world that women know how to use the power we have for good ends—to show that we know how to be effective. And we do have an advantage. As Barbara Mikulski—the dean of the women senators, the ranking member of the Appropriations Committee, and the queen of witty quips—once said, "Women view issues not just on the macro level, but also on the macaroni and cheese level."

Our challenge is to use the different views and experiences we bring into government to make change for the better. We must remember that although the road to power may not be easy, our work has gained us more than a few seats at the table. And as I once heard said at an EMILY's List event, it is always better to be at the table than to be on the menu.

I think a strong case can be made that we are now coming into our own in the U.S. Senate. Increasingly, what we don't have in numbers, we have made up for in power. On the Democratic side, in 2014 eight of the Senate committees were chaired by women. In 2015, most of these women are now ranking members of various Senate committees with Republican Susan Collins chairing the Committee on Aging and Lisa Murkowski chairing Energy and Natural Resources.

I have consistently found that these women are leaders who enjoy getting things done. Partly that's because most of the women who have risen to this level in politics have come up through what I call the accountability route. To get to where they are, they've really had to prove themselves to the people they represent. When I was county attorney, I would scan websites, looking for the sites of other women officeholders such as Janet Napolitano of Arizona and Kathleen Sebelius of Kansas. I would study the speeches and the practical policy approaches of then U.S. Senator Hillary Clinton. Almost invariably, women elected officials would spell out goals and offer up data to show the public what they had actually done.

As someone once said, women politicians need to "speak softly and carry a big statistic." Though I don't agree with the "speak softly" part, time and time again I have seen elected women leaders focus on accountability and results.

In the Senate, many of our bipartisan victories over the difficult last few years have been achieved by the women senators. Debbie Stabenow ushered the farm bill through; Barbara Boxer led the way for both the transportation and water resources bills; Barbara Mikulski and Patty Murray pushed through the budget and appropriations bills. I worked together with Senator Leahy to successfully spearhead bipartisan support for the Violence Against Women Act, with every woman senator voting for it, making it difficult for certain Republican members of the House to push for their weaker version. Kirsten Gillibrand, Claire McCaskill, and so many others were successful in changing the way the military is handling sexual assaults.

When that needless government shutdown occurred in 2013, my husband kept calling me at work and saying, "What are you doing about it? This is absurd. This is an embarrassment." The breakthrough happened when Republican Susan Collins made the floor speech that sparked the formation of our bipartisan group to end the shutdown. I was the first Democrat who called her, and the plan the fourteen of us—half women—came up with was basically the plan the leaders adopted to get us out of that mess.

To ensure that women gain more positions of power, we need to make sure citizens know about these successes. We need them to know that more women equals better governing. We spend a lot of time talking about and batting down sexist comments or stereotypes. But to truly move forward, we need to sell the successes of women in power.

To date, much of the attention on the women senators has focused on the every-other-month bipartisan dinners we have to build good relationships and trust. But the story should be about much more than twenty women eating dinner together. What really matters is what we've accomplished. The story should be about what has come out of our comradery. Passing a budget, managing appropriations, ending a shutdown, getting a highway bill done, and ushering through a groundbreaking report on torture? Those are—to borrow the phrase of former Minnesota congresswoman Coya Knutson's 1958 six-foot-four-inch opponent—"man-sized jobs" successfully led by the women of the Senate. The more the electorate hears these stories, the more women will be elected to the Senate, to governors' offices, and yes, even to the presidency.

December 13, 2014

On a cold Saturday in December 2014, something pretty interesting happened in the Senate. No one noticed it much, because it was a Saturday and not many of the regular reporters were there. It was also a month after an election in which the Republicans had taken back the Senate, our Democratic leadership was in the waning weeks of power, and everyone was focused on which Republicans would be chairing what committees in 2015.

But then, just as things were in something of a no-one-will-remember-these-last-few-weeks-before-Christmas Rip Van Winkle fog, Senator Ted Cruz of Texas did something that could only be described as just too grinchy for even the grinchiest of partisans. Late on Friday evening, hours after Senate leaders Harry Reid and Mitch McConnell had publicly announced that we were finished for the weekend and would vote next on nominations the following Monday, Cruz decided to go for broke. He called for a vote the next day—Saturday, December 13, 2014—on a "constitutional point of order" that attacked President Obama's executive order on immigration.

Never mind that Cruz knew he wouldn't succeed. Never mind that the business at the end of the year was focused on passing the omnibus spending bill and dealing with a raft of nominations for such important jobs as Surgeon General, Director of National Intelligence, general counsel and chief financial officer of the Department of Veterans Affairs, Administrator of the National Highway Traffic Safety Administration, as well as the nominations of a number of ambassadors and federal judges. And never mind that many senators were already heading home for the weekend after both leaders gave them the green light to leave.

Ted Cruz was on a mission. And under existing Senate rules, his call for a vote on a constitutional point of order meant that there was no stopping him. Everyone had to come back to Washington, and everyone had to come back by noon the next day.

Senators who had just flown home flew back for the Saturday votes. Joe Manchin was driving to Pittsburgh for a family gathering. He stopped in a hotel and drove back. Kelly Ayotte had already returned to New Hampshire and was planning to see *The Nutcracker* with her daughter.

Of course, no one feels sorry for politicians who lose a weekend day or have their regular weekend schedule disrupted. And they shouldn't. Senators learn to expect the unexpected, and that means knowing that anything can happen. (Okay, Kelly Ayotte's daughter had the right to feel more than a little disappointed.) The question one should ask, however, is this: what was the vote's purpose? It wasn't to govern. It wasn't to compromise. It wasn't to accomplish some pressing piece of end-of-the-year business. The purpose was to make a point—or, more accurately, to score a political point.

Senator Cruz would go on to lose his vote, but what happened on the way to that loss was what made it all so interesting. Many of the Republicans were angry with him; more than one said publicly, "I think it's counterproductive."

At some point in the early hours of the afternoon, our side decided to turn the tables and go for it. We were all back anyway, so why not vote on more and more of the president's nominations. All in all, including the procedural votes, we pushed through twenty-eight roll call votes, with some arguments in between. Senator Cruz offered to end it late in the afternoon, but we said *no*, let's just keep going. We are all here for the weekend anyway.

Now, at the beginning, it wasn't exactly a charged-up group. It was a pissed-off group. A lot of people had lost their elections and a lot of people had gotten very little sleep. So one important goal was to keep everyone there and voting. As one of the proponents for the don't-stop-till-we-drop strategy, I brought in the electric piano from our apartment (something we had gotten for Abigail when she was taking lessons). We plugged it in in a back room and sang Christmas carols in between votes. At one point Mark Warner (a leader in business, the Senate, and, apparently, the communal art of Christmas caroling) led an impressive round of "The Twelve

Days of Christmas" that involved forty senators singing different parts. Cory Booker tweeted out a photo of a group of us, including Roger Wicker, singing around the piano.

In the end, we got a whole lot of people confirmed and Senator Cruz lost his point of order vote 22–74, with twenty Republicans voting against it, including Mitch McConnell. Harry Reid had played it smart and gotten a number of people unexpectedly confirmed; Cruz—perhaps realizing that, this time, even he'd gone too far—would go on to apologize to his colleagues.

That day, as absurd as it was, provides a good example of what seems to be an emerging coalition in the Senate over the last few years. When things get really out of whack, or there is an especially important bill to pass, a good number of Republicans have joined with a good number of Democrats to get the job done. That is the model—a pragmatic, bipartisan approach to problem solving—we have to embrace to move forward as a country.

Since that December day, things have ebbed and flowed, with high points and low points. But in the months that followed, there were several other glimmers of hope. Speaker John Boehner and House Minority Leader Nancy Pelosi negotiated a long-term fix to what had become a yearly issue of impending cuts to Medicare payments to doctors and the potential loss of services to patients; Speaker Boehner even planted a kiss on Leader Pelosi's cheek at a Rose Garden ceremony to celebrate their bipartisan achievement. Senators Bob Corker and Ben Cardin, with help from Tim Kaine, amicably negotiated a review process for any agreement coming out of the Iran nuclear negotiations; Senators Patty Murray and Lamar Alexander negotiated an education bill; a group of seven of us, led by Senators Leahy and Grassley, announced a long-awaited compromise on patent reform; Jeanne Shaheen and Rob Portman passed an energy efficiency bill they'd been trying to pass for more than a year; and we reformed intelligence-gathering laws and reached a compromise to end the two-party stand-off over Senator Cornyn's and my bill to combat sex trafficking.

The coalition of compromisers changes from issue to issue, a reflection of the senators' different views and different constituencies. But what most defines those willing to cross the special interest divides and the parties' chasms is something you don't often see on the Sunday TV shows. It is moderation. And as David Brooks points out in his book *The Road to Character*, a "moderate" is not always someone who takes a position halfway between two opposing views, nor does the term necessarily mean someone who is moderate in temperament. What truly defines moderation in politics is instead a philosophy "based on an awareness of the inevitability of conflict . . . and the idea that things do not fit neatly together."

In his analysis of the virtue of moderation in governing, Brooks makes this point:

> Great matters cannot be settled by taking into account just one principle or one viewpoint. Governing is more like sailing in a storm: shift your weight one way when the boat tilts to starboard, shift your weight the other when it tilts to port—adjust and adjust and adjust to circumstances to keep the semblance and equanimity of an even keel.

As a Midwesterner who gets sick on ships in stormy weather, this isn't the easiest of analogies for me, but I do think it's helpful. And to those who feel queasy when reading this passage on the grounds that it could be interpreted to mean we shouldn't take on big challenges or attempt to make major progress, I suggest a different reading. In the end our ship of state can travel from one place to another only if we are willing to move out into those choppy waters and hoist the sails.

As I always like to remind myself when the storm clouds look particularly threatening, those of us who try to forge alliances do have history on our side. It's important to keep in mind that in none of the country's milestone legislative battles, including epic ones over the Social Security Act of 1935 or the passage of the Voting Rights Act and Medicare in 1965, was there originally unanimous support. What led to those landmark laws was not unanimity but a shared commitment by a bipartisan group of Democratic and Republican lawmakers to advance the welfare—and the rights and interests—of the American people.

If legislators decades ago found the courage and the will and the wherewithal to come together to accomplish great things, surely we can too. And if we can't do that, why are we here in the first place?

Epilogue

A couple of years ago our family visited Slovenia, the home of my ancestors. While we were there, we heard a story about a writer who was dying of cancer and decided to write her own obituary to leave behind for her children. In it, she left them with this wisdom: "[M]ay you always remember that obstacles in the path are not obstacles, they ARE the path."

Our trip happened to take place only a few weeks before Abigail started college, so for the rest of the vacation John and I kept hammering her with that sage advice. The obstacles are the path. The obstacles are the path. It got so bad that she later wrote a commentary about the experience for her college newspaper, describing how the phrase became our mantra for the entire trip. As Abigail wrote: "Plane delayed? Menu all in Slovene? Over 100 degrees and no air conditioning? The obstacles are the path."

Okay, maybe we got a little carried away. But there's actually a lot of truth in those five simple words.

Throughout my journey in life and politics, I've found that obstacles that initially appear insurmountable often turn out to be the best route to a solution. My dad's approach to journalism was grounded in his immigrant family's roots and the simple idea that ordinary people can do extraordinary things. How could he have called the national presidential race in 1960 if he hadn't grown up in that hardscrabble mining town and understood how people on Minnesota's Iron Range would vote? Would he have worked as hard as he did in college if my grandma hadn't pushed him to pursue his dreams? My grandpa and grandma devoted their entire lives to their family, with my grandpa giving up everything to work underground in the mines so his two sons could get ahead. Would my dad have ended up where he did if not for his parents' sacrifice?

In my own life, each challenge has taught me to take on an even bigger one. My dad's alcoholism, my parents' divorce, and the ups and downs of a big public high school all made it impossible for me to view the world through a narrow lens. There were no black-or-white solutions to what was right or wrong in my family, and no time or space to follow a rigid philosophy or ideology. I learned how to forgive and move on by seeing my mom's fortitude and good humor. I saw how redemption and faith saved my dad. Later, it was always my instinct to look for the good in people and the common ground in conflicts because when I was growing up, that's what I did to survive.

What if my first law firm hadn't decided to terminate my biggest client, forcing me to choose between the stability of my newly earned partnership and starting anew at another firm? If it hadn't happened, I might still be working as a telecommunications lawyer. Or if Abigail hadn't been so sick when she was born—and our life so suddenly different from what they said it would be like in those parenting books—would I have been given the gift of having at least some understanding of the lives of parents with kids with disabilities? Would I have ever been inspired to go into politics? Would I have known that true love was seeing my husband taking care of our daughter night after night after night?

The obstacles were my path.

Every tough election, grueling debate, and difficult decision as a prosecutor taught me the value of character and gave me one more dose of courage. And when I got to Washington and saw the roadblocks in the way of progress for the people of this country, and observed the big money and the pall it casts on the place, it only increased my resolve to do everything possible to find a way forward.

Over the past few years, I've seen far too many people in politics play on the extremes to get attention, raise money, and expand their power base. I've had a front row seat to the flame throwing and the saber rattling, the shutdowns and the slowdowns. Yet instead of viewing every tumultuous event in our nation's capital as an end, I've decided to see each one as a beginning.

If members of Congress refuse to act like grown-ups and rejoice in shutting down the government, the American people will call them on it. If elected officials insist on playing politics with such important issues as immigration reform and foreign policy, the people will see through the charade. If our leaders want to close their eyes to major long-term problems such as income inequality, out-of-date infrastructure, climate change, and the national debt, or insulate themselves from the rest of the world just because a policy is currently unpopular, the American people will eventually challenge them to do better.

And when people finally get sick and tired of all the big money in Washington, the citizens of this country will decide that enough is enough. Eventually, we will change the rules and maybe even the U.S. Constitution.

But to make our country a better place and to bring back that shared duty and purpose, we need advocates for change *and* we need people who can find common ground. We need rabble rousers, but we also need those who are willing to cross the partisan divide and push and prod for compromise. As biographer Walter Isaacson says about America's founders, and Benjamin Franklin in particular, "Compromisers may not make great heroes, but they do make great democracies."

In a time of instant TV heroes, political Twitterstorms, and single-issue Super PACs, it's harder than ever to be a compromiser. Today those who reach for the middle are more likely to encounter protests than praise, and brambles instead of bouquets. But I take solace in the fact that even some of the Senate's most fiery advocates—such as Minnesota's own Hubert Humphrey—were also adept at the art of compromise.

A few years into my first term, I brought my staff together to watch a documentary about Humphrey's life called *Hubert H. Humphrey: The Art of the Possible*. All of us were awed by the closing credits, which included a scrolling list of the bipartisan bills Humphrey had passed as a senator. Humphrey's ability to get things done was one of the many reasons why, soon after I arrived in Washington, I requested his desk in the Senate chamber. The small wooden desk finally arrived a few months later, and when I opened the desktop and saw the carved names of the senators who had used the desk, I immediately spotted the bold printed name "Humphrey." The problem? The first name wasn't "Hubert," it was "Gordon." They had mistakenly given me the desk of little-known former Republican Senator Gordon Humphrey of New Hampshire.

By this time I had already learned to pick my battles. I used Gordon Humphrey's desk for a long time. Then one day, soon after a new Congress had been sworn in, I was talking to my seatmate and friend Jeanne Shaheen of New Hampshire. I told her the story of my Gordon Humphrey desk, and she asked how I knew it was his. "Well, they carve their names in the desks when they leave," I explained as I opened the desktop. But to my surprise the names I found were completely different. During the Senate's winter recess they had made the switch—I finally had Hubert Humphrey's desk.

Years later I still have that desk. And if this Humphrey treasure isn't enough to get me through the most acrimonious days, there is always the bipartisan women senators' group, as well as the weekly Senate prayer breakfast meetings. These get-togethers allow people from across the political spectrum to get to know one another. Just as we maintain friendships back home with friends and neighbors we don't always see eye to eye with politically, Democrats and Republicans in Washington, D.C., must learn to get along for the greater good.

In "The Road Not Taken," the American poet Robert Frost famously penned these lines: *Two roads diverged in a wood, and I— / I took the one less traveled by, / And that has made all the difference.* But in "Mending Wall," Frost also wrote of two neighbors who met "at spring mending-time" to repair a stone wall separating their plots of land, an apple orchard and a grove of pines. "Good fences make good neighbors," one man says twice as the two, in their annual ritual, *meet to walk the line / And set the wall between us once again.* In speaking for the other man walking that line, Frost ponders whether such fences—such barriers—are truly necessary, asking: *"Why* do they make good neighbors?" As Frost's evocative poem reads: *Before I built a wall I'd ask to know / What I was walling in or walling out, / And to whom I was like to give offense.*

In the U.S. Senate I've tried my best to be a good citizen and a good neighbor. Whenever possible I've worked to tear down the stone walls that have been built up over the years and so often get in the way of friendship, dialogue, and mutual respect. I've focused on finding common

ground with my colleagues, no matter how many times I disagree with
their views. I have built up a good record for introducing and passing
bills on a bipartisan basis, and I always try to be civil. I'm not in the habit
of taking potshots at my colleagues, on TV or elsewhere. When I travel
to another senator's state to speak at a political event such as a Democratic dinner, for instance, I let them know I'm coming, if only as a
common courtesy. And I've even gone so far as to check with my fellow
senators before ribbing them in humorous speeches I've made at the
National Press Club, the Congressional Correspondents' Dinner, and the
Gridiron Club.

None of this means I don't stand my ground on matters of principle.
Legitimate policy disagreements are to be expected in politics—and are
certainly fair game. What I object to is all the needless bickering that gets
in the way of needed compromise. You can't legislate without coalitions
and relationships built on trust. And you can't have trust if you don't like
the people you work with. Respect and trust make the work much more
satisfying—and yes, even joyful from time to time—but that respect and
trust also prepare you for that one moment when you can actually get
something done.

My colleague Sherrod Brown always wears a lapel pin with a yellow
bird in a cage on it. "The canary," he says, "represents the struggle for economic and social justice." For decades, miners in Ohio depended on the
canaries—the little birds were, quite literally, their lifeline. With no mine
safety laws and no trade unions to protect them, early American coal miners would carry canaries into the mines; if the birds died, they knew the
air was too toxic to breathe.

Sometimes, when I see that pin on Sherrod's suit coat, I think that his
canary is not just a symbol of economic justice; it's also a statement about
the toxicity of our politics. There are days when I almost feel as if I can't
breathe in the Capitol, and I just want to run out its heavy gilded doors
to somewhere nicer and quieter and much more pleasant. I think of the
vast prairies and farmland of my home state, the beautiful lakes and
streams of the heartland, and the rugged hikes on Minnesota's North
Shore along Lake Superior.

But then I remember why I came to Washington in the first place.

One day a woman from Sherrod's state came to Washington to speak to a group of us about her life. She had fallen on tough times, and she and her husband were having trouble keeping up with their mortgage and couldn't imagine how they could ever afford to send their kids to college. For years, she said, she thought the words "Restore the Middle Class" were nothing more than a slogan on a political bumper sticker. But when her husband was laid off, when her family began struggling to make ends meet, she had come to see those words as nothing less than "a prayer."

And then she asked one heartbreaking question: "Why does the American Dream have to end with me?"

I've now spent more than eight years working to govern in the Senate, and I've served with many people of good will. They, too, don't want the American Dream to end with them. While all of us can be tossed to and fro by the ever-present pull of interest groups and partisan politics, for the most part we share a common goal: to make America a better nation. Everyone genuinely wants their children and grandchildren to inherit a better world.

There is, I know, no panacea to curing the ills of modern-day politics. Because I can't control what others do, all I can do is try to stay true to myself, to stay focused, and to keep my eyes on the North Star. And as for all those obstacles, all those hurdles and fences and stone walls I've run into and around and over through the years? Every one of them has taught me something. And what I've learned so far is this: far more often than not, when you really want to get somewhere or do something and move ahead, the obstacles aren't really obstacles—the obstacles are your path.

NOTES

CHAPTER 1

5   GI loan: Jim Klobuchar, *Minstrel: My Adventure in Newspapering* (Minneapolis: University of Minnesota Press, 1997), p. 11.

6   only teach until you were five months pregnant: Interview with Gwen Mosberg; "Second School Vote April 22 at La Crescent," *The Winona Daily News* (Winona, MN), Mar. 13, 1967 ("The pregnancy policy of not allowing a teacher to teach after five months of pregnancy will remain, but the board may review each case on an individual basis."). Such policies were, after much advocacy, later changed by school districts around the country. "Virginia News Briefs," *The Danville Register* (Danville, VA), Nov. 20, 1971; John Carmody, "Expectant Mothers Fight to Keep Teaching," *Anderson Sunday Herald* (Anderson, IN), Jan. 30, 1972.

8   "independent merchant running against a chain store": Hubert H. Humphrey, *The Education of a Public Man: My Life and Politics* (Minneapolis: The University of Minnesota Press, 1991), p. 152. For more on the 1960 primaries and general election, see Chris Matthews, *Jack Kennedy: Elusive Hero* (New York: Simon & Schuster, 2011).

8   my dad: Jim Klobuchar, *Minstrel*, pp. 1–24.

9   five electoral votes shy: *Triumph and Tragedy: The Story of the Kennedys* (New York: The Associated Press, 1968), p. 155 ("Sometime during the night, Michigan went into the Kennedy column to stay. Jack Kennedy was five votes short of the magic 269. Minnesota decided it. At 12:33 p.m. on November 9, The Associated Press bulletined that the state's eleven electoral votes were assured for Kennedy. Illinois fell to him later. California's decision was not known until November 16. It went for Nixon by 35,000."); *compare* Associated Press, "Eight Electoral Votes Needed in Tight Race," *The Progress-Index* (Petersburg-Colonial Heights, VA), Nov. 9, 1960.

9   Minnesota, Illinois, and California: Gary A. Donaldson, *The First Modern*

Campaign: Kennedy, Nixon, and the Election of 1960 (Lanham, MD: Rowman & Littlefield, 2007), pp. 146–47; James Reston, "Kennedy's Victory Won by Close Margin," *New York Times*, Nov. 10, 1960.

9   thousands of votes were still unreported: Reporters of the Associated Press, *Breaking News: How the Associated Press Has Covered War, Peace, and Everything Else* (New York: Princeton Architectural Press, 2007), p. 180.

9   "If you grew up on Minnesota's Iron Range": Jim Klobuchar, *Minstrel*, p. 3.

10   Silence followed: Jim Klobuchar, "Sweaty Fingers in Minneapolis, and an Election," May 31, 2012, http://www.ecumen.org/blog/jim-klobuchar-sweaty-fingers -minneapolis-and-election#.VPIS5mTF84Q.

10   sent out across the wires: "AP Also Was Winner in Presidential Race," Associated Press, Winter 1960–61, p. 7. A special thanks to Dave Espo, an AP special correspondent, for locating—and passing along—this in-house AP publication.

10   As James Reston: Reston, "Kennedy's Victory Won by Close Margin."

10   three pigs: Jim Klobuchar, "Sweaty Fingers in Minneapolis, and an Election," May 31, 2012.

11   a cover showing Jackie Kennedy: "Jackie Kennedy: A Front Runner's Appealing Wife," *Life*, Aug. 24, 1959. At the time that 1959 photograph of Jackie Kennedy was taken, John F. Kennedy was of course still a presidential *candidate*.

11   President Roosevelt's funeral: Jonathan Alter, *The Promise: President Obama, Year One* (New York: Simon & Schuster, 2010), p. 423.

11   "There'll be great Presidents again": Theodore H. White, "For President Kennedy: An Epilogue," *Life*, Dec. 6, 1963, pp. 158–59.

12   Minnesota's beaming Governor Wendell Anderson: *TIME*, Aug. 13, 1973.

13   in 1947: "Reading Boosts School Average," *Manitowoc Herald Times*, Feb. 5, 1947 ("The board approved employment of four new kindergarten teachers to start next September. They are Mary Louise Harman and Harriet Gass of Wauwatosa and Rose Katherine Heuberger and Gwendolyn Gehring of Milwaukee. All are graduates of Milwaukee State Teachers college.").

13   Manitowoc Shipbuilding Company: William Hakala, *Voyage of Vision: The Manitowoc Company, a Century of Extraordinary Growth* (2002); Wisconsin Maritime Museum, *Maritime Manitowoc 1847–1947* (Charleston, SC: Arcadia Publishing, 2006), p. 99.

13   an afternoon tea: "100 Attend Tea Held by Mothers Club Wednesday," *Manitowoc Herald Times*, Nov. 18, 1948.

13   walking the picket line: "Vacation Ends in Minneapolis: Teachers Halt Strike," *Milwaukee Journal*, Feb. 14, 1951.

15   she died: Tim Nelson, "Rose Klobuchar, Mother of Sen. Amy Klobuchar, Dies," MPR News, Aug. 2, 2010, http://www.mprnews.org/story/2010/08/02/rose -klobuchar.

16   "lived at several cheese factories": "John Wuetrich, 68, Dies; Cheesemaker," *Monroe Evening Times*, Aug. 16, 1945. "Wuetrich" is a variant of Wuthrich, the spelling that is used in his Petition of Naturalization filed on October 31, 1916.

16   arrived at Ellis Island: List or Manifest of Alien Passengers for the United States Immigration Officer at Port of Arrival (S.S. *Orbita*, Passengers Sailing from Cherbourg, arriving at Port of New York, Oct. 22, 1923); Record of Aliens Held for Special Inquiry, S.S. *Orbita*, arrived "10/23/23," with "Cause of Detention" listed as "QE & Can. Insp." QE stands for "Quota Exceeded," a reference to the 1921 Emergency Quota Act, also known as the Emergency Immigration

Act or the Immigration Restriction Act of 1921, Pub. L. 67-5, 42 Stat. 5 (May 19, 1921).

16 U.S. quotas for Swiss immigrants: "Immigration Lists Show Small Quotas," *The Fort Wayne Journal-Gazette* (Fort Wayne, IN), Apr. 12, 1923; "An Indignant Swiss," *The Indianapolis News* (Indianapolis, IN), July 19, 1923 (noting how one Swiss immigrant was refused entry to the U.S. after arriving at Ellis Island—and promptly sent back to Europe—because "the Swiss quota . . . was full and that he could not be admitted"). As 1920s news reports show, the timing of a ship's arrival could be critical to a hopeful immigrant's chances of entry. "New Immigration Policy Is Needed," *Wise County Messenger* (Decatur, TX), Dec. 21, 1923 ("Under the present restrictive measure, steamship companies race their vessels across the ocean in an effort to land their passengers before the monthly quota has been filled. Many vessels arrive too late and aliens who have disposed of their property at a great sacrifice are forced to return to their old home in a penniless condition."); "No More Races with Immigrants," *The Logansport Morning Press* (Logansport, IN), Aug. 9, 1921 (noting "[f]rantic midnight racing of immigrant laden steamers into American harbors to land monthly quotas in the first minutes of the first day of new months").

16 traveled by train: List or Manifest of Alien Passengers Applying for Admission to the United States from Foreign Contiguous Territory, U.S. Department of Labor Immigration Service (Port of Detroit, Michigan), Nov. 24, 1923.

16 Canadian immigration sources: Canadian Museum of Immigration at Pier 21, "Canadian Immigration Process," http://www.virtualmuseum.ca/Exhibitions/Pier21/eng/chronologie-evenements-immigration-timeline-events-immigration-eng.html; Michael C. LeMay, *From Open Door to Dutch Door: An Analysis of U.S. Immigration Policy Since 1820* (Westport, CT: Praeger Publishers, 1987), p. 82; Mae M. Ngai, *Impossible Subjects: Illegal Aliens and the Making of Modern America* (Princeton, NJ: Princeton University Press, 2004), pp. 64–66; Immigration Act of 1924, Pub. L. 68-139, 43 Stat. 153 (May 26, 1924).

17 register as an alien: Alien Registration Act of 1940, Pub. L. 76-670, 54 Stat. 670 (June 28, 1940); U.S. Immigration and Naturalization Service, Alien Registration Form for Martin Heuberger, Sept. 4, 1940.

17 The next year: Letter from the U.S. Department of Justice, Immigration and Naturalization Service, Apr. 21, 1941, File No. 11-285658.

17 applied for citizenship: Petition for Naturalization of Martin Heuberger dated Sept. 5, 1941, with Oath of Allegiance taken by Martin Heuberger on November 18, 1941.

17 our country declared war: Frank L. Kluckhohn, "U.S. Now at War with Germany and Italy," *New York Times*, Dec. 12, 1941; Charles A. Beard, *President Roosevelt and the Coming of the War, 1941: Appearances and Realities* (New Brunswick, NJ: Transaction Publishers, 2011), pp. 209–10.

17 In 2013: Seung Min Kim, "Immigration Reform 2013: Senate Passes Legislation 68–32," *Politico*, June 27, 2013, http://www.politico.com/story/2013/06/immigration-bill-2013-senate-passes-93530.html.

18 floor speeches: Lisa Mascaro, "For These Senators, Immigration Is a Personal Story," *Los Angeles Times,* June 23, 2013; Amy Klobuchar Floor Speech, June 18, 2013; Amy Klobuchar Floor Speech, June 25, 2013.

19 "mad hatter": Lyndon Comstock, *Annie Clemenc and the Great Keweenaw*

Copper Strike (Austin, TX: CreateSpace, 2013), p. 142; Leon Brimer, *Chemical Food Safety* (Oxfordshire, UK: CABI, 2011), p. 144; Sharon L. Zuber and Michael C. Newman, eds., *Mercury Pollution: A Transdisciplinary Treatment* (Boca Raton, FL: CRC Press, 2012), p. 2.

19   the Habsburg Dynasty: Oto Luthar, ed., *The Land Between: A History of Slovenia* (Frankfurt: Peter Lang, 2008), pp. 123–40; Leopoldina Plut-Pregelj and Carole Rogel, *The A to Z of Slovenia* (Lanham, MD: Scarecrow Press, 2007), pp. xxi–xxiii, 94.

19   Minnesota's Iron Range: Jim Klobuchar, *Minstrel*, pp. 25–51; Jim Klobuchar, *Over Minnesota* (San Francisco, CA: Weldon Owen, 1992), pp. 33–39 (photography by Jerry Stebbins); Jim Klobuchar, "A Miner's Son Goes Home," *The Minneapolis Star*, Mar. 4, 1978 (Saturday magazine).

19   "If the New World": Jim Klobuchar, "An Iron Ranger's Roots: Grandmother's Birth Record Rekindles Story," *Minneapolis Star and Tribune*, Aug. 19, 1985. This column was one of a series that ran in the newspaper from August 18–23, 1985.

19   my grandpa Mike: Jim Klobuchar, *Pieces of My Heart: Everyone Has an Everest* (Minneapolis: Nodin Press, 2007), pp. 168–74.

20   Mike and Mary: "Mary Klobuchar, 91, Former Columnist's Mother," *StarTribune*, Apr. 23, 1999 (obituary); "Obituaries: Mary Klobuchar," *The Ely Echo*, Apr. 26, 1999; Chick Beel, "Bush Pilots: Mining, Part III," *The Ely Echo*, May 31, 1999.

22   tiger mom: Amy Chua, *Battle Hymn of the Tiger Mother* (London: Bloomsbury, 2011).

22   Simon Bourgin: Simon Bourgin, *An Odyssey That Began in Ely* (Ely, MN: Ely-Winton Historical Society, 2010); Angie Riebe, "Ely's Simon Bourgin," *Mesabi Daily News* (Virginia, MN), Aug. 11, 2007; Megan McDonough, "Simon E. Bourgin, Journalist, Policy Advisor, Dies at 99," *Washington Post*, Oct. 4, 2013; Tom Rose, "Early Ely Had Several Jewish Families," *Ely Echo*, Aug. 31, 2013; "Simon Bourgin Writes," HometownFocus.US, http://www.hometownfocus.us/news/2011-03-25/Features/Simon_Bourgin_writes.html.

23   George Sanders: Alfred Hitchcock, *Foreign Correspondent* (1940).

23   Tyne Souja: Jim Klobuchar, *Heroes Among Us: Uncommon Minnesotans* (Duluth, MN: Pfeifer-Hamilton, 1996), pp. 189–91.

23   Wordsworth: William Wordsworth, "Composed Upon Westminster Bridge, September 3, 1802," in Geoffrey Durrant, *Wordsworth and the Great System: A Study of Wordsworth's Poetic Universe* (Cambridge: Cambridge University Press, 1970), p. 58.

23   Sigurd Olson: Sigurd F. Olson, *The Singing Wilderness* (Minneapolis: University of Minnesota Press, 1997); David Backes, *A Wilderness Within: The Life of Sigurd F. Olson* (Minneapolis: University of Minnesota Press, 1997), pp. 246–47; Jim Klobuchar, *Minstrel*, p. 48; Jim Klobuchar, "Silence of the Forest Pays Tribute to Olson," *The Minneapolis Star*, Jan. 14, 1982.

24   Boundary Waters: Kevin Proescholdt, Rip Rapson, and Miron L. Heinselman, *Troubled Waters: The Fight for the Boundary Waters Canoe Area Wilderness* (St. Cloud, MN: North Star Press of St. Cloud, 1995), pp. 7, 10, 277; Dave Kenney, *Northern Lights: The Stories of Minnesota's Past*, 2d ed. (St. Paul: Minnesota Historical Society Press, 2003), pp. 304–5. In the U.S. House of Representatives, Minnesota Congressman Bruce Vento was also very involved in efforts to preserve the Boundary Waters.

25   my dad wrote a book: Jim Klobuchar, *Will the Vikings Ever Win the Super Bowl?* (New York: Harper & Row, 1977). In the 1970s, my dad also wrote a book about

the Vikings and a biography of their popular quarterback Fran Tarkenton. Jim Klobuchar, *True Hearts and Purple Heads: An Unauthorized Biography of a Football Team* (Minneapolis: Ross & Haines, 1970); Jim Klobuchar and Fran Tarkenton, *Tarkenton* (New York: Harper & Row, 1976). Through the years, my dad has continued writing about the team, ever hopeful that one day they *will* win the Super Bowl. Jim Klobuchar, *Purple Hearts and Golden Memories: 35 Years with the Minnesota Vikings* (Coal Valley, IL: Quality Sports Publications, 1999); Jim Klobuchar, *Knights and Knaves of Autumn: 40 Years of Pro Football and the Minnesota Vikings* (Cambridge, MN: Adventure Publications, 2000).

25   "Fred and Ginger of daily newspaper columnists": William Swanson, "Barbara and Jim," *Mpls.-St. Paul Magazine*, Mar. 1, 1999 (interview).

25   He loved to do crazy things: Jim Klobuchar, *Minstrel* (photos of my dad skydiving, playing "Minnesota Fats" in a game of pool, ice climbing at 22,000 feet in the Peruvian Andes, and of the piece of chalk—pursed between his lips—exploding after being shot out of his mouth by a sharpshooter). My dad's passion for mountaineering, trekking, and wilderness adventures led him to write several other books. Jim Klobuchar, *Where the Wind Blows Bittersweet* (Wayzata, MN: Ralph Turtinen Publishing Co., 1975); Jim Klobuchar, *Wild Places and Gentle Breezes* (Stillwater, MN: Voyageur Press, 1990); Jim Klobuchar, *Pieces of My Heart*, pp. 168–74.

25   *The Wrestler*: Jim Westerman, *The Wrestler* (1974) (produced by professional wrestler Verne Gagne and W. R. Frank).

26   "If they are going to carry off their seats": "Columnist Suspended," *New York Times*, Dec. 24, 1981.

26   Munich hofbrauhaus and Mousey's Bar: Jim Klobuchar, *The Zest (and Best) of Jim Klobuchar* (Minneapolis: Minneapolis Star and Tribune Co., 1967), pp. 45, 52.

26   alcohol-related driving offenses: Jim Klobuchar, *Pursued by Grace: A Newspaperman's Own Story of Spiritual Recovery* (Minneapolis: Augsburg Fortress Publishers, 1998), pp. 38, 91–102; Lisa DePaulo, "The Audacity of Minnesota: Senator Amy Klobuchar," *Elle*, Mar. 30, 2010.

26   response to the 1993 arrest: Jim Klobuchar and Tim McGuire's editor's note, "An Apology for an Act of Reckless Behavior, a Violation of Trust," *StarTribune*, May 4, 1993. After his DWI arrest in Maple Plain, Minnesota, my dad—in a book chapter titled "The Mirror Is Not Always Kind"—later reflected on his dangerous behavior, describing his prior alcohol-related driving violations this way before confronting the fact that he was an alcoholic: "I drank because I was an alcoholic. The reason wasn't any more complicated than that." Jim Klobuchar, *Minstrel*, pp. 217–18; Jim Klobuchar, *Pursued by Grace*, pp. 91–93.

27   "heroes among us": Jim Klobuchar, *Heroes Among Us*.

27   a five-year-old girl: Jim Klobuchar, *The Zest (and Best) of Jim Klobuchar*, pp. 95–97 (column titled "A Little Girl's Last Train Ride").

28   "Was it worth it?": Jim Klobuchar, *Minstrel*, pp. ix–xiv.

28   "outstanding columnist": He was named outstanding columnist for newspapers with a circulation of more than 100,000 readers. "Former 'Star-Tribune' Sportswriter Klobuchar Joins MinnPost," *Editor & Publisher*, Aug. 19, 2009.

28   "a champion of those on the outside": Amy Kay Nelson, "*Star Tribune*'s Klobuchar 'Roasted' in Alumni Society Event," *The Murphy Reporter, University of Minnesota: School of Journalism and Mass Communication* (Spring 1996), p. 3.

28   my dad retired: Chuck Haga, "For a Minnesota Minstrel, a Rich Ride," *StarTribune*, Dec. 24, 1995.

CHAPTER 2

29   Plymouth was a pioneer town: "Plymouth Schools," Plymouth Historical Soci-
        ety newsletter, vol. 16, no. 1 (Apr. 1998), pp. 3–5; "Beacon Heights School,"
        Plymouth Historical Society newsletter, vol. 7, no. 2 (Sept. 1990), pp. 2–4; and
        "Exploring Plymouth's Past," www.plymouthmnhistoricalsociety.com.

31   read the whole book in one sitting: Laura Ingalls Wilder, *Little House in the Big
        Woods* (New York: HarperCollins, 1961).

34   "The Law of the Camp Fire Girls": *Remarkable Women, Remarkable Wisdom:
        A Daybook of Reflections* (Cincinnati, OH: St. Anthony Messenger Press, 2001),
        p. 112.

38   "Take home a jug of fun": *Daily Journal* (Fergus Falls, MN), June 24, 1977, p. 8
        (containing an ad from that era with A&W's "Take home a jug of fun!" slogan).
        During my 2006 U.S. Senate race, I campaigned at an A&W and told this story.
        Pauline Schreiber, "Amy Klobuchar Makes Campaign Stop at A&W," *Owatonna
        People's Press*, June 10, 2006.

39   Amy's Bread: Amy Scherber and Toy Kim Dupree, *Amy's Bread: Artisan-Style
        Breads, Sandwiches, Pizzas, and More from New York City's Favorite Bakery*,
        rev. & updated (Hoboken, NJ: John Wiley & Sons, 2010), pp. 1–11.

40   David Cassidy's birthday: Phil Hardy and David Laing, eds., *The Encyclopedia
        of Rock* (Frogmore, UK: Panther Books, 1976), vol. 3, p. 59.

40   Molly: Jim Klobuchar, "There Go His Socks!," *The Minneapolis Star*, May 14,
        1974 (noting Molly's arrival in our house three days earlier); Herbert W. Chil-
        strom, *My Friend Jonah and Other Dogs I've Loved* (Edina, MN: Huff Publishing
        Associates, 2014), pp. ix–xi (my foreword to Bishop Chilstrom's book describing
        Molly, our family dog).

41   *Jim Klobuchar's Merry-Go-Round*: *The Working Press of the Nation* (Chicago,
        IL: The National Research Bureau, 1970), p. 526.

42   my dad pledged to join AA: Jim Klobuchar, *Minstrel: My Adventure in News-
        papering* (Minneapolis: University of Minnesota Press, 1997), p. 205.

43   "pursued by grace": Jim Klobuchar, *Pursued by Grace: A Newspaperman's Own
        Story of Spiritual Recovery* (Minneapolis: Augsburg Fortress Publishers, 1998),
        pp. 101, 136–44.

44   the divorce: Jim Klobuchar, *Minstrel*, p. 206; Jim Klobuchar, "Four Days Short
        of an Anniversary," *The Minneapolis Star*, Aug. 3, 1976. My mom did not start
        to learn to drive until August 1972, after eighteen years of marriage. Jim Klo-
        buchar, "She Comes Down from Olympus," *The Minneapolis Star*, Aug. 28,
        1972.

46   long-distance bike rides: For thirty-nine years, from 1974 to 2013, my dad
        led his "Jaunt with Jim" bicycle ride, almost always in Minnesota. The "Klobu-
        char Ride" tradition has now been taken over by Bob Lincoln. *See* Tour of Min-
        nesota Bicycle Tours of Minnesota, "Our History," www.tourofminnesota.com.

47   a historic firestorm: Daniel James Brown, *Under a Flaming Sky: The Great
        Hinckley Firestorm of 1894* (Guilford, CT: The Lyons Press, 2006); Hinckley Fire
        Museum, http://hinckleyfiremuseum.com.

47   challenging bike trips: Jim Klobuchar, "A Thousand Mile Ride Ends in Blue,"
        The Minneapolis Star, May 31, 1975; Jim Klobuchar, "Around the Bend, a
        Moose at Breakfast," *The Minneapolis Star*, June 16, 1975; Jim Klobuchar, "His
        Mother Rescues Him from Folly," *The Minneapolis Star*, June 11, 1976 ("My
        1,000 mile exploration of Minnesota from the seat of a 10-speed brought me

into the land of my ancestors today."). I often accompanied my dad on his bicycling adventures, including the long-distance bike ride I helped plan after my freshman year of college. Jim Klobuchar, "She Twists Him Around Her Spokes," *The Minneapolis Star*, Mar. 24, 1979 (Saturday magazine); Jim Klobuchar, "Nature's Hands Grasp Bikers," *The Minneapolis Star*, May 19, 1979 (Saturday magazine); Jim Klobuchar, "Bruised But Tough, We Ride Together," *The Minneapolis Star*, Dec. 28, 1979.

49   "Happy Warrior": Ralph G. Martin, *A Man for All People: Hubert H. Humphrey* (New York: Grosset & Dunlap, 1968) (containing a photo of Hubert Humphrey's campaign plane emblazoned with the words "HAPPY WARRIOR").

49   "Stairway to Heaven": Led Zeppelin, *Led Zeppelin IV*, "Stairway to Heaven" (1971).

53   "lean in": Sheryl Sandberg with Nell Scovell, *Lean In: Women, Work, and the Will to Lead* (New York: Alfred A. Knopf, 2013).

CHAPTER 3

56   Steve Isaacs: William Yardley, "Stephen D. Isaacs, Journalist and Educator, Dies at 76," *The New York Times*, Sept. 4, 2014 ("Mr. Isaacs was 39 when he left to become editor of *The Minneapolis Star* in 1978. *The Star*, an afternoon paper, was struggling with declining circulation, and Mr. Isaacs sought to revive it by promoting longer, investigative articles on local issues. He left four years later, after *The Star* agreed to merge with *The Minneapolis Tribune*."). At the time of the merger, Mr. Isaacs was called "a big, indiscreet, intimidating Easterner in a town known for its Scandinavian reserve." Ibid.

57   a credit card: At that time, my dad frequently complained about people having to pay fees to credit card companies. *See, e.g.,* Jim Klobuchar, "Without a Credit Card You Are Zero," *Minneapolis Tribune*, Jan. 7, 1978.

58   Nathan Hale: *Nathan Hale*, 1913, Bela Lyon Pratt (1867–1917) (Location: Old Campus); M. William Phelps, *Nathan Hale: The Life and Death of America's First Spy* (Lebanon, NH: University Press of New England, 2014), ix ("Today Nathan Hale is recognized as Connecticut's state hero, known to most for his rumored last words, 'I only regret that I have but one life to lose for my country.'"). Yale's innovative residential college system puts students into twelve—soon to be fourteen—separate colleges within the larger university. This gives every student a nice place "to live, eat, and associate" while creating "a small-college 'feel' together with the resources of a great research university." Mark B. Ryan, *A Collegiate Way of Living: Residential Colleges and a Yale Education* (New Haven, CT: Jonathan Edwards College/Yale University, 2001), p. 9.

58   freshmen roommates: In my freshman year, I also had a fifth roommate who spent nearly all of the fall semester living in another dorm with a friend. She did not come back to our room for the spring semester.

60   I would pull out: Wilfred Funk and Norman Lewis, *30 Days to a More Powerful Vocabulary* (New York: Pocket Books, 1971).

61   cast in a play: Marsha Norman, *Getting Out* (New York: Dramatists Play Service Inc., 1979).

62   John Hinckley Jr.: Mike Mayo, *American Murder: Criminals, Crime, and the Media* (Canton, MI: Visible Ink Press, 2008), p. 155.

62   Whiffenpoofs: Joshua S. Duchan, *Powerful Voices: The Musical and Social World of Collegiate A Cappella* (Ann Arbor: University of Michigan Press, 2012), p. 191

n. 2 (noting the Whiffenpoofs' appearance on NBC's *Saturday Night Live* on December 12, 1981).

62   Senate Watergate hearings: Stanley I. Kutler, *The Wars of Watergate: The Last Crisis of Richard Nixon* (New York: W. W. Norton & Co., 1990), pp. 350–82.

63   Eldridge Cleaver: In the 1968 election, Richard Nixon received 3,467,664 votes in California compared to Hubert Humphrey's 3,244,318. Eldridge Cleaver's California vote total—27,707—would not have made up the gap. *The World Almanac and Book of Facts 1985* (New York: World Almanac Books, 1985), p. 43.

63   if Eugene McCarthy: Albert Eisele, *Almost to the Presidency: A Biography of Two American Politicians* (Blue Earth, MN: Piper Co., 1972).

63   Emily Anne Staples: Barbara J. Love, ed., *Feminists Who Changed America, 1963–1975* (Urbana: University of Illinois Press, 2006), p. 469; Lori Sturdevant, *Her Honor: Rosalie Wahl and the Minnesota Women's Movement* (St. Paul: Minnesota Historical Society Press, 2014), pp. 61–62, 134; Barbara Stuhler and Gretchen Kreuter, eds., *Women of Minnesota: Selected Biographical Essays* (St. Paul: Minnesota Historical Society Press, 1998), p. 274.

64   Orville Freeman's son Mike: Howard Lestrud, "Hennepin County Attorney Mike Freeman's Father's Boss Was President Kennedy," ABC Newspapers, June 27, 2013, http://abcnewspapers.com/2013/06/27/hennepin-county-attorney -mike-freemans-fathers-boss-was-president-kennedy/.

64   I was particularly inspired: Robert A. Dahl, *Who Governs? Democracy and Power in an American City*, 2nd ed. (New Haven, CT: Yale University Press, 2005).

64   power elite: C. Wright Mills, *The Power Elite* (New York: Oxford University Press, 1956).

64   Dahl would also write: Robert A. Dahl, *Modern Political Analysis*, 5th ed. (Englewood Cliffs, NJ: Prentice Hall, 1991), pp. 37–43.

64   Charles Sumner: Doris Kearns Goodwin, *Team of Rivals: The Political Genius of Abraham Lincoln* (New York: Simon & Schuster, 2005), p. 184.

65   Ted's superb book: Theodore R. Marmor, *The Politics of Medicare*, 2nd ed. (Hawthorne, NY: Aldine de Gruyter, 2000).

65   sixty-eight senators: Sean J. Savage, *JFK, LBJ, and the Democratic Party* (Albany: State University of New York Press, 2004), p. 130 ("the Senate passed the Medicare bill by a vote of 68 to 21 on July 9, 1965").

65   Fifty years later, Medicare: Robert I. Field, *Mother of Invention: How the Government Created "Free-Market" Health Care* (Oxford: Oxford University Press, 2013), p. 177 ("Medicare is widely championed as a public policy success. Polls show that more than 90 percent of its beneficiaries are satisfied, the highest rating for any insurance plan in the United States."); Jennie Jacobs Kronenfeld, Wendy E. Parmet, and Mark A. Zezza, eds., *Debates on U.S. Health Care* (Thousand Oaks, CA: SAGE Publications, 2012), p. 113 ("In a 2011 Pew Research Center survey, 88 percent said that Medicare had been good or very good for the country, and only 10 percent said it had been bad or very bad."); "Poll: Public Strongly Supports Medicare, Opposes Cuts," McKnight's, Jan. 28, 2013, http://www.mcknights.com/poll-public-strongly-supports-medicare -opposes-cuts/article/277675/ ("The Medicare program is working well, according to 60% of total respondents and 80% of seniors."). Medicare was popular even before the law's passage. Lawrence R. Jacobs, *The Health of Nations: Public Opinion and the Making of American and British Health Policy*

(Ithaca, NY: Cornell University Press, 1993), p. 139 ("A November 1964 survey by Michigan's Survey Research Center found that 75 percent would favor a federal law to provide medical care for the elderly.").

65   Matt Hamel: Nancy Flagg, "To Succeed in Business, Move to Sweden," *Forefront Magazine*, Sept. 9, 2013.

66   a new sports stadium: Amy Klobuchar, *Uncovering the Dome* (Chicago: Waveland Press, 1986). In writing my book, I used the decision-making analysis laid out in Professor Graham Allison's book, *Essence of Decision: Explaining the Cuban Missile Crisis* (Boston: Little, Brown, 1971). I confess that the political battles and intrigue over the building of a domed stadium in Minneapolis has little in common with the threat of a nuclear war brought on by the Cuban Missile Crisis. But as I did my research in college for *Uncovering the Dome*, I found Graham Allison's mode of analysis interesting, so I used it.

66   business advice books: Harvey B. Mackay, *Swim with the Sharks Without Being Eaten Alive: Outsell, Outmanage, Outmotivate, and Outnegotiate Your Competition* (New York: HarperBusiness, 2005).

67   Vice President Mondale: Walter Mondale with David Hage, *The Good Fight: A Life in Liberal Politics* (New York: Simon & Schuster, 2010). After my internship with Vice President Mondale, I wrote him a thank-you note that emphasized: "I left the office with an understanding of government and politics far beyond that which could have come from any textbook or lecture." As I wrote in my letter: "My experience was not only worthwhile and broadening but it piqued my interest in politics in the future." Amy Klobuchar to Vice President Walter Mondale, Sept. 9, 1980.

68   Tom Nides: Paul R. Lawrence and Mark A. Abramson, *What Government Does: How Political Executives Manage* (Lanham, MD: Rowman & Littlefield, 2014), pp. 58–60.

68   Marianne Herrmann: Marianne now lives in Minnesota and is a fiction writer. Marianne Herrmann, *Signaling for Rescue* (Moorhead, MN: New Rivers Press, 2007).

69   right to counsel: Gideon v. Wainwright, 372 U.S. 335 (1963).

69   eleven days before an election: Terry Gydesen, *Twelve Years and Thirteen Days: Remembering Paul and Sheila Wellstone* (Minneapolis: University of Minnesota Press, 2003); Bill Lofy, *Paul Wellstone: The Life of a Passionate Progressive* (Ann Arbor: University of Michigan Press, 2005), p. 124.

70   Judge Neil Riley: Jim Klobuchar, "Don't Show Your Flat Head in Court," *The Minneapolis Star*, July 15, 1977 (taking note of my visit to Judge Riley's courtroom, with my dad quipping at the beginning of his column: "In the ultimate act of revenge for my despotism during her kindergarten years, my oldest daughter has decided she would like to become a lawyer.").

72   "Law and Economics": Robin I. Mordfin and Marsha Ferziger Nagorsky, "Chicago and Law and Economics: A History," *The Record* (Alumni Magazine), Fall 2011. The University of Chicago has produced much law and economics scholarship. *E.g.*, R. H. Coase, "The Problem of Social Cost," *Journal of Law and Economics* 3 (Oct. 1960): 1; Richard Posner, *Economic Analysis of Law*, 7th ed. (New York: Aspen Publishers, 2007); Frank H. Easterbrook and Daniel R. Fischel, *The Economic Structure of Corporate Law* (Cambridge, MA: Harvard University Press, 1991).

73   "Foreseeability": Richard A. Epstein, "Beyond Foreseeability: Consequential Damages in the Law of Contract," *Journal of Legal Studies* 18 (Jan. 1989):

105. The law's use of the concept of foreseeability, both in torts and contracts, goes back a long way. William H. Hardie, Jr., "Foreseeability: A Murky Crystal Ball for Predicting Liability," 23 *Cumberland Law Review* 349, 349–50 ("The doctrine of foreseeability, which creates a duty for foreseeable harm, is derived from the Utilitarian philosophy of John Stuart Mill. . . . Although foreseeability has had a long tradition in the law, the doctrine was most prominently used by Judge Benjamin N. Cardozo in *Palsgraf v. Long Island Railroad.*"); Melvin Aron Eisenberg, "The Principle of *Hadley v. Baxendale*," 80 *California Law Review* 563, 565–66 (1999) ("*Hadley v. Baxendale* has traditionally been conceptualized to mean that consequential damages can be recovered only if, at the time the contract was made, the seller had reason to foresee that the consequential damages were the probable result of the breach."). Professor Epstein continues to be a critic of the law's use of the concept of foreseeability to determine damages. Richard A. Epstein, "The Remote Causes of Affirmative Action, or School Desegregation in Kansas City, Missouri," 84 *California Law Review* 1101, 1111–12 (1996) ("The formal ideal of perfect rectification requires one to reconstruct the past out of whole cloth and is often recognized as unattainable in ordinary contract disputes. Parties frequently substitute liquidated damages provisions for expectation damages to obviate the need for reconstructing 'what might have been,' even on a small compass.").

74   Cass Sunstein: Richard H. Thaler and Cass R. Sunstein, *Nudge: Improving Decisions About Health, Wealth, and Happiness* (New York: Penguin Books, 2009); Cass R. Sunstein and Martha C. Nussbaum, eds., *Animal Rights: Current Debates and New Directions* (Oxford: Oxford University Press, 2004); Alex Isenstadt, "Cass Sunstein Confirmed in 57–40 Vote," *Politico*, Sept. 11, 2009.

76   Jim Comey: "FBI Director Nomination Hearing," C-SPAN, July 9, 2013, http://www.c-span.org/video/?313811-1/cmte-hears-fbi-director-nominee-james-comey; Ralph G. Carter, ed., *Contemporary Cases in U.S. Foreign Policy: From Terrorism to Trade* (Thousand Oaks, CA: SAGE Publications, 2014), pp. 388–89.

76   "the happy class": FBI Director Nomination Hearing for James Comey, C-SPAN, July 9, 2013. In addition to Karen Cornelius and others mentioned in this chapter, other friends who got me through those law school years included Stephanie Brett, who now lives in Ohio; Chicago booster Tom Sax; my third-year roommate, Melissa Nachman; Tony Bouza, son of the former Minneapolis police chief of the same name; and California securities lawyer Dan Tyukody. On fundraising trips to L.A. in 2006, I stayed in Dan's basement to save money, sharing space with his family's parrot. In the morning, their bird would wake me up with the words—repeated over and over—"Go to work, go to work."

CHAPTER 4

77   Fortune 500 companies: Christie Washam, "18 MN Cos. Make Fortune 500; 9 Move Up in Rank," *Twin Cities Business*, June 2, 2014.

77   Dorsey: Tinsley E. Yarbrough, *Harry A. Blackmun: The Outsider Justice* (New York: Oxford University Press, 2008), pp. 40–45. The Dorsey firm was founded in 1912. National Association for Law Placement, *Directory of Legal Employers* (1995), p. 130.

78   summer associate program: 1984 Dorsey & Whitney recruiting brochure, p. 15.

78   Jack Mason: Jackie Crosby, "John M. Mason, Magistrate Judge, Dies at 63," *Star-Tribune*, June 10, 2002; Jackie Crosby, "Magistrate Judge Jack Mason Dies," *StarTribune*, June 11, 2002.

79   "Hockeytown, U.S.A.": Wayne Coffey, *The Boys of Winter: The Untold Story of a Coach, a Dream, and the 1980 U.S. Olympic Hockey Team* (New York: Three Rivers Press, 2005), p. 202.

79   Warren Spannaus: John Watson Milton, *For the Good of the Order: Nick Coleman and the High Tide of Liberal Politics in Minnesota, 1971–1981* (Bloomington, IN: Xlibris Corp., 2012), pp. 135, 257, 312.

79   Judge Gerald Heaney: Gerald Heaney (1918–2010) enlisted in the Army in World War II, trained as an Army Ranger, and landed on Omaha Beach in Normandy, heroically leading his men ashore after his superiors were "cut down by gunfire." Congressman Jim Oberstar and I were able to get the federal courthouse in Duluth named in his honor before his death. Congressional Record, Vol. 153, Pt. 3, pp. H3388–3389 (Feb. 7, 2007) (statement of Rep. James Oberstar).

80   University of Minnesota Law School: *The Law School Buzz Book* (New York: Vault, 2006), pp. 267–72 (the law school building is now called Walter F. Mondale Hall).

80   Walter Mondale's arrival: "Mondale Runs for Fish in Minnesota," *Santa Cruz Sentinel* (Santa Cruz, CA), June 7, 1987 ("Former Vice President Walter Mondale said Friday in St. Paul he's returning to Minnesota to practice law, write, lecture and fish. . . . [I]t was announced that he is becoming a partner in the Minneapolis law firm of Dorsey & Whitney Sept. 1.").

81   six criminal jury trials: Back then, the jury trials I did were before twelve-person juries. Before 1971, all Minnesota juries consisted of twelve jurors. In 1971, Minnesota's legislature authorized six-person juries for all cases except felonies and gross misdemeanors (Minn. Stat. § 593.01, subd. 1), but that law was challenged seventeen years later. In 1988, the Minnesota Supreme Court ruled that the state constitution mandated twelve-person juries, thus declaring unconstitutional the six-person criminal jury statute. State v. Hamm, 423 N.W.2d 379 (Minn. 1988). The Minnesota Constitution was amended in 1988 to allow for six-person juries, Baker v. State of Minnesota, 590 N.W.2d 636 (Minn. 1999), but the cases I handled at the Minneapolis City Attorney's Office predated that state constitutional amendment. I worked full time at the Minneapolis City Attorney's Office from April through August of 1988 and tried and won six jury trials—three domestic assaults, two DWIs, and one theft case. Minnesota's constitutional amendment was approved by the voters in November of 1988. Research Department, Minnesota House of Representatives, Minnesota Constitutional Amendments: History and Legal Principles (Mar. 2013), p. 76.

81   Jan Sanderson: "Janet Sanderson, 32, Partner at Law Firm, Dies," *StarTribune*, Feb. 23, 1990; Annual Hennepin County Bar Memorial Session, Hennepin County Government Center, Apr. 25, 1990, pp. 24–25 (Barb Frey's remembrance of my mentor, Janet S. Sanderson [1957–1990], "only the third woman to be named partner in the trial department of Dorsey & Whitney's Minnesota offices").

84   "dinner parties, lunches, visits to Garrison Keillor's *A Prairie Home Companion*": 1984 Dorsey & Whitney recruiting brochure, p. 15. One of the pleasures of running for office (yes, there actually are some) has been getting to know

Garrison Keillor, a fellow Democrat and the legendary host of *A Prairie Home Companion*. Garrison Keillor, *Homegrown Democrat: A Few Plain Thoughts from the Heart of America*, rev. ed. (New York: Penguin Books, 2006). On the fortieth anniversary of Garrison Keillor's radio show, I had the honor to present him with a congratulatory Senate resolution—and do a little sing-along—before the start of his show at Macalester College in St. Paul. S. Res. 492, 113th Cong., 2nd Sess. (adopted June 26, 2014) ("Congratulating 'A Prairie Home Companion' on its 40 years of engaging, humorous, and quality radio programming").

84   Bill Bessler: John's dad became the director of the Regional Science and Engineering Fair in Mankato in the 1970s, and over the course of five decades, he—with his wife Marilyn's help—grew the fair from about 275 annual participants to approximately 2,000 students at its peak. Minnesota State University-Mankato, Southern Minnesota Regional Science and Engineering Fair, "History and Archives," http://www.mnsu.edu/sciencefair/about/history.html. We need more people like my in-laws to get kids excited about science and engineering.

85   After the fourth boy: Actually, when Bill and Marilyn got married at St. Lawrence Catholic Church in Lawrenceburg, Indiana, they vowed to be open to children and hoped simply to be blessed with healthy children. As John's mom puts it, "And we were." As Marilyn and Bill like to say, they still consider "our six sons, and the lives that they have created for themselves and their families, as the most creative, significant, and positive aspect of our lives."

86   Mondale Fellow session: Hubert H. Humphrey Institute of Public Affairs, University of Minnesota, "Politics and the Media: Improving the Public Dialogue" (Feb. 6–7, 1992), pp. 16–17, 59, 61.

87   *Wayne's World*: Penelope Spheeris, *Wayne's World* (1992) (starring Mike Myers, Dana Carvey, and Rob Lowe).

89   he proposed to me: The Hungry Mind, which closed its doors in 2004 after changing its name to Ruminator Books, was located on Grand Avenue in St. Paul. Before John proposed, we had dinner together at the then adjoining and popular Table of Contents Café. Paul Deblinger, *Culpepper's Minneapolis and Saint Paul: The Essential Guide to the Twin Cities* (Minneapolis, MN: Culpepper Press, 1990), pp. 88, 128. Garrison Keillor's new independent bookstore, Common Good Books, near Snelling Avenue and Grand Avenue in St. Paul, is not far from where The Hungry Mind bookstore used to be. Laurie Hertzel, "Keillor's Bookstore Is Moving, Joining Macalester," *StarTribune*, Dec. 3, 2011.

90   My sister: Jim Klobuchar, *Pursued by Grace: A Newspaperman's Own Story of Spiritual Recovery* (Minneapolis: Augsburg Fortress Publishers, 1998), pp. 94–95; Jim Klobuchar, *Minstrel: My Adventure in Newspapering* (Minneapolis: University of Minnesota Press, 1997), p. 205.

92   My dad: Jim Klobuchar, *Minstrel*, pp. 206–21; Jim Klobuchar, *Pursued by Grace*, pp. 95–102.

94   Susan Wilkes: "About Jim: The Worlds of Jim Klobuchar," Jim Klobuchar's Adventures, http://www.jimklobuchar.com/?page_id=17. My dad and Susan later wrote a book together on one of Susan's great passions, the use of microcredit—or small loans—to help people in developing nations lift themselves out of poverty. Jim Klobuchar and Susan Cornell Wilkes, *The Miracles of Barefoot Capitalism: A Compelling Case for Microcredit* (Minneapolis, MN: Kirk House Publishers, 2003).

95   distracted driving: Maggie Jackson, *Distracted: The Erosion of Attention and the Coming Dark Age* (Amherst, NY: Prometheus Books, 2008), pp. 74, 77.

97   a children's book: Helme Heine, *The Pigs' Wedding* (New York: Macmillan, 1991).

97   Lions Club: Jim Klobuchar, "An Urban Woman Reconciles with the International Lions," *StarTribune*, July 7, 1993.

98   "Donald Segretti": Donald Segretti is a figure from the Watergate era. Carl Bernstein and Bob Woodward, *All the President's Men* (New York: Simon & Schuster, 1974), p. 120. Segretti—a California lawyer close to staffers for President Nixon—has been called "the dark prince of dirty tricks." Joseph Cummins, *Anything for a Vote: Dirty Tricks, Cheap Shots, and October Surprises in U.S. Presidential Campaigns* (Philadelphia, PA: Quirk Books, 2007), p. 243.

100   Tom Moe: Tom Moe, the Golden Gophers' "Most Valuable Player" in 1959, had a distinguished athletic career before heading up Dorsey & Whitney. "Tom Moe, Former Gopher Athletic Director and Chairman of Dorsey & Whitney law firm, to receive Bud Grant Distinguished Minnesotan Award," National Football Foundation—Minnesota Chapter, 3/27/14 press release, http://assets .ngin.com/attachments/document/0054/5709/Tom_Moe_Press_Release.pdf.

102   I would keep up my friendships: I remain close friends to this day with many Dorsey lawyers and alums. I still get together on a regular basis for dinners with some of the women lawyers I befriended at the firm—Leslie Anderson, Kathleen Sheehy, Margaret Zverinova, and Lisa Hondros.

102   John Mooty: "John Mooty: Franchise Player," *Twin Cities Business*, July 1, 2003; "Buffett to Acquire Dairy Queen Chain for $585 Million," *Los Angeles Times*, Oct. 22, 1997 (from *Bloomberg News*); Adam Belz, "Obituary: John Mooty, Powerful Lawyer and Former Dairy Queen Chairman," *StarTribune*, Apr. 22, 2015.

104   Vinton Cerf: Laura Lambert, *The Internet: A Historical Encyclopedia* (Santa Barbara, CA: ABC-CLIO, 2005), pp. 62–63.

105   Telecommunications Act of 1996: Telecommunications Act of 1996, Pub. L. 104-104, 110 Stat. 56 (Feb. 8, 1996).

105   terrific colleagues: Among my many good friends and mentors at Gray Plant were Tamara Olsen (whom we lost way too early), Laura Hein, Mike Flom, Myron Frans, Jim Carroll, Dick Hackett, Sarah Duniway, Mike Sullivan Jr. and Sr., Tom Johnson, Bill Fisher, Susan Segal, Bill Kline, Ben Omorogbe, Steve Wilson, Jim Simonson, Clint Schroeder, David Lebedoff, Bruce Mooty, and of course Mr. Gray. Steve Alexander, "Tamara Hjelle Olsen, Top Corporate Lawyer," *StarTribune*, July 7, 2011.

CHAPTER 5

106   Gloria Segal: Pat Pheifer, "Former Rep. Gloria Segal, Champion of Programs for the Mentally Ill, Dies at 65," *StarTribune*, Oct. 28, 1993.

107   Milt and Rosalie: *Crossing the Barriers, The Autobiography of Allan H. Spear* (Minneapolis: University of Minnesota Press, 2010), pp. 115–16.

108   Mark Andrew: Mark Andrew, http://en.wikipedia.org/wiki/Mark_Andrew _(politician).

108   Wellstone's come-from-behind victory: Dennis J. McGrath and Dane Smith, *Professor Wellstone Goes to Washington: The Inside Story of a Grassroots U.S. Senate Campaign* (Minneapolis: University of Minnesota Press, 1995),

pp. 145–51, 178, 275. Paul Wellstone's style of campaigning has inspired countless candidates and campaign staffers. Jeff Blodgett and Bill Lofy, *Winning Your Election the Wellstone Way: A Comprehensive Guide for Candidates and Campaign Workers* (Minneapolis: University of Minnesota Press, 2008).

109   DFL Education Foundation: This foundation was started in 1985 to encourage political participation through discussion of issues.

109   "In this era of sound bites": Wendy Webb, "At a Glance: Amy Klobuchar," *Skyway News*, Feb. 5, 1991.

109   a quarterly newsletter: *Idea News*. This newsletter was published by the DFL Education Foundation. See https://dfleducationfoundation.wordpress.com/about /contact-us/.

109   Tim Penny: Timothy J. Penny with Major Garrett, *Common Cents: A Retiring Six-Term Congressman Reveals How Congress Really Works—and What We Must Do to Fix It* (Boston, MA: Little, Brown & Co., 1995).

110   "rapid response team": Hillary Rodham Clinton, *Living History* (New York: Scribner, 2003), p. 114.

111   Office of the County Attorney: http://www.hennepinattorney.org.

112   Mike Freeman: "After Losing DFL Endorsement to Marty, Freeman Says He'll Seek Second 4-year Term," *StarTribune*, June 10, 1994.

112   I announced my bid: "Minnesota Politicians Hurry Off to the '94 Races," *Star-Tribune*, Jan. 16, 1994.

116   the latest edition: Arlene Eisenberg, Heidi E. Murkoff, and Sandee E. Hathaway, *What to Expect When You're Expecting*, 2nd rev. and expanded ed. (New York: Workman, 1991).

117   "Drive-by births": Robert F. Rich and Christopher T. Erb, *Consumer Choice: Social Welfare and Health Policy* (New Brunswick, NJ: Transaction Publishers, 2005), pp. 37–38.

118   twenty-four-hour policy: Congressional Record, vol. 147, pt. 6, pp. 8837–38 (May 21, 2001), Hon. Fortney Pete Stark of California in the House of Representatives (submitting into the congressional record an article published in the *Washington Monthly* that was written by Dr. Ronald J. Glasser, a practicing pediatrician at Children's Hospital in Minneapolis, stating in part: "Managed care's first great PR disaster was the early discharge of new mothers within 24 hours of delivery. . . . Beginning in the early 1990s, HMOs began demanding that their obstetricians discharge women who had uncomplicated vaginal deliveries within 24 hours of giving birth.").

119   extraordinary pediatricians: Abigail's regular pediatrician, Dr. Steven Inman, did an amazing job of coordinating all of Abigail's care. Pediatric Services, P.A., http://www.pspa.md/meet-us/our-providers.php#inman.

120   "it takes a village": Hillary Rodham Clinton, *It Takes a Village: And Other Lessons Children Teach Us* (New York: Simon and Schuster, 2012).

120   "my father's joy": Ronald H. Isaacs, *Why Hebrew Goes from Right to Left: 201 Things You Never Knew About Judaism* (Jersey City, NJ: Ktav Publishing House, 2008), p. 6.

122   Patty Murray: Barbara Palmer and Dennis Simon, *Breaking the Political Glass Ceiling: Women and Congressional Elections*, 2nd ed. (New York: Routledge, 2008), p. 59; Susan J. Carroll and Richard L. Fox, *Gender and Elections: Shaping the Future of American Politics* (Cambridge: Cambridge University Press, 2006), p. 169; "Biography," United States Senator Patty Murray, http: //www.murray.senate.gov/public/index.cfm/biography.

123 I became determined to change the policy: Maria Douglas Reeve, "Maternity 'Policy' Criticized," *St. Paul Pioneer Press*, Nov. 17, 1995.

123 I testified: Legislative Testimony of Amy Klobuchar Regarding 24-hour Maternity Stay Requirement before the Senate Commerce Committee, Jan. 22, 1996, p. 4.

123 Christine Todd Whitman: Jon Nordheimer, "New Mothers Gain 2d Day in Hospital," *New York Times*, June 29, 1995.

123 Governor Arne Carlson signed the bill: Minnesota House of Representatives Public Information Office, "Hospital Stays After Birth," Session Summary: New Laws 1996, p. 39.

123 under President Clinton's leadership: President Clinton called for a similar law on the federal level less than two months after Minnesota's law took effect. Ronald Brownstein, "Clinton Calls for 2-Day Hospital Birth Coverage," *Los Angeles Times*, May 12, 1996 ("Using Mother's Day as a backdrop, President Clinton on Saturday endorsed legislation that would require health insurance companies to guarantee hospital stays of at least 48 hours for newborn infants and their mothers.").

124 I announced: David Chanen, "Amy Klobuchar Seeks Hennepin Attorney Post," *StarTribune*, Nov. 15, 1997; Ka Vang, "Minneapolis Lawyer to Run for County Attorney Post," *St. Paul Pioneer Press*, Nov. 16, 1997.

124 "More than 1,000 lawyers": This ad ran in the *StarTribune*.

125 "Murderapolis": Dirk Johnson, "Nice City's Nasty Distinction: Murders Soar in Minneapolis," *New York Times*, June 30, 1996.

125 forty-eight-page leadership plan: We published this plan on our campaign website, and after the campaign was over, I fully intended to implement the plan. Rachel E. Stassen-Berger, "Klobuchar Plans Changes for Attorney's Office," *St. Paul Pioneer Press*, Jan. 2, 1999.

126 a formidable candidate: Mark Brunswick, "Citing Her Experience, Ramstad Hvass Enters Hennepin County Attorney Race," *StarTribune*, Feb. 10, 1998; "Ramstad Hvass Quits Bar Post," *StarTribune*, Mar. 3, 1998.

127 money was clearly going to be a problem: Mark Brunswick, "Spending Limit Rejected in Hennepin Attorney Race," *StarTribune*, Apr. 10, 1998 ("Ramstad Hvass, who is expected to raise big money in her campaign, declined the offer."). To raise the necessary funds, I reached out to countless friends and my law school classmates. The ability to solicit campaign contributions is, like it or not, critical to any political candidate's chances of success these days. Rebecca Sive, *Every Day Is Election Day: A Woman's Guide to Winning Any Office, from the PTA to the White House* (Chicago: Chicago Review Press, 2013), pp. 173–76.

128 I knew I would be badly outspent: Mark Brunswick, "Rivals Share Tough Ideas About Crime," *StarTribune*, Aug. 10, 1998 ("Ramstad Hvass expects to spend more than $500,000, while Klobuchar is expecting to raise about $300,000. The total would exceed the previous record spent. While no one keeps a failsafe accounting, the previous spending record for a county race was likely set in 1986, when Hennepin County Attorney Tom Johnson, a DFLer, spent $196,274 to fend off a challenge by Tom Heffelfinger, an Independent-Republican who spent $201,153.").

130 Minneapolis Aquatennial: In addition to its fabulous torchlight parade, the Minneapolis Aquatennial—an annual civic celebration—features fireworks, a sand castle competition, and milk-carton boat races. www.aquatennial.com.

130 Sarah Rathke: Sarah is now an extremely accomplished litigator in Cleveland, Ohio, who lectures on trial advocacy. "Sarah K. Rathke," http://www.squirepattonboggs.com/professionals/r/sarah-rathke.

130   the race heated up: Mark Brunswick, "Attacking Resumes in County Campaign," *StarTribune*, Oct. 4, 1998; Rachel E. Stassen-Berger, "Prosecutor Candidates Spar over Records, Ideas," *St. Paul Pioneer Press*, Oct. 26, 1998.

131   the last word: Brunswick, "Attacking Resumes in County Campaign."

131   "If any of you get hasty with a girlfriend": Association of Trial Lawyers of America, National College of Advocacy, "Handling the Criminal Case from Pre-trial Through Appeal" (Harvard Law School, 1974), p. 489; American Trial Lawyers Association, New Frontiers for the Trial Lawyer (W. H. Anderson Co., 1968), p. 153.

131   I received the endorsement: *StarTribune* Endorsements," *StarTribune*, Oct. 24, 1998.

132   "C.J.": Michele St. Martin, "Klobuchar Wins!" Minnesota Politics, Nov. 4, 1998, https://groups.yahoo.com/neo/groups/mn-politics/conversations/topics/1922.

132   Tim Klobuchar: Ibid.; Cheryl Johnson, "A Campaign Blood Feud," *StarTribune*, Oct. 29, 1998.

133   Kramarczuk's: Donna Tabbert Long, *Tastes of Minnesota: A Food Lover's Tour* (Black Earth, WI: Trails Books, 2001), pp. 134–35; Nathaniel Minor, "Kramarczuk's Wins James Beard Award," MPR News, Feb. 28, 2013.

133   The outcome of my race remained in limbo: Mark Brunswick, "Hennepin County Attorney's Race a Very Tight One," *StarTribune*, Nov. 4, 1998; Rachel E. Stassen-Berger, "Klobuchar Takes Attorney Post in Hennepin," *St. Paul Pioneer Press*, Nov. 5, 1998 ("At the end of a long and expensive race, DFLer Amy Klobuchar managed to squeak past her Republican opponent. . . . Results from all 431 precincts weren't complete until Wednesday afternoon, and Klobuchar won with just over 50 percent of the more than 441,000 total votes counted. Her opponent, Sheryl Ramstad Hvass, received a little more than 49 percent of the vote. Only 3,738 votes separated the two candidates at the final count.").

133   Jesse Ventura was declared: Jesse Ventura, *I Ain't Got Time to Bleed: Reworking the Body Politic from the Bottom Up* (New York: Random House, 2000); Jake Tapper, *Body Slam: The Jesse Ventura Story* (New York: Macmillan, 2014).

134   they finally called the race: Mark Brunswick, "Klobuchar Hangs On in County Attorney Cliffhanger," *StarTribune*, Nov. 5, 1998.

134   outspent: Mark Brunswick, "Ramstad Hvass Far Ahead of Klobuchar in Fundraising," *StarTribune*, Oct. 29, 1998; Brunswick, "Hennepin County Attorney's Race a Very Tight One." To try to offset this fundraising disadvantage as best I could, Dee Dee Myers—President Clinton's former press secretary—graciously agreed to be a special guest and headline an event for me in 1998. That fundraiser took place at the historic State Theatre in Minneapolis. By using that venue, the State Theatre also put up this message in big letters on its colorful marquee on heavily trafficked Hennepin Avenue for a couple of days: "Amy Klobuchar" / "The Next Hennepin County Attorney." Talk about a great package deal!

CHAPTER 6

136   swearing-in ceremony: Mark Brunswick, "Local Officials Take Their Oaths," *StarTribune*, Jan. 5, 1999.

136   Kay Hagan: Samantha Lachman, "Winning, with Women," *Chronicle*, Oct. 30, 2013, http://www.dukechronicle.com/articles/2012/10/30/winning-women#.VPuMJIcbBBw.

137 "bait cars": Robert Siegel, "Bait Cars Ruin Joyrides for Auto Thieves," MPR News, Mar. 23, 2007, http://www.mprnews.org/story/npr/9075820.

137 truancy: "Hennepin County Reports Priorities," InsightNews.com, July 27, 2004, http://208.113.232.90/news/1431-hennepin-county-reports-priorities.

139 Hennepin County Attorney's Office: As county attorney, I had the honor to work with some incredibly talented county commissioners. When I started, the commissioners were Mike Opat, Mark Stenglein, Mark Andrew, Peter McLaughlin, Penny Steele, Mary Tambornino, and Randy Johnson. Starting in early 1999, I also got to serve with Gail Dorfman, who was elected in a special election to fill Mark Andrew's seat after he left the board. Linda Koblick also became a commissioner after her election in 2002.

139 Pete Cahill: Brian Rosemeyer, "Plymouth's Peter Cahill Re-elected as Chief Judge in Hennepin County," *Sun Sailor*, July 12, 2014.

139 *Yes Minister*: *Yes Minister* (TV series) (1980–1984).

140 Cindy Jesson: Biographical Note, Lucinda E. Jesson, Minnesota Department of Human Services Commissioner, http://mn.gov/dhs/images/Lucinda_Jesson_bio.pdf. After Cindy left the Hennepin County's Attorney's Office, Jim Jacobson—now the general counsel at Medica Health Plans—took over. Other great managers of the office's civil work included David Hough, Susan Segal, Mark Chapin, and Peggy Gunn.

140 Kathryn Quaintance: Judge Profile, Judge Kathryn L. Quaintance, http://www.mncourts.gov/default.aspx?ID=30276&page=31&printFriendly=true.

141 leadership plan: "Amy's Leadership Plan" (Oct. 1, 1998) ("Safe Streets. Real Consequences.").

141 hundred-day and year-end goals: James Walsh, "Klobuchar Says Plan Will Make Justice System Accountable," *StarTribune*, Jan. 13, 1990; Margaret Zack, "Klobuchar Says Her Office Is Right on (Crime's) Track," *StarTribune*, Apr. 20, 1999.

141 first plan: Hennepin County Attorney Amy Klobuchar, 100-Day Plan Results, Apr. 20, 1999.

141 75 percent rate: 2006 Minnesota Sentencing Guidelines Commission Report to the Legislature (Jan. 2006), p. 101 (Mandatory Minimum Sentences Imposed and Executed; Cases Disposed from July 1, 2004 to July 1, 2005).

141 last word in final arguments: Paul Gustafson, "Criminal Prosecutors Want Last Word," *StarTribune*, Feb. 20, 1999; "Last Word for Prosecutors," Session Weekly: A Nonpartisan Publication of the Minnesota House of Representatives, vol. 16, no. 14, Apr. 9, 1999, p. 11; "New Laws Effective Aug. 1, 1999"—"Crime: Last Word for Prosecutors," http://www.house.leg.state.mn.us/HINFO/NL8199.

141 F. Lee Bailey: Stephen Redding, "DNA Testing Evidence in Minnesota: Vanguard or Rearguard?", *Hennepin Lawyer*, vol. 63, no. 1 (Sept.–Oct. 1993), pp. 16, 21.

141 signed the bill into law: "Last Word for Prosecutors," Session Weekly: A Nonpartisan Publication of the Minnesota House of Representatives, vol. 16, no. 8 (Feb. 26, 1999), p. 6.

142 property crime team: James Walsh and Richard Meryhew, "Catch & Release: 8,700 Chronic Offenders Evade Justice, Cost Millions," *StarTribune*, July 17, 1999 ("Hennepin County Attorney Amy Klobuchar notes that her property crime team recently started targeting car thieves, burglars and other kinds of property offenders, and it already has successfully prosecuted some as 'career criminals.'"); Office of the Legislative Auditor, State of Minnesota, Report #01-05, Program Evaluation Report: Chronic Offenders (Feb. 2001), p. 54

("The use of the career offender statute has increased over the last three years, particularly in Hennepin County during 1999.").

142   child support and protection cases: *See, e.g.,* Hennepin County Attorney Amy Klobuchar, 2000 Annual Report, p. 9 ("Court appearances by child support attorneys increased more than 25% over 1999. A record total of more than $107 million in current and past support payments due to children was collected in 2000."); Hennepin County Attorney's Office, 2004 Annual Report, p. 10 (discussing procedures developed by Hennepin County and the County Attorney's Office for expediting child support payments and better responding to child protection cases).

143   sixty-nine murder convictions in 1999: Hennepin County Attorney Amy Klobuchar, 1999 Annual Report, p. 5 ("The number of homicide convictions in 1999 was a significant increase over 1997 and 1998. More than two-thirds of the homicide cases resolved in 1999 involved crimes that had been committed in 1998 or earlier.").

146   nearly four hundred homicide convictions: Hennepin County Attorney Amy Klobuchar, 1999 Annual Report, p. 5 (69 homicide convictions); Hennepin County Attorney Amy Klobuchar, 2000 Annual Report, p. 1 (53 homicide convictions); Hennepin County Attorney Amy Klobuchar, 2001 Annual Report, p. 1 (44 homicide convictions); Hennepin County Attorney Amy Klobuchar, 2002 Annual Report, p. 9 (40 homicide convictions); Hennepin County Attorney Amy Klobuchar, 2003 Annual Report, p. 5 (50 homicide convictions); Hennepin County Attorney Amy Klobuchar, 2004 Annual Report, p. 11 (more than 40 homicide convictions); Hennepin County Attorney Amy Klobuchar, 2005 Annual Report, p. 1 (53 homicide convictions). The office also got a number of homicide convictions in 2006. *See, e.g.,* Margaret Zack, "Man Who Killed Two Men at Office Is Sentenced," *StarTribune,* May 10, 2006; Margaret Zack, "Man Gets 45 Years in Fatal Shooting," *StarTribune,* July 26, 2006; Margaret Zack, "New Hope Man Gets 30-Year Term in Minneapolis Killing," *StarTribune,* Sept. 20, 2006; Chao Xiong, "Killer Sentenced to Life in Prison in Block E Slaying," *StarTribune,* Dec. 12, 2006; Margaret Zack, "Man Convicted in Gang Shooting," *StarTribune,* Dec. 13, 2006; Margaret Zack, "New Trial Brings 2nd Conviction in Shooting Death of Housemate in 2003," *StarTribune,* Dec. 15, 2006.

146   convenience store clerk: David Chanen and Randy Furst, "Gas Station Clerk Killed After Defending a Friend," *StarTribune,* Oct. 6, 2004.

146   three children whose father stabbed their mother: Amy Mayron, "Man Guilty of Killing Wife in Front of Kids," *St. Paul Pioneer Press,* Sept. 20, 2000 ("A man who repeatedly stabbed his estranged wife in front of her three children pleaded guilty to murder Tuesday in Hennepin County District Court. Leevoice S. Washington, 33, pleaded guilty to second-degree intentional murder in the March 7 death of Nikki Washington.").

146   Pa Nhia Lor: Minnesota Coalition for Battered Women, Special Femicide Report: Strangulation and Women and Children Murdered in Minnesota, 1989–2005, p. 20; Margaret Zack, "Man Admits Killing Sixth-Grade Girl in Brooklyn Park," *StarTribune,* Apr. 23, 1999; Jim Adams, "Man, 18, Pleads Guilty, Gets 24 Years for Murder of Brooklyn Park Girl," *StarTribune,* July 3, 1999; Margaret Zack, "Teen Pleads Guilty in Rape of Girl Who Was Killed," *StarTribune,* May 20, 1999; Margaret Zack, "Two Plead Guilty to Helping Hide Body," *StarTribune,* Feb. 2, 1999; Rachel E. Stassen-Berger, "Fifth Teen Pleads Guilty in Lor Murder," *St. Paul Pioneer Press,* July 3, 1999. Pa Nhia Lor, the

thirteen-year-old girl from St. Paul, was raped and murdered in Brooklyn Park, a Minneapolis suburb, which is why our office handled the case. David Chanen, "A Free Spirit, a Family's Heartache," *StarTribune*, Oct. 2, 1998; Tom LaVenture, "Amy Klobuchar Meets Hmong Community Leaders," *Asian American Press* (St. Paul, MN), June 9, 2006.

146   a state of refugees: Dave Kenney, *Northern Lights: The Stories of Minnesota's Past*, 2nd ed. (St. Paul: Minnesota Historical Society, 2003), p. 317; Kathleen R. Arnold, ed., *Contemporary Immigration in America: A State-by-State Encyclopedia* (Santa Barbara, CA: ABC-CLIO, 2015), pp. 421–42.

147   high on meth: David Chanen and Warren Wolfe, "2 Men Linked to 5 Killings," *StarTribune*, May 2, 2003; David Chanen and Randy Furst, "Confessed Killer of Five Kills Himself," *StarTribune*, July 12, 2003; "Earl Sentenced in Second Set of Killings: Man, 88, and Daughter Were Slain in Home," *St. Paul Pioneer Press*, Feb. 18, 2005; Paul Levy, "Previous Murders Ruled Admissible in Earl Trial," *StarTribune*, Feb. 13, 2004; Margaret Zack, "Lifer Is Back in Court on New Charges," *StarTribune*, Dec. 2, 2004; State v. Earl, 702 N.W.2d 711 (Minn. 2005); Fighting Meth in America's Heartland: Assessing Federal, State, and Local Efforts, Hearing Before the Subcommittee on Criminal Justice, Drug Policy, and Human Resources of the Committee on Government Reform, House of Representatives, 109th Cong., 1st Sess., June 27, 2005, Serial No. 109-97 (Washington, DC: U.S. Government Printing Office, 2006), pp. 130–33 (reprinting my letter to Mark Souder, the chair of the U.S. House Subcommittee on Criminal Justice, Drug Policy, and Human Resources dated June 27, 2005, that describes the murders).

147   Byron Phillips: "FYI," *StarTribune*, July 31, 1997; Jim Adams, "A Billboard's Poignant Plea," *StarTribune*, July 25, 1997; David Chanen, "Three Indicted in '96 Slaying of Byron Phillips," *StarTribune*, July 1, 1998; Chris Graves, Margaret Zack, and Andrew Tellijohn, "Guilty Verdicts in Byron Phillips Case," *StarTribune*, Mar. 28, 1999; Chris Graves, "Anti-gang Push Nets 9 Bogus Boyz," *StarTribune*, June 18, 1997; Margaret Zack, "Byron's Killer Faces 41 Years in Prison; Man Convicted of Conspiracy Gets 12-Year Minimum Term," *StarTribune*, Apr. 13, 1999; State v. Blanche, 696 N.W.2d 351 (Minn. 2005); State v. Bernard, 2000 WL 1015418 (Minn. Ct. App.), *rev. denied* (Minn. Sept. 27, 2000).

148   Melissa Schmidt: "Melissa Jayne Schmidt," Officer Down Memorial Page, http://www.odmp.org/officer/16343-police-officer-melissa-jayne-schmidt.

148   Pamela Ragland: State v. Francis, 729 N.W.2d 584, 588 (Minn. 2007); Margaret Zack, "Man Gets Life Term in Shooting Death," *StarTribune*, Nov. 2, 2004; Howie Padilla, "Man Found Guilty of Killing Woman—The Shooting Resulted from an Argument Over a Set of Wheel Rims," *StarTribune*, Oct. 9, 2004.

148   Shelley Joseph-Kordell: Mike Kaszuba, "Stiffer Security Urged for Government Center," *StarTribune*, Apr. 21, 2004; Margaret Zack, "Berkovitz Is Sentenced to Life," *StarTribune*, June 19, 2004; Art Hughes, "Weapons Screening Begins at Hennepin County Government Center," Minnesota Public Radio, Mar. 14, 2005.

149   Victor Cossette: Chris Ison and Paul McEnroe, "Case Reopens 23 Years After 2 Firemen Died," *StarTribune*, Jan. 30, 2000; Paul McEnroe and Chris Ison, "Man Indicted in Fatal '77 Arson," *StarTribune*, June 9, 2000; Pam Louwagie and Paul McEnroe, "Decades Later, Shop Owner Pleads Guilty in Fatal Arson," *StarTribune*, Mar. 6, 2001; Margaret Zack, "Man Sentenced for '77 Fire That Killed 2 Firefighters," *StarTribune*, May 10, 2001. As KARE 11-TV also reported

on the day of Victor Cossette's sentencing: "After serving his prison sentence, Cossette must serve another year in jail and will be on probation for ten years." "Man Sentenced for 1977 Fire that Killed Firefighters," http://archive.kare11 .com/news/article/8987/0/Man-Sentenced-For-1977-Fire-That-Killed -Firefighters.

149   Glen Miller: Jon Melegrito, "Crimebusters Offstage," AFSCME newsletter (Sept./Oct. 2002).

150   how victims felt about "the system": Amy Klobuchar, Floor Speech, Sexual Assault in the Military, Nov. 19, 2013.

151   preserve records of sexual assaults: Rick Maze, "Bill Would Make DoD Keep Sexual Assault Records," *Army Times*, Mar. 28, 2011; "Klobuchar Award for Work Against Sexual Assault in Military," *Jackson County Pilot*, http://www .jacksoncountypilot.com/Stories/Story.cfm?SID=41952.

151   Pyotr Shmelev: Jim Adams, "Man Charged with Stabbing Wife, Dismembering Body," *StarTribune*, Mar. 17, 2001; Minnesota Coalition for Battered Women, 2001 Femicide Report: Women and Children Murdered, p. 2; Rubén Rosario, "Should Russian Murderer Be Sent Home to Finish Sentence?," *St. Paul Pioneer Press*, Feb. 8, 2015.

152   Todd Jones: Elizabeth Murphy, "Obama to Nominate B. Todd Jones to Serve as Permanent ATF Director," Main Justice, Jan. 16, 2003, http://www.mainjustice .com/2013/01/16/obama-to-nominate-b-todd-jones-to-serve-as-permanent -atf-director/.

152   Tom Heffelfinger: Pam Louwagie, "Bush to Nominate Tom Heffelfinger as U.S. Attorney," *StarTribune*, Aug. 4, 2001.

153   hate crimes conference: Senate Bill 622, 106th Cong., 1st Sess. (Hate Crimes Prevention Act of 1999); News Release, "Hennepin County Attorney and U.S. Attorney Participate in White House Meeting on Hate Crimes," Apr. 25, 2000.

153   crimes motivated by hate: Andrew Tellijohn, "Teen Charged with Burning Crosses at Minneapolis School," *StarTribune*, May 22, 1999; David Chanen, "Man Accused of Vandalizing Minneapolis Church," *StarTribune*, Jan. 26, 2000; Tom Hamburger, "Twin Cities Prosecutors Join Clinton, Reno in Push for Hate Crimes Statute," *StarTribune*, Apr. 26, 2000; Howie Padilla, "Man Gets 15 Years for Shooting Black Teen on King Day," *StarTribune*, Aug. 9, 2000; David Hawley, "Man Charged with Painting Hate Graffiti," *St. Paul Pioneer Press*, Jan. 26, 2000; Amy Mayron, "Man Admits Painting Hate Messages on Korean Church," *St. Paul Pioneer Press*, May 19, 2000.

153   hitting one of his workers over the head for speaking Spanish: Kermit Pattison, "Spanish Is Alleged Motive in Attack," *St. Paul Pioneer Press*, Nov. 18, 2000; Maria Elena Baca, "Business Owner Charged with Beating Man," *StarTribune*, Nov. 18, 2000; Doug Grow, "Violent Episode Shatters Immigrant's Body, Spirit: As Teen Struggles to Recover, Police Say He Was Attacked for Speaking Spanish," *StarTribune*, Dec. 20, 2000; Margaret Zack, "Business Owner Convicted of Assault in Bloomington," *StarTribune*, Apr. 7, 2001; Margaret Zack, "Assault Brings 7 Years, 7 Months," *StarTribune*, June 8, 2001. The business owner ended up getting a new trial, but he later pleaded guilty to first-degree assault. Margaret Zack, "Business Owner Gets New Trial in Assault Case," *StarTribune*, May 22, 2002; Pam Louwagie, "Businessman Pleads Guilty to Assault," *StarTribune*, Mar. 2, 2004.

154   investigation of Matthew Shepard's murder: Matthew Shepard Foundation, "Matthew's Story," http://www.matthewshepard.org/our-story/matthews-story.

154   "public square in Ljubljana": William J. Clinton, *Public Papers of the Presidents of the United States* (Washington, DC: Government Printing Office), pp. 988–99 (President Clinton's remarks of June 21, 1999, in Slovenia); Charles Babington, "Clinton Touts Slovenia as Model for Serbia," *Washington Post*, June 22, 1999.

154   pulling out the stool: Cheryl Johnson, "Clinton Gives Klobuchar a Lift at White House Event," *StarTribune*, May 2, 2000.

155   introduced President Clinton: Remarks, White House Hate Crimes Strategy Session, Hennepin County Attorney Amy Klobuchar, Apr. 25, 2000; Transcript of Clinton Remarks on Hate Crimes, Apr. 25, 2000; "Capitol Briefing," *St. Paul Pioneer Press*, Apr. 26, 2000; "Hate Crimes," C-SPAN, Apr. 25, 2000, http://www.c-span.org/video/?156747-1/hate-crimes; The White House, Hate Crimes Strategy Session and Statement (Apr. 24, 2000), http://www.clintonlibrary.gov/assets/storage/Research-Digital-Library/dpc/reed-subject/111/647386-hate-crimes.pdf.

155   Matthew Shepard and James Byrd, Jr. Hate Crimes Prevention Act: http://www.justice.gov/crt/about/crm/matthewshepard.php; "Remarks by the President at Reception Commemorating the Enactment of the Matthew Shepard and James Byrd, Jr. Hate Crimes Prevention Act," The White House, Office of the Press Secretary, Oct. 28, 2009.

156   joined by five Republicans: David A. Graham, "George Voinovich: Unsung Moderate Hero of the Senate," *Newsweek*, Sept. 10, 2010.

CHAPTER 7

158   Amiruddin Quassim: David Shaffer, "Suspect Charged in Death of Man Pushed Off Bus," *StarTribune*, Sept. 21, 2000; Margaret Zack, "St. Paul Man Sentenced in Shoving Death on Bus," *StarTribune*, July 20, 2001.

159   batting average: Rachel A. Koestler-Grack, *Kirby Puckett* (New York: Chelsea House, 2007), p. 102.

160   he worked with a lot of charities: Bob Sansevere, "The Secret Life of Kirby Puckett," *St. Paul Pioneer Press*, Dec. 17, 2002.

160   Baseball Hall of Fame: Kirby Puckett, National Baseball Hall of Fame, http://baseballhall.org/hof/puckett-kirby; Text of Kirby Puckett's Hall of Fame Induction Speech, http://sports.espn.go.com/mlb/news/story?id=2357373.

160   Puckett's wife, Tonya: Jim Adams, Pam Louwagie, and La Velle E. Neal III, "Tonya Puckett Seeks Divorce from Kirby After Alleged Threat," *StarTribune*, Jan. 12, 2002; Bob Sansevere, "Pucketts Getting a Divorce: Popular Ballplayer's Wife Reports Threatening Phone Call," *St. Paul Pioneer Press*, Jan. 12, 2002.

161   "Like most Minnesotans": Tom Scheck, "Hall of Famer Puckett Charged in Alleged Sexual Assault," Minnesota Public Radio, Oct. 18, 2002; Jim Adams and Randy Furst, "Puckett Is Charged in Sex Case," *StarTribune*, Oct. 19, 2002.

161   "It seems strange to me": Sherrie L. Wilson, "Kirby Puckett: A Middle American Tragedy," in David C. Ogden and Joel Nathan Rosen, eds., *Fame to Infamy: Race, Sport, and the Fall from Grace* (Jackson: University Press of Mississippi, 2010), p. 40.

161   The trial: Margaret Zack, "Judge Won't Delay Kirby Puckett Trial," *StarTribune*, Mar. 18, 2003; Jay Weiner, "Puckett Trial: A Peek Inside," *StarTribune*, Mar. 30, 2003. Kirby Puckett was also represented by Christopher Madel, a lawyer at Robins Kaplan.

162   "Take Me Out to the Ballgame": Jay Weiner, "Kirby Puckett Trial Draws a Crowd, But Not a Circus," *StarTribune*, Mar. 30, 2003.

162   After more than eight hours of deliberations: Michael Hirsley, "Jurors Need a 2nd Day," *Chicago Tribune*, Apr. 3, 2003; Amy Mayron, "Kirby Puckett Cleared of Sexual Assault Charges," *St. Paul Pioneer Press*, Apr. 4, 2003; Bob Sansevere, "Kirby Puckett Walks Away, But Not Untarnished," *St. Paul Pioneer Press*, Apr. 3, 2003; Patrick Reusse, "Verdict Doesn't Save Reputation," *StarTribune*, Apr. 4, 2003; Elizabeth Stawicki, "Puckett Acquitted of Assault Charges," Minnesota Public Radio, Apr. 3, 2003.

162   "beyond a reasonable doubt": Jay Weiner and Pam Louwagie, "Puckett Found Not Guilty in Sexual-Assault Case," *StarTribune*, Apr. 4, 2003; Pam Louwagie and Margaret Zack, "Case Against Puckett Was Sign of the Times," *StarTribune*, Apr. 6, 2003; "Puckett Prosecution Was Uphill Battle," Minnesota Public Radio, Apr. 4, 2003. Kirby Puckett tragically died of a massive stroke three years later, just short of his forty-sixth birthday. Richard Goldstein, "Kirby Puckett, 45, Hall of Fame Outfielder, Dies," *New York Times*, Mar. 7, 2006.

163   he saw her kiss another guy: Jim Adams, "Spurned Boyfriend Held in Stabbing Death at Megamall," *StarTribune*, May 6, 1999; Kimberly Hayes Taylor, "Teen's Death Puts Painful Light on Strife in Somali Community," *StarTribune*, May 14, 1999; Jim Adams, "Suspect in Mall Slaying Is Charged, Says He Was Jealous of Another Man," *StarTribune*, May 7, 1999; David Chanen, "Man Indicted in Mall Slaying of Ex-Girlfriend," *StarTribune*, May 19, 1999.

163   first-degree murder: Heron Marquez Estrada and Margaret Zack, "Man Convicted of Killing Woman at Mall," *StarTribune*, Dec. 6, 1999; Margaret Zack, "Man Gets 25 Years for Killing His Ex-Girlfriend at Megamall," *StarTribune*, Jan. 5, 2000.

165   *New Yorker* cartoon: Kim Warp, *New Yorker* cartoon, Condé Nast Collection, http://www.condenaststore.com/-sp/And-I-m-sure-no-one-will-mind-if-we-fold-a-few-clothes-while-we-talk-New-Yorker-Cartoon-Prints_i8479106_.htm.

165   divided up the housework: Ellen Tomson, "A Life of Achievement . . . and Individuality," *St. Paul Pioneer Press*, Oct. 27, 2006. One now decades-old article noted that I was "not the first" Hennepin County Attorney "to balance home and work," but that I was "the first mother" to do so as evidenced by the wall of photos in my office of my all-male predecessors. Jon Tevlin, "Chasing Amy," *StarTribune*, Aug. 31, 2003. Toward the end of that profile, however, the reporter editorialized a bit. In a bit of prose that generated more than a bit of discussion around Twin Cities office water coolers, he wrote that my husband "seems to do more than his share of parenting duties." Ibid. Naturally, I didn't think that was fair, and I told the reporter—a very good one by the way who, I think, just underestimated how working women would react to that line—how I felt about it. The reporter, Jon Tevlin, later told me about the reception that line got from working moms, but of course that didn't stop my John—my husband—from proudly tacking up the article on the refrigerator! The lesson: what's a "fair share" of household chores and parenting duties is all in the eye of the beholder. I suppose men and women will be debating this one well into the next century. Anyway, no hard feelings Jon (and John, *I think*).

165   Dale Carnegie: Dale Carnegie, *How to Stop Worrying and Start Living: Time-Tested Methods for Conquering Worry* (New York: Pocket Books, 1984).

166   bank robber in Detroit: "Rules for Bank Robbers," http://www.frivolity.com /teatime/Miscellaneous/bank_robbery.html.

166   record all interrogations: In *State v. Scales*, 518 N.W.2d 587 (Minn. 1994), the Minnesota Supreme Court required that all custodial interrogations be recorded. To guarantee "the fair administration of justice," the court ruled, "we hold that all custodial interrogation including any information about rights, any waiver of those rights, and all questioning shall be electronically recorded where feasible and must be recorded when questioning occurs at a place of detention." "If law enforcement officers fail to comply with this recording requirement," the court added, "any statements the suspect makes in response to the interrogation may be suppressed at trial."

166   caught the suspect reading a piece of paper: Shannon Prather, "Lights, Camera, Confession," *St. Paul Pioneer Press*, July 17, 2006.

166   picked up on videotape saying: Frank Main, "Cops to Start Taping Interrogations: 'We Will Get Better Confessions' in Murder Cases," *Chicago Sun-Times*, July 3, 2005.

166   News of the Weird: Chuck Shepherd's News of the Weird, Mar. 7, 2004 (citing Canadian Broadcasting Corp., Jan. 12, 2004, and *StarTribune*, Feb. 3, 2004).

166   the police officer on duty: "Nude Man Pulled from Chimney on Christmas," *USA Today*, Dec. 26, 2003.

167   "meter eater": Margaret Zack, "Man Charged with Tampering with Meters," *StarTribune*, July 10, 1999; Amy Mayron, "No Such Thing as Free Parking: Man Charged with Breaking Meters," *St. Paul Pioneer Press*, July 10, 1999.

167   nuclear secrets: Joseph Masco, *The Nuclear Borderlands: The Manhattan Project in Post–Cold War New Mexico* (Princeton, NJ: Princeton University Press, 2006), p. 280; James Risen and Jeff Gerth, "Breach at Los Alamos: China Stole Nuclear Secrets for Bombs, U.S. Aides Say," *New York Times*, Mar. 6, 1999. Espionage allegations were leveled against Dr. Wen Ho Lee, a nuclear engineer at the Los Alamos National Laboratory in New Mexico, who spent 278 days in solitary confinement, but he ended up pleading guilty to only one of the government's fifty-nine counts—using an unsecure computer to download national defense information. The espionage charges against Dr. Lee were ultimately dropped. Wen Ho Lee with Helen Zia, *My Country Versus Me: The First-Hand Account by the Los Alamos Scientist Who Was Falsely Accused of Being a Spy* (New York: Hyperion, 2001), pp. 1–7.

167   protect the innocent: Amy Klobuchar and Hilary Lindell Caligiuri, "Protecting the Innocent/Convicting the Guilty: Hennepin County's Pilot Project in Blind Sequential Eyewitness Identification," *William Mitchell Law Review* vol. 32, iss. 1 (2005); Conrad deFiebre, "Police Plan to Reshuffle the Lineup," *StarTribune*, Aug. 31, 2003; "Witness IDs: Piloting a Smarter System," *StarTribune*, Nov. 10, 2003 (editorial); Jim Adams, "Police Test New Tactic for Lineups," *StarTribune*, Feb. 10, 2005.

167   videotaping interrogations: Steven E. Barkan and George J. Bryjak, *Myths and Realities of Crime and Justice: What Every American Should Know*, 2nd ed. (Burlington, MA: Jones & Bartlett Learning, 2014), p. 283; Press Release, New York County Lawyers' Association, "NYCLA's Report on Videotaping of Custodial Interrogations Approved by ABA's House of Delegates," Feb. 9, 2004 (reporting on forum featuring Richard A. Brown, the Queens County district attorney, and me, titled "Beware of False Confessions!: Should All Custodial Interrogations Be Videotaped?").

168   "Career Offender Statute": Margaret Zack, "Klobuchar Touts Increased Use of
       Career-Offender Sentencing," *StarTribune*, Jan. 19, 2000; Margaret Zack, "Hen-
       nepin Prosecutors Tally Up Stiff Penalties," *StarTribune*, Jan. 30, 2001.

168   legislative auditor's report: Report #01-05, Office of the Legislative Auditor, State
       of Minnesota Program Evaluation Report (Feb. 2001).

168   community prosecution initiative: David Hawley, "Community Prosecutor
       System Wins Recognition," *St. Paul Pioneer Press*, July 6, 2001; Robert V. Wolf
       and John L. Worrall, *Lessons from the Field: Ten Community Prosecution
       Leadership Profiles* (Alexandria, VA: American Prosecutors Research Insti-
       tute, Nov. 2004), pp. vi, xi, 23–28; U.S. Department of Justice, Office of Justice
       Programs, Bureau of Justice Assistance, Community Prosecution Strategies
       (Aug. 2003), pp. vi, 74; Margaret Zack, "Hennepin Honored for Anticrime
       Work," *StarTribune*, July 6, 2001.

168   truancy: Mark Brunswick, "Hennepin County Turns a Spotlight on Truancy,"
       StarTribune, Jan. 29, 2001; Allie Shah, "Battle Against Truancy Revs Up," *Star-
       Tribune*, Aug. 21, 2001.

169   drunk driving: Margaret Zack, "Woman Pleads Guilty to 10th Charge Linked
       to Driving Drunk," *StarTribune*, Dec. 2, 1999; David Hawley, "Woman's 10th
       DWI Conviction Fuels Get-Tough Bill," *St. Paul Pioneer Press*, Jan. 25, 2000;
       David Chanen, "Case Is Used to Seek Tougher Legislation on Drunken Driv-
       ing," *StarTribune*, Jan. 25, 2000; Margaret Zack, "Repeat Drunken Driver Is Sent
       to Prison," *StarTribune*, June 29, 2002; Rachel E. Stassen-Berger, "Repeat
       Drunken Driver Finally Faces Felony," *St. Paul Pioneer Press*, Dec. 28, 1999.

169   Malik Sealy: Joy Powell, "Charges: Man Was Drunk in Sealy Crash," *StarTri-
       bune*, May 25, 2000; Margaret Zack, "Driver Who Killed Sealy Gets Four Years
       in Prison," *StarTribune*, Oct. 19, 2000.

170   twenty-year-old woman: Howie Padilla, "Eagan Man Pleads Guilty to Fatal
       Wrong-Way Crash," *StarTribune*, Mar. 6, 2001; Margaret Zack, "Drunken Driver
       Gets 4 Years for Fatal Crash," *StarTribune*, May 15, 2001. This vibrant young
       woman, just short of her twenty-first birthday, was the only child of former
       Minnesota Secretary of State Mark Ritchie and his wife, Nancy. Doug Grow,
       "Secretary of State Ritchie Q-A: 'I Have a Long List of Things I Want to Do
       Before Leaving,'" *MinnPost*, June 10, 2013.

170   felony DWI: Conrad deFiebre, "New Felony DWI Law Getting Broken in Fast,"
       StarTribune, Aug. 8, 2002; Margaret Zack, "Hennepin Charges 2 with Felony
       DWI Under New Statute," *StarTribune*, Aug. 13, 2002; Jim Adams, "A Chase
       Ends with Driver's DWI," *StarTribune*, June 25, 2004; Howie Padilla, "Driver
       Pleads Guilty to DWI Charge," *StarTribune*, Oct. 2, 2004; Margaret Zack,
       "Chronic DWI Offender Is Heading to Prison," *StarTribune*, Nov. 5, 2004;
       Minnesotans for Safe Driving, http://mnsafedriving.com/drunk-a-drugged
       -driving/felony-dwi.html (describing the felony DWI law that passed the Min-
       nesota legislature in August 2002).

170   ".10 to a .08": Tom Scheck, "Last in the Nation, Minnesota Tightens Drunk Driv-
       ing Limit," Minnesota Public Radio, July 29, 2005.

170   Tommy Rukavina: Quotes of the Session, Capitol Watch, http://www
       .larkinhoffman.com/files/OTHER/CapWatch05End.pdf, Larkin Hoffman
       newsletter (2005), p. 3.

170   up to twenty DWIs: David Hawley, "Man Guilty of 23rd DWI: Man Faces Five
       Years under Felony Law," *St. Paul Pioneer Press*, Oct. 2, 2004; Oversight Hear-
       ing on Effectiveness of Federal Drunk Driving Programs, Subcommittee on

Transportation Safety, Infrastructure Security, and Water Quality of the Committee on Environment and Public Works, United States Senate, 110th Cong., 1st Sess. (Oct. 25, 2007), pp. 3–5.

170   within five months we had charged ninety-two felony DWI cases: Hennepin County Attorney Amy Klobuchar, 2002 Annual Report, p. 2. We continued using the law throughout my tenure. "Minn. Man Charged with DUI for 23rd Time," AP Online, June 26, 2004 ("During the first 18 months of the new law, 920 people were sentenced for felony drunken-driving offenses, according to the state Sentencing Guidelines Commission. Hennepin County has filed felony drunken-driving charges in 350 cases since the new law was enacted.").

171   investment swindles: Margaret Zack, "Coin Dealer Pleads Guilty to Swindle, Gets Prison Time," *StarTribune*, June 6, 2006; Margaret Zack, "Fraudulent Schemes Netted $1.3 Million, Charges Say," *StarTribune*, Apr. 3, 2002; Margaret Zack, "Not a Billionaire Businessman After All: He Lured Investors But Kept Money," *StarTribune*, Feb. 7, 2003.

171   contractor fraud: Amy Sherman, "Contractor Charged in Major Swindle," *St. Paul Pioneer Press*, Jan. 31, 2003; Margaret Zack, "Home Remodeler Sentenced for Fraud," *StarTribune*, Jan. 16, 2004; Amy Sherman, "St. Paul, Minn.–Area Contractor Gets Two Years for Fraud," *St. Paul Pioneer Press*, Jan. 16, 2004. Our white-collar prosecutions often ended in convictions and prison sentences. Occasionally, however, we did not always get the prison sentences we sought. Terry Fiedler, "Builder Faces 46 Months in Fraud," *StarTribune*, Jan. 6, 2006; Joy Powell, "Builder Bren Avoids Prison in Swindle: Bruce Bren Pleaded Guilty to Eight Counts of Pocketing Customers' Money, But a Judge Decided on Probation," *StarTribune*, May 20, 2006.

171   tax evasion: Margaret Zack, "Day Care Provider Admits Fraud in $660,000 Case," *StarTribune*, Apr. 7, 2004.

171   identity theft: Margaret Zack, "Ringleader Found Guilty in Patient-ID-Theft Case," *StarTribune*, Apr. 15, 2004; Bill Gardner "Seventh Defendant Guilty in ID Theft Ring," *St. Paul Pioneer Press*, Apr. 15, 2004; Margaret Zack, "Tougher Penalty Law Applied in ID Theft Case," *StarTribune*, June 6, 2006.

172   pilots' tax evasion: Howie Padilla, "Tax Inquiry Looks at 13 NWA Pilots," *StarTribune*, Nov. 29, 2001; Liz Fedor, "Northwest Pilot Is Found Guilty of Tax Evasion," *StarTribune*, Oct. 22, 2002; Ed Lotterman, "Taxes Are a Necessary Evil; Tax Evaders Really Are Evil," Real World Economics, October 27, 2002, www .edlotterman.com; Liz Fedor, "Pilot Faces Jail for Tax Evasion," *StarTribune*, Dec. 13, 2002; Associated Press, "Pilot Convicted of Tax Evasion," *Rochester Post-Bulletin*, Dec. 21, 2002; Dave Beal, "Minnesota Widens Tax Evasion Probe of Northwest Airline Employees," *St. Paul Pioneer Press*, Jan. 29, 2003; Liz Fedor, "Third Northwest Pilot Convicted of Tax Evasion," *StarTribune*, Feb. 20, 2003; Liz Fedor, "Fourth NWA Pilot Guilty of Tax Evasion," *StarTribune*, Mar. 26, 2003; Hennepin County Attorney Amy Klobuchar, 2003 Annual Report, p. 9 ("The County Attorney's Office successfully completed the prosecutions of seven commercial airline pilots for evading Minnesota income taxes by falsely claiming to live in states with no personal income tax when they actually resided in Minnesota.").

173   "President Bartlet": *The West Wing* (NBC, 1999–2006).

173   Judge Roland Amundson: Craig Gustafson, "Judge Is Investigated in Handling of Trust," *StarTribune*, Jan. 17, 2002; Margaret Zack, "Judge Resigns as Trustee for Disabled Woman," *StarTribune*, Jan. 24, 2002; Pam Louwagie, "Amundson

Resigns from Appeals Court," *StarTribune*, Feb. 26, 2002; Pam Louwagie and Randy Furst, "Judge Charged with Theft," *StarTribune*, Feb. 27, 2002; Phillip Piña, "Ex-Judge Pleads Guilty to Theft: Amundson Swindled More Than $400,000," *St. Paul Pioneer Press*, Apr. 2, 2002; Margaret Zack, "Ex-Judge Gets 69 Months for Swindling Disabled Woman," *StarTribune*, June 8, 2002; Ruben Rosario, "Judge's Penitence Doesn't Shine Through in Lawsuit," *St. Paul Pioneer Press*, Jan. 5, 2004 ("disabled Minneapolis woman" had "the mental capacity of a 3-year-old").

174   a reporter for the paper interviewed me: Kate Zernike, "A Fallen Judge Rethinks Crime and Punishment," *New York Times*, Jan. 13, 2006.

175   "Miss Skyway News": "Ms. Skyway News: Amy Klobuchar," *Skyway News*, Mar. 17, 1988; David Brauer, "Senate Candidate Reveals Her Sordid Past," *The Journal*, Apr. 25, 2005 ("According to our records, Amy Klobuchar ascended to the lofty title of Ms. Skyway, on March 17, 1988, reigning for a week until a new winner was awarded the newsprint tiara."). "Ms. Skyway, a feature of this newspaper for 20 years, was discontinued in the early '90s." Ibid.

176   John Marshall Harlan: Timothy L. Hall, *Supreme Court Justices: A Biographical Dictionary* (New York: Facts on File, 2001), p. 176.

176   Paul Wellstone: Dennis J. McGrath and Dane Smith, *Professor Wellstone Goes to Washington: The Inside Story of a Grassroots U.S. Senate Campaign* (Minneapolis: University of Minnesota Press, 1995), pp. xix–xx, 89.

176   98.7 percent of the votes!: Minnesota Secretary of State, Official Results: General Election, County Attorney.

176   no opponent: "Hennepin Attorney: Amy Klobuchar, Unchallenged or Not," *StarTribune*, Oct. 22, 2002. After not drawing an opponent in 2002, my husband John joked that State Representative Frank Hornstein and I should start a Society for Unopposed Candidates, the sole purpose of which would be to explain to our respective spouses why we still needed to campaign that year. Frank is married to Rabbi Marcia Zimmerman at Minneapolis's Temple Israel and—like John—has a great sense of humor. Frank even does impressions. Needless to say, John's suggestion was purely in jest, with Frank and I both vigorously campaigning—at parades, at festivals, the whole nine yards—in the lead-up to the 2002 general election, doing our best to help our fellow DFL candidates.

176   multiple sclerosis: Marisa Helms, "U.S. Sen. Paul Wellstone Diagnosed with Multiple Sclerosis," Minnesota Public Radio, Feb. 24, 2002.

176   his wife, Sheila: Kay Harvey, "Sheila Wellstone: 'Driven by Principle and Passion' on Domestic-Abuse Issue," *MinnPost*, Oct. 25, 2012.

176   famous green bus: Larry Sabato, ed., *Midterm Madness: The Elections of 2002* (Lanham, MD: Rowman & Littlefield, 2003), p. 89 (noting of Paul Wellstone and his famous bus: "The populism of his grassroots campaign was symbolized by a tattered green school bus that Wellstone used in all his Senate races.").

177   voted against the Iraqi war resolution: Mark Richard Ireland, ed., *Wellstone, Conscience of the Senate: The Collected Floor Speeches of Senator Paul Wellstone* (St. Cloud, MN: North Star Press of St. Cloud, 2008), pp. 188–93.

177   tragic plane crash: Paul David Wellstone Jr., *Becoming Wellstone: Healing from Tragedy and Carrying on My Father's Legacy* (Center City, MN: Hazelden Publishing, 2012).

178   Camp Wellstone: http://www.wellstone.org/programs/camp-wellstone; Jeff

Blodgett, "Ten Years Later: We Still Need the 'Wellstone Way,'" *MinnPost*, Oct. 25, 2012.

178   insurance parity to those with mental illnesses: Paul Wellstone and Pete Domenici Mental Health Parity and Addiction Equity Act of 2008, Pub. L. 110-343, 122 Stat. 3765 (Oct. 3, 2008).

178   tenth anniversary of the deaths: "Sens. Klobuchar, Franken: Paul Wellstone's Legacy," *StarTribune*, Oct. 24, 2012; Dan Kraker, "Wellstones, Crash Victims Remembered 10 Years After Their Deaths," Minnesota Public Radio, Oct. 25, 2012.

179   John Kerry came to St. Paul: Bill Salisbury, "Kerry Rally Draws Overflow Crowd: Democratic Front-Runner Keeps Focus on Bush," *St. Paul Pioneer Press*, Feb. 26, 2004.

180   the Democratic National Convention: Eric Black, "Anatomy of an Opportunity: Klobuchar's Speech Is a Chance to Shine," *StarTribune*, July 28, 2004; "Convention Journal: Scenes from Inside and Out," *StarTribune*, July 29, 2004.

180   "Barbara Jordan": In Congresswoman Barbara Jordan's own words: "What the people want is very simple. They want an America as good as its promise." Clara Villarosa, *The Words of African-American Heroes* (New York: Newmarket Press, 2011), p. 102.

181   The teleprompter had gone dark: C-SPAN, "Democratic National Convention, Day 3 Afternoon," July 28, 2004.

CHAPTER 8

182   Mike Hatch: Conrad deFiebre, "GOP Rep. Johnson Will Run for Hatch's Job," *StarTribune*, Feb. 16, 2005; Dane Smith, "Mighty Shuffle Could Be Ahead in '06 Elections," *StarTribune*, Feb. 13, 2005.

183   a surprise announcement: Dane Smith, Eric Black, and Patricia Lopez, "Plenty of Contenders for That Vacant Seat," *StarTribune*, Feb. 10, 2005; Bill Salisbury, "Dayton Won't Run Again in '06," *St. Paul Pioneer Press*, Feb. 10, 2005.

184   Jennifer Thompson-Cannino: "Guilt, Innocence: Seeking True Justice for All," *StarTribune*, Feb. 15, 2005 (editorial); Jennifer Thompson-Cannino and Ronald Cotton with Erin Torneo, *Picking Cotton: Our Memoir of Injustice and Redemption* (New York: St. Martin's Press, 2009).

184   Keith Ellison: Keith Ellison, *My Country, 'Tis of Thee: My Faith, My Family, Our Future* (New York: Simon & Schuster, 2014).

185   "follow candidates around": My 2006 Republican tracker, Ryan Flynn, actually became a public supporter of mine in the 2012 election. Tom Scheck, "Candidates Have Few Secrets from Campaign 'Trackers,'" MPR News, Oct. 18, 2006; Rachel E. Stassen-Berger, "The Trackers and the Tracked," Hot Dish Politics Blog (*StarTribune*), May 27, 2014. Thanks for your support, Ryan!

187   Minnesota had twice rejected qualified women candidates: Anne E. Kornblut, *Notes from the Cracked Ceiling: What It Will Take for a Woman to Win* (New York: Random House, 2011), p. 138.

187   Mark Kennedy: Eric Black, "Kennedy Is Off and Running," *StarTribune*, Feb. 12, 2005; Rachel E. Stassen-Berger, "Kennedy First Out of Gate to Chase U.S. Senate Seat," *St. Paul Pioneer Press*, Feb. 12, 2005.

188   International Eelpout Festival: http://www.eelpoutfestival.com; Dean Morrill, "Klobuchar Brings U.S. Senate Campaign to Walker," *Pilot-Independent*

(Walker, MN), Aug. 15, 2006. That year's International Eelpout Festival took place from February 11–13, 2005. Dave Scroppo, "The Greatest Shows on Ice," *Field & Stream*, Dec. 2004–Jan. 2005, p. 32. I jumped into the Senate race not long thereafter. Rob Hotakainen, "Klobuchar to File Candidacy Papers," *Star-Tribune*, Feb. 24, 2005; Kevin Duchschere, "DFLers Klobuchar, Wetterling Move Closer to Senate Race," *StarTribune*, Mar. 19, 2005; Toni Coleman, "Klobuchar Edges 'Closer' to Entering Senate Race," *St. Paul Pioneer Press*, Mar. 19, 2005.

189   I made the decision to run: Josephine Marcotty, "Painful Times with Dad Helped Create Drive to Succeed," *StarTribune*, Oct. 8, 2006.

190   dispute about how to say my last name: Marshall Helmberger, "Klobuchar Rounds Up Support During Iron Range Visit," *Cook-Orr Timberjay* (Cook, MN), Jan. 21, 2006; Mike Hillman, "Is There One Right Way to Say Klobuchar?," *Ely Timberjay* (Tower, MN), Jan. 21, 2006; Mike Hillman, "Ahh, the Differing Ways to Pronounce 'Klobuchar,'" *Timberjay News* (Tower, MN), Jan. 28, 2006.

190   Joan Growe: "Capitol Ideas," *The Hour* (Norwalk, CT), July 10, 1985 ("Joan Growe, the Minnesota Democrat who lost her 1984 campaign to unseat incumbent Sen. Rudy Boschwitz, R-Minn., but who may make another go at a Senate race next time around, defines sexual parity in politics this way: 'We'll have equality when we've elected as many mediocre women as mediocre men.'"). Joan Growe told me she got this quip from other women and passed it on.

192   Burt Bacharach: Burt Bacharach did, however, contribute significantly to Al's campaign. But hearing Burt perform live at a small venue: priceless.

193     $17,000 from ex-boyfriends: Anne Schroeder Mullins, "Klobuchar Brings Down the House," *Politico*, Feb. 5, 2009.

194   I ended up raising $592,000: Greg Gordon, "Coffers for Senate Race Grow," *Star-Tribune*, Apr. 6, 2005; Eric Black, "Klobuchar Is Set to Announce," *Star Tribune*, Apr. 16, 2005.

194   my formal announcement: Eric Black, "Klobuchar Is First DFL Candidate in U.S. Senate Race," *StarTribune*, Apr. 18, 2005; Bill Salisbury, "Klobuchar Vows to Bring 'Common Sense' to Congress," *St. Paul Pioneer Press*, Apr. 18, 2005; Gregg Hennigan, "Local Ties: Klobuchar's In-Laws Live in Mankato," *Free Press* (Mankato, MN), Apr. 19, 2005.

195   Patty Wetterling: Dane Smith and Kevin Duchschere, "Many Women Seek Top Offices," *StarTribune*, Feb. 26, 2005; Bill Salisbury, "Wetterling a Stronger Senate Candidate, She Says," *St. Paul Pioneer Press*, Apr. 20, 2005; Greg Gordon, "Klobuchar, Wetterling Raising Lots of Cash," *StarTribune*, July 7, 2005; Janet Moore, "Wetterling Makes Her Senate Bid Official," *StarTribune*, Oct. 10, 2005.

196   Kelly Doran: Greg Gordon, "Developer Doran Joins Race for Dayton's Seat," *StarTribune*, May 17, 2005; Jill Burcum, "Developer Seeks DFL Nod for Senate Seat," *StarTribune*, June 6, 2005; "Doran's Assets Worth Between $57 Million and $210 Million," *St. Paul Pioneer Press*, June 18, 2005.

196   federal budget: Associated Press, "Klobuchar Calls for Attacking Deficit," *St. Paul Pioneer Press*, Aug. 30, 2006.

196   Ford Bell: Patricia Lopez, "DFL's Bell Throws Hat in Senate Ring," *StarTribune*, July 23, 2005; Rachel E. Stassen-Berger, "DFLer Bell Seeks U.S. Senate Seat," *St. Paul Pioneer Press*, July 23, 2005.

197   I needed the party's support: Dane Smith, "Senate Hopefuls Already on Move," *StarTribune*, Aug. 21, 2005.

197   Rod Grams: Amy Forliti, "Grams Drops Out of 2006 Senate Race," *St. Paul Pioneer Press*, Apr. 25, 2005.

197   Mark Kennedy: Rachel E. Stassen-Berger, "Kennedy Gets GOP Nod, Stresses His Independence," *St. Paul Pioneer Press*, June 2, 2006; Jay Weiner, "The Life of Mark Kennedy: From 'Dull' to Determined Candidate," *StarTribune*, Oct. 1, 2006; Tom Scheck, "Mark Kennedy Touts Experience in Re-election Bid," Minnesota Public Radio, Aug. 12, 2004.

197   EMILY's List: Greg Gordon, "EMILY's List Backs Klobuchar for Senate," *StarTribune*, Sept. 30, 2005; Frederic J. Frommer, "Kennedy Draws GOP Senate Cash; EMILY's List Backing Democrat Klobuchar," *St. Paul Pioneer Press*, Feb. 17, 2006.

198   grassroots operation: Linda Vanderwerf, "Klobuchar Building Grassroots Network," *West Central Tribune* (Willmar, MN), Apr. 21, 2005.

198   other Democrats left the race: Rachel E. Stassen-Berger, "Doran's Switch Shakes Up Races," *St. Paul Pioneer Press*, Sept. 22, 2005; Brian Bakst, "Wetterling Endorses Klobuchar for Senate," *Post-Bulletin* (Rochester, MN), Jan. 21, 2006.

198   Mike Ciresi: Greg Gordon, "FEC Filings Show Mark Kennedy $1 Million Ahead of Klobuchar; Eyes Are on Ciresi," *StarTribune*, Feb. 1, 2006; Rachel E. Stassen-Berger and Patrick Sweeney, "Potential Successors Lining Up: Ciresi, Klobuchar Lead Democrats Among Political Punditocracy," *St. Paul Pioneer Press*, Feb. 10, 2005.

198   decided not to run: Rachel E. Stassen-Berger, "Ciresi Won't Run for Senate," *St. Paul Pioneer Press*, Feb. 9, 2006; Patricia Lopez, "Ciresi Says He Will Not Run for U.S. Senate," *StarTribune*, Feb. 7, 2006.

198   duke it out for quite a while longer: "Three U.S. Senate Candidates in Debate at Noon," *St. Paul Pioneer Press*, Mar. 3, 2006; Dane Smith, "DFLers Square Off; Bell Signals Primary Battle," *StarTribune*, May 27, 2006; Rachel E. Stassen-Berger, "Bell Concedes DFL Party Nod to Klobuchar But Veterinarian Still Will Run in Primary," *St. Paul Pioneer Press*, May 27, 2006.

198   precinct caucuses: Dane Smith and Patricia Lopez, "Klobuchar, Hatch Win Their DFL Straw Polls," *StarTribune*, Mar. 9, 2006; Bill Salisbury, "Hatch, Klobuchar Dominate DFL Rivals at Precinct Caucuses," *St. Paul Pioneer Press*, Mar. 8, 2006. There were more than four thousand precinct caucuses to organize. Bill Salisbury, "Caucuses Kick Off Campaigns: Tuesday's Gatherings Will Launch Large Number of Races," *St. Paul Pioneer Press*, Mar. 6, 2006 (noting caucuses were held "in 4,111 precincts across the state").

198   Ford announced that he was pulling out of the race: Patricia Lopez, "DFL Candidate Ford Bell Pulls Out of U.S. Senate Race," *StarTribune*, July 12, 2006.

198   allowing me to focus all of my energies: Eric Black, "Kennedy, Klobuchar Win Primaries by Wide Margins," *StarTribune*, Sept. 13, 2006.

198   the DFL convention: Patricia Lopez, "DFL Backs Klobuchar as She Girds for Battle," *StarTribune*, June 10, 2006; Rachel E. Stassen-Berger, "Klobuchar Sews Up Endorsement," *St. Paul Pioneer Press*, June 10, 2006.

199   fundraising efforts: Greg Gordon, "There's No Off-Season for Senate Fund Drive," *StarTribune*, Aug. 22, 2005; Greg Gordon, "Klobuchar Leads Wetterling in Race for Dollars," *StarTribune*, Oct. 15, 2005.

200   Minnesota Nice: John Radzilowski, *Minnesota* (Northampton, MA: Interlink Books, 2006), p. ix; Martin Schwabacher and Patricia K. Kummer, *Minnesota: Celebrate the States* (Tarrytown, NY: Marshall Cavendish Benchmark, 2008), p. 51.

200   judging a chili-tasting contest: Juliana Thill, "DFLers Turn Up the Heat at Chili Cookoff," *Independent Review* (Litchfield, MN), Oct. 20, 2005.

201   One of my favorite stories Al tells: "On Eve of Trial, Franken Jokes with His
        Radio Base," *Huffington Post*, Feb. 27, 2009, http://www.huffingtonpost.com/the
        -uptake/on-eve-of-trial-franken-j_b_160682.html; Heather M. Gray, "Renowned
        Columnist Jim Klobuchar Stumps for His Daughter While in Town," *Spring
        Grove Herald* (Spring Grove, MN), Aug. 30, 2006.

201   Justin Buoen: Doug Grow, "Sen. Amy Klobuchar Names Justin Buoen to Run
        Re-Election Campaign," *MinnPost*, Nov. 1, 2011.

202   Jessica Vanden Berg: Elizabeth Noll, "Behind the Scenes," *Minnesota Women's
        Press*, Apr. 10, 2015.

202   Ben Goldfarb: "Klobuchar Names Goldfarb Campaign Manager," *St. Paul Pio-
        neer Press*, Feb. 22, 2006; Craig Cox, "Managing to Win," *Rake Magazine* (Nov.
        2006), pp. 46–47.

202   Sara Grewing: Frederick Melo, "St. Paul City Attorney Appointed District Court
        Judge," *St. Paul Pioneer Press*, Dec. 23, 2014.

203   Jake Sullivan: Devin Henry, "Biden Names Minnesotan Jake Sullivan Top
        National Security Adviser," *MinnPost*, Feb. 26, 2013.

204   "in the toss-up column": Charlie Cook, "Senate's '06 Races Point Parties to Sep-
        arate Paths," *National Journal*, Apr. 16, 2005, p. 1174 ("The Cook Report").

204   "I'll follow the North Star": Amy Klobuchar, Speech to the State Democratic
        Party Convention, June 9, 2006.

205   Kennedy raised lots of money: David Chanen, "Sen. Bill Frist Campaigns for
        Kennedy," *StarTribune*, June 27, 2005; Greg Gordon, "Candidates Report Their
        Donations Raised in the Past Quarter," *StarTribune*, July 15, 2005; Rochelle
        Olson, "Cheney Makes Quiet Visit to Back Kennedy," *StarTribune*, July 23,
        2005; Dane Smith, Rochelle Olson, and Conrad deFiebre, "Bush Pops In," *Star-
        Tribune*, Dec. 10, 2005; Greg Gordon, "With Bush's Help, Kennedy Raised $1.5
        Million in Last Quarter of '05," *StarTribune*, Jan. 31, 2006; Patricia Lopez,
        "Rove to Fit in Senate Fundraiser Friday," *StarTribune*, July 19, 2006; Patricia
        Lopez, "Laura Bush Stumps for Kennedy," *StarTribune*, June 7, 2006. Polls con-
        ducted in early 2006 showed that the Minnesota Senate race would be a close
        one. Minnesota Senate Race, Real Clear Politics, http://www.realclearpolitics
        .com.

205   TV ads: Patricia Lopez, "Kennedy's First TV Ad in Senate Race Treads Lightly,"
        StarTribune, July 26, 2006; Patricia Lopez, "Kennedy, Klobuchar Quicken Pace
        of Race," *StarTribune*, July 25, 2006; "Kessler's Top 4 Political Stories of the
        Week," WCCO-TV Channel 4, July 30, 2006 (Pat Kessler's "Top 4 Political Sto-
        ries of the Week").

206   "without fear or favor": Patricia Lopez, "Klobuchar Opens Senate Ad Season
        with Portrayal as a Crimefighter," *StarTribune*, July 11, 2006.

206   our best ad of the campaign: Eric Black, "Klobuchar's Ad Hedges When the Real
        Story Is Better," *StarTribune*, Oct. 7, 2006; Melinda Rogers, "Ads Show Fierce-
        ness of Senate Race," *Detroit Lakes Tribune*, Oct. 15, 2006.

207   Tyesha: Amy Mayron and Maja Beckstrom, "Peace for Tyesha as an 11-Year-
        Old Girl Is Laid to Rest in a Small Blue Casket," *St. Paul Pioneer Press*, Dec. 1,
        2002; Phillip Pina, "Suspect Guilty in Tyesha's Slaying," *St. Paul Pioneer Press*,
        Mar. 4, 2003; State v. Burrell, 772 N.W.2d 459 (Minn. 2009). Thanks to the
        excellent work of our prosecutors Paul Scoggin and Bob Streitz, and later Mike
        Furnstahl in the retrial, all three of the gang members involved in the shoot-
        ing went to prison. "Final Defendant Guilty: Getaway Driver in Girl's Shooting
        Death Enters Plea," *St. Paul Pioneer Press*, June 3, 2003.

207   negative ads continued: Rachel E. Stassen-Berger, "Mark Kennedy Launches Attack Ad," *St. Paul Pioneer Press*, Sept. 16, 2006.

207   immigration: Eric Black, "Kennedy Ad Claim About Klobuchar Is False," *StarTribune*, Oct. 14, 2006. Immigration was a hot topic in the 2006 race. Jean Hopfensperger, "Immigration," *StarTribune*, Oct. 7, 2006.

207   prescription drugs: Patricia Lopez, "Attack of the Attack Ads," *StarTribune*, Oct. 21, 2006; Associated Press, "Klobuchar Disputes Drug Ad," *Brainerd Dispatch*, Oct. 17, 2006. All the negative ads that Kennedy ran in the race actually became an issue in and of itself. "Attack Ads Hurt Rather Than Help Kennedy," *Grand Forks Herald* (Grand Forks, ND), Oct. 10, 2006 (editorial). The profusion of negative TV ads is just one of the reasons that—as E. J. Dionne puts it—Americans hate politics. E. J. Dionne Jr., *Why Americans Hate Politics* (New York: Simon & Schuster, 1991), pp. 15–17.

209   hip replacement: Matthew Stolle, "Amy Klobuchar Has Hip Surgery at Mayo Clinic," *Post-Bulletin* (Rochester, MN), July 27, 2006.

209   Farmfest debate: Pat Doyle, "Kennedy, Klobuchar, Others Spar at Farmfest," *StarTribune*, Aug. 2, 2006; Patrick Condon, "Candidates Sow Seeds at Farmfest," *St. Paul Pioneer Press*, Aug. 2, 2006; "At Farmfest, Time for Candidates to Show Their Country Sides," *Owatonna People's Press*, Aug. 2, 2006; Don Davis, "Candidates Agree: Manure Not Toxic," *Forum* (Fargo, ND), Aug. 2, 2006.

210   a fierce competitor: Rachel E. Stassen-Berger, "Senate Race Picks Up Speed," *St. Paul Pioneer Press*, Oct. 17, 2006.

210   the headline: "Politicians Spread Manure at Farmfest," *The Free Press* (Mankato, MN), Aug. 15, 2006.

210   "doesn't pass the smell test": "Politicians Spread Out Something at Farmfest," *West Central Tribune* (Willmar, MN), Aug. 3, 2006 (editorial).

210   Robert Fitzgerald: Pat Doyle, "Fitzgerald Is Driven by Much More Than Biodiesel," *StarTribune*, Sept. 30, 2006.

210   the Minnesota State Fair: Kathryn Strand Koutsky and Linda Koutsky, *Minnesota State Fair: An Illustrated History* (Minneapolis, MN: Coffee House Press, 2007); Eric Black, "State Fair Fare: Politics Finds a Niche at the Get-Together," *StarTribune*, Sept. 2, 2005; Patrick Condon, "Fair a Chance for Senate Candidates to Tout Minnesota Roots," *Duluth News Tribune*, Aug. 28, 2006; Rachel E. Stassen-Berger, "Shaking Hands, Wooing Voters," *St. Paul Pioneer Press*, Aug. 29, 2005; "Politics on a Stick," *St. Paul Pioneer Press*, Aug. 29, 2005 ("Politics and the State Fair go together like mustard and Pronto Pups."). The State Fair is always a great way to interact with Minnesotans—and to sample some great, if occasionally unusual, offerings. I went down the Fair's ever-popular Giant Slide with local news anchor Randy Meier, took the ALS ice bucket challenge with Fox 9's Jeff Passolt, and enjoy doing spin art—and strolling the Midway—with our daughter. "Randy, Klobuchar Go for Slide Ride," http://www.myfoxtwincities.com/clip/7655248/Randy,%20Klobuchar%20go%20for%20slide%20ride; "Jeff Passolt and Amy Klobuchar Take Ice Bucket Challenge," Aug. 21, 2014, https://m.facebook.com/fox9kmsp/posts/10152646950469138. In 2013, I sampled the State Fair Doughnut-Flavored Beer, which—I discovered—was actually beer with powdered sugar on the rim of the glass. "It's basically a Minnesota margarita," I explained to Minnesota Public Radio. Bob Collins, "It's OK to Love the State Fair," Minnesota Public Radio, Aug. 23, 2013, http://blogs.mprnews.org/newscut/2013/08/its-ok-to-love-the-state-fair/. Just for the record, I declined reporter M. A. Rosko's request that I

eat lamb testicles. "M.A. Tries the Lamb Balls, Sen. Klobuchar Sticks with the Fruit," FOX9.com, Aug. 23, 2012.

211 Jonathan Demme: Karal Ann Marling, *Blue Ribbon: A Social and Pictorial History of the Minnesota State Fair* (St. Paul: Minnesota Historical Society Press, 1990), preface (describing filmmaker Jonathan Demme's State Fair visit to the "Ladies' Sheep Lead").

211 Bob's Snake Zoo: Bob's Snake Zoo was started by Bob Duerr, a former Como zookeeper, more than forty years ago. John Brewer, "Each Day at the Fair, He Heads into a Snake Pit," *St. Paul Pioneer Press*, Aug. 29, 2007. Price of admission: $1.00. (Note: it's free for kids five and younger and those aged 65 and above. http://www.mnstatefair.org/entertainment/adventure_park.html). Bob's Snake Zoo has always been a good neighbor.

211 State Fair debate: Rachel E. Stassen-Berger, "U.S. Senate Race Off to a Testy Start," *St. Paul Pioneer Press*, Sept. 2, 2006; Don Davis, "Senate Debate Full of Fire," *West Central Tribune* (Willmar, MN), Sept. 2, 2006; Patrick Condon, "Kennedy, Klobuchar Square Off at State Fair," *New Ulm Journal* (New Ulm, MN), Sept. 2, 2006; Patricia Lopez, "Kennedy, Klobuchar Come Out Swinging in State Fair Debate," *StarTribune*, Sept. 2, 2006.

212 Tim Russert: Tim Russert, with a preface by Luke Russert, *Big Russ & Me, Father and Son: Lessons of Life* (New York: Weinstein Books, 2014).

212 the *StarTribune* billed it: Patricia Lopez, "Senate Candidates to Face Off at Fair," *StarTribune*, Aug. 25, 2006.

213 "where Nixon and Kennedy debated": John L. Moore, *Elections A-Z* (New York: Routledge, 1999), p. 508.

213 the debate went well: Rob Hotakainen, "Sharp Exchanges in National Spotlight," *StarTribune*, Oct. 16, 2006; Rachel E. Stassen-Berger, "A Familiar Fight, But on National TV Kennedy, Klobuchar Trade Barbs on the Iraq War in NBC Debate," *St. Paul Pioneer Press*, Oct. 16, 2006.

214 Bills/Vikings game: Scott Pitoniak, *The Good, the Bad, and the Ugly: Heart-Pounding, Jaw-Dropping, and Gut-Wrenching Moments in Buffalo Bills History* (Chicago: Triumph Books, 2007), p. 98.

214 Chuck Foreman: Chris Tomasson, "Vikings: Chuck Foreman Still Struck by '75 Snowball Fiasco," *St. Paul Pioneer Press*, Oct. 16, 2014; Sid Hartman, "Hit by Snowball in Game, Foreman Has Blurred Vision," *Minneapolis Tribune*, Dec. 21, 1975.

214 President Clinton came to town: Josephine Marcotty, "Clinton Stars at Klobuchar Event," *StarTribune*, Sept. 17, 2006.

214 got a tremendous boost: Patricia Lopez, "Sen. Clinton Among the Big Names Stumping for Minnesota Candidates," *StarTribune*, Oct. 18, 2006.

214 a visit from Senator Barack Obama: Bob von Sternberg, "Obama Knows How to Attract a Crowd," *StarTribune*, Oct. 31, 2006; Associated Press, "Obama Thrills Rochester Democrats," *St. Paul Pioneer Press*, Oct. 31, 2006; Meggen Lindsay, "Obama Inspires His Minnesota Fans," *St. Paul Pioneer Press*, Oct. 31, 2006.

214 "the movie": *Broadcast News* (1987); Deborah Caulfield Rybak, "Obama Gets DFLers on Their Feet," *StarTribune*, Apr. 9, 2006; Rob Hotakainen, "Riding High, Obama Hits the Road for His Party," *StarTribune*, Apr. 8, 2006.

215 Al Gore: Pat Doyle, "Gore Visits to Boost Klobuchar Campaign," *StarTribune*, Nov. 3, 2006; Rachel E. Stassen-Berger and Craig Borck, "Gore Tells Democrats the Race Isn't Over Yet," *St. Paul Pioneer Press*, Nov. 3, 2006.

215   Byron Dorgan: Byron L. Dorgan, *Reckless!: How Debt, Deregulation, and Dark Money Nearly Bankrupted America (And How We Can Fix It!)* (New York: St. Martin's Press, 2009).

216   poll: Patricia Lopez, "Wide Gap a Surprise in Senate Race," *StarTribune*, July 17, 2006. The Hopkins Raspberry Festival and Parade took place on Sunday, July 16, 2006. "Becky Lourey and Tim Baylor to Appear at Rondo Days and Hopkins Raspberry Festival," *Insight News*, July 15, 2006.

216   Election Night: Dane Smith, "It's Pawlenty Again; Klobuchar Wins Big," *StarTribune*, Nov. 8, 2006; Pat Doyle, "Klobuchar's Winning Ways," *StarTribune*, Nov. 9, 2006; Rachel E. Stassen-Berger, "Klobuchar Off to a Divided Senate: DFLer Will Be First Elected Female U.S. Senator for State," *St. Paul Pioneer Press*, Nov. 8, 2006.

216   declared the projected winner: Dane Smith, "It's Pawlenty Again; Klobuchar Wins Big," *StarTribune*, Nov. 8, 2006; Mark Zdechlik, "Klobuchar Races to Easy Victory in Senate Race," MPR News, Nov. 8, 2006.

216   Congressman Kennedy faced an uphill battle: Charlie Cook, "Financial Hurdles," *National Journal*, May 2, 2006, www.govexec.com; Patrick Condon, "Iraq Casts Long Shadow over Minnesota Senate Race," *West Central Tribune* (Willmar, MN), Nov. 7, 2006; Dane Smith, "Ticket Splitters Favor Pawlenty, Klobuchar," *StarTribune*, Oct. 12, 2006; Sharon Schmickle, "Feelings About Bush, War Drive High State Turnout," *StarTribune*, Nov. 8, 2006; David Broder, "Bush Looms Over Minnesota Race," *The Free Press* (Mankato, MN), July 11, 2006; Brian Voerding, "Klobuchar Hopes to Woo Moderate Republicans," *Winona Daily News* (Winona, MN), July 11, 2006.

217   Joan Growe and Ann Wynia: Sarah Janecek, "A New Insult to Toss at Female Candidates," *StarTribune*, Feb. 23, 2006.

217   "never highlighted gender": Patricia Lopez, "Klobuchar Cruises to Senate Victory," *StarTribune*, Nov. 8, 2006.

217   "a street fighter from the Iron Range": Bill Hanna, "Klobuchar's Iron Range Roots Run Deep," *Mesabi Daily News* (Virginia, MN), Sept. 11, 2005; Charles Ramsay, "Steelworkers Give Early Nod to Hatch for Governor, Klobuchar for U.S. Senate," *Mesabi Daily News* (Virginia, MN), Nov. 2, 2005; Patrick Condon, "For Klobuchar, Dad's Story Is Key to Her Own Rapid Rise," *St. Paul Pioneer Press*, Oct. 25, 2006. One of the most important endorsements I got in 2006 came from an Iron Ranger, my future colleague Congressman Jim Oberstar. Bill Hanna, "Oberstar Endorses Klobuchar for Senate," *Mesabi Daily News* (Virginia, MN), Jan. 12, 2006; Tom Coombe, "Klobuchar Brings Campaign to Ely," *Ely Echo*, Jan. 14, 2006. Jim was a tremendous mentor to me, and his sudden death in 2014 was a shock. John Myers, "Oberstar Remembered as 'a Man of Purpose and Grit,'" *Duluth News Tribune*, May 8, 2014.

218   twenty-seven promises: Rob Hotakainen, "Klobuchar's To-Do List Keeps Growing," *StarTribune*, Nov. 27, 2006.

CHAPTER 9

219   drive to Washington, D.C.: "Road Trip! Klobuchar Sets Off for Washington by Car," *StarTribune*, Dec. 28, 2006.

219   Rosslyn, Virginia: "About Rosslyn," http://projects.arlingtonva.us/projects /rosslyn/.

220 Our daughter would later describe: Abigail Bessler, "Growing Up: A Senator's Daughter Goes to Washington," *Faces*, Sept. 1, 2008.

221 Our new class of senators: Terence Samuel, *The Upper House: A Journey Behind the Closed Doors of the U.S. Senate* (New York: Palgrave Macmillan, 2010), pp. 59–82.

224 "submarine mom": I got to use the "submarine mom" line at a party in honor of the commissioning of the U.S. Navy's new Virginia-class submarine, the U.S.S. *Minnesota*, in Norfolk, Virginia. My husband and I were there with Virginia Senator Mark Warner who, for obvious reasons, does a lot more commissioning and christening of ships than any Minnesota senator. The families of the crew of the U.S.S. *Minnesota*—the first U.S. Navy ship to be named after our state since 1921—were there along with the submariners and an array of Minnesotans, from media mogul Stan Hubbard to the ship's sponsor, Minneapolis-born Ellen Roughhead, the daughter of a World War II Navy veteran. *Commissioning of USS* Minnesota *(SSN 783) 7 September 2013* (Eden Prairie, MN: Lifetouch Inc., 2013), p. 115. The "submarine mom" line got an enthusiastic response—about as good a response as I've ever experienced in public life. Then again, these were actual *bona fide* submarine moms! Thanks to all—submariners and your families—for your service.

224 Spouses of the Senate: Nikki Schwab, "Sign of the Times: Husbands Happily Join Senate Spouses," *U.S. News & World Report*, Sept. 22, 2014.

226 Talking Heads song: Talking Heads, "Once in a Lifetime" (single released Feb. 2, 1981).

227 Thinking I had all kinds of new powers: Congressional Record: Proceedings and Debates of the 110th Congress, 1st Sess., vol. 153, no. 19, p. S1397 (Jan. 31, 2007).

228 "Senator Byrd": David A. Corbin, *The Last Great Senator: Robert C. Byrd's Encounters with Eleven U.S. Presidents* (Washington, DC: Potomac Books, 2012), p. 221.

228 "pull up your shirt": Emily Heil and Elizabeth Brotherton, "Heard on the Hill: Book Reveals Klobuchar's Peekaboo Moment," *Roll Call*, May 26, 2010.

229 Hillary Clinton: Robin Givhan, "Hillary Clinton's Tentative Dip into New Neckline Territory," *Washington Post*, July 20, 2007.

229 Jon Tester: Samuel, *The Upper House*, pp. 23–25.

229 Harry Reid: Harry Reid with Mark Warren, *The Good Fight: Hard Lessons from Searchlight to Washington* (New York: G. P. Putnam's Sons, 2008).

229 fifth in agriculture: Su Ye, Minnesota Agricultural Profile, Minnesota Department of Agriculture (2014), https://www.mda.state.mn.us/~/media/Files/agprofile.ashx.

229 first in turkeys: Minnesota Turkey Growers Association, http://minnesotaturkey.com.

230 congressional ethics rules: Patrick Condon, "Senate Race Becomes Referendum on Ethics," *Duluth News Tribune*, June 30, 2006; "Democrats Push Hard in Heartland Senate Campaigns: In Montana, Sen. Conrad Burns, Linked to Jack Abramoff, Faces a Tough Race," *StarTribune*, Aug. 5, 2006; "Ethics Reform Good Idea, Senator-Elect," *St. Paul Pioneer Press*, Dec. 20, 2006 (editorial); Rachel E. Stassen-Berger, "Klobuchar Outlines Her Ethics Proposal," *St. Paul Pioneer Press*, Dec. 19, 2006.

230 Senator Barack Obama: Pete Souza, *The Rise of Barack Obama* (Chicago: Triumph Books, 2008), pp. 80, 84.

230   lobbyists paying for overseas trips: Peter H. Stone, *Heist: Superlobbyist Jack Abramoff, His Republican Allies, and the Buying of Washington* (New York: Farrar, Straus and Giroux, 2006), pp. 16–17; Paul Finkelman, ed., *Encyclopedia of African American History* (New York: Oxford University Press, 2009), p. 24 ("A 2005 FBI sting caught [Congressman William] Jefferson taking cash from one of [his] donors. An FBI raid found $90,000 of that cash in his home freezer. . . . On 4 June 2007 a federal grand jury indicted Jefferson on sixteen corruption charges, including for racketeering, bribe taking, obstruction of justice, money laundering, and violation of the Foreign Corrupt Practices Act—crimes with a total potential penalty of 235 years.").

230   a press conference: Brady Averill, "Klobuchar Backs Ethics Reform in Her First Press Conference," *StarTribune*, Jan. 8, 2007.

230   Traditionally: Carl Hulse, "On the Hill; High Turnover Brings Age Shift to Senate, Injecting More Youthful Feel," *New York Times*, Feb. 1, 2009.

230   my first floor speech: Brady Averill, "Klobuchar Focuses on Ethics in First Senate Speech," *StarTribune*, Jan. 13, 2007; Senate Session, Jan. 12, 2007, C-SPAN video.

231   Trent Lott: Congressional Record: Proceedings and Debates of the 110th Congress, 1st Sess., vol. 153, pt. 1 (Washington, DC: United States Government Printing Office, 2007), pp. 429–30 (Trent Lott's remarks on January 9, 2007).

231   Jon Tester: Ibid., pp. 428–29.

231   Russell Senate Office Building: Bruce J. Schulman, ed., *Student's Guide to Congress* (Washington, DC: CQ Press, 2009), pp. 115–16; Nancy Erickson, *Russell Senate Office Building: The First Century* (Washington, DC: Senate Historical Office, 2009), p. 28.

232   in the basement: Noelle Straub, "Tester Takes Seat in U.S. Senate," *Montana Standard*, Jan. 4, 2007.

232   lost three fingers: "Montana: Senate—Jon Tester (D)," *National Journal* 38 (2006), p. 59.

232   time-worn wooden desks: Senate Chamber Desks, "Desk History & Mystery," http://www.senate.gov/artandhistory/art/special/Desks/history.cfm.

232   the first bill: Honest Leadership and Open Government Act of 2007, Pub. L. 110-81, 121 Stat. 735 (Sept. 14, 2007).

233   more than three thousand U.S. military men and women: "Operation Iraqi Freedom," Iraq Coalition Casualty Count, http://icasualties.org.

233   forty-five: "Faces of the Fallen," *Washington Post*, http://apps.washingtonpost.com/national/fallen/maps/states/ (last visited Apr. 25, 2015); Hart Van Denburg and Sara Meyer, "Remembering Minnesota's Fallen Troops in Afghanistan, Iraq and Beyond," MPR News, May 23, 2014, http://www.mprnews.org/story/2013/03/18/war/minnesota-war-casualties#2005. Another Minnesota soldier died in a non-combat-related incident in Kuwait. Ibid.

233   more than $300 billion: "Estimated War-Related Costs, Iraq and Afghanistan," Infoplease (2012), http://www.infoplease.com/ipa/A0933935.html (citing Amy Belasco, "The Cost of Iraq, Afghanistan, and Other Global War on Terror Operations Since 9/11," Congressional Research Service Report for Congress, RL33110, p. CRSb9).

233   homily: Leon Lillie, "In Honor of Sgt. Bryan McDonough," LillieNews.com, Jan. 31, 2007, http://southwestreviewnews.com/print/167896; News Column, "In Honor of Sergeant Bryan McDonough," http://www.house.leg.state.mn

.us/members/pressrelease.asp?pressid=1873&party=1&memid=12269; John Brewer, "His Death Made War 'More Real,'" *St. Paul Pioneer Press*, Dec. 13, 2006.

233 I flew to Iraq: Mike Mulcahy and Jessica Mador, "Klobuchar Travels to Iraq," Minnesota Public Radio, Mar. 18, 2007.

233 almost three thousand Minnesota National Guard and Reserve troops in Iraq: Nick Coleman, "Minnesota Guard Tops '06 'People' Awards," *StarTribune*, Dec. 24, 2006.

233 nine firefighters: "Senator Klobuchar Delivers Speech on Iraq," July 17, 2007, http://www.klobuchar.senate.gov/public/events-speeches-and-floor -statements?ID=d3483f6e-1b0e-45a3-ba8a-5f6b638c1c9f.

234 six caskets: Michael Luo, "Many Lawmakers Go to Iraq, But Few Change Their Minds," *New York Times*, Apr. 3, 2007.

234 response to President Bush's weekly radio address: "Klobuchar, in Democratic Radio Address, Calls for Change of Course in Iraq," Apr. 20, 2007, http://www .keyc.com/story/6405595/klobuchar-in-democratic-radio-address-calls-for -change-of-course-in-iraq.

234 traumatic brain injuries: Tim Hennagir, "Former Monticello Resident with Traumatic Brain Injury Gets Purple Heart," *Monticello Times*, Oct. 4, 2014.

234 "wasn't a waiting line": "Senator Amy Klobuchar Is Reaching Out to Veterans in East Grand Forks," WDAY News, Nov. 12, 2011; "Klobuchar Speaks to Veterans at American Legion National Convention in Minneapolis," ECM Archives, Aug. 30, 2011.

234 Walter Reed: Dana Priest and Anne Hull, "Soldiers Face Neglect, Frustration at Army's Top Medical Facility," *Washington Post*, Feb. 18, 2007; Edward Felker, "Senators Vary in Tone over Walter Reed Scandal," *Post-Bulletin* (Rochester, MN), Mar. 8, 2007; Tom Bowman, "Walter Reed Was the Army's Wake-Up Call in 2007," NPR, Aug. 31, 2011.

234 voted to dramatically increase funding for veterans' health care: Veterans' Mental Health and Other Care Improvements Act of 2008, Pub. L. 110-387 (Oct. 10, 2008); Caregivers and Veterans Omnibus Health Services Act of 2010, Pub. L. 111-163 (May 5, 2010).

235 under Senator Jim Webb's leadership: Post-9/11 Veterans Educational Assistance Act of 2008, Title V of the Supplemental Appropriations Act of 2008, Pub. L. 110-252 (June 30, 2008); "President Bush Signs H.R. 2642, the Supplemental Appropriations Act, 2008," White House, http://georgewbush-white house.archives.gov/news/releases/2008/06/20080630.html. As a veteran himself, Senator Jim Webb was the perfect person to lead this effort. "This bill," President Bush said at the time, "shows the American people that even in an election year, Republicans and Democrats can come together to stand behind our troops and their families." Ibid.; Jim Webb, *A Time to Fight: Reclaiming a Fair and Just America* (New York: Broadway Books, 2008); Paul Rieckhoff, "History Is Made: New GI Bill Signed into Law," *Huffington Post*, July 8, 2008.

235 "Beyond the Yellow Ribbon": http://www.beyondtheyellowribbon.org; Nina Petersen-Perlman, "Vet Aid Draws on Minnesota Model," *StarTribune*, Dec. 11, 2007.

235 John Kline: News Release, "Klobuchar, Kline Bipartisan Legislation to Ensure National Guard and Reserve's Ability to Assist Victims of Sexual Assault Passes Senate, Heads to President's Desk to Be Signed into Law," Dec. 12, 2014.

235   Tim Walz: New Release, "Klobuchar-Backed Bill to Prevent Veteran Suicides Passes Senate, Heads to President's Desk to Be Signed into Law," Feb. 3, 2015 ("Congressman Tim Walz [D-MN] led the bill in the House.").

235   pass legislation: KBJR News 1, "Klobuchar's Bipartisan Bill Supports Homeless Veterans Signed into Law," Aug. 6, 2012, http://www.northlandsnewscenter .com/news/local/Klobuchars-Bipartisan-Bill-Supports-Homeless-Veterans -Signedin-into-Law-165179246.html; Jim Ragsdale, "Dayton, Klobuchar Help Dedicate Veterans Home Building," StarTribune, Aug. 15, 2012.

235   Ryan Hallberg: Mark Brunswick, "Lost a Leg in Iraq, All But Forgotten at Home," StarTribune, June, 1, 2010; Mark Brunswick, "Amputee Wins His Battle with the Army Over Bomb Injuries," StarTribune, June 7, 2010.

236   Frankie Valli: "Can't Take My Eyes Off of You," The Very Best of Frankie Valli and the Four Seasons (2002).

236   "a catastrophe of historic proportions": Paul Levy, "To the Ballgame, on the Bus, Drivers Plunge into Terror," StarTribune, Aug. 2, 2007; Patricia Lopez and Mark Brunswick, "Pawlenty May Call Special Session," StarTribune, Aug. 3, 2007.

237   Security camera footage: https://www.youtube.com/watch?v=z1uscpZt8EQ.

237   thirteen people lost their lives: Dan Olson, "Hundreds Turn Out to Dedication of 35W Bridge Memorial," MPR News, Aug. 2, 2011.

237   Shannon Hanson: Tim Nelson, "Minneapolis Bridge Collapse Heroes," St. Paul Pioneer Press, Aug. 3, 2007 (as updated), http://www.twincities.com/localnews /ci_23774668/minneapolis-bridge-collapse-heroes.

237   Taystee semi-truck: Kevin Diaz, "America Celebrates Another I-35W Hero," StarTribune, March 25, 2009.

237   Jeremy Hernandez: Diaz, "America Celebrates Another I-35W Hero"; Kevin Harter, "Minneapolis Bridge Collapse Heroes."

238   we needed to get the actual money: Congressional Record: Proceedings and Debates of the 110th Congress, vol. 153, pt. 17, p. S24156 (Sept. 11, 2007) (including Sept. 11, 2007, letter from Bob McFarlin, assistant to the commissioner of the Minnesota Department of Transportation).

240   "will the Senator yield": Ibid., p. S24133.

240   NTSB's report: National Transportation Safety Board, "Collapse of I-35W Highway Bridge, Minneapolis, Minnesota, August 1, 2007," Accident Report, NTSB/HAR-08/03 (Washington, DC, Nov. 14, 2008), pp. ii, xiii–xiv, 28.

241   Representative Michele Bachmann: "Michele Bachmann Really Glad to Meet Bush," Talking Points Memo, https://www.youtube.com/watch?v=s_uiudt_Kiw. Later, on Dave Lee's WCCO morning radio show, Representative Bachmann spoke of her own interactions with the president that day, saying she pulled back at one point after the president reached over, offering her a kiss on the cheek. "What? You don't want an embrace?" Bush reportedly teased her. "You know, the people of Minnesota love you, Mr. President," Representative Bachmann replied, "but I think one kiss was enough." "Rep. Michele Bachmann on the Dave Lee Show on WCCO Radio Wednesday Morning," Post of Sept. 20, 2007, http://www.truthsurfer.com/2007_09_01_archive.html; http://blogs.mprnews .org/capitol-view/2007/12/the_top_politic/.

241   Red Bulls: Mark Brunswick, "Minnesota Guardsmen Begin Heading Home," StarTribune, June 20, 2007 ("The 2,600 members of the Minnesota Guard have received confirmation that they soon will be leaving Iraq. All are expected back by Aug. 1. The 16 months spent in a combat zone by the 1st Brigade Combat Team 34th Infantry Division will be the longest tour of any unit fighting in the

Iraq war. Nine Minnesotans have been killed in action."); Richard Meryhew, "Minnesota National Guard on Way Back from Iraq," *StarTribune*, June 24, 2007; Curt Brown, "The Green, Green Grass of Home: As Minnesota's Red Bulls Return from Iraq, the Task of Preparing Them for Civilian Life Begins in Earnest," *StarTribune*, July 11, 2007; "Sen. Klobuchar Goes to Fort McCoy, Meets with Returning National Guard Troops," U.S. Fed. News Service, July 23, 2007 ("U.S. Senator Amy Klobuchar visited Fort McCoy on Sunday, July 22, and met with Minnesota National Guard troops from the First Brigade Combat Team who had just returned from duty in Iraq.").

242   1992 presidential campaign: Bill Clinton and Al Gore, *Putting People First: How We Can All Change America* (New York: Times Books, 1992).

242   Abbey Taylor: http://www.abbeyshope.org (the foundation established by the Taylors in Abbey's name); Josephine Marcotty, "Abigail Taylor Was a Fighter to the End," *StarTribune*, Mar. 22, 2008; Maura Lerner, "Abigail Faces Another Setback: Cancer Treatment," *StarTribune*, Mar. 7, 2008; Maura Lerner, "Pool Staff Was Aware of Drain Dangers," *StarTribune*, Sept. 4, 2008; Joy Powell, "Transplants Rebuild What Pool Mangled," *StarTribune*, Dec. 20, 2007; Julie Pfitzinger, "A Promise to Abbey," *StarTribune*, Aug. 16, 2009; Scott Taylor, "Letter of the Day," *StarTribune*, Apr. 18, 2011.

242   When I saw the story about Abbey: Jeff Strickler and Susan Feyder, "Pool-Drain Victim Undergoes Surgery," *StarTribune*, July 5, 2007; Jeff Shelman, "6-Year-Old Edina Girl Severely Injured in Pool," *StarTribune*, July 4, 2007.

243   I went to work: Maura Lerner, "Pool-Drain Trauma May Prod New Law," *StarTribune*, July 7, 2007; "Grievous Injury Leads to Safety Measure," *StarTribune*, Dec. 18, 2007 (editorial); Nina Petersen-Perlman, "Senate OKs Pool Drain Safety Bill," *StarTribune*, Dec. 15, 2007.

243   her parents knew this bill could be her legacy: Maura Lerner and Jake Sherman, "'Amazing Abigail' Inspires D.C. to Act," *StarTribune*, July 24, 2007; Pat Pheifer, "Safety Law for Public Pools Now Requires Suction Shutoffs," *StarTribune*, Sept. 28, 2011.

244   signed into law by President Bush: Joy Powell, "Abigail Pulls Through—With a Smile," *StarTribune*, Dec. 21, 2007.

244   consumer protection bills: Kevin Diaz, "Klobuchar: Aiming for the Middle Ground," *StarTribune*, Mar. 29, 2010.

246   Axel Zirbes: Press Release, Amy Klobuchar, "Klobuchar Calls for Swift Action to Prevent Critical Drug Shortages," Jan. 26, 2012.

246   Dr. Jon LaPook: "Emmy Winning Reports: Cancer Drug Shortages Lower Children's Survival Rate," CBS News, Oct. 4, 2013.

246   Cheryl Burt: Jessica Mador, "Senate Bill Named for Two Poisoned Kimball, MN Brothers Moves Ahead," Rick Kupchella's Bring Me the News, http://bringmethenews.com/2014/04/10/nicholas-and-zachary-burt-memorial-carbon-monoxide-poisoning-prevention-act/.

246   contaminated peanut butter: I particularly want to thank Jeff Almer for testifying before Congress about the 2008 death of his mother—a Perham, Minnesota, cancer survivor—after she ate salmonella-contaminated peanut butter on her toast. Jeff's advocacy for stronger food safety regulations made a big difference. When he testified, Jeff prominently displayed a photo of his late mother, Shirley Mae Almer. Mitch Anderson, "Minnesota Families Testify, But Peanut Plant Owner Won't Talk," *StarTribune*, Feb. 12, 2009; David Shaffer, "A Heartbreaking Lawsuit: Surviving Cancer, Done in by Salmonella," *StarTribune*, Sept. 18, 2014.

246   Jarnell Brown: Sarah Lemagie, "Reebok's Deadly Lead Charm Draws $1 Million Federal Fine," *StarTribune*, Mar. 18, 2008.
247   lead standard: H.R. 4040, 110th Cong.: Consumer Product Safety Improvement Act of 2008, https://www.govtrack.us/congress/votes/110-2008/s41 (noting passage of bill in the Senate by a 79–13 vote). Before the bill was signed into law, a conference report in the Senate was adopted by an even wider margin. H.R. 4040, 110th Cong.: Consumer Project Safety Improvement Act of 2008, https://www.govtrack.us/congress/votes/110-2008/s193 (noting the conference report was agreed to by the Senate on a 89–3 vote).
247   the Merkouris family: Rachel Kytonen, "Klobuchar Recognizes Cambridge Couple as 'Angels in Adoption,'" Oct. 13, 2010, http://archives.ecmpublishers.info/2010/10/13/klobuchar-recognizes-cambridge-couple-as-angels-in-adoption/. The children's birth father had kept the children together before their adoption and made sure they stayed together at the orphanage. To see Tim and Renee Merkouris and the children they adopted from the Children's Shelter of Cebu, watch the joint interview we did on Fox News with Gretchen Carlson about the adoption bill. "Senator Klobuchar Working to Simplify Adoption Laws," Dec. 21, 2010, http://video.foxnews.com/v/4469828/sen-klobuchar-working-to-simplify-adoption-laws/?playlist_id=87937#sp=show-clips.

CHAPTER 10

249   2008 financial collapse: U.S. Senate Permanent Subcommittee on Investigations, *Wall Street and the Financial Crisis: Anatomy of a Financial Collapse* (New York: Cosimo, 2011), p. 47. This report was prepared under the direction of Michigan Senator Carl Levin, the chair of the Permanent Subcommittee on Investigations.
250   AIG: AIG is the acronym for American International Group, the large property and casualty insurer.
250   they made their case: David M. Herszenhorn, "Congressional Leaders Stunned by Warnings," *New York Times*, Sept. 19, 2008.
250   "we may not have an economy on Monday": Andrew Ross Sorkin, Diana B. Henriques, Edmund L. Andrews, and Joe Nocera, "As Credit Crisis Spiraled, Alarm Led to Action," *New York Times*, Oct. 1, 2008.
251   our banks: Chris Serres and Glenn Howatt, "Minnesota Banks Leaned on the Fed During Financial Crisis," *Star Tribune*, Mar. 31, 2011 ("Even healthy banks with solid balance sheets borrowed repeatedly from the Fed's discount window well into 2009, a sign that the cash crunch in the financial system was longer and more severe than previously thought, according to banking experts.").
251   Sheila Bair: Ryan Lizza, "The Contrarian: Sheila Bair and the White House Financial Debate," *New Yorker*, July 6, 2009.
251   Senate floor speech: Congressional Record, vol. 154, no. 150 (Sept. 22, 2008), pp. S9186–S9187.
251   authorizing $700 billion: Steven M. Davidoff, *Gods at War: Shotgun Takeovers, Government by Deal, and the Private Equity Implosion* (Hoboken, NJ: John Wiley & Sons, 2009), p. 265.
251   three-page document: UPI, "Bush Pushes Quick Bailout Bill Passage," Sept. 22, 2008, http://www.upi.com/Top_News/2008/09/22/Bush-pushes-quick-bailout-bill-passage/19211222098639/.

251   Bernie Sanders: Bernie Sanders with Huck Gutman, *Outsider in the House* (New York: Verso, 1997), pp. 13–14, 123.

252   the TARP bill: U.S. Senate Permanent Subcommittee on Investigations, *Wall Street and the Financial Crisis*, p. 43.

252   stimulus funding: *Stimulus: American Recovery and Reinvestment Act of 2009—Essential Documents* (Lanham, MD: Scarecrow Press, 2009).

253   American auto industry was in deep trouble: Baird Webel and Marc Labonte, *Government Interventions in Response to Financial Turmoil*, Congressional Research Service (Feb. 1, 2010), p. 13.

253   "Legislator of the Year": "Sen. Amy Klobuchar Honored by Minnesota Auto Dealers," *Ortonville Independent* (Ortonville, MN), Dec. 8, 2009.

254   "Banks That Had a Brain": Amy Klobuchar, "Banks That Had a Brain," *Washington Post*, Feb. 24, 2009.

254   the initial margin was 215 votes: Jay Weiner, *This Is Not Florida: How Al Franken Won the Minnesota Senate Recount* (Minneapolis: University of Minnesota Press, 2010), p. 50.

254   more than 2.9 million cast: Ibid., p. 224.

256   Fortune 500 companies: Christie Washam, "18 MN Cos. Make Fortune 500; 9 Move Up in Rank," *Twin Cities Business*, June 2, 2014.

257   declared the victor: Perry Bacon Jr., "Minnesota Supreme Court Declares Franken Winner in U.S. Senate Race," *Washington Post*, July 1, 2009; Rachel Stassen-Berger, "Minnesota Sen. Al Franken Sworn In with Paul Wellstone Bible," *St. Paul Pioneer Press*, July 7, 2009. Actually, for a short time I was not the only "only senator." After Barack Obama won his election, he resigned from his Senate seat in mid-November 2008. Then Illinois Governor Rod Blagojevich was responsible for naming his successor, but the man he chose—Roland Burris—was not immediately seated because Governor Blagojevich got caught up in a corruption scandal. From mid-November 2008 to mid-January 2009 my Senate colleague Dick Durbin was also his state's only senator. James Oliphant, "Roland Burris Sworn In as Illinois' Junior Senator," *Chicago Tribune*, Jan. 16, 2009.

259   fiscal cliff: Walter J. Oleszek, *Congressional Procedures and the Policy Process*, 9th ed. (Thousand Oaks, CA: SAGE Publications, 2014), p. 83.

260   Erskine Bowles and Alan Simpson: National Commission on Fiscal Responsibility and Reform, http://www.fiscalcommission.gov.

261   a management matrix: Stephen Covey, *The Seven Habits of Highly Effective People* (New York: Simon & Schuster, 1989), pp. 149–56.

261   President Eisenhower: "The Eisenhower Decision Matrix: How to Distinguish Between Urgent and Important Tasks and Make Real Progress in Your Life," http://www.artofmanliness.com/2013/10/23/eisenhower-decision-matrix/.

261   Chuck Schumer: Dana Rubinstein, "Revenge of the Nerd?," *Observer*, Apr. 7, 2009, http://observer.com/2009/04/revenge-of-the-nerd-2/ (noting that Chuck Schumer refers to this management matrix as "the Genovesi Box," named for Senator Schumer's late mentor, Assemblyman Anthony Genovesi).

262   Bush's decision to "fly over" New Orleans: The Institute of Politics, John F. Kennedy School of Government, Harvard University, *Campaign for President: The Managers Look at 2008* (Lanham, MD: Rowman & Littlefield, 2009), p. 57 n. 6.

263    $2.13 an hour, plus tips: Patrick M. Sheridan, "Living on $2.13 an Hour, Plus Tips," CNN Money, May 5, 2014, http://money.cnn.com/2014/05/05/news/economy/tipped-worker-minimum-wage/.

263 gas-mileage standards: "Sen. Klobuchar Highlights New Gas Mileage Standards as She Fuels Up for Statewide 'Main Street Tour,'" *Farmers Independent* (Bagley, MN), Jan. 9, 2008; Carl Hulse, "Mileage Vote Reveals New Configuration in Senate," *New York Times,* June 23, 2007; Virginia McConnell, "The New CAFE Standards: Are They Enough on Their Own?," Discussion Paper (Washington, DC: Resources for the Future, May 2013), p. 5.

263 Affordable Care Act: After working with high-quality medical institutions in my state, I was successful in getting a quality index provision added to the Affordable Care Act. Jeff Hansel, "Mayo Clinic's Noseworthy to Nation's Leaders: Talk to Us," *Post-Bulletin* (Rochester, MN), Nov. 8, 2012.

264 illegal dumping: John Myers, "Minnesota Lawmakers Meet with Federal Trade Officials to Discuss Steel Industry Woes," *Duluth News Tribune,* Mar. 27, 2015.

265 a law professor: Steve Karnowski, "Minnesota Law Prof Detained in Rwanda Returns Home," Boston.com, June 22, 2010, http://www.boston.com/news /nation/articles/2010/06/22/minn_lawyer_jailed_in_rwanda_heading_home/.

265 imprisoned for nine months: Corey Mitchell, "United Arab Emirates to Release Minnesota Man Imprisoned for YouTube Video," *StarTribune,* Jan. 4, 2014.

265 three hikers: Shane Bauer, Joshua Fattal, and Sarah Shourd, *A Sliver of Light: Three Americans Imprisoned in Iran* (New York: Houghton Mifflin Harcourt, 2014).

265 Harold Knutson: "The Presidency: He Told Us," *TIME,* Nov. 3, 1947, vol. 50, p. 19 ("Said Knutson: 'Give them a paddle and then tell 'em—'Go paddle your own canoe.'").

265 Henrik Shipstead: Barbara Stuhler, *Ten Men of Minnesota and American Foreign Policy* (St. Paul: Minnesota Historical Society Press, 1973), pp. 94–97.

265 refugees from the world over: Kathleen R. Arnold, ed., *Contemporary Immigration in America: A State-by-State Encyclopedia* (Santa Barbara, CA: ABC-CLIO, 2015), p. 421; Chris Williams, "New Census Data: Minnesota Somali Population Grows," *StarTribune,* Apr. 13, 2015.

266 a column: David Ignatius, "The Internationalism of the Heartland," *Washington Post,* Feb. 21, 2014.

267 increasing exports: "Klobuchar Concludes 'Exporting Minnesota' Tour with Business Leader Roundtable," HometownSource.com, Feb. 20, 2013, http: //hometownsource.com/2013/02/20/klobuchar-concludes-exporting -minnesota-tour-with-business-leader-roundtable/.

268 Cuba: A special thanks to Brian Burton, my deputy legislative director, for all his good work on my bill to lift the Cuban embargo. The Minnesota Orchestra just visited Cuba for the first time since 1930, and historic, exciting changes are on the horizon. Tom Hauser, "5 EYEWITNESS NEWS Travels with MN Orchestra on Historic Trip to Cuba," KSTP.com, May 13, 2015, http://kstp.com /article/stories/s3794862.shtml.

268 a major foreign policy shift: Statement by the President on Cuba Policy Changes, The White House, Office of the Press Secretary, Dec. 17, 2014.

269 in their book: Nicholas D. Kristof and Sheryl WuDunn, *Half the Sky: Turning Oppression into Opportunity for Women Worldwide* (New York: Alfred A. Knopf, 2009).

269 Cindy McCain: John Croman, "Klobuchar, Cindy McCain Fight Human Trafficking," KARE-11 (Aug. 20, 2014) (describing our joint appearance in Minneapolis at the National Conference of State Legislatures).

270 Farewell Address: Ralph Ketcham, *Presidents Above Party: The First American*

Presidency, 1789–1829 (Chapel Hill: The University of North Carolina Press, 1984), p. 92.

272   "80 percent rule": Mike Enzi, "Good Wishes for Senator Kennedy," in Congressional Record, vol. 154, no. 85 (May 22, 2008), pp. S4774–S4776.

272   *Washingtonian* magazine: "Least Likely to Star in a Scandal," *Washingtonian*, Sept. 13, 2010 (also listing Russ Feingold and Olympia Snowe).

273   *Grand Forks Herald*: *Grand Forks Herald*, May 10, 2012. I always do my best to work across the aisle, looking for cosponsors of bills where I can find them. Allison Sherry, "Klobuchar Manages to Cross Senate's Partisan Divide," *Seattle Times*, Dec. 20, 2014; Kevin Diaz, "Klobuchar: Aiming for the Middle Ground," *StarTribune*, Mar. 29, 2010; 2014 Report Card for Sen. Amy Klobucher, www .govtrack.us.

273   a tragic plane crash: "Plane Crash Kills Son of Oklahoma Sen. Inhofe," FoxNews .com, Nov. 11, 2013, http://www.foxnews.com/politics/2013/11/11/plane-crash -kills-oklahoma-sen-inhofe-son/.

275   U.S.S. *John S. McCain*: http://www.mccain.navy.mil.

276   women carpenters: United Brotherhood of Carpenters, https://www.carpenters .org/Todays_UBC_Top_Nav/Sisters/SIB_Landing.aspx ("Sisters in the Brotherhood").

277   only forty-six women: Women in the Senate, https://www.senate.gov/artand history/history/common/briefing/Women_senators.htm.

277   Elena Kagan's 2010 Supreme Court confirmation hearing: Senate Committee on the Judiciary Holds a Hearing on the Elena Kagan Nomination, June 30, 2010, http://www.washingtonpost.com/wp-srv/politics/documents/KAGAN HEARINGSDAY3.pdf.

278   Coya Knutson: Liz Halloran, "The Congresswoman Whose Husband Called Her Home," NPR, May 10, 2014, http://www.npr.org/blogs/itsallpolitics/2014/05 /10/310996960/the-congresswoman-whose-husband-called-her-home.

278   Patty Murray: Gloria Feldt, *No Excuses: 9 Ways Women Can Change How We Think About Power* (Berkeley, CA: Seal Press, 2010), pp. 222–23.

278   Claire McCaskill's U.S. Senate opponent: Claire McCaskill with Terry Ganey, *Plenty Ladylike: A Memoir* (New York: Simon & Schuster, 2015), p. 133.

279   "Daddy's little girl": Ibid., p. 165; Pat Kessler, "Bills Aiming to Raise the Heat on Klobuchar," CBS Minnesota, Oct. 10, 2012, http://minnesota.cbslocal.com /2012/10/10/bills-raising-the-heat-on-klobuchar/; Rachel E. Stassen-Berger, "In Uphill Battle for Senate Seat, Bills Is Driven to 'Stop the Debt,'" *StarTribune*, Oct. 20, 2012.

280   when I came in there were only sixteen of us: Vicki Donlan with Helen French Graves, *Her Turn: Why It's Time for Women to Lead in America* (Westport, CT: Praeger Publishers, 2007), p. 173. The number of women in the Senate has gradually been growing over time. Barbara Mikulski, Kay Bailey Hutchison, Dianne Feinstein, Barbara Boxer, Patty Murray, Olympia Snowe, Susan Collins, Mary Landrieu, and Blanche L. Lincoln with Catherine Whitney, *Nine and Counting: The Women of the Senate* (New York: Perennial, 2001). Since my election in 2006, the U.S. Senate has added even more strong women to its ranks—women who are taking center stage in American politics. *See, e.g.*, Elizabeth Warren, *A Fighting Chance* (New York: Metropolitan Books, 2014); Kirsten Gillibrand, *Off the Sidelines: Raise Your Voice, Change the World* (New York: Random House, 2014).

282   "speak softly and carry a big statistic": At the Minnesota State Fair, Theodore

Roosevelt once quoted a West African proverb that goes, "Speak softly and carry a big stick—you will go far." Donald J. Davidson, ed., *The Wisdom of Theodore Roosevelt* (New York: Citadel Press Books, 2003), p. 9 (quoting "National Duties," speech delivered on Sep. 2, 1901). Kathleen Hall Jamieson, the director of the Annenberg Public Policy Center at the University of Pennsylvania, later said of women candidates that they should "speak softly and carry a big statistic." Barbara Lee, who—for decades—has helped women in their bids for local, state, and federal office, has quoted this aphorism in her own speeches. Julia Watson, "Feature: Women Train for Governor Office," UPI, Dec. 3, 2004, http://www.upi.com/Business_News/Security-Industry/2004/12/03/Feature -Women-train-for-governor-office/34801102107191/.

284   *The Nutcracker*: Manu Raju, Burgess Everett, and John Bresnahan, "Ted Cruz Does It Again," *Politico*, Dec. 13, 2014, http://www.politico.com/story/2014 /12/ted-cruz-does-it-again-113560.html. We need more civility—and less extremism—in the halls of Congress and in our political discourse. Thomas E. Mann and Norman J. Ornstein, *It's Even Worse Than It Looks: How the American Constitutional System Collided with the New Politics of Extremism* (New York: Basic Books, 2012); Faiz Shakir, "McClatchy: Rachel Maddow Brings 'Civility' to Cable News," ThinkProgress, Apr. 22, 2009, http://thinkprogress .org/politics/2009/04/22/37746/maddow-civility/.

286   moderation: David Brooks, *The Road to Character* (New York: Random House, 2015).

EPILOGUE

288   kids with disabilities: For many years I served on the advisory board of PACER, an amazing nonprofit organization cofounded and led by my friend Paula Goldberg. Its core mission is to provide assistance and information to parents of children with disabilities and to enhance the lives of those children. Its recent anti-bullying initiative is just the latest of its many good works. Thanks, Paula, for all you do. You're the best.

289   Walter Isaacson: Walter Isaacson, *Benjamin Franklin: An American Life* (New York: Simon & Schuster, 2003), p. 491.

289   a documentary: Mick Caouette, *Hubert H. Humphrey: The Art of the Possible* (2010).

290   Robert Frost: Edward Connery Lathem, ed., *The Poetry of Robert Frost* (New York: Henry Holt and Co., 1969), pp. 33–34, 105.

ACKNOWLEDGMENTS

In many book acknowledgments, the spouse is an add-on, appearing in the last paragraph with the obligatory "love and gratitude" lead-in. For me, John goes first. He not only encouraged me to write this book; he was also at my side for half the story. A law professor and the author of six books himself, he had a keen eye for keeping me out of book trouble and was always quick to make me get to the crux of vague memories and old stories. He was a stickler for cites (and, boy, did he find them). Our marriage has withstood many tests—from two careers to a sick child to political campaigns—but nothing prepared me for watching my husband rifle through box after box of old newspaper clippings in search of a farm debate quote from the Owatonna newspaper that I just *knew* existed. I have now found a new definition of true love.

My eighty-seven-year-old dad spent hours in his "base camp" basement/den filled with mountaineering/adventure photos telling me stories about his life (and those of a few others as well). His collected works (more than twenty books and collections of columns at last count) were incredibly helpful in bringing our family heritage on Minnesota's Iron Range to life, and key to understanding the high-flying career (yes, he actually flew a plane, skydived, hot-air ballooned, and hang glided) of a newspaper columnist throughout the sixties, seventies, and eighties. I hope that the wisdom he has shared with me over the years about the great virtues and beauty of our wonderful state jumps off the pages of this book, or I didn't do my job. I love you, Dad.

Although my mom is no longer with us, I think she would have enjoyed her role in this book in not only the stories about her life and her teaching career but also the use of her collected works. She saved everything from my dad's first columns to my report cards and writings to notes from elementary school and postcards. Nearly everything was painstakingly glued into scrapbooks and done with much love.

Both my uncle Dicks were of enormous help. My dad's brother, Dick Klobuchar, himself an author of a book on Pearl Harbor, has an excellent memory that I truly appreciate. He was always quick to e-mail back with detailed facts and photos. My mom's Milwaukee brother, Dick Heuberger, gave me some very important information about my mom and their parents. His memory also stood the test of time! His recollections were supplemented by the stellar research of my sister-in-law, Lori Bessler, a reference librarian and genealogist for the Wisconsin Historical Society, as well as by some facts, figures, and a family tree from the Swiss themselves in the form of Silvia Engli and Martin Heuberger. A family tree put together years ago by MIT graduate and Raytheon inventor Robert Pucel was also a research treasure trove on the Klobuchar/Pucel side of our family.

Also helpful was a conversation with E. Jack Williams, a relative and retired teacher/playwright/theater director from Waseca High School who wrote an entire play, *To the Left of the Moon*, based on the early life of Hannah Klobuchar, his mother and the youngest sister of my grandpa Mike. When my grandpa and his nine siblings were orphaned, it was ten-year-old Hannah who was sent to a Duluth orphanage, and it was my grandpa—her oldest brother and one of two brothers left to support the entire family—who borrowed a car and picked her up a year and a half later to bring her home.

My sister, Meagan, an accomplished accountant with an eye for detail, provided some excellent insights, as did my in-laws, Bill and Marilyn Bessler. My dad's wife, Susan, was also quite helpful and a good and upbeat reader!

And last but not least when it comes to family members, a special note of acknowledgment to our daughter, Abigail, for dutifully (with an emphasis on the word *duty*) reading the text. Abigail is a writer herself—she just won a Mark of Excellence Award from the Society of Professional Journalists for a nonfiction college magazine piece—and I valued her comments. (Next year she will be the editor of one of her college's magazines, so she will have more than enough opportunity to look for other people's typos!)

She was also good-natured about allowing me to tell the stories about her in this book, which many twenty-year-olds might not be.

A lot of politicians have ghostwriters or coauthors for these kinds of books. This was all me, which is somewhat unusual but also taxing for the editor. John Sterling, editor at Henry Holt and Company (a book publishing company in business since 1866, and now located in New York City's historic Flatiron Building), took a risk with this project, and the book is much better because of his superb editorial skills. He never flinched but sometimes backed down, which was in my mind perfect. I especially enjoyed our debates about parentheses and semicolons (just kidding). Thanks to him and the rest of the Henry Holt crew—associate editor Emi Ikkanda, publicity director Pat Eisemann, and the entire production staff—for their great work. And thanks for taking a chance on a political memoir from someone from the Midwest, John. We will not let you down (right, Midwest?). Jay Sures and Paul Fedorko and Samantha Bina at United Talent Agency and N. S. Bienstock were very helpful in guiding me through this process. And way to go, Paul, getting the rights to the Talking Heads song stanza.

While many friends who are mentioned in the text reviewed portions of this book, I particularly want to thank Sara Grewing, Cindy Jesson, Mandy Grunwald, Rose Baumann, Kathleen Sheehy, Kathryn Quaintance, Justin Buoen, Tim Kaine, Byron Dorgan, Jonathan Becker, Pete Cahill, Paul Scoggin, Andy LeFevour, Marc Elias, and Tom and Victoria Johnson, all of whom read drafts and offered detailed comments. My high school buddies Amy Scherber, Amy Anderson, Heidi Dick, and Steve Bergman were of great help. My college roommates Meg Symington, Alex Johnston, and Becca Lish, and my law school classmates Kate Stacy, Adam Emmerich, Linda Benfield, et al., as well as law professors Cass Sunstein, Richard Epstein, and Geoffrey Stone, also reviewed portions of the book. Dean Michael Schill of the University of Chicago Law School (now the University of Oregon's president) and Master Penelope Laurens of Jonathan Edwards College at Yale were wonderful resources.

It was a lot of fun connecting with old neighbors and friends from Plymouth. At age ninety-two, Ila Ronning is as sharp as a tack, remembering the spelling of everyone's last names on Oakview Lane. Sue Samela and Lois Rogers—who gave me some of my first babysitting jobs—were also great to talk to again, and my mom's dear friends Gwen Mosberg and Mary Beaudin were amazing. (For years I thought my mom and Mary had rented that RV and driven to southern California to see the monarchs, but now I know it was the total eclipse. Thanks, Mary.)

For the section of the book about Slovenia, I was able to go straight to the top. Through my work, I'd gotten to know Joseph Mussomeli, the former U.S. Ambassador to Slovenia, and one of his top-flight State Department aides, Christopher Wurst. Both Chris and the former ambassador were helpful in answering questions as I wrote that portion of the book. In addition, the detailed record-keeping of the U.S. Immigration Service allowed me to re-create my Swiss grandpa's first failed attempt at entering the U.S., his decision to go through Canada to try again, and, twenty years later, his alien registration and citizenship proceedings. That was a good investment for twenty dollars!

Thanks to Mike Cunningham and Mike Flom at Gray, Plant, Mooty law firm and Judge Bill Fisher and Commissioner Myron Frans (both formerly at Gray Plant), as well as Ken Cutler and Alison Humphrey at Dorsey & Whitney, for the trips down memory lane. I worked with so many wonderful people at these firms that the publisher wouldn't let me list them. Bill Levis, my former client at MCI, was kind enough to listen to and remember the MCI story, and Verizon (which now owns MCI) attorneys Randal Milch and Mike Glover were nice enough to let me use it. Hennepin County prosecutors and former prosecutors Pete Cahill, Paul Scoggin, Al Harris, Bob Streitz, Carrie Lennon, Judith Hawley, Mike Furnstahl, Dave Brown, and Teresa Froehlke and nearly every prosecutor and victim-witness advocate mentioned in the book were generous to verify and review old cases.

I also should acknowledge my fellow prosecutors during my time as president of the Minnesota County Attorneys Association, including Jim Backstrom, Lisa Borgen, Susan Gaertner, Bob Johnson, Doug Johnson, Janelle Kendall, Craig Nelson, Ray Schmitz, and the late Alan Mitchell. And to John Kingrey, the association's recently retired executive director, thanks for always being so responsive. Thanks, too, to former U.S. Attorneys David Lillehaug, B. Todd Jones, and Tom Heffelfinger, Hennepin County Attorney Mike Freeman, and current U.S. Attorney Andy Luger.

Several journalists were of kind help in verifying stories: Dave Espo, veteran national AP reporter, went out of his way to find an old AP report about the role of the Minneapolis AP office in the 1960 presidential race election coverage; Eric Black of *MinnPost* was great; and Tim McGuire, former *StarTribune* editor, and Steve Roland, the newspaper's former deputy managing editor, helped me re-create my dad's last day at the office.

Many friends from law and politics helped me with facts and stories and with good advice: Walter Mondale, Governor Mark Dayton, Al Franken, Norm Coleman, Trent Lott, Kent Conrad, Rick Nolan, Tina Flint Smith, Sam and Sylvia Kaplan, Vin Weber, Mark Ritchie, Warren Spannaus, Dee Long, Phyllis Kahn, Tom Nides, Jeff Blodgett, Stephanie Schriock, Neera Tanden, Rosalie Rosoff, Emily Anne Staples, Joan Growe, Guy Cecil, Steve Hunegs, Susan Segal, Ross Corson, Lynda Pedersen, Lee Sheehy, Jim Andrews, Jean Manas, Rebecca Haile, Pat Diamond, David Hough, and Mondale alums Mike Berman, Jim Johnson, Norm Sherman and Al Eisele. And, in addition to the senators and former senators who were mentioned in the text (see index), thanks to my current and former committee chairs/ranking members Pat Roberts, Bill Nelson, Dan Coates, and Jay Rockefeller, as well as Senators Tom Daschle, Ben Nelson, Carl Levin, Jon Kyl, George LeMieux, Gordon Smith, Evan Bayh, Judd Gregg, George Voinovich, Mo Cowan, Jeff Chiesa, Ted Kaufman, Elizabeth Dole, Herb Kohl, Bob Kerrey, Ron Wyden, Tom Udall, Rand Paul, Jeff Merkley, Brian Schatz, Joe Donnelly, Shelley Capito, Ed Markey, Mark Udall, Chris Murphy, Gary Peters, John Barrasso, and Martin Heinrich, for giving me insights and advice, or simply being great colleagues.

There are a few senators mentioned in the text whom I must also acknowledge here: Elizabeth Warren, who knew I was writing this book since we share an editor and a publisher, but was kind enough to keep my confidence while I finished it up (a rarity in Washington . . . as I like to say, Minnesota may be the "Land of 10,000 Lakes" but Washington is the "Land of 10,000 Leaks"); Claire McCaskill and Kirsten Gillibrand, who have both written excellent books and were kind enough to share their experiences (and words) with me; my colleague Al Franken, who provided me with some good stories for this book and who trusted me enough that he didn't even ask to read it until it was published; and Bob Casey, who once listened to me read a chapter for a really long time on a Friday night as he drove from D.C. to Pennsylvania. (If he got bored, I never knew. Thanks, Bob.) And thanks to Harry Reid, Chuck Schumer, Dick Durbin, Patty Murray, and Debbie Stabenow for not only their leadership, but also for being the characters they are. After all, interesting people make for a much better book, not to mention a much better life.

I wouldn't have this story to tell without the wonderful people of the State of Minnesota. I am so proud of our state, and I hope it shows. I also wouldn't be here without the campaign volunteers who have marched in those parades, made those get-out-the-vote calls, and put up those lawn signs, as well as my loyal donors and fundraiser hosts over the years. You all know who you are. Thank you.

I thank my staff, both in the County Attorney's Office and in the U.S. Senate, for the tremendous work they have done for the people of our state and this country. I also thank the staff of my political campaigns for helping me get into office in the first place.

Justin Buoen has been a rock for me, starting in 2004, when I didn't even know what statewide office I was running for, and continuing on to become my state fundraiser in the 2006 Senate campaign and my campaign manager in 2012. I have seen him go from a kid carrying signs in a parade to a husband and a dad of two great kids, with more to come (as in politics, not kids). Along with media guru Mandy Grunwald, consultant Al Quinlan, advisor Jeff Blodgett, treasurer Brigid McDonough, fundraiser Tina Stoll, lawyer Marc Elias, accounting volunteer Jerry Halbach, and direct-mail guy Pete Giangreco, Justin and his friends and staff have been the core of "Team Klobuchar" since day one in the Senate campaigns.

Rose Baumann has also been a star. She started on our 2006 campaign while she was still at Gustavus Adolphus College, then joined our state office as a health care outreach worker. She moved to D.C. and did my health care policy work during the year-plus-long debate on and passage of the Affordable Care Act, became legislative director, and finally chief of staff (somewhere along the way dating and becoming engaged to my former deputy chief of staff, Tom Sullivan).

Campaign staff/volunteers from those early county attorney campaigns who weren't mentioned in the book but deserve a shout-out include treasurers Walter Duffy and John Eisberg, as well as Matt Anderson, Barbara Bearman, Kristin Beckmann, Dale Dramstad, Bob Elliott, Don Gerdesmeier, Tricia Hull, Brian Strub, Julie Johns, Josie Johnson, the late Matthew Little, Amanda Mahnke, Kathy Nelson, Heather Peterson, Steve Rathke, Dan Rogan, Charlie Rounds, Chris Milder, Joanne Spencer, and Ray Waldron. Thanks, too, to DFL Party Chairs—past and present—Rick Stafford, Mark Andrew, Dick Senese, Mike Erlandson, Brian Melendez, and Ken Martin. And, Dave Hartman and Kate Nilan, way to go winning that uncontested county attorney's race in 2002 and somehow motivating our volunteers to put up three thousand lawn signs when we didn't have an opponent.

Thanks are in order for our tremendous 2006 Senate campaign. Staff and key volunteers not mentioned in chapter 8 include Heather Abraham,

Nimco Ahmed, Ben Alsdurf, Steve Barrows, Sarah Berns, Laura Cederberg, Jeannette Cleland and Tim Schumann (now married), Becky Rothmeier Loewen and Gordie Loewen (ditto), Micah Clemens, Brian Doory, Robert Giesler, Becky Groen, Simone Hardeman-Jones, Julie Hottinger, Bob Hume, Megan Kinninger, Sara Mursky-Fuller, Melissa Parker, Kirsten Petersen, Dan Pollock, Ken Sanguin, Zach Stephenson, and Renee Willette. And finally, our fantastic 2012 campaign staff includes a few people not already mentioned in the book: Madeline Coles, Aram Desteian, Erick Garcia Luna, Ben Garmisa, Rommel Lee, Brian O'Shea, Joe Radosevich, Gia Vitali, Francesca Capodilupo, Anna Widowson, and Sara Bryant (a true unsung hero, first on Tina Stoll's team, and then as my finance director).

In addition to Rose Baumann, there are many, many hardworking staff to thank in our Washington, D.C., office who have drafted bills, helped pass legislation, solved problems for our constituents, and steadfastly done their jobs through shutdowns and worse. I am so proud of all of you and your work! I particularly want to mention Jonathan Becker, my counsel and later chief of staff for many years; Tom Sullivan, my long-time foreign relations expert and deputy chief of staff who is now John Kerry's deputy chief of staff; Travis Talvitie, my legislative director, who knows practically every mayor and county commissioner in our state (at least the ones who sought federal funding for transportation projects); Linden Zakula and Brigit Helgen, two great communications directors who were willing to dig in and learn the policies behind the rhetoric; and Lizzy Peluso, my chief of staff. And for years Joe Radosevich, Danny Carlson, Matt Manning, Emily Anfinson, Kate Nilan, Lauren Mandelker, Renee Coe, Lindsey Nienstedt, Caroline Selby, Asal Sayas, Sally Cluthe, Bonnie Berry, and Paul Zygmunt made sure I knew what I needed to know and where I was supposed to be. Most of the time, they kept me precisely on schedule. When I wasn't on time it was my fault, not theirs.

On our state staff, I want to acknowledge the work of Kali Cruz and Clara Haycraft, my former and current deputies/constituent services managers. Their belief that every constituent should be treated with dignity and respect has defined the work of our office. Also, Chuck Ackman, Andy Martin, and Jerry Fallos, our longtime regional office heads, have been a godsend, not to mention a lot of fun. Jerry, a former steelworker who headed up our northern Minnesota office for eight years, is now retiring, leaving him with much more time to enter his award-winning homemade wine in the State Fair contest, fruit wine category. Bring that blue ribbon home, Jerry!

We have a great community outreach staff, and five stand out for their long-standing service: Greg Swanholm (always a hit at Game Fair), Siad Ali (now a member of the Minneapolis School Board), retired General Tim Cossalter, former deputy Erika Nelson, and deputy Megan Lahr (who has done an extraordinary job in both D.C. and Minnesota). I also want to call out four state directors: Sammy Clark (I was so happy for Sammy when Mayor Chris Coleman recently appointed him as the St. Paul City Attorney); Sara Grewing (she is now a judge, but Sara was there at the beginning when our temporary office space wouldn't allow anyone to flush the toilets on the weekend and it got so cold in the winter that the pipes burst, sending torrents of water into her staff's workspaces); Zach Rodvold (my field director in the 2006 campaign and all-around good guy); and Ben Hill (my current state director). And thanks to Allison O'Toole, Deb Calvert, Steve Huser, Teresa DeTrempe, Peter Grafstrom, Kaleb Rumicho, and Alexandra Griffin for being my pals out on the road and planning and making those yearly rounds of the eighty-seven counties.

Finally, a lot of people went out of their way to help me with the photos: my dad's friend Rod Wilson, my uncle Dick, Katie Beirne Fallon and the White House, the Ely-Winton Historical Society, Linda Messenger and Bob Distad, John and Meg Symington, the Minnesota Historical Society, Hennepin County, Bill Cameron, John's graphic artist brother Andrew, the AP, the Minneapolis *StarTribune*, the *Downtown Journal*, and KSTP-TV. And thanks to my husband, John, for being my scanner-in-chief.

Last but not least, I'd like to thank the folks at Apple for developing the iPad Notes app, which allowed me to write this book wherever I was over the past few years. As much as I'd like to say I had a romantic writing room somewhere in the heartland in which to write the book, it was in fact written in airport gate areas, on planes and trains, in hotel rooms and coffee shops and restaurants, and on my own kitchen and dining room tables. Thanks to all my airport seatmates, neighboring Minnesota-coffee-shop patrons, and total strangers who listened and read paragraphs and pages and gave me their own two cents. Being a senator makes you accessible to a lot of people, and a whole bunch of kind strangers helped out in their own ways. I don't know all of you by name, but you were really nice about it. Thanks.

INDEX

ABOUT THE AUTHOR

AMY KLOBUCHAR, the daughter of a newspaperman and a schoolteacher, is Minnesota's senior United States Senator. A Democrat, she was first elected to the Senate in 2006; she was later reelected in a landslide and named to Senate leadership. A national leader, she has a well-earned reputation for working across the aisle to pass legislation that supports families, workers, and businesses. She and her husband, John, have a daughter, Abigail, who is in college.